p752

The International Lawyer's Guide to Legal Analysis and Communication in the United States

Brief.

红 F.

橙 C/A.

黄 PH.

深绿 SI.

浅绿 PI.

蓝 H.

紫 J.

粉 Relevant Rules

灰 Court's Reasoning.

红

蓝

《 Gettn to Mayle 》

Jiang Yiyun

Eve.

ASPEN PUBLISHERS

The International Lawyer's Guide to Legal Analysis and Communication in the United States

Deborah B. McGregor
Clinical Professor of Law
Indiana University School of Law

Cynthia M. Adams
Clinical Professor of Law
Indiana University School of Law

Wolters Kluwer
Law & Business

AUSTIN   BOSTON   CHICAGO   NEW YORK   THE NETHERLANDS

To contact Customer Care, e-mail customer.care@aspenpublishers.com, call 1-800-234-1660, fax 1-800-901-9075, or mail correspondence to:

Aspen Publishers
Attn: Order Department
PO Box 990
Frederick, MD 21705

Printed in the United States of America.

1 2 3 4 5 6 7 8 9 0

ISBN 978-0-7355-6477-0

Library of Congress Cataloging-in-Publication Data

McGregor, Deborah B., 1951-
    The international lawyer's guide to legal analysis and communication in the United States / Deborah B. McGregor, Cynthia M. Adams.
        p. cm.
    Includes bibliographical references and index.
    ISBN 978-0-7355-6477-0
    1. Law — United States — Interpretation and construction. 2. Legal composition. 3. Law — Study and teaching — United States. I. Adams, Cynthia M. II. Title.

KF250.M38 2008
340.071'173 — dc22

2008019881

About Wolters Kluwer Law & Business

Wolters Kluwer Law & Business is a leading provider of research information and workflow solutions in key specialty areas. The strengths of the individual brands of Aspen Publishers, CCH, Kluwer Law International and Loislaw are aligned within Wolters Kluwer Law & Business to provide comprehensive, in-depth solutions and expert-authored content for the legal, professional and education markets.

CCH was founded in 1913 and has served more than four generations of business professionals and their clients. The CCH products in the Wolters Kluwer Law & Business group are highly regarded electronic and print resources for legal, securities, antitrust and trade regulation, government contracting, banking, pension, payroll, employment and labor, and healthcare reimbursement and compliance professionals.

Aspen Publishers is a leading information provider for attorneys, business professionals and law students. Written by preeminent authorities, Aspen products offer analytical and practical information in a range of specialty practice areas from securities law and intellectual property to mergers and acquisitions and pension/benefits. Aspen's trusted legal education resources provide professors and students with high-quality, up-to-date and effective resources for successful instruction and study in all areas of the law.

Kluwer Law International supplies the global business community with comprehensive English-language international legal information. Legal practitioners, corporate counsel and business executives around the world rely on the Kluwer Law International journals, loose-leafs, books and electronic products for authoritative information in many areas of international legal practice.

Loislaw is a premier provider of digitized legal content to small law firm practitioners of various specializations. Loislaw provides attorneys with the ability to quickly and efficiently find the necessary legal information they need, when and where they need it, by facilitating access to primary law as well as state-specific law, records, forms and treatises.

Wolters Kluwer Law & Business, a unit of Wolters Kluwer, is headquartered in New York and Riverwoods, Illinois. Wolters Kluwer is a leading multinational publisher and information services company.

Dedication

To my parents, William A. Matson and Mary Katharine Geimer Matson.
— CMA

To my sons, Geoff and Dan, for their love, patience, and never-ending humor.
— DBM

SUMMARY OF CONTENTS

CONTENTS

Part Two.
AN INTRODUCTION TO WRITING
IN THE U.S. LEGAL SYSTEM   71

Chapter 5. The Legal Writing Process   73

Part Six.
LAW SCHOOL EXAMINATIONS   351

Appendices   375

PREFACE

The world is, indeed, becoming smaller. With the increasing number of agreements between international and U.S. interests the need to understand one another's legal system becomes pronounced. Our goal is to help you, the international lawyer from a different legal system, to understand how the U.S. legal system works.

Many of you work in a civil or mixed legal system and are most interested in learning about the U.S. common law system. While many texts exist that include instruction on common law analysis, there is no book to date that provides the level of detail provided in this one.

We wanted to focus on the types of communications that you are most likely to read from U.S. lawyers or need to write to U.S. lawyers. Cultural differences and tradition may influence how a single document, a contract, for example, is written in any individual country. By introducing you to the techniques U.S. lawyers use when drafting communications you will have a better understanding of why something is written the way it is, and how, in turn, to most effectively communicate with U.S. lawyers. For these reasons, we have introduced techniques for drafting objective legal analyses, client letters, demand letters, and e-mail communications. In addition, a separate section, Part Five, is devoted to both substantive considerations in drafting contracts as well as to basic techniques for drafting contracts that provide a single, clear understanding of the agreement between the parties. Finally, for those of you attending a U.S. law school, we have provided in Part Three an overview of how to properly cite to legal resources and in Part Six some suggestions for taking law school examinations.

We chose not to explore research sources and techniques in the United States, knowing there are other exceptional books available that provide that guidance.

We are thankful to our assistant, Janice White, for her help throughout this process. We would also like to thank ESL Specialist M. Catherine Beck for her advice and support. Thanks, too, to Aspen's anonymous reviewers, who read our manuscript and offered valuable commentary. And a special thank you to our research assistants, including Hongbin Bao, Shishir Deshpande, Anna Dyuzheva, Kristen Davis Edmundson, Nathan Lundquist, Koichi Nishioka, James Porter, and Thomas Vandenabeele. All helped shape the final version of this text. Thanks also to our students who were assigned early drafts of this book and helped us refine both the substance and the style.

We welcome feedback from faculty and students who use this book. You may contact Professor McGregor at dmcgreg@iupui.edu or Professor Adams at cmadams@iupui.edu.

May 2008   *Deborah B. McGregor and Cynthia M. Adams*

PART ONE

Introduction to the Study of the U.S. Legal System

CHAPTER

1

The U.S. System of Government

HIGHLIGHTS

- The United States has a dual system government, composed of a federal system and a state system.
- Each government system derives its law from four sources: (1) constitutions, (2) statutes, (3) case decisions, and (4) administrative regulations.
- The federal and state constitutions provide a framework for governance at the federal and state levels, creating three branches: the legislative branch, the executive branch, and the judicial branch.
- The legislative branch enacts statutes that are subject only to constitutional restraints.
- The executive branch enforces and implements statutes.
- The judicial branch comprises courts that interpret statutes and create laws in situations not addressed by statute.
- The rules and principles created by courts to respond to situations not addressed by statute are referred to as the common law.
- The federal system and the state system each has its own set of courts with its own trial courts and appellate courts.

4

1. U.S Constitution
2. federal statutes
3. ad. reg promulgated by Fed. Ag
4. fed court des.
5. State Constitution
2. state statutes } by st. Ag.
3. ad reg
st court des

 ## A. A Dual System of Government

The United States has a dual system of government, the federal system and the state system. The federal system derives its law from four sources: the U.S. Constitution, federal statutes, administrative regulations promulgated by federal agencies, and federal court decisions. State law is derived from the following four sources: state constitutions, state statutes, administrative regulations promulgated by state agencies, and state court decisions. (See Figure 1-1.) Although states do make their own laws, they still cannot disregard federal law.

Primary Sources of the Law

Federal System	State System
• United States Constitution • Statutory laws enacted by the United States Congress • Common law found in federal case decisions involving special matters (e.g., international disputes) • Administrative regulations promulgated by federal agencies (e.g., the Environmental Protection Agency)	• State Constitution • Statutory laws enacted by a state legislature • Common law found in state appellate court decisions • Administrative regulations promulgated by state agencies (e.g., the Bureau of Motor Vehicles)

Figure 1-1

Why not state trial court decisions? Trial courts don't have the right to make law?

 ## B. The Constitutionally-Created Three Branches of Government

The U.S. Constitution, which consists of 7 articles and 27 amendments, is the foundation of the U.S. legal system. The Constitution allocates responsibility for governance between the federal and state governments. In its first 10 amendments, known as the Bill of Rights, the Constitution also mandates fundamental rights and protections for people. The Bill of Rights limits the federal government's power by guaranteeing certain rights to the people, including the freedom of speech, the freedom of religion, the freedom of assembly, the freedom of the press, the right to bear arms, the right to be secure from unreasonable searches and seizures, the right to a speedy trial, the right not to make incriminating statements against one's self, the right to a trial by jury, and the right to protection against cruel and unusual punishment. A state constitution can grant additional or greater rights and protections to individuals within its boundaries than does the U.S. Constitution. At a minimum, though, a state constitution must provide the same degree of rights and protections as is afforded under the U.S. Constitution.

Both federal and state constitutions also provide a framework for governing the jurisdictions to which they apply. The constitutions divide the responsibility of governance into three branches: the executive branch, the legislative branch, and the judicial branch. (See Figure 1-2.) Each branch is assigned a particular role, but all branches may create law. Each one serves as a check and balance of power over the other two.

The legislative branches in both the federal and state legal systems possess supreme law-making powers. The legislative branch may respond to issues and problems by enacting statutes that protect the welfare of the public. These statutes are subject only to the limitations laid down by the federal and applicable state constitutions.

The executive branch's primary role is to enforce the statutes created by the legislative branch. The executive branch and its administrative agencies may be called on by the legislative branch to enforce and implement statutes by promulgating regulations that further define a statute.[1] In 1991, for instance, the U.S. Congress enacted the Telephone Consumer Protection Act (TCPA) and mandated an independent administrative agency known as the Federal Communications Commission (FCC) to promulgate regulations protecting residential telephone subscribers from receiving unwanted telephone solicitations.[2] The regulations promulgated by the FCC under the TCPA have the same force and effect as statutory laws.[3] By promulgating regulations, the administrative agencies create law as they have been assigned to do by statute.

The judicial branch plays a strong role in the U.S. legal system. The judiciary interprets existing statutes and may review statutes to determine whether they are consistent with the federal and state constitutions. The judiciary can declare a statute unenforceable if it finds the statute unconstitutional.[4] In addition, the judiciary possesses the power to create law by establishing rules and principles that respond to issues not otherwise addressed by statute. This body of law created by the judiciary is called the common law.[5] In this way, the U.S. legal system is quite different from civil code legal systems where the courts may only interpret and apply the civil code. Because of the judiciary's unusually strong law-making role in the U.S. legal system, the remainder of this chapter will focus on the hierarchal levels in the federal and state court systems.

---

1. For example, an administrative agency may be directed by statute to create regulations in situations where the legislative branch lacks the technical expertise or the time to create detailed laws that fully address more complex issues or problems.

2. 47 U.S.C. § 227(c)(1-4) (2000).

3. 47 U.S.C. § 227(c)(5) (2000).

4. *See Marbury v. Madison*, 5 U.S. (1 Cranch) 137 (1803).

5. Although the United States Supreme Court in *Erie R.R. Co. v. Tompkins*, 304 U.S. 64, 78 (1938), stated there is no "general common law," federal courts have continued to develop federal common law in limited circumstances involving important federal interests, such as in admiralty and maritime cases and international disputes.

U.S. Dual System of Government

The Constitutionally Created Three Branches of Government

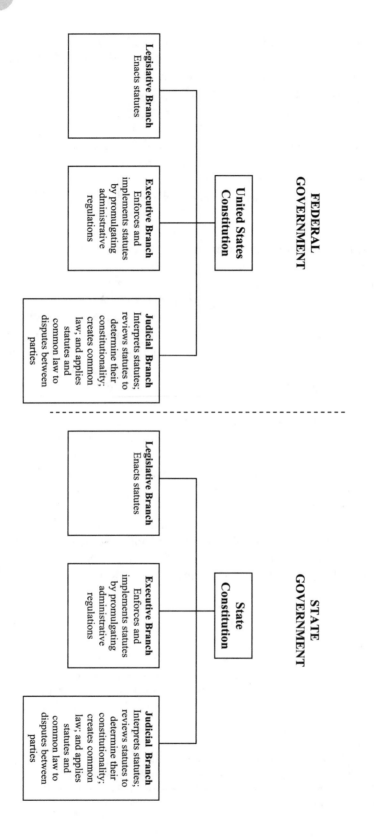

Figure 1-2

FEDERAL GOVERNMENT

United States Constitution

Legislative Branch
Enacts statutes

Executive Branch
Enforces and implements statutes by promulgating administrative regulations

Judicial Branch
Interprets statutes; reviews statutes to determine their constitutionality; creates common law; and applies statutes and common law to disputes between parties

STATE GOVERNMENT

State Constitution

Legislative Branch
Enacts statutes

Executive Branch
Enforces and implements statutes by promulgating administrative regulations

Judicial Branch
Interprets statutes; reviews statutes to determine their constitutionality; creates common law; and applies statutes and common law to disputes between parties

C. A Dual Court System

Both the federal court system and the state court system comprise a pyramid-like hierarchy of courts, with the trial courts at the base of the pyramid, usually followed by intermediate courts of appeals, and then a court of final appeal at the apex of the pyramid. (See Figure 1-3.) This dual court system reflects the dual law-making authority of the federal and state governments. Generally, the federal courts interpret and apply federal law, while the state courts interpret and apply state law.

Court Hierarchy

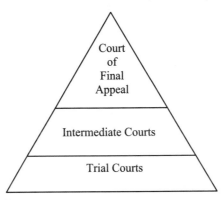

Figure 1-3

1. The federal court system

The federal courts hear disputes involving federal law, including those disputes arising from the U.S. Constitution, federal statutes, and federal regulations. A federal court will also hear disputes where the United States is named as a party and will even hear state law issues if the parties are citizens of different states and the dispute involves more than $75,000. For example, if two people, a citizen of Oregon and a citizen of California, are involved in a car accident resulting in injuries and damages exceeding $75,000, a lawsuit can be brought in federal court.

Issues involving federal civil or criminal law are usually heard in a federal trial court, called a district court.[6] Each state has at least one district court. Because each district court serves an approximately equal population, the more sparsely populated states may have only a single district court and the more densely populated states may have several district courts. Oregon, for example, has only one district court, but California has four district courts. These courts may hear civil or criminal cases.

---

6. In addition to district courts that hear disputes involving general federal law, the federal court system includes courts that have jurisdiction over special disputes, such as the military courts, the bankruptcy courts, and the United States Tax Court.

The district court's jurisdiction is limited to the area within the territorial boundaries of its district. There are 94 judicial districts located in the United States, the District of Columbia (D.C.), the Commonwealth of Puerto Rico, and the three territories of the United States—Guam, the Virgin Islands, and the Northern Mariana Islands. (See Figures 1-4 and 1-5.)

A party has a right to appeal the final judgment of a district court or, if permitted by statute, certain orders of the court made during the course of the trial to the intermediate court of appeals having jurisdiction over the district court. In the federal court system, the intermediate courts of appeals are known as the United States Circuit Courts of Appeals. Congress has divided the United States into 13 circuits.[7] Eleven of these circuits are numbered. The two other federal circuits are the United States District Court for the District of Columbia and the United States Court of Appeals for the Federal Circuit. (See Figures 1-4 and 1-5.) The total number of judges serving on the court of appeals in each circuit varies from 6 judgeships in the First Circuit to 28 judgeships in the Ninth Circuit,[8] but appeals are heard by three-judge panels.[9]

Each of the numbered circuits includes district courts from various states and sometimes territories, such as Guam. For example, the United States Court of Appeals for the Ninth Circuit hears appeals from district courts located in Alaska, Arizona, California, Guam, Hawaii, Idaho, Montana, Nevada, Northern Mariana Islands, Oregon, and Washington. The United States Court of Appeals for the Second Circuit hears appeals from district courts located in New York, Connecticut, and Vermont. The numbered circuits and the D.C. Court of Appeals also hear appeals from decisions of some federal administrative agencies. (See Figures 1-4 and 1-5.)

Unlike the jurisdictions of the numbered circuits and the D.C. circuit that are based on territorial boundaries, the jurisdiction of the Court of Appeals for the Federal Circuit is nationwide and based on special claims, such as those involving international trade disputes and patents. (See Figures 1-4 and 1-5.) In some instances, the Court of Appeals for the Federal Circuit also may hear cases against the U.S. government, including disputes arising out of U.S. government contracts, claims for money from the U.S. government, and claims related to veteran's benefits.

The United States Supreme Court, comprising nine justices, is the court of last resort for appeals in the federal system and for appeals of state court decisions involving federal issues. (See Figure 1-5.) Although the Supreme Court is required by law to hear appeals regarding certain matters,[10] its docket[11] of mandatory cases is quite small. Most of the cases on the Court's docket are discretionary. Thousands of petitions for

---

7. 28 U.S.C. § 41 (2000).

8. 28 U.S.C. § 44 (2000).

9. The United States Code provides that the Federal Circuit may have panels of more than three judges, if permitted by the Federal Circuit's court rules. 28 U.S.C. § 46(c) (2000).

10. *See, e.g.,* 28 U.S.C. § 1253 (2000) (providing for a direct appeal to the Supreme Court for review of decisions from three-judge district courts granting or denying an injunction); 47 U.S.C. § 555(c)(2) (2000) (Cable Act) (providing for a direct appeal to the Supreme Court for review of decisions from a three-judge court holding that § 534 or § 535 of the Cable Act unconstitutional).

11. A court docket refers to a record of the cases pending in the court.

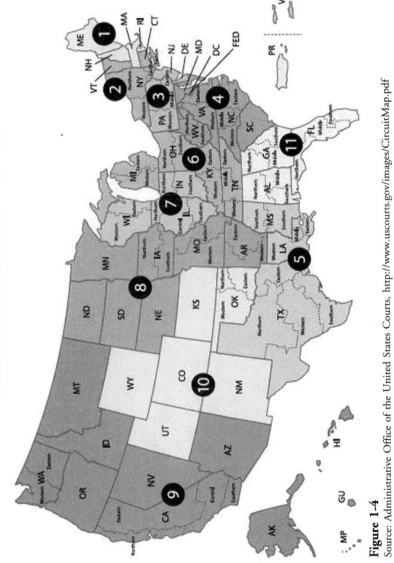

Figure 1-4

Source: Administrative Office of the United States Courts, http://www.uscourts.gov/images/CircuitMap.pdf

Hierarchy of the Federal Court System

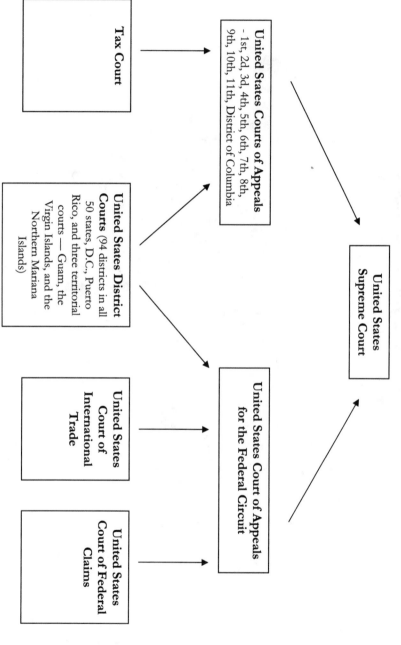

Figure 1-5

Source: Administrative Office of the United States Courts, http://www.uscourts.gov/
Note: Military, Bankruptcy, and Veterans Claims Courts are not shown.

appeal are filed each year with the Court. The Court is constrained by time, however, and grants permission to hear only a small number of these cases, usually those requiring an interpretation of federal constitutional or statutory provisions, or those requiring the resolution of pressing issues of federal law.[12]

2. The state court system

Each of the 50 states, as well as the District of Columbia and the Commonwealth of Puerto Rico, has its own court system. Similar to the federal system, many state court systems are composed of a three-tiered hierarchy consisting of a trial court, an intermediate court of appeals, and the highest court of appeals or the court of last resort. A minority of states with smaller populations, such as Maine, have two-tiered systems only, with trial courts and appellate courts. The names of the appellate courts vary from state to state. For example, California refers to its intermediate court of appeals as the court of appeal and its court of last resort as the supreme court. (See Figure 1-6.) Conversely, New York refers to one of its intermediate courts of appeals as the supreme court and its court of last resort as the court of appeals.[13]

A trial court may be of general or limited jurisdiction. A court of limited jurisdiction can hear only certain types of cases. For example, a small claims court may hear only cases involving claims for small debts, and a state criminal court of limited jurisdiction may hear only criminal cases. Still other courts have specialized roles, such as a juvenile court, which hears matters involving delinquent or dependent children.

Similar to the federal court system, most states allow a right of appeal to the intermediate appellate court.[14] A party that is dissatisfied with the outcome of a civil case decided by a state trial court may ask an appellate court in the state to review the trial court's judgment, order, or decision to determine whether the trial court committed a legal error that requires a reversal, a modification, or a new trial. If there is a third tier to the state court system, a party dissatisfied with the outcome in the intermediate appellate court may appeal the intermediate appellate court's decision

---

12. The Court receives annually over 8,500 petitions for certiorari per court term but agrees to hear far less. In the 2005 term, for example, only 87 cases were argued before the reviewing Court. United States Supreme Court Chief Justice Roberts, *The 2006 Year-End Report on the Federal Judiciary* 9, http://www.uscourts.gov/newsroom/yearend06.pdf.

13. A quick way to determine the names of the courts in the various state jurisdictions is to refer to Table 1 in *The Bluebook: A Uniform System of Citation* (18th ed., Harvard Law Review Assn. 2005) or Appendix 1 in Association of Legal Writing Directors & Darby Dickerson, *ALWD Citation Manual: A Professional System of Citation* (3d ed., Aspen Publishers 2006). The states are listed alphabetically, and as a part of each state entry, the names of the courts in the state that publish decisions are identified along with the names of the reporters in which these decisions are published.

14. There are exceptions: Hawaii and North Dakota, for example, do not provide for a direct right of appeal to the intermediate appellate court. Instead, the state supreme court assigns cases to the intermediate appellate court.

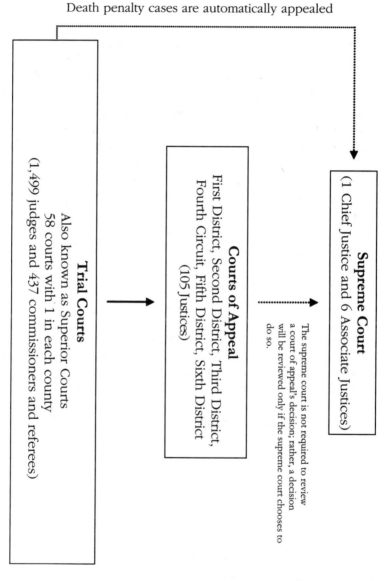

Hierarchy of the California Court System

Death penalty cases are automatically appealed

Supreme Court
(1 Chief Justice and 6 Associate Justices)

The supreme court is not required to review a court of appeal's decision; rather, a decision will be reviewed only if the supreme court chooses to do so.

Courts of Appeal
First District, Second District, Third District, Fourth Circuit, Fifth District, Sixth District
(105 Justices)

Trial Courts
Also known as Superior Courts
58 courts with 1 in each county
(1,499 judges and 437 commissioners and referees)

Figure 1-6
Judgeship numbers are current as of 2007.
Source: The Judicial Council of California, http://www.courtinfo.ca.gov/about/#cjb

to the state's highest court. In most instances, the highest court in a three-tiered court system is not required to hear an appeal. Like the United States Supreme Court, most dockets are discretionary in state courts of last resort. Unless the decision of a state court involves a federal constitutional question or federal law, the decision of the highest state court is final and cannot be appealed to any other court. For an example of one state's court system (California), see Figure 1-6.

CHAPTER

2

The Common Law in the United States

HIGHLIGHTS

- Precedents are holdings in prior cases used by a court to reach a decision in a current case.
- Under the doctrine of stare decisis, a court is required to reconcile a new decision with that court's prior decisions and higher court decisions in the same jurisdiction involving similar legal issues and substantially similar facts.
- Mandatory precedents are prior court decisions that a court must follow when reaching a decision in a current case.
- Persuasive precedents are prior court decisions that a court may be persuaded to follow but aren't obligated to follow when reaching a decision in a current case.
- When faced with an issue of first impression (an issue that has never been decided within a jurisdiction), a court may give greater consideration to persuasive precedent and may pay particular attention to public policy concerns, as well as social and economic considerations related to the new issue.
- If a court must address an issue that arguably involves a statute, a court will first determine whether the statute applies to the case and, if so, will apply the statute to the case. A court will not enforce an unconstitutional statute.
- A court is not required to follow its own or higher courts' prior decisions when the facts of the present case are substantially different from the facts of prior cases.
- A court may overrule precedent when (1) a development in the law results in a conflict between two precedents, (2) the rule underlying the precedent has become unworkable, or (3) the policy supporting the precedent does not reflect current public policy interests and concerns.

A. The Common Law as Precedent

The U.S. judiciary plays a vital role in the law-making process. Although one of the judiciary's primary responsibilities is to interpret and apply statutes, the judiciary also has the power to create and develop rules and legal principles in situations not addressed by statute. Courts often rely on prior case decisions to help their decision making in a current case that involves similar legal issues and facts. These prior case decisions are referred to as precedent. Precedent makes up the common law.

 ## B. The Judicial Self-Governing Doctrine of Stare Decisis

Under the doctrine of stare decisis, a court is required to reconcile new decisions with its own prior decisions or with those of a higher court in its jurisdiction. Advocates of stare decisis contend that the following objectives are realized when judges abide by precedent:

1. *Certainty in the law:* When judges consistently apply the same rules to substantially similar fact situations, people can plan their actions with a measure of confidence because they are better able to predict the legal consequences of their actions.[1]
2. *Fairness:* The consistent application of rules will result in equal treatment of parties similarly situated.[2]
3. *Court efficiency:* Relying on precedent frees judges from the burden of recreating rules and principles.[3]
4. *Justice and judicial impartiality:* Requiring judges to base their decisions on precedent promotes the appearance of justice and judicial impartiality in the decision-making process. The public has greater confidence in the judiciary when there is less opportunity for judges' personal opinions to influence their decisions.[4]

Precedent that a court is bound to follow is called mandatory or binding precedent. Courts, however, can also seek guidance from nonbinding precedent, which is frequently referred to as persuasive precedent.

---

1. *See* Frederick Schauer, *Precedent*, 39 Stan. L. Rev. 571, 597-598 (1987).

2. *See id.* at 595-597.

3. Justice Benjamin N. Cardozo, one of the greatest U.S. jurists, noted that "the labor of judges would be increased almost to the breaking point if every past decision could be reopened in every case, and one could not lay one's own course of bricks on the secure foundation of the courses laid by others who had gone before him." Benjamin N. Cardozo, *The Nature of the Judicial Process* 149 (Yale U. Press 1921).

4. Earl Maltz, *The Nature of Precedent*, 66 N.C. L. Rev. 367, 371 (1988).

1. Mandatory precedent

In the state court system, a trial court is bound by the previous decisions of the higher courts within its jurisdictional borders and federal statutory and constitutional decisions of the United States Supreme Court. State trial courts cannot make precedent for other courts. If the state has a three-tiered court system, the intermediate appeals court is bound by (1) its previous decisions, (2) previous decisions of the court of last resort in the state, and (3) previous federal statutory and constitutional decisions of the United States Supreme Court. The state court of last resort is bound only by (1) its own previous decisions and (2) the previous federal statutory and constitutional decisions of the United States Supreme Court. (See Figure 2-1 for a chart of a state court system's general appeals hierarchy.) Using the California three-tiered court system as an example, a California trial court must abide by (1) previous decisions of the California Court of Appeals in its region, (2) the previous decisions of the California Supreme Court, and (3) the previous federal statutory and constitutional decisions of the United States Supreme Court. A California Court of Appeals, however, is bound only by (1) previous decisions within its own region,[5] (2) previous California Supreme Court decisions, and (3) previous federal statutory and constitutional decisions of the United States Supreme Court. The California Supreme Court is bound only by (1) its own previous decisions and (2) previous federal statutory and constitutional decisions of the United States Supreme Court. (See Figure 1-6 in Chapter 1 for a chart of the California court hierarchy.)

In the federal court system, a district or trial court is bound by (1) the previous decisions of the United States Supreme Court, (2) the previous decisions of the court of appeals of the circuit in which the district court is located, and (3) its own previous decisions. (See Figure 2-1 for the federal court system's general appeals hierarchy. A more descriptive federal court hierarchy chart is found in Figure 1-5 in Chapter 1.) Therefore, a federal district court in California must abide by (1) the previous decisions of the United States Supreme Court, (2) the previous decisions of the United States Court of Appeals for the Ninth Circuit (the circuit in which the California district courts reside), and (3) its own previous decisions.

Courts of appeals, such as the United States Court of Appeals for the Ninth Circuit, are not bound by previous decisions of district courts or previous decisions from other circuit courts of appeal. Nevertheless, these courts of appeals are required to abide by (1) their own previous decisions and (2) those of the United States Supreme Court. Of course, the United States Supreme Court is bound only by its own previous decisions.

A special situation, however, arises when a federal court is deciding a matter of state law. A federal court may assert jurisdiction over certain disputes arising under state law when the claimed losses exceed $75,000 and the dispute is between:

(1) citizens of different [s]tates;
(2) citizens of a [s]tate and citizens or subjects of a foreign [country];

---

5. *See, e.g., Estate of Cleveland*, 17 Cal. App. 4th 1700, 1709 (2d Dist. 1993) (the California Court of Appeals for the Second District stated that it was not bound to follow a prior decision of the California Court of Appeals for the Sixth District on a similar issue and rejected the Sixth District's decision).

18

Figure 2-1

Hierarchy of Appeals

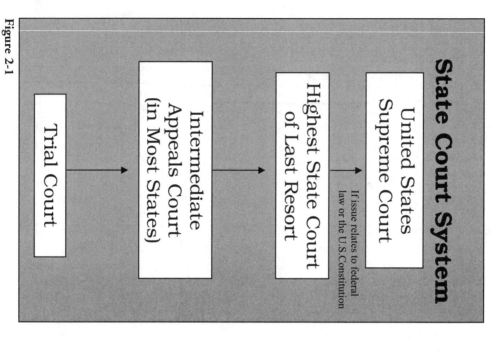

State Court System

Trial Court → Intermediate Appeals Court (in Most States) → Highest State Court of Last Resort → United States Supreme Court

If issue relates to federal law or the U.S.Constitution

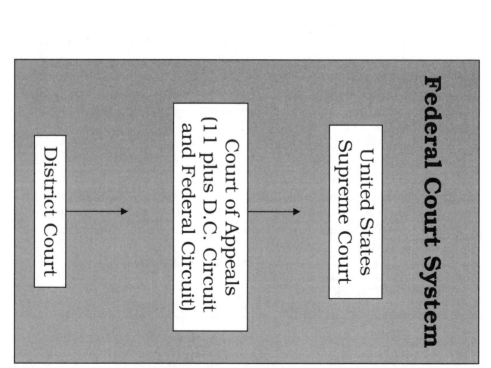

Federal Court System

District Court → Court of Appeals (11 plus D.C. Circuit and Federal Circuit) → United States Supreme Court

(3) citizens of different [s]tates and in which citizens or subjects of a foreign state are additional parties; [or]

(4) a foreign state . . . as plaintiff and citizens of a [s]tate or different [s]tates.[6]

A federal court's jurisdiction in these cases is based on the different citizenships of the parties. Here, the federal court applies the law that it thinks the state's court of last resort would apply if the state court was faced with the same issue. While the federal court's decision is binding on the parties in that dispute, the state court is not bound by the federal court's decision. Remember, a state court is bound only by (1) previous decisions of its own court, (2) previous decisions of higher courts within its jurisdiction, and (3) previous federal statutory and constitutional decisions of the United States Supreme Court. The federal court is not within a state court's jurisdiction. As previously mentioned, the federal court system is a separate court system from the state court system. (See also Figure 2-1.)

2. Persuasive precedent

If no mandatory precedent exists, a court may seek guidance from persuasive precedent in addition to other sources.[7] Persuasive precedent consists of all precedent that is not binding on the court. For instance, the California Supreme Court may be persuaded by a decision of the California Court of Appeals. A court may also look at persuasive case decisions outside its jurisdiction. The California Supreme Court, for example, may look to an Arizona decision on the same issue for guidance. In the federal court system, a comparable example would be the United States Court of Appeals for the Ninth Circuit being persuaded by a decision from the United States Court of Appeals for the Second Circuit.

● Exercise 2-A

1. The California Supreme Court decided a case based on California law. On which courts is this decision binding? On which courts is this decision persuasive?

COURT	BINDING	PERSUASIVE
California Court of Appeal for the First District	✓	✓
Oregon Supreme Court		✓
United States Court of Appeals for the Ninth Circuit, applying California law	✓	✓
United States Supreme Court, applying California law		✓

---

6. 28 U.S.C. § 1332(a)(1)&(2) (2000).

7. Courts may also seek guidance from other authorities, such as statutes from other jurisdictions and so-called secondary authorities, such as law review articles or treatises. Research texts provide extensive discussion of secondary authorities. Examples of good research texts include Christina Kunz et al., *The Process of Legal Research* (6th ed., Aspen Publishers 2004), and Amy Sloan, *Basic Legal Research* (2d ed., Aspen Publishers 2003).

2. The United States Court of Appeals for the Ninth Circuit applied California law in deciding a diversity case. On which courts is this decision binding? On which courts is this decision persuasive?

COURT	BINDING	PERSUASIVE
United States Court of Appeals for the Second Circuit		✓
United States Supreme Court, applying California law	✓	
California trial court		✓
California Court of Appeals for the First District		✓
California Supreme Court		✓

3. The California Court of Appeals for the First District, sitting in San Francisco, decided a case based on California law. On which courts is this decision binding? On which courts is this persuasive?

COURT	BINDING	PERSUASIVE
United States District Court for the Northern District of California (which includes San Francisco), applying California law		✓
California Supreme Court	✓	
California Court of Appeals for the Second District		✓
Superior (trial) Court in Sacramento, California (located in the Third District of the California Court of Appeals)		✓
Superior (trial) Court in Fresno, California (located in the Fifth District of the California Court of Appeals)		✓

C. The Evolving Common Law

1. Creating and developing the common law

The judge's role of creating and developing rules and principles that comprise the common law is a difficult one. When forming a new rule, the conscientious judge will want to craft a rule that brings a just result to the current dispute but also makes clear what future factual situations will be subject to the rule. During this decision-making process, the judge also may consider the interest of the public, whether the rule will promote the social or economic well-being of society (also known as public policy).

If a judge crafts a rule using language that is too narrowly drawn, the rule will give insufficient notice to the public of its application. This could result in courts being overwhelmed with litigation involving similar situations. For the sake of certainty in the law and judicial efficiency, a court strives to create a rule that is not too narrow. For example, suppose Landowner A has an apple tree on his property situated near the boundary line between his and Landowner B's property. Apples drop off the tree, and some fall in the yard of Landowner B. Landowner A walks onto Landowner B's property and picks up the apples. Landowner B sues Landowner A for entering onto his property without permission. A court deciding this issue must first determine whether there is a statute governing this situation. If there is no applicable statute, a court will rely on prior similar court decisions to determine whether there is mandatory precedent on this issue. If no mandatory precedent exists, the court is faced with a new, unresolved issue in its jurisdiction, often referred to as an issue of first impression. During the decision-making process, the court may look to persuasive precedent and other resources of law for guidance.[8] In addition, the court will consider how the decision will serve justice in the immediate situation and how the decision will support or further the goals of the public's interest in the future.

In Landowner A's situation, let's say the court decides that in the interest of fairness and in the interest of the public, Landowner A should have the right to go onto Landowner B's property to pick up the apples. The court must then draft the language of the rule. A rule that states, "Owners of apple trees have the right to walk on adjoining property to pick up apples that have fallen from their trees," certainly addresses the current case. But how does this rule affect future situations? Should an owner of peach trees, for example, have the same right to pick up peaches that have fallen onto a neighboring property? Is there any real difference between apples and peaches in this situation? If there is no real difference between apples and peaches, then the rule may have been drafted too narrowly.

Conversely, a rule that is written too broadly can also create problems. A broadly constructed rule can unintentionally affect fact situations far outside the intended scope of the rule. As with a rule that is too narrowly stated, a rule that uses overly broad language can create uncertainty in the law. This can result in a flood of litigation attempting to weaken the rule by arguing for exceptions to the rule.

Referring again to the case of Landowner A's retrieval of apples from Landowner B's property, a rule that states, "A person has the right to enter the land of another in order to retrieve his property," is unquestionably broad. This rule, as written, would seem to give anyone the right to walk onto someone else's property. This could be especially burdensome, for instance, to a homeowner whose land borders a golf course. The broadly worded rule would give all golfers the right to retrieve their golf balls landing on the homeowner's property. This scenario may result in numerous people walking onto the homeowner's property and arguably gives rise to fairness and perhaps public interest concerns that are quite different from Landowner B's situation, which merely involves an adjoining landowner's right to retrieve his property.

A court deciding the issue of whether a landowner can retrieve apples from neighboring property would probably not want to construct a rule that has such a far-reaching effect. Perhaps it would be better to leave the decision regarding the

---

8. *See supra* n. 7.

retrieval of golf balls to a time when such an issue arises and the court is in a better position to contemplate the particular concerns of that issue.

Therefore, the court must carefully draft rules that are neither too narrow or too broad. Ideally, it chooses words that include those groups intended to be affected by the rule and excludes all others. Limiting the landowner's right to enter another's property only to retrieve apples leaves open the question of whether the rule should also apply to retrieving other fruit. Conversely, permitting persons the right to retrieve any of their property from another's land may give rights far beyond those contemplated by the current situation before the court.

Ideally, a judge not only drafts a rule that provides a fair result for the parties in the current case but also provides guidance to potential parties in future cases. The following exercise and those in the remainder of this chapter, inspired by stories from Greek mythology, are designed to give you a sense of a judge's difficult task in creating and developing precedent.

● Exercise 2-B[9]

Murder, violence, and plots for power trouble the ancient country of Fairland. In an effort to bring justice and order to the land, the people created a citizens' Assembly and a Court. The Assembly, made up of representatives elected from various regions of Fairland, enacts the laws. The Court, comprising a panel of six judges, interprets and applies enacted laws to disputes between parties. The Court also creates and applies common law to disputes when no enacted law governs the situation. You are one of the judges appointed to the Court. All legal disputes regarding civil matters (involving the private rights of citizens) are submitted to your Court for judgment.

The first case to come before the Court is the following: Nicholas, the commander of Fairland's armies, returned triumphant from a great war. As part of his spoils from the war, he brought home his mistress, Cassandra, a princess from the defeated country. Nicholas's jealous wife, Selena, kills Nicholas and his mistress. Under his Last Will and Testament, created before he set sail for the war, Nicholas had left his entire estate to Selena, if she should survive him. Otis, the son of Nicholas and Selena, argues before the Court that his mother should not have any of his father's estate because she caused his death. Otis claims that, as next in line to inherit, he should receive his father's estate.

Although the Assembly had passed a law providing that one who intentionally causes the death of another may be imprisoned, there are no enacted laws addressing whether a murderer can inherit the property from his or her victim. Selena pled guilty

---

9. This exercise is loosely based on the triumphant return of Agamemnon, the commander of the Greek armies, from the Trojan War, bringing with him a princess of Troy and invoking the jealous anger of his wife, Clytemnestra.

to intentionally killing her husband and his mistress. The Court must decide whether Selena should inherit Nicholas's estate.

   a. In addition to the argument previously mentioned, are there any additional arguments Otis might use to support his position that he should receive Nicholas's estate?

   b. What arguments might Selena use to support her position that she should inherit Nicholas's estate?

   c. How will you decide this case?

   d. In addition to the parties' arguments, will you be guided by social customs, religious convictions, and/or philosophical ideals?

   e. Draft a rule on which you will base your decision. Make sure that you carefully word the decision-making rule to address Selena's case adequately.

   f. When constructing your rule, were you mindful as to how your rule might have an impact on future cases?

2. The interaction between the common law and other forms of law

The federal constitution is the supreme law of the land. On the state level, a state constitution follows right behind the federal constitution in level of importance. All other laws — federal and state statutes, regulations promulgated under statutes, and common law — cannot infringe on federal constitutional law. On the state level, a state's statutes, regulations promulgated under state statutes, and common law cannot violate federal or state constitutional law.

Courts, as guardians of the federal and state constitutions, must ensure that constitutional rights and protections are not violated by statutes, regulations, or court decisions. Sometimes legislatures enact a statute that may inadvertently infringe on rights and protections provided under the U.S. Constitution or a state's constitution. In these instances, the court must determine whether the statute violates the constitutional law. If the court finds a statute applied in any circumstance would be unconstitutional, then the statute will no longer be given force and effect. For example, the Washington Supreme Court in a 2003 decision found a Washington statute unconstitutional, and thus unenforceable, because it exempted in-state wine producers from a statute that required out-of-state wine producers to give notice and cause before terminating contracts with distributors in the state.[10] The statute at issue violated the Commerce Clause of the U.S. Constitution[11] because the exemption impermissibly "protect[ed] in-state wine producers and discriminate[d] against out-of-state producers" by allowing in-state producers more flexibility to do business.[12]

---

   10. *Mt. Hood Beverage Co. v. Constellation Brands*, 63 P.3d 779 (Wash. 2003) (finding § 19.126.040 of the Washington Code unconstitutional).

   11. U.S. Const. art. I, § 8, cl. 3.

   12. *Mt. Hood Beverage*, 63 P.3d at 786–787.

If a statute is constitutional, a court must abide by the statute. A court cannot create precedent that runs contrary to a statute enacted by the legislature. Because the legislature has supremacy over the courts in its law-making power, a constitutional statute has paramount authority over common law.

Sometimes, though, a statute can be ambiguous or vague as written or as applied to a certain factual situation. In these instances, the court's role is to interpret the statute to determine whether the statute applies to the case facts currently before the court.[13] As a part of this determination, the court may also decide whether the statute takes the place of any prior common law, reflects the common law, or supplements the common law. If the legislature does not agree with the court's interpretation of the statute, the legislature may amend the statute to express more clearly the legislative intent behind the statute.

Even if a statute does not directly apply to the factual circumstances of a case before the court, the public policy that motivated the enactment of the statute may or may not influence a court in determining whether to extend the law expressed in the statute to other factual situations.

● Exercise 2-C[14]

After the case of Selena, the Assembly hurriedly passed the following statute without debate or discussion:

> No person who intentionally causes the death of another shall in any way benefit by the death. All property of the decedent[15] and all money shall pass as if the guilty person had predeceased[16] the decedent.

Several months after the enactment of this "slayer statute," you are now faced with the following case:

A huge wild pig was ravaging the countryside in northern Fairland. Cyril, a wealthy man in that region, ordered his son, Stephen, to kill the wild pig. Thinking to make it a great sport, Stephen invited Fairland's best hunters from all reaches of the country to help him hunt the wild pig. Part of the reward would be the wild pig's hide and tusks. Among those to answer his call were his two uncles. Diana, a beautiful huntress, also joined the hunt. During the hunt, Stephen and his uncles fell in love with Diana. Although Diana dealt the first blow to the wild pig, Stephen gave the wild pig the lethal strike. Stephen gave the wild pig's hide and tusks to Diana in an effort to win her heart. His plan worked. Stephen's uncles, jealous of Stephen's victory and his wooing of Diana, fought with him, using their spears. One uncle's spear tip actually cut Stephen's shoulder, just above his heart. Fearing for his life, Stephen killed his uncles.

self - defense?

---

13. A more detailed explanation of the court's role in statutory interpretation is given in Chapter 13.

14. This exercise is loosely based on a Greek myth often referred to as the Calydonian Boar Hunt.

15. *Decedent* means a deceased person.

16. *Predeceased* as used in the statute means the guilty party will be treated for purposes of inheritance as though he died before the decedent.

Stephen's uncles, who were on good terms with Stephen until that fateful day, had named Stephen as the heir[17] to their property. Stephen's mother, outraged that Stephen killed her brothers, does not want Stephen to receive the inheritance. The Court must determine whether Stephen may inherit from his uncles' estates.

   a. What arguments might Stephen use to support his position that he should inherit his uncles' estates? *[handwritten: ① Trust & Will is a gift, rather than a trade] [handwritten margin: ② self-defense trade between estates and uncles might reconsider being good to me]*
   b. What arguments might Stephen's mother use to support her position that Stephen should not inherit his uncles' estates?
   c. Should Stephen receive his inheritance from his uncles' estates? Why or why not? *[handwritten: Yes]*
   d. Does the statute or the precedent from Selena's case apply to Stephen? Explain. *[handwritten margin: No, self-defense]*
   e. Consider the public policy that perhaps motivated the legislature to enact the statute. Is that public policy applicable to Stephen's situation? Why or why not? *[handwritten margin: No. It was Uncles who started the fight out of jealousy]*
   f. Does the statute replace the common law expressed in the prior case involving Selena, or does it reflect or supplement the common law?
   g. If the statute is not applicable to Stephen's situation, construct a rule that reflects your decision in this case. Remember, you must reconcile the rule created in Selena's case with the rule in Stephen's situation. Be mindful too how the new rule will affect future cases.

[handwritten: Exception: A person who causes the death or of self-defense in an appropriate way may not be subject to the foregoing statute (slayer)]

3. The living law

A court must adhere to the constraints of mandatory precedent, as well as constitutional and statutory law, but this does not mean that the common law is stagnant and unchanging. On the contrary, the common law is "living law." It is constantly evolving to keep abreast of scientific and technological advancements, as well as changing social customs and economic considerations.

Traditionally, courts have used three rationales to depart from mandatory precedent:[18] (1) a development in the law has created a conflict between two precedents,[19]

---

17. *Heir* means a person who stands to inherit property.

18. Amy L. Padden, *Overruling Decisions in the Supreme Court: The Role of a Decision's Vote, Age, and Subject Matter in the Application of Stare Decisis after* Payne v. Tennessee, 82 Geo. L.J. 1689, 1694 (1994).

19. *See generally* Maltz, *supra* n. 4, at 383. In his article, Professor Maltz cites as an example the United States Supreme Court decision in *City of New Orleans v. Dukes*, 427 U.S. 297 (1976), which overruled the Court's prior decision in *Morey v. Doud*, 354 U.S. 457 (1957). *Id.* In *Morey*, the Court held that the special exemption of the American Express Company from the Illinois Currency Act was unconstitutional because the classification lacked a rational basis for doing so. *Morey*, 354 U.S. at 466-469, *cited in* Maltz, *supra* n. 4, at 383 n. 81. Since *Morey*, there had been an "unbroken line of cases that left states free to make classifications in cases involving purely economic regulations"; however, in an effort to avoid further confusion in the lower courts that sometimes relied on *Morey* to strike down local business regulations, the *Dukes* court overruled *Morey*. *Maltz, supra* n. 4, at 383 (citing *Dukes*, 427 U.S. at 306).

(2) the rule underlying the precedent is flawed[20] or has become unworkable,[21] or (3) the policy supporting the precedent does not reflect contemporary public policy interests and concerns.[22] In these instances, the court, typically the highest court in the jurisdiction, will reject the governing precedent by overruling the precedent and creating a new rule of law that will serve as precedent in future cases.

● Exercise 2-D[23]

After reaching a decision as to whether Stephen can inherit his uncles' estates (see Exercise 2-C), the Court is faced with yet another inheritance issue that may involve Fairland's "slayer statute." Early in his career as an adventurer and soldier, Titus married Helen. Helen inherited a large estate from her father. Several years passed, and Titus began experiencing mental problems. In a fit of madness, he killed Helen. Titus was not punished for the murder because of his insanity. Helen's Last Will and Testament names Titus as the sole beneficiary of her estate. Helen's surviving brother, Derek, does not want Titus to receive any of Helen's estate. The Court must determine whether Titus may inherit Helen's estate.

    a. What arguments might Derek use to support his position that Titus should not receive any of Helen's estate?

    b. What arguments might Titus use to support his position that he should inherit Helen's estate?

    c. Should the statute or the precedent from the cases of Selena and Stephen apply to Titus's situation? Explain.

    d. State a rule that supports your decision as to whether Titus can inherit from Helen's estate.

● Exercise 2-E[24]

Titus eventually recovered his sanity and went on to many grand adventures. He became quite famous and wealthy. During one of his adventures, he fell in love with

---

20. *See, e.g., Proctor v. State*, 967 S.W.2d 840, 845 & n. 4 (Tex. Crim. App. 1998) (noting that prior decisions by the court were "poorly reasoned," the court overruled precedent requiring the state to prove beyond a reasonable doubt that prosecution was not barred by the statute of limitations, even when the defendant does not raise the issue).

21. *See, e.g., Padilla v. State Farm Mut. Auto. Ins. Co.*, 68 P.3d 901 (N.M. 2003) (reasoning the prior rule unworkable, the court overruled precedent that upheld arbitration provisions in automobile insurance contracts providing for binding arbitration so long as the award did not exceed the limits under statute and would be subject to de novo appeal by either party). *See also Payne v. Tennessee*, 501 U.S. 808, 827 (1991) (finding that a departure from stare decisis is permissible "when governing decisions are unworkable or are badly reasoned"), *cited in Padilla*, 68 P.3d at 907.

22. *See, e.g., State v. Valentine*, 935 P.2d 1294 (Wash. 1997) (court relied on a perceived change in public policy to overrule prior common law that permitted citizens to resist unlawful arrests).

23. This exercise is loosely based on one of the many tales involving the Grecian adventurer and hero Herakles.

24. This exercise is loosely based on one of the many tales involving the Grecian adventurer and hero Herakles.

[handwritten: Titus fell in love with.]

his archenemy's daughter, Iris. Even so, he married Alexa. Titus eventually defeated his archenemy and carried off his longtime lover, Iris, despite being married still. When Alexa heard about this, she mixed a love potion and soaked one of Titus's shirts with it. She had been told that the potion would guarantee the return of her straying husband. She sent the shirt to Titus by way of a messenger. When Titus put on the shirt, the potion began burning his flesh. He twisted and squirmed in agony. Convinced his death was imminent, he had a funeral pyre[25] built, laid himself on it, and begged someone to light it to put him out of his misery. No one wanted to do it. Finally, his friend Philip, a great archer, took pity on Titus's suffering and lit the pyre. Unknown to Philip at the time, he stood to inherit a large amount of land and money under Titus's Last Will and Testament.

Philip received the minimum prison sentence for intentionally causing the death of Titus. Jason, the son of Titus and Alexa, has decided to contest Philip's inheritance. The Court must determine whether Philip may inherit from Titus's estate.

  a. What arguments might Jason use to support his position that Philip should not receive any of Titus's estate? *[handwritten: slayer statute.   intentional killer]*
  b. What arguments might Philip use to support his position that he should receive the estate? *[handwritten: killing out of good will / consent]*
  c. For a. and b., consider how you can use the statute and precedent to support arguments for each position. Explain.
  d. State a rule that supports your decision whether Philip should receive Titus's estate. *[handwritten: Exception: A person who causes the death with the dead's consent and out of good-will may not be subject to the slayer statute]*

● Exercise 2-F

Philip writes a play about Titus's death. He presents the play at Fairland's spring festival where his play competes against other plays for the honor of the best play of the festival. Philip's play wins the competition, and he receives a valuable prize of gold. Jason, the son of Titus and Alexa, has decided to contest Philip's receipt of the prize. The Court must determine whether Philip may keep the prize.

  a. What arguments might be used to support the position that Philip should keep the prize? *[handwritten: He wins the prize through beating others in the competition]*
  b. What arguments might be used to support the position that Philip must forfeit the prize? *[handwritten: Without the son's consent. Jason cares about how his parents are portrayed in the play and is vulnerable to others']*
  c. For a. and b., consider how you might use the statute and precedent to support arguments for each position. Explain. *[handwritten: unrelated std prod w Will & Testament others' comments on his parents.]*
  d. Should Philip be permitted to keep the prize? State the reasons supporting your decision. *[handwritten: Yeah. he wins to the way stated by the festival host.]*

[handwritten: Yet, he shall pay damages to Jason]
[handwritten: P.S. Did Philip use Titus & Alexa's real names in the play?]

---

25. *Pyre* is a mound of flammable materials on which a dead body is placed and burned as part of a funeral ritual.

CHAPTER
3

The Anatomy of the Civil Litigation Process

eric bodnar @ sandiego.edu

HIGHLIGHTS

- Parties to a legal dispute may seek resolution of a dispute through informal negotiations, mediation, or arbitration, or a party may seek a more formal means of resolving a dispute by filing a complaint in court.
- The complaint must be filed in a court that has personal jurisdiction over the parties and subject matter jurisdiction over the dispute.
- The pleadings stage is the first stage of the formal litigation process, which includes the complaint and the defendant's response to the complaint.
- During the discovery stage, the parties investigate and collect information related to the dispute through methods such as interrogatories, depositions, and requests for production of documents.
- A dispute may be resolved without going to trial in one of the following ways: the court enters a default judgment against a party, the parties agree to dismiss the complaint, or the court grants a party's motion to dismiss or a motion for summary judgment. Prior to trial, a pretrial conference may be held to manage and expedite the trial proceedings.
- At trial, each party to the dispute has an opportunity to present its case through witness testimony and the presentation of evidence.
- A losing party may appeal the trial court's final judgment and any judicial orders made by the judge during the trial.
- Once a dispute has been fully litigated and a final judgment entered, the parties are barred from re-litigating the dispute.

This chapter provides an overview of the basic civil litigation process. It is not intended as an exhaustive discussion of civil procedure.[1] Unless otherwise noted, this chapter focuses on the rules of procedure for a civil matter in federal court, though many states pattern their rules of procedure after the federal rules.[2]

 ## A. The Client Interview

The U.S. civil litigation process begins when the client meets with the lawyer for the first time to discuss a legal problem. The objectives of the client will vary. The client may want the lawyer to bring on his behalf a legal action against another person or entity. Alternatively, the client may have been named a party in a lawsuit and wants the lawyer to represent him in the matter. Or, the client may want the lawyer to negotiate on his behalf a resolution to the legal problem without court involvement. In any event, the lawyer will want to collect the following information:

(1) The identification of the parties involved, including (if possible) addresses, telephone numbers, fax numbers, and email addresses.
(2) Where the key events of the problem arose.
(3) All facts related to or giving rise to the legal problem.
(4) When the events related to or giving rise to the legal problem occurred.
(5) Copies of all writings, papers, and documents related to the legal problem.

As part of assessing the client's case, a lawyer may summarize the important facts of the case gathered from the above listed information before researching the problem. In this way the lawyer brings some order to the interview notes, identifies follow-up questions that she needs to ask, and becomes more familiar with the facts.

 ## B. Assessing the Law and a Course of Action

The next step usually is to research the law to determine the legal issues and the strength of the client's case. A good U.S. law library contains a massive collection of legal resources for researching the law in the United States. Most of these resources also are found on the Internet. Before opening a book or turning on a computer, however,

---

1. Neither does this chapter discuss procedure involving criminal law nor special cases such as those presented in military court, bankruptcy court, and tax court. The types of procedure used in these cases move through stages similar to those in civil actions, but they also include significant differences.

2. *See, e.g.,* Charles Alan Wright, *Law of Federal Courts* 430 (5th ed., West 1994). Generally, the Federal Rules of Civil Procedure "govern the procedure in the United States district courts in all suits of a civil nature. . . ." Fed. R. Civ. P. 1. Each state has its own set of trial rules for governing the procedure of civil lawsuits.

it is best to create a research plan, which helps a lawyer avoid becoming overwhelmed or losing focus while researching. (Developing a research plan is discussed in Chapter 5.) Sometimes a junior member of a law firm is asked to perform the research and write for a senior lawyer's review a memorandum analyzing the client's legal question in light of the controlling law. (Writing a legal memorandum is discussed in Part Three, Chapters 7 through 10.)

A lawyer is in a better position to assess the client's legal position and determine a course of action that best protects the client's interests after completing the research or after reviewing a legal memorandum discussing the client's situation. The lawyer may discuss the findings with the client and make recommendations for possible courses of action in a personal meeting or in a more formal letter. (Writing a client letter is covered in Chapter 16.)

Contrary to what perhaps is popular belief, a U.S. lawyer who finds that a client has a viable legal action does not always immediately rush to court with a written complaint in hand. At this early stage, the lawyer's role is one of negotiator on behalf of the client. As a negotiator, the lawyer often attempts to seek a resolution to the client's problem outside of the courtroom, even before commencing any legal action. For example, if the client wants another party to take a particular action, the lawyer may write a letter on the client's behalf to the other party insisting on this action. (Chapter 16 discusses drafting a demand letter.) Negotiating a resolution to the client's problem also can involve oral communication between the lawyer and the other parties or, if the other parties are represented by legal counsel, the other parties' attorneys. This informal negotiation process may continue even while the parties are engaged in the pleading, discovery, or trial stage of the litigation process.

C. Alternative Dispute Resolution

Over the past 20 years, alternative dispute resolution (ADR) methods have been used increasingly to resolve civil disputes in the United States. Parties may be reluctant to resolve a dispute through formal litigation. Litigation in court can be quite costly and time consuming. In addition, pleadings and accompanying documents are available to the public. This gives rise to concern when parties want to keep certain information private. In some circumstances, ADR methods can lead to quicker resolution of the dispute and result in less cost than court-centered litigation. ADR methods also preserve the parties' privacy.

ADR methods that can be used prior to commencement of formal litigation in court include mediation and the more structured process of arbitration. In mediation, the parties seek to resolve issues through cooperation and problem solving with a neutral third party acting as a mediator. Arbitration follows a process similar to formal litigation in the courts, but the parties have more control over the arbitration procedure. In arbitration, the parties present their respective positions to a neutral fact-finder (the arbitrator) who then issues a decision in the matter. The parties may agree beforehand as to whether the arbitrator's judgment will be binding on the parties or merely advisory.

Mediation and arbitration also are available in some jurisdictions after formal litigation has commenced. In these jurisdictions, courts may order the parties to seek mediation. Alternatively, the parties may ask the court to order mediation or the parties may agree to arbitrate in an attempt to resolve some or all issues before the court. The case remains on the court's docket while mediation or arbitration is pursued. The court is available to issue orders, if necessary, to ensure that the parties continue to participate in the ADR process. If no resolution can be reached, mediation or arbitration may be abandoned and the case resumes moving forward in court.

In the interest of conserving judicial resources in a busy court system, some jurisdictions also may provide for additional ADR mechanisms, such as mini-trials, summary jury trials, and the appointment of a private judge. All parties must agree to the process before any of these options may be used.

D. Formal Litigation in the U.S. Civil Court System

Sometimes, despite a lawyer's best efforts at negotiating a resolution to the problem, the only way to obtain relief is to bring the matter to court. The following is a brief introduction to aspects of the civil litigation process. See also Figure 3-1, which charts the basic stages in the civil litigation process.

1. Choice of forum

In the preliminary stage of the formal litigation process, the parties must decide in which court to bring the lawsuit. A court must have personal jurisdiction over the parties so the judgment reached by the court will be enforceable over the parties.[3] A court must also possess the power to adjudicate the disputed claims, more commonly referred to as subject matter jurisdiction.[4]

In addition to the personal jurisdiction and subject matter jurisdiction requirements, the parties must give some thought to a variety of venue[5] considerations when deciding which court should hear the controversy. Considerations may include trying the case in a court presided over by a sympathetic judge, in a court that follows more favorable procedural court rules, or in a court situated in a location convenient to the parties, testifying witnesses, or physical evidence.[6]

---

3. *Ruhrgas AG v. Marathon Oil Co.*, 526 U.S. 574, 584 (1999).

4. *Id.* (citing Fed. R. Civ. P. 12(h)(3)).

5. "Venue deals with the locality of the suit, that is, with the question of which [c]ourt, or [c]ourts, of those that possess adequate personal and subject matter jurisdiction may hear the specific suit in question." *Japan Gas Lighter Assn. v. Ronson Corp.*, 257 F. Supp. 219, 221 (D.N.J. 1966).

6. *See, e.g., Goggins v. Alliance Capital Mgmt.*, 279 F. Supp. 228 (S.D.N.Y. 2003).

Basic Stages in Formal Civil Litigation

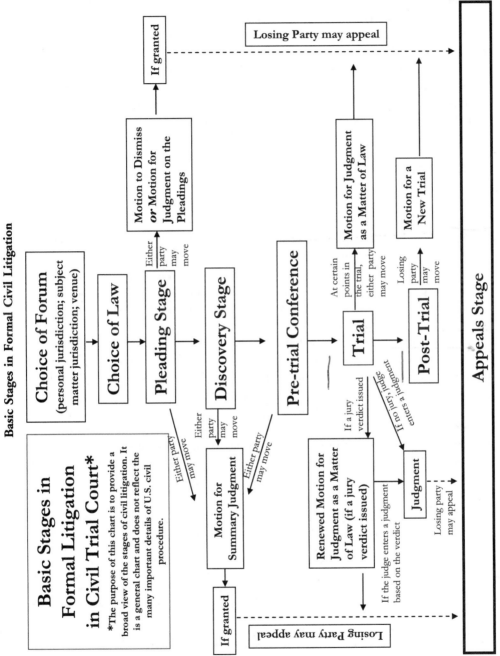

Basic Stages in Formal Litigation in Civil Trial Court*

*The purpose of this chart is to provide a broad view of the stages of civil litigation. It is a general chart and does not reflect the many important details of U.S. civil procedure.

Choice of Forum (personal jurisdiction; subject matter jurisdiction; venue)

Choice of Law

Pleading Stage

Discovery Stage

Pre-trial Conference

Trial

Post-Trial

Appeals Stage

Motion to Dismiss *or* Motion for Judgment on the Pleadings

Either party may move

If granted

Losing Party may appeal

Motion for Summary Judgment

Either party may move

Either party may move

If granted

Losing Party may appeal

Motion for Judgment as a Matter of Law

At certain points in the trial, either party may move

Motion for a New Trial

Losing party may move

Renewed Motion for Judgment as a Matter of Law (if a jury verdict issued)

If a jury verdict issued

If no jury, judge enters a judgment

If the judge enters a judgment based on the verdict

Judgment

Losing party may appeal

Figure 3-1

The plaintiff, as the party bringing the action, will choose the court in which to file the complaint. But this does not guarantee that the plaintiff's chosen court will hear the matter. The defendant in the action may object to the forum chosen by the plaintiff for a variety of reasons and may be able to convince the court in the original forum that another court is more suitable to hear the dispute. For example, a defendant may request removal of a case originally filed in a state court to a federal court if the case involves a federal law question. And, in a case brought in a state court, the defendant might request a change of venue to another court in the state that is more conveniently located to all parties or is more impartial to the plaintiff.

2. Choice of law

When deciding on a court in which to litigate a case, the lawyer must consider the procedural and substantive laws[7] the court will apply to resolve the controversy. A court applies the law of its own forum to procedural matters. But predicting which substantive law a court will apply is not always as straightforward as it seems. It would be natural to assume that a court will always apply the substantive law of its own forum. Indeed, this is the case where a state court is faced with a state law question, and the parties and the events giving rise to the dispute are within the state's jurisdictional boundaries.

In some instances, however, a court will use the substantive law of another jurisdiction. A federal court, for example, will apply state substantive law to a state law question raised in a diversity jurisdiction action.[8] A state court will apply federal substantive law in actions where federal statutes permit a claimant to bring an action in state court for a violation of federal law.[9] And where transactions or occurrences surrounding the dispute have significant connections to more than one jurisdiction, the court will decide which jurisdiction's substantive law will determine the parties' rights and obligations. A court may consider factors, such as where the parties reside;

---

7. Substantive laws determine the parties' rights and obligations that are at issue in the pleadings. Procedural law governs the process that will determine these rights and obligations.

8. The exercise at the end of this chapter provides an example. In the exercise, a client from Illinois seeks the return of a painting stolen from her home. The painting is in the possession of a doctor, a citizen of the fictitious state of East Carolina, who refuses to return the painting. The client will have to bring a legal action in a court that has jurisdiction over the doctor so that, if the client prevails, the court will have the power to order the doctor to return the painting. The client and the doctor are citizens of different States, and the painting is valued at more than $75,000. Therefore, although the return of personal property (such as the painting) is governed by state law, the client may consider bringing the action in a federal district court located in East Carolina, rather than a state trial court in East Carolina. Federal district courts located in the citizen's home state are presumed to be more impartial to a citizen than a state court from that citizen's home state. If the client brings the action in federal district court, the court will need to decide whether to apply the law of Illinois or East Carolina to determine the respective parties' rights to the painting.

9. *Schneider v. Susquehanna Radio Corp.*, 581 S.E.2d 603 (Ga. App. 2003), provides an example of a state court applying federal law. In this case, claimant filed a cause of action against a radio station for allegedly violating the federal Telephone Consumer Protection Act (TCPA). Under 47 U.S.C. § 227(b)(3) (1999), a claimant can bring an action in state court for a violation of the TCPA.

the particular claims raised by the pleadings; the location of the subject matter of the lawsuit, if relevant; and the location(s) where the events giving rise to the dispute took place.[10]

3. The pleading stage

Once the plaintiff has determined the most appropriate forum for the dispute, the plaintiff will file a pleading with the court setting out the claims against the defendant, the basis for the court's jurisdiction, and a request for the court to grant specific relief.

In federal courts, a legal action commences with the filing of the complaint.[11] What constitutes the official commencement of an action in a state court varies from state to state. In some states, the legal action begins with the filing of the complaint. In other states, the action begins when all defendants to the action are served with a copy of the complaint along with a summons to appear in court and respond to the plaintiff's claims ("service of process"). The Federal Rules of Civil Procedure set out federal compliance requirements for service of process.[12] What constitutes adequate service of the complaint and summons on all state court defendants varies from state to state.

A defendant may respond to the complaint by either filing with the court an answer to the complaint, a motion for the court to dismiss the complaint, or both.[13] If the defendant fails to respond to the complaint in one of these ways within the period of time specified by the court rules, the clerk of the court will enter a default judgment in favor of the plaintiff.[14] Obviously, the defendant will want to avoid this outcome.

The defendant's answer will specifically respond to each allegation raised in the plaintiff's complaint. As to each allegation, the defendant may elect to admit, deny, or plead that he "lacks knowledge or information sufficient to form a belief about the truth of an allegation. . . ."[15] The last response will be treated, in effect, as a denial.[16]

In addition, the defendant may raise any available affirmative defense.[17] An affirmative defense pleads a new matter not raised by the allegations in the complaint. An affirmative defense asserts that if this new matter is true, the defendant will prevail regardless of whether the plaintiff's allegations are true. For example, most claims have statutorily imposed time limits for filing a complaint. These so-called statutes of

---

10. *See, e.g., Restatement (Second) of Conflicts of Law* §§ 145, 188(2) (1971). Restatements, prepared by legal scholars, practitioners, and judges, cover areas of law such as contracts, torts, or, as here, conflicts of law. Courts are not required, but may be persuaded, to apply a Restatement's guidance to resolve disputes. Conflicts of law, a topic typically covered in upper-level law courses at U.S. law schools, focuses on determining which law applies to resolve a dispute when the subject matter of the dispute has a connection to more than one jurisdiction.

11. Fed. R. Civ. P. 3.

12. Fed. R. Civ. P. 4.

13. Fed. R. Civ. P. 12.

14. Fed. R. Civ. P. 55(a).

15. Fed. R. Civ. P. 8(b).

16. *Id.*

17. Fed. R. Civ. P. 8(c).

limitations protect defendants from loss of evidence that might have helped defeat the claim and from "the emotional stress and financial uncertainty" of possibly being brought into court on an old claim.[18] The expiration of a statute of limitations is an affirmative defense that can be raised if the plaintiff fails to file a timely claim. Rule 8(c) of the Federal Rules of Civil Procedure provides a long, but incomplete, list of other examples of affirmative defenses.

A defendant also may assert a claim against any codefendant, called a cross-claim, arising from an opposing party's claims.[19] A defendant may also bring claims against a plaintiff, called a counterclaim, which may or may not relate to the claims arising from the plaintiff's complaint.[20] In turn, the party against whom the counterclaim or cross-claim is asserted must file a reply to the claim.[21]

As an alternative or in addition to filing an answer, the defendant may file a motion to dismiss the plaintiff's complaint or a motion to dismiss certain claims contained in the plaintiff's complaint.[22] A judge may dismiss a complaint because the complaint failed to state a valid claim in the complaint on which relief can be granted, the court lacked personal jurisdiction over the defendant, or the court lacked subject matter jurisdiction over the dispute.[23]

In a motion to dismiss, the defendant asserts that even if the facts alleged in the plaintiff's complaint are true, the complaint must be dismissed as a matter of law because there is no legal basis for the claim.[24] If the court grants the defendant's motion to dismiss, a judgment is entered in favor of the defendant, dismissing the entire complaint or specific claims stated in the complaint. If the judge denies the motion to dismiss, the defendant must respond to the allegations in the complaint, if she has not already done so.

Additionally, any time between the close of pleadings[25] and prior to trial, a party may move for a judgment on the pleadings.[26] The party moving for a judgment on the pleadings asserts that, based on the pleadings filed by the parties, the court should enter judgment for the moving party as a matter of law. The basis for this motion and the standard the court uses for determining whether to grant it are the same as for a motion to dismiss. If the court grants the motion, a judgment is entered for the moving party. If the court denies the motion, the litigation proceeds with discovery or, if discovery has already begun, the discovery process continues.

---

18. Gene R. Shreve & Peter Raven-Hansen, *Understanding Civil Procedure* 240 (3d ed., LexisNexis 2002).

19. Fed. R. Civ. P. 13(g).

20. Fed. R. Civ. P. 13(a) & (b). A counterclaim is litigated between opposing parties in the original action, whereas a cross-claim is litigated by parties on the same side in the original action.

21. Fed. R. Civ. P. 7(a).

22. Fed. R. Civ. P. 12(b).

23. Fed. R. Civ. P. 12(b).

24. *See, e.g., Rippy* ex rel. *Rippy v. Hattaway,* 270 F.2d 416, 419 (6th Cir. 2001).

25. Pleadings are deemed closed when the defendants have filed their answers to the complaint and the parties have filed replies to any cross-claims and counterclaims.

26. Fed. R. Civ. P. 12(c).

4. The discovery stage

During the discovery stage, the parties have the opportunity to investigate and collect information related to any claims or defenses raised in the pleadings. This not only assists the parties in preparing for trial but also helps the parties identify issues and determine the strengths or weaknesses of their respective positions.

There are several methods of discovery. Interrogatories are a series of written questions that must be answered in writing by the opposing party.[27] Depositions are an oral means of discovery where a party or witness is questioned either orally[28] or in writing[29] about matters related to the controversy and the deposed party responds orally to the questions. A court reporter records the questions and answers, and prepares a transcript of the deposition for the parties.

In addition to interrogatories and depositions, a party also may request documents relating to the dispute, such as a contract in the case of a contractual dispute.[30] A party also may request an inspection of a physical site, provided it is relevant to the controversy.[31] If the mental or physical condition of a party is at issue, a court may order the party to submit to an examination.[32]

Finally, as a part of discovery, a party may ask the court to submit to an opposing party written fact statements, which the opposing party must admit or deny.[33] If any statement is admitted, then the admission is binding at trial, meaning that the court will treat the fact as established, making it unnecessary to prove it at trial.[34]

5. Resolution of the dispute prior to trial

Most cases are settled or dismissed prior to trial.[35] For example, a dispute can be resolved without going to trial if the plaintiff voluntarily withdraws the complaint as permitted under the trial rules or if all parties agree to dismiss the case because they have reached an out-of-court settlement.[36] A court also has the power to involuntarily

---

27. Fed. R. Civ. P. 33.

28. Fed. R. Civ. P. 30.

29. Fed. R. Civ. P. 31. In a "written" deposition, the deposer provides written questions to the deponent (the person being questioned) ahead of time. Here, the deposer's attorney is not present to observe the deponent when he answers the questions. Rather, a court reporter reads the questions to the deponent, who orally answers the questions, and the court reporter records the answer. The advantage of this form of deposition is that it is cheaper for the party who requests the deposition because that party avoids the costs of having an attorney present during the deposition.

30. Fed. R. Civ. P. 34.

31. *Id.*

32. Fed. R. Civ. P. 35.

33. Fed. R. Civ. P. 36.

34. Fed. R. Civ. P. 36(b).

35. *See generally* Chris Guthrie, *Understanding Settlement in Damages (and Beyond),* 2004 J. Dis. Res. 89, 89 (noting that "roughly two-thirds of all cases settle and most of the rest are resolved through motions").

36. Fed. R. Civ. P. 41(a).

dismiss an action before it reaches trial in situations where the plaintiff fails to timely pursue the case or fails to comply with trial rules or court orders.[37]

An action can also be resolved prior to trial if the court grants a party's motion for summary judgment and the judgment resolves all claims and requests for relief.[38] In a summary judgment motion, the moving party asks the court to enter a judgment in its favor on some or all of the claims. The moving party must assert that there are no genuine issues of material fact as to these claims and thus the moving party is "entitled to judgment as a matter of law."[39] In a supporting brief or during a hearing on a motion for summary judgment, the parties may use evidence outside the pleadings, including information uncovered during discovery, to support a motion for summary judgment.[40]

A claimant may move for summary judgment at any time after 20 days from the commencement of the action or any time after being served with a motion for summary judgment by the opposing party.[41] A defending party may move for summary judgment at any time.[42] If the court grants summary judgment as to any or all claims, the court will enter judgment in favor of the moving party as to those claims. If the court denies the motion, the parties continue with discovery or, if discovery is complete, the trial begins.

6. The pretrial conference

Prior to trial, the judge may order the attorneys representing opposing parties to attend a pretrial conference.[43] Pretrial conferences can help in the management and expedition of the trial. For instance, a conference gives the parties the opportunity to discuss such matters as limiting or restricting testimony at trial, stipulating matters of law, narrowing issues, identifying witnesses and documents, and reaching a settlement of the dispute.[44] The judge will issue a pretrial order stating any action taken at the pretrial conference. The pretrial order controls the proceedings of the case at trial, unless modified by subsequent order of the court.[45]

---

37. Fed. R. Civ. P. 41(b).

38. Fed. R. Civ. P. 56(d).

39. Fed. R. Civ. P. 56(c).

40. A motion for a judgment on the pleadings will be treated as a motion for summary judgment if the court permits the parties to introduce evidence beyond the pleadings to support their arguments. Fed. R. Civ. P. 12(c).

41. Fed. R. Civ. P. 56(a).

42. Fed. R. Civ. P. 56(b).

43. Fed. R. Civ. P. 16.

44. Fed. R. Civ. P. 16(c)(2).

45. Fed. R. Civ. P. 16(e).

7. The trial

In situations where a party fails to make a timely demand for a jury trial or where a party waives the right to a jury trial,[46] the case will be tried before the judge in a "bench trial" unless the court, in its discretion, orders a jury trial.[47] In bench trials, the judge will make findings of fact[48] and rulings of law.[49] In jury trials, the jury makes findings of fact, and the judge makes rulings of law.

The number of people serving on a civil jury varies. For example, the federal courts require at least six but not more than twelve jurors.[50] The members of a jury are determined by a proceeding known as voir dire. In voir dire, the attorneys or the judge asks questions of potential jurors and listens to their responses to determine whether the potential jurors will be fair and impartial when weighing the evidence.[51]

After the selection of a jury (if there is one), the trial begins with the attorney for the plaintiff making an opening statement, which is then followed by the opening statement by the attorney for the defendant. Next, the attorney for the plaintiff presents the plaintiff's case by asking questions of the plaintiff's witnesses on direct examination and introducing evidence in order to prove the claims alleged in the complaint. Here and throughout the trial, the judge supervises the conduct of those in the courtroom and determines what evidence is admissible.

The attorney for the defendant may cross-examine any of the plaintiff's witnesses. The attorney for either defendant or plaintiff can object to any question asked during direct examination or cross-examination. The attorney also can object to the introduction of any evidence that may violate the rules of evidence.[52] It is important for the attorney to promptly state her objection and the grounds on which she bases this objection. In this way, the objection is preserved in the trial record so that the issue can be raised, if appropriate, in the event of an appeal.[53] If the attorney fails to make a timely and specific objection, the alleged error is usually treated as waived unless there is "plain error."[54]

---

46. Fed. R. Civ. P. 38.

47. Fed. R. Civ. P. 39(b) & (c). According to the U.S. Department of Justice, in 2001 "there were an estimated 11,908 tort, contract, and real property cases" tried in 75 of the largest counties in the United States. Of this number, 8,859 cases were jury trials and 2,828 cases were bench trials. U.S. Dept. of Justice, Bureau of Justice Statistics, *Civil Justice Statistics*, http://www.ojp.usdoj.gov/bjs/civil.htm (last modified Mar. 25, 2007).

48. Findings of fact "generally respond to inquiries about who, when, what and where." Henry P. Monaghan, *Constitutional Fact Review*, 85 Colum. L. Rev. 229, 235 (1985).

49. "Rulings of law" determine what law will apply to the facts.

50. Fed. R. Civ. P. 48.

51. Fed. R. Civ. P. 47(a).

52. Rules of evidence are promulgated by state and federal courts to govern the admission of evidence during trials and hearings in the courts.

53. Fed. R. Evid. 103(a)(1). *See, e.g., Stringel v. Methodist Hosp. of Ind., Inc.*, 89 F.3d 415, 421 (7th Cir. 1996).

54. Fed. R. Evid. 103(d). "The plain error doctrine may be available to review evidentiary rulings to which no objection was made at trial if a moving party can demonstrate (1) that exceptional circumstances exist, (2) that substantial rights are affected, and (3) that a miscarriage of justice will result if the doctrine is not applied." *Stringel*, 89 F.3d at 421 (quoting *Prymer v. Ogden*, 29 F.3d 1208, 1214 (7th Cir. 1994)).

After the plaintiff's attorney has introduced all testimony or other evidence necessary to prove the allegations in the complaint, the attorney will rest the plaintiff's case. At this point, the attorney for the defendant may move for a judgment as a matter of law (JMOL), asking the court to direct a verdict in the defendant's favor based on the argument that "there is no legally sufficient evidentiary basis for a reasonable jury to find for [the plaintiff]. . . ."[55] If the court grants the JMOL, then a judgment is entered in favor of the defendants. In essence, the matter for adjudication is taken away from the jury (if there is one), and the judge enters a judgment for the defendant as a matter of law. In the event the court denies the JMOL, however, the trial will proceed with the defendant presenting his case.

The attorney's presentation of the defendant's case includes direct examination of the defendant's witnesses and the offering of evidence into the record. This time the attorney for the plaintiff has the opportunity to cross-examine any of the defendant's witnesses. Again, the judge presides over courtroom conduct and determines whether evidence is admissible.

After the close of the defendant's case but before the case is given to the jury, either party can move for a JMOL, directing the court to rule in its favor.[56] If the judge grants the motion, then the judge will enter a judgment in favor of the moving party, and the trial ends. If the judge denies a JMOL after the close of the defendant's case, the plaintiff has the opportunity to provide evidence that rebuts any evidence introduced by the defendant. The defendant, in turn, is given a chance to present evidence that rebuts the evidence introduced in the plaintiff's rebuttal. Finally, the attorneys for the plaintiff and defendant present their closing arguments.

After the closing arguments in a bench trial, the judge considers the evidence presented in the case in light of the applicable law, reaches a decision, and enters a judgment. If it is a jury trial, the jury will deliberate over the facts of the case in light of instructions of law from the judge to reach a decision about the case.

When the jury returns its decision, called a verdict, the losing party may renew its motion for JMOL (often referred to as RJMOL or, under old terminology, a judgment notwithstanding the verdict or JNOV). The losing party moving for a RJMOL requests the judge to enter a judgment in that party's favor, despite the jury's verdict against that party.[57] If the judge finds insufficient evidence to support the verdict, then the judge grants the RJMOL.[58] If the judge finds the verdict reasonable, the judge enters a judgment reflecting the jury verdict.[59]

---

55. Fed. R. Civ. P. 50(a)(1).
56. Fed. R. Civ. P. 50(a).
57. Fed. R. Civ. P. 50(b).
58. *Id.*
59. Fed. R. Civ. P. 50(b)(1).

8. Post-trial stage

The losing party may move for a new trial.[60] This motion can be filed as an alternative motion at the same time as the filing of a RJMOL.[61] Although the judge has broad discretion to order a new trial, a judge will not liberally grant new trials in deference to the jury and in light of the time and cost of conducting a new trial.[62] A judge will grant a new trial if it can be shown the "jury has reached a 'seriously erroneous result' such as [when]: (1) the verdict [is] against the weight of the evidence; (2) the damages [are] excessive; or (3) the trial [is] unfair to the moving party in some fashion, e.g., the proceedings are influenced by prejudice or bias."[63] If the judge grants a new trial, the verdict is set aside, and the dispute is tried for a second time in front of the judge or a new jury.

The losing party can also appeal any final judgment[64] of the trial court to a higher court in that court system. With some limited exceptions, judicial orders made by a judge during a trial, including most denials of summary judgment or partial summary judgments, may not be appealed until the trial concludes and final judgment has been entered in the case.

9. The appeals stage

Usually it is the losing party who seeks appellate review. A prevailing party, however, may also seek appellate review if, for example, the prevailing party wants an increase in the amount of damages awarded by the trial court in its judgment.[65] The party seeking the appeal must give notice of appeal in the manner and within a time period specified in the applicable appellate rules.[66]

On the federal level and in states where there are two levels of appellate courts, the case will be reviewed by the intermediate appeals court. A copy of the trial court record will be sent to the appeals court for review. Each party will also write a brief, which sometimes can be a lengthy document, arguing its respective position. In their briefs, the parties will attempt to persuade the court, which comprises a panel of judges, to

---

60. Fed. R. Civ. P. 59(b).

61. Fed. R. Civ. P. 50(b). In the case of alternative motions, the judge can decide whether to grant the RJMOL or the motion for a new trial, or to deny both motions.

62. *See also* Fed. R. Civ. P. 61.

63. *Holmes v. City of Massillon, Ohio,* 78 F.3d 1041, 1045-1046 (6th Cir. 1996) (citing *Montgomery Ward & Co. v. Duncan,* 311 U.S. 243, 251 (1940); *Cygnar v. City of Chicago,* 865 F.2d 827, 835 (7th Cir. 1989); *Mallis v. Bankers Trust Co.,* 717 F.2d 683, 691 (2d Cir. 1983)).

64. Fed. R. Civ. P. 54(a).

65. According to the U.S. Department of Justice, "[a]mong the tort cases concluded in 2001, litigants filed appeals in approximately 33% of product liability and 18% of medical malpractice trials." Of civil cases appealed, "[f]orty-three percent were dismissed or withdrawn prior to disposition." U.S. Dept. of Justice, Bureau of Justice Statistics, *Appeals from General Civil Trials in 46 Large Counties, 2001-2005,* http://www.ojp.usdoj.gov/bjs/abstract/agctlc05.htm (last modified July 6, 2006).

66. *See, e.g.,* Fed. R. App. P. 3, 4, & 5.

rule in their favor. Sometimes the court will want to hear oral arguments from the opposing parties and have an opportunity to ask questions. The court will not hear the testimony of any witnesses.

The decision of the appeals court is issued in the form of a written opinion, explaining the court's reasons for affirming or reversing the trial court's decision and perhaps "remanding the case" (sending the case back to the trial court) for retrial. An appeals court reverses or modifies the trial court's decision only if it finds the trial court committed an error that affected the substantial rights of the parties, meaning that it must have affected the outcome of the case.[67]

The losing party on appeal may request the highest court in the court system to review the case. Except in strictly limited circumstances, the highest court, however, is not required to grant a review. In the event that the highest court in its discretion agrees to review a case, its judgment is final. On appeal, the parties again file briefs in support of their respective positions, and the court may hear oral arguments on the matter. The highest court will issue a written opinion, explaining the reason for its decision.

 ## E. Res Judicata

Once a claim has been fully litigated and a valid, final judgment on the merits has been issued, the parties cannot relitigate in a subsequent action an issue raised or an issue that could have been raised in this case.[68] The doctrine precluding relitigation of issues is referred to as res judicata.[69]

For example, a golfer (A) sues a homeowner (B) whose land abuts a golf course for injuries sustained when he went on the defendant B's land to retrieve his golf ball and was bitten by the homeowner's dog. This is an issue that has never been decided by a court in defendant B's state. The trial court finds that defendant B owed no duty of care to A to protect him from B's dog. Plaintiff A appeals the case of *A v. B* all the way to the highest court in the state, and the highest court affirms the trial court's decision. The case is now res judicata, which means that plaintiff A can never sue defendant B again for these particular injuries.

Let us say that, after the decision in *A v. B*, another golfer (X) is injured when he is bitten by defendant Y's dog while retrieving a golf ball from Y's property. Plaintiff X pursues his claim to the state's highest court, which, after agreeing to hear the case, decides that its prior decision in *A v. B* does not reflect current public policy and so

---

67. *Beck v. Haik*, 377 F.3d 624, 634 (6th Cir. 2004) (quoting *Kotteakos v. United States*, 328 U.S. 750, 765 (1946)); *Crabtree v. National Steel Corp.*, 261 F.3d 715, 719 (7th Cir. 2001).

68. *Allen v. McCurry*, 449 U.S. 90, 94 (1980).

69. Res judicata is based on "the generally recognized public policy that there must be some end to litigation and that when one appears in court to present his case, is fully heard, and the contested issue is decided against him, he may not later renew the litigation in another court." *Heiser v. Woodruff*, 327 U.S. 726, 733 (1946).

overturns the decision by finding that defendant Y owed a duty to plaintiff X to protect him from the dog. Plaintiff A (from the previous case of *A v. B*) cannot bring a new action against defendant B for his prior injuries, even though the law has changed in his state to allow for such an action. It would be possible, however, after the decision in *X v. Y* for plaintiff A to bring an action against defendant B if he is again injured by defendant B's dog while retrieving another golf ball from defendant B's land because res judicata applies only to the injuries alleged in the original dispute.

● Exercise 3-A

You recently met with Edina Broward. Ms. Broward has asked your help in obtaining the return of a painting stolen from her home. You taped the interview. The following is a transcript of the interview. Prepare a summary statement of the situation. Include in your summary (1) the identity of the parties, (2) any important "when" facts, (3) any important "where" facts, and (4) all other facts you believe might be relevant.

Transcript of the Interview with Edina Broward

Lawyer: Good afternoon, Ms. Broward. We have talked about your problem over the phone, but now I'd like to start at the beginning, if you don't mind.

Edina: Yes, that would be fine.

Lawyer: Good. Let's start by getting your full name and where you live.

Edina: I'm Edina Lawton Broward. I live at 303 Forest Drive, in Oak Park, Illinois.

Lawyer: And is this the same residence where you lived when the painting was stolen?

Edina: Yes. It happened in 1975 when I was moving out of my house. A temporary move, you see. The house was in need of repairs and major renovation. I thought it would be best to move everything out of the house so that the workers could do their job, and I wouldn't have to worry about their ruining my antique furniture and rugs. I inherited the house from my father when he passed away in the 1960s. It's a lovely home; the famous architect Frank Lloyd Wright built it in 1903. Unfortunately, my father didn't keep up repairs during his final years.

Lawyer: Before we talk any further, tell me about the painting.

Edina: I inherited the painting, too, from my father. He was an attorney, just like yourself, though he practiced law in Chicago. Samuel Bryce Broward IV. He was the founding partner in the firm Broward & Fromm. He loved practicing law, but his real passion was art, especially the sketches and paintings of the Impressionists. The stolen painting was by the American Impressionist James Singer Sargent and had been his pride and joy. It was an oil on canvas of the Rialto Bridge, which Sargent had painted in 1913 during one of his many visits to Venice, Italy.

Lawyer: Do you remember when your father acquired it and how much he paid for it?

Edina: He kept documents on it. The records show he purchased the painting in 1925 for $800.

Lawyer: Did you ever have the painting appraised for insurance purposes?

Edina: No. I really don't know why. I thought the painting was covered by the insurance policy on the house. I didn't realize until the painting became missing that it wasn't covered under the policy. I do know that Dr. Warren, the man who has the painting now, paid $200,000 for it.

Lawyer: Let's go back to when the painting was stolen. You told me earlier that the painting was stolen when you moved your furnishings from the house.

Edina: Well, I didn't know immediately that the painting had been stolen. For several days, I thought the painting had just been lost in the move.

Lawyer: Do you remember the date you moved from the house?

Edina: October 5, 1975.

Lawyer: And can you tell me what you remember about that day?

Edina: I had taken the painting down from the wall. And I had wrapped it in brown paper and had tied it with a string. I wrote on the front of the paper, "Don't Move" in black marker and placed it in the corner of the room. I had planned for the movers to transport some of the furnishings down to my winter home in Florida, rather than risk putting them in storage. But I had planned to take the painting with me when I traveled to Florida. There were a lot of men from the moving company, packing and taking things out to the van. Also, some workers from the home restoration company were there that day, working on the second floor of the house. The workers sometimes passed through the front hall, next to the parlor, to get equipment and supplies from their truck. I was busy directing the movers on which furnishings to take to storage and which furnishings would be sent to Florida. When the movers were ready to leave, I noticed that the painting was missing. I asked the movers whether they remembered seeing the painting, and I even asked the workers from the restoration company whether they had seen the painting, but no one could recall. I assumed the painting must have been inadvertently put into one of the vans. The moving supervisor said that they would take careful inventory of my furnishings when they moved them off the truck into storage. If they found the painting, he would contact me. When the other van arrived at my Florida home several days later, they unloaded my furnishings, but the painting was not there.

Lawyer: Had the van stopped en route to Florida to pick up other transports?

Edina: No. The movers said that they had closed the van before it left my home, locked it, and had not reopened it until they arrived at my Florida home.

Lawyer: And what about the van going to the storage facility?

Edina: The moving supervisor told me that the painting had not been found in that van, either.

Lawyer: So what did you do?

Edina: I called a partner from my father's old firm, William McIntyre. He called the police. We filled out a theft report with the police. The police wanted a photograph of the painting, but I didn't have one. I just gave them a description of the painting. Mr. McIntyre also helped me hire a private investigator to track down the painting.

Lawyer: And what was the investigator's name?

Edina: James Morgan. He had done some work for Mr. McIntyre in the past. I doubt he is still in the business. He was an older man. I suppose he's retired now.

Lawyer: Did Mr. Morgan find any leads?

Edina: No, he spent several weeks investigating the moving company, the restoration company, and their workers. He also questioned neighbors to determine whether they saw anything. He really didn't do any more than what the police did. Neither Mr. Morgan nor the police were able to turn up any information. It was about this same time that the insurance company told me that the painting was not insured.

Lawyer: When was that?

Edina: January of 1976. The police continued to investigate, though not as actively. I called them in October 1976, almost one year after the painting had disappeared, to see if they had turned up anything. But after talking with a detective, it became clear to me that finding the missing painting was not a top priority for them. I guess that the file remains open to this day. I was so sad. It wasn't so much the loss of the value of the painting. I'm not an art collector or art fan, and I don't subscribe to art magazines or regularly visit museums. For me, the painting had sentimental value. My father adored the painting. It was like losing a part of my father when I lost that painting.

Lawyer: Did you do anything else to try to find the painting?

Edina: Mr. McIntyre wrote the local museums, including the Art Institute of Chicago, the Terra Museum of American Art, and the Smart Museum of Art, and some local art dealers and auction houses. In the letters, he described the missing painting and requested that anyone who may have seen the painting or knew of its whereabouts contact the police, Mr. McIntyre, or me. I even offered an award of $25,000 for information that would lead to finding the painting. Mr. McIntyre followed up his letters with telephone calls to these places. No one had any helpful information.

Lawyer: Did you just give up looking for the painting at that point?

Edina: No, no. I never gave up looking for the painting. But Mr. McIntyre died in September of 1976. He was a close family friend, and after he was gone I never felt comfortable hiring another attorney. I never married, and I didn't have any family living nearby. I just didn't know who to ask to help me. Then I started suffering periodic dizzy spells that left me bedridden for days. I was only 55, but the doctor said that I had a disease of the inner ear. I had hoped that the police and Mr. McIntyre's letters would result in someone finding my painting.

Lawyer: But you, personally, haven't done anything else to find the painting?

Edina: Last year, I was reading the *Chicago Tribune* and came across an article reporting on the renewed popularity in artwork of American Impressionist painters. The article made me think that maybe, with the renewed popularity, whoever had my painting would try to sell it or exhibit it. I had kept copies of Mr. McIntyre's letters to the museums, auction houses, and art dealers. I wrote my own letters to these places, reminding them about my stolen painting and asking them to contact me if they saw or heard about my painting.

Lawyer: And did anything come of this?

Edina: No, but a curator at the Art Institute of Chicago recommended that I file a theft report with IFAR.

Lawyer: What is IFAR?

Edina: The International Foundation for Art Research. It's a global organization that reports stolen art to museums, galleries, auction houses, and other businesses and experts that deal in fine art.

Lawyer: What didn't you do this earlier?

Edina: I didn't know about IFAR until then. It wasn't in existence when my painting was stolen.

Lawyer: When did you file the report?

Edina: July 25 of last year.

Lawyer: And is that how you learned about the painting's whereabouts?

Edina: No. My grand-niece, Susan Broward, has a friend, Mary Carter, who is an art student at the University of East Carolina. She attended an art exhibit last month at the university and saw my painting. She had talked with Susan some time ago about my stolen painting. A painting on exhibit at the university reminded Mary of my painting. Mary called Susan and told her about the painting. Susan gave my phone number to Mary, and Mary called me. Mary told me that the plaque by the painting noted that it was "owned" by Dr. Thomas Warren of Flora, East Carolina. I was able to track down Dr. Warren's phone number and called him. I explained to him what had happened to my painting and described my painting to him.

Lawyer: And what did he say?

Edina: He admitted that the painting I described was the painting in his possession. But, when I asked him to return the painting to me, he refused. He said that he had purchased the painting in June of 1978 from a reputable art gallery in Flora, the Nigel Townsend Gallery. The painting had been sold as part of the estate of Jeremy Thorne, a wealthy Flora art collector who had a special interest in American Impressionists. He died in 1977. There were no existing records as to where or how Mr. Thorne had acquired the painting. Dr. Warren purchased the painting for $200,000.

Lawyer: Did you ask Dr. Warren whether he looked into the prior history of the painting's ownership before he purchased it?

Edina: Dr. Warren said that Mr. Thorne was well respected. He didn't think Mr. Thorne would have a stolen painting in his collection, and the painting was in perfect condition. Dr. Warren said that he had no reason to suspect the painting was stolen.

Lawyer: Was last month the first time Dr. Warren had publicly exhibited the painting?

Edina: He had exhibited the painting several times since he purchased it. He said that he had exhibited the painting in 1980, 1985, 1990, and 1995, mostly at local art galleries in Flora but once at the East Carolina Museum of Art. Each time the painting was on exhibit for about a month, except at the Museum of Art, where it was on exhibit for six months as part of a special show celebrating American Impressionist artists. Otherwise, the painting has been kept at Dr. Warren's private residence in Flora.

Lawyer: Is there anything else you can tell me about the painting and your search for it?

Edina: Not that I can think of. I want the painting back. It was my father's, and it was stolen from me. I don't care how much Dr. Warren paid for it or how long he has kept it, he bought a stolen painting. The painting belongs to me. If he refuses to give it back to me, I want to take him to court. Surely, a judge will order him to return it to me.

Lawyer: I will look into the matter and get back with you, Ms. Broward. Then, we can discuss what action you may want to take.

CHAPTER

4

The U.S. Legal Education System:
Studying the Law and Briefing Cases

HIGHLIGHTS

- The study of court opinions is essential to understanding the U.S. legal system.
- Most court opinions found in casebooks are appellate or reviewing court opinions.
- Preparing a case brief for class and using it later when studying for examinations is an essential part of the U.S. educational process.
- When preparing a case brief for class, it is essential to understand the procedural posture of a case, or what aspect of the case was appealed.
  - A motion to dismiss challenges the legal basis for a cause of action or court claim.
  - A motion for summary judgment challenges whether sufficient relevant disputable facts are at issue to justify sending the case to trial.
- A court opinion includes essential information (the "holding") and sometimes also includes unessential comments ("dicta").
- Many law school professors use a question and answer method (Socratic method) in the classroom, rather than just lecturing to students.
- Tips for taking notes in class include the use of abbreviations and a system for keeping track of new language and definitions.

A. Why We Study Cases as a Means to Learn the Law

Studying U.S. law involves studying more than rules and codes. It requires you to critically review U.S. constitutional provisions, statutes, and cases. The overriding goal is to learn (1) what legal principles and policies are relevant to a legal issue; (2) how to analyze and apply those legal principles and policies to a client's set of facts; and (3) how to create arguments on behalf of parties in a legal dispute.

In the U.S. legal system, the specific language of constitutional provisions, statutes, and legal principles developed through court decisions (the common law) is essential to legal analysis.[1] And yet that language does not mean a great deal when studied by itself. The language of a statute, for example, takes on real meaning when a court must interpret it and apply it to to the facts in a case. And although the development of the common law results in rules or legal principles similar to statutes, these rules are flexible; they change or are further defined each time a court applies them to a different set of facts. Benjamin Cardozo[2] once stated, "The rules and principles of case law have never been treated as final truths, but as working hypotheses [theories], continually retested in those great laboratories of the law, the courts of justice."[3]

Thus, while federal and state constitutions, statutes, and cases all provide the foundation for any legal analysis and argument, the outcome of each case depends on how the court interprets and applies the law to a new set of facts. In his book, *The Nature of the Judicial Process*, Justice Cardozo commented on the process from a judge's perspective. He longed for certain answers in the prior case law — clear mandates as to how to decide a new case before the court. He finally realized that

> [a]s the years have gone by, and as I have reflected more and more upon the nature of the judicial process, I have become reconciled to the uncertainty, because I have grown to see it as inevitable. I have grown to see that the process in its highest reaches is not discovery, but creation. . . . [The change is inevitable, where] principles that have served their day expire, and new principles are born.[4]

---

1. See Chapter 2 on the U.S. legal system.

2. Benjamin Nathan Cardozo was an Associate Justice of the United States Supreme Court from 1932-1938. Before serving on the Supreme Court, he served as a justice with the New York Court of Appeals for 14 years (Chief Judge for his last 4 years). He was named as the "great common law jurist of America . . . who spoke of the way the Constitution should be approached and the proper job of the judiciary in the American system," and the "outstanding common-law jurist of the twentieth century." Sidney Asch, *The Supreme Court and Its Great Justices*, 159 (Arco 1993).

3. Benjamin N. Cardozo, *The Nature of the Judicial Process* 23 (Yale U. Press 1949).

4. *Id.*

In the exercises in Chapter 2, a statute was passed to preclude those who killed another from benefiting in any way from the death they caused. The statute read:

No person who intentionally causes the death of another shall in any way benefit by the death. All property of the decedent and all money shall pass as if the guilty person had predeceased the decedent.

Since the statute does not include any definitions of the words used in the section, it is the judge's job to determine what the words mean. Determining how to interpret and apply the language of the statute raises a question of law (also referred to as a legal issue or law-based issue, discussed in Chapter 14). For example, what is not easily apparent from the statutory language is what *intentionally* means. The court must determine what *intentionally* means and then apply that meaning to the facts of the case before it.

The lawyer's job, then, is to argue to the judge what the correct interpretation of the law is and why, in applying that interpretation to the case facts, the outcome favors her client. To prove a client's case, a lawyer must show how the client's position conforms to the authority that is binding in the controlling jurisdiction.[5] In particular, a lawyer must show that the facts of the client's case are sufficiently similar to the facts of other cases addressing the same legal issue(s), so that the same outcome reached in the earlier cases should apply in the client's case. Further, the lawyer must show why the facts of a client's case are sufficiently different[6] from the facts in those cases decided in opposition to the client's position, so that a different outcome should apply in the client's case.

Finally, once a judge interprets the language of a statute or a rule, it is the fact-finder's job to answer all questions of fact (also referred to as a fact-based issue or a fact-sensitive issue). In the example referring to a "person who intentionally causes the death of another," the fact-finder would decide whether the defendant acted intentionally based on the judge's interpretation of what *intentionally* means. A judge's interpretation of the word *intentionally* would become known when the judge decides procedural issues or jury instructions.

B. Where the Use of Case Law Fits in the Process

If you have watched a trial on U.S. television, you may have questioned how the use of past cases and other authority actually fits in the overall legal process. Lawyers do

---

5. Note, however, that on occasion a legal issue is raised where there is no controlling authority in the jurisdiction. This is known as a case of first impression. Lawyers will look to authority (statutes and cases) from other jurisdictions to help argue the client's position, and judges will look to these outside authorities to decide a legal issue. (More on addressing cases of first impression is found in Chapter 14.)

6. When used in a legal context, the terms *factual similarities and differences* are used interchangeably with *factual analogies and distinctions* and *comparing and contrasting facts*.

not argue the similarity or difference between facts of past cases and the client's case to a U.S. jury.[7] Attorneys argue the importance of the relevant case law to the trial judge when addressing the following issues:

1. Procedural consideration: when determining whether a legal issue will be presented to the fact-finder

As discussed in Chapter 3, when a plaintiff files a complaint in a civil court, the defendant may file pretrial motions challenging, among other things, the validity of the complaint. If the defendant files a motion to dismiss,[8] the defendant is challenging whether a legal basis for the claim exists. If there is no recognized legal claim or cause of action, the plaintiff has no legal means to recover from the defendant. The plaintiff's lawyer will argue that the client's facts fall within the class of cases covered by a particular law, while the defendant's lawyer will argue that the facts of the case do not fall within the class of cases covered by the plaintiff's claim, so the case should be dismissed.

2. Procedural consideration: when determining whether an issue is in dispute and the case should proceed to trial

Before a case goes to trial, either or both parties may file a motion for summary judgment,[9] arguing that no genuine issue of material fact is in dispute and the case can be dismissed as a matter of law.[10] If the motion is granted, the judge dismisses the case, and the case never proceeds to trial, unless the decision is reversed on appeal.

This motion for summary judgment is different from a motion to dismiss. In a motion to dismiss, one party is claiming that no legal basis exists for the claim. When moving for summary judgment, the moving party is arguing that, based on the legal claim, no reasonable juror could find for the nonmoving party, even when viewing the facts in a way that is most favorable to the nonmoving party.

[Handwritten margin note, left:] legal basis → legal claim / cause of action

[Handwritten note, bottom:] procedural considerations: a motion to dismiss : no legal basis ; no legal claim / no cause of action. a motion for summary judgment : legal claim ✓ / no reasonable juror could find for the nonmoving party.

---

7. Sometimes there is no jury, in which case the judge serves as the fact-finder and decides questions of fact as well as questions of law. See Chapter 3.

8. Fed. R. Civ. P. 12(b)(6).

9. Fed. R. Civ. P. 56(a).

10. The exact language used in the rule addressing summary judgment motions is whether a "genuine issue of material fact exists." *Id.*

3. Substantive considerations: when determining other questions of law

a. Determining which rule of law applies

A judge must sometimes determine which rule of law, among alternative choices, is proper to apply in a particular case. This responsibility requires the court to consider the underlying public policy reasons for creating the law — why the law was created in the first place. Different, sometimes opposing, public policy considerations may exist for adopting one rule of law over others, and it is the court's duty to determine which policy reasons are stronger and more consistent with other laws in the controlling jurisdiction. (Public policy is discussed in further detail in Chapter 8.)

b. Determining how to interpret the rule of law

As discussed previously, a court may also need to determine what the relevant law actually says. This responsibility requires the court to interpret the language of the relevant law, whether that law originates in a constitutional provision, a statute, or a binding case. In interpreting the language, the court will consider the underlying public policy reasons supporting the law. One of the judiciary's goals is to determine the original legislative intent in creating a rule of law. A court will review, among other things, how other courts have interpreted and applied the same rules of law. (For more on statutory interpretation, see Chapter 13.)

C. The Study of Appellate Court Cases

In the U.S. legal education system, much of the discussion in a typical class focuses on the study of federal and state appellate court cases. Only rarely are trial court decisions included in a casebook. Appellate cases are studied because the appellate court judges must ensure that the laws are interpreted and applied in a similar way by the lower courts in the same jurisdiction. As explained in Chapter 2, appellate court decisions are binding on decisions reached by lower courts in the same jurisdiction; thus, the intermediate appellate court cases are binding on trial courts in the same jurisdiction, and the highest court decisions are binding on both the intermediate appellate courts and the trial courts within the same jurisdiction.

As Figure 4-1 shows, the U.S. federal and state court systems are separate. In some circumstances, however, federal courts may consider cases that include state law issues, such as when the two parties in a dispute involving state law live in two different states and the claim exceeds $75,000. State courts may also consider federal issues, for example, when a constitutional question is at issue and the court must consider both the federal and state constitutions. State cases addressing questions of federal law and constitutional issues may be appealed to the United States Supreme Court. (For a more detailed description of the U.S. federal and state court systems, see Chapter 1.)

Court Hierarchy

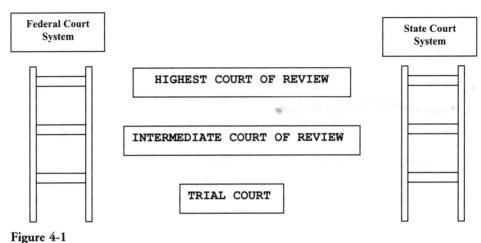

Figure 4-1

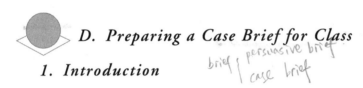

D. Preparing a Case Brief for Class

1. Introduction

The term *brief* is used in the study of U.S. law in two ways: First, a *persuasive brief* is what a lawyer writes and submits to a court. In a persuasive brief, a lawyer explains the law relevant to the legal issues before the court and tries to convince the court that the position of the lawyer's client is correct. Second, a *case brief* is what a U.S. law student writes to prepare for class and to use later when studying for examinations. Lawyers often continue briefing cases when they enter law practice. The remaining sections of this chapter explain why briefing cases in a U.S. law school is necessary and how to brief cases when preparing for class, especially for those classes where the Socratic method is used by the professor. (The Socratic method is explained in part G of this chapter.)

A court opinion includes many of the same sections found in a typical piece of fiction writing. In a fictitious story, the writer creates an overall plan for the story (the plot). The plot oftentimes raises questions that are answered as the reader moves through the story. Any good story includes one or more conflicts and a cast of characters who are struggling with these conflicts. Most stories have a beginning, a middle, and an end. By the end, the good writer answers the questions raised in the story and explains how and why the conflicts are resolved.

A court opinion includes many of the same sections as a work of fiction, though they have different labels. A court opinion introduces the characters ("parties") who are in court because they have different opinions about the story ("facts"). These differences about the story and the legal meaning of the story create one or more legal conflicts ("issues"), which may be resolved in a court of law. In answering the questions raised in the dispute, the court resolves the conflicts (by issuing a "holding" and a "judgment"). The court also explains why it resolved the conflict the way it did ("court's reasoning"). Similarly, the writer of a good fictitious story takes care to explain the reasons for the resolutions in the story before ending the story. If this does not happen, the reader often feels frustrated and disappointed.

To better understand how to recognize these sections of a court opinion, read the following case excerpt.

This is the heading as the court has rendered it. It includes the case name and the citation to the case. In citing this case name, however, you would shorten it as instructed in a legal citation manual such as the *ALWD Citation Manual* or the *Bluebook*.

Supreme Court of Alaska
In the Matter of the Estate
of Richard Blodgett
147 P.3d 702 (Alaska 2006)[11]

This is the justice who wrote the majority opinion.

CARPENETI, Justice.

*****

On September 14, 2003, Robert Blodgett caused the death of his father, Richard Blodgett. Blodgett was indicted for murder in * **704** the second degree, and in January 2004 he was convicted of criminally negligent homicide and given a three-and-one-half-year term of imprisonment.

Blodgett was named in the final Will and Testament (Will) of his father, which left "all properties, Bank accounts, stocks, and insurance policies" to his children. In April 2004 Blodgett petitioned the superior court for a hearing to determine his right to participate in the probate proceedings under the Alaska probate code and the slayer statute. The other beneficiaries of Richard Blodgett's

Will consented to the hearing but argued that Robert intentionally killed his father, so the slayer statute precluded him from receiving any property under the Will.

The superior court denied Robert Blodgett's petition, preventing him from obtaining any benefits under the Will. The court explained that under the slayer statute he couldn't benefit unless he proved by a preponderance of the evidence that this would result in manifest injustice, which Blodgett failed to do. The court considered, and rejected, possible factors it thought might support finding manifest injustice, including past family relationships and Blodgett's monetary needs. The court found the "great deal of testimony about the nature of the past relationship" between Blodgett and his father "unhelpful" and irrelevant in determining "the justice of denying or allowing recovery." The court also concluded that "Blodgett retained sufficient income-earning capacity and property holdings that he would not be destitute if he did not receive these funds." Blodgett appeals.

Because the statutory subsection that governs this case provides that the superior court "may" set aside the application of the slayer statute if manifest injustice would result, we review the superior court's decision for abuse of discretion.[12] We find an abuse of discretion "only if, based on a review of the whole record, we are left with a definite and firm conviction that a mistake has been made [by the trial judge]."

---

11. This case has been heavily edited, so the page numbers are marked throughout the case by an asterisk (*) followed by the number where the new page of the original case begins. All footnotes have been eliminated.

12. Reviewing courts' powers to review a lower court decision vary according to the issue on appeal. In this case, the review power is limited to whether the judge abused his discretion in reaching the decision. — EDS.

* 705 The common law has long followed the policy that "no one should be allowed to profit from his own wrong." *Riggs v. Palmer*, 22 N.E. 188 (N.Y. 1889). Over the years most legislatures enacted statutes covering these rules, known as "slayer statutes."

The original Alaska slayer statute, passed in 1972, prevented only those who feloniously and intentionally killed from benefiting. In 1988 the legislature passed an amendment removing the words "intentionally" from the statute, so the statute applied to crimes, including criminally negligent homicide. Ch. 164, §§ 3-8, SLA 1988.

Shortly after the legislature passed this amendment, the Alaska governor expressed concern that under unusual circumstances it might be unjust to prohibit a killer from taking the property of the victim, such as in the case of an unintentional felonious killing. Accordingly, another amendment was adopted in 1989, creating the manifest injustice exception for unintentional homicides now found in Alaska Stat. § 13.12.803(k):

> In the case of an unintentional felonious killing, a court may set aside the application of [the slayer statute] if the court makes special findings of fact and conclusions of law that the application of the subsection would result in a manifest injustice and that the subsection should not be applied.

*****

Thus, the legislature broadened the application of the slayer statute — by extending it to unintentional killings — and created an escape clause — by enacting the manifest injustice exception.

Under the current Alaska criminal code, all unjustified killings are considered felonies. This includes murders in the first and second degree, manslaughter, and criminally negligent homicide. Thus, Alaska's slayer statute encompasses intentional as well as unintentional homicides. Criminally negligent homicide occurs when "the person causes the death of another person." A.S. § 11.41.130.

* 707 The legislature limited the broad reach of the slayer statute by giving trial court judges the discretion to allow killers to benefit from the victim's assets if manifest injustice would result otherwise. Should an inheritance be denied to the unskilled teenager who drives his car in a criminally negligent manner and accidentally causes the death of his sole remaining parent? The legislature clearly decided that in such a case there should be discretion in the court to consider the specific facts of the homicide and, if denial of the inheritance would be manifestly unjust, to permit it. Where the killer's act was not intentional, and especially where the act was not even reckless, and where other circumstances lessen the overall effect of the crime, the application of the slayer statute may lead to unnecessarily harsh results. Indeed, the unintended killing of a loved one, as in the example above, would likely cause the killer far greater personal ruin than monetary gain.

In this case, Blodgett was convicted of criminally negligent homicide, which is an unintentional homicide. Therefore, under subsection (k) Blodgett can avoid the effects of the slayer statute only if he proves by a preponderance of the evidence that applying the statute to him will result in manifest injustice.

* 708 We have not had occasion to define the phrase "manifest injustice" as used in the slayer statute, or to set out the relevant factors that a trial judge should consider when ruling on this question. Similarly, because no other slayer statute contains a provision similar to subsection (k), out-of-jurisdiction case law provides no ready assistance. However, the Alaska Court of Appeals has interpreted this phrase in another, similar context, describing manifest injustice as something that is "plainly unfair" as applied "to a particular defendant." *Beltz v. State*, 980 P.2d 474, 480 (Alaska App. 1999). Before finding manifest injustice, the court held that the "judge must articulate specific circumstances that make the defendant significantly different from a typical offender within that category or that makes the defendant's conduct significantly different from a typical offense." *Id.* We adopt *Beltz's* approach for the purpose of applying subsection (k) of Alaska's slayer statute.

Thus, the relevant comparison here is between Blodgett's conduct and that of a typical offender convicted of negligent homicide. In the criminal proceedings, Blodgett was sentenced to three and one-half years in prison, which is not the lowest possible sentence for negligent homicide. This suggests that the superior court did not believe Blodgett's acts fell at the lowest level of culpability and that the court below considered Blodgett's conduct in relation to other similarly situated defendants when it rejected his claim of manifest injustice.

To try and prove manifest injustice, Blodgett introduced evidence regarding (1) past family relationships, and (2) possible financial hardship if denied the benefits of inheritance. The court found that Blodgett failed to meet his burden of proving, by a preponderance of the evidence, extraordinary circumstances that would have made it manifestly unjust to exclude him from his father's Will. We agree.

The court described the evidence regarding his family relationships as "unhelpful." Witnesses testified that Blodgett and his father shared a "good relationship" marked with occasional fights typical of father-son relationships. Such testimony neither proves nor disproves the fairness of prohibiting Blodgett's inheritance. The court did not abuse its discretion in deciding that Blodgett failed to prove manifest injustice on this basis.

The court also examined Blodgett's argument that "it would be unjust to deny benefits under the Will to someone who is physically disabled, who faces unknowable future medical expenses, who has a compromised earning capacity, and who has ongoing psychological needs." The superior court noted that, although Blodgett suffered some medical disabilities, Blodgett's own witness testified that he "is capable at the operation of heavy equipment and has skills as a mechanic." The * **709** court found that these skills could lead to employment with yearly compensation ranging between $40,000 and $50,000 per year. It also found that Blodgett owns other property and that future medical expenses will likely be met through the Alaska Native Health Service. In light of this testimony, the court concluded that Blodgett would not endure financial hardship if he did not receive these funds. Consequently, the court found that Blodgett failed to prove manifest injustice based on monetary need.

While we believe the court did not abuse its discretion in making this determination, we are concerned that the court's analysis could lead to the conclusion that a showing of manifest injustice may turn on predictions concerning the future financial health of the defendant. Such an approach would allow slayers of their victims to inherit if they are poor, but not if they are financially stable. We doubt that this distinction — between different slayers based on their personal wealth — reflects the legislature's purpose in enacting the manifest injustice provision.

Despite these concerns, we conclude that the superior court did not abuse its discretion in finding that Blodgett failed to prove manifest injustice by a preponderance of the evidence.

*****

Affirmed.

2. The basic sections of a case brief

Case briefs include all or most of the following sections:

- Heading
- Facts (F)
- Procedural History (PH)
- Statement of the Issue (I)
- Holding (H)
- Judgment (J)
- Relevant Rules/Legal Principles Applied in the Case
- Court's Reasoning
- Concurrence and Dissent
- Personal Comments/Reactions

a. Heading

The heading includes the following information:

Case Name	•	Volume #	•	Reporter Abbreviation	•	Page #	•	(Name of Court & Year Decided)

- **Case Name:** Case names are found at the beginning of each court opinion. The name provided in the actual case, however, may not be written using proper citation form. Specific instructions regarding what to include and how to write case names are found in citation manuals.
- **Volume Number and Reporter:** Cases are provided in publications called reporters. The abbreviations for these reporters are found in citation manuals, such as the *ALWD Citation Manual*,[13] or at the beginning of any reporter volume. The volume number is found on the spine of each book and at the top of the page of the case found online.
- **Page Number:** The page number in the citation refers to the page where the court opinion begins.
- **Court Decision and Year (in parentheses)**[14]**:** The name of the court varies, depending on which court decided the case. (See Chapter 15 on citation.) The year is the year when the case was decided.

In briefing the sample case, the heading would appear as follows.

---

13. See Chapter 15 on citation form.
14. The court designation and year are enclosed by parentheses. Material within parentheses is sometimes referred to as a parenthetical.

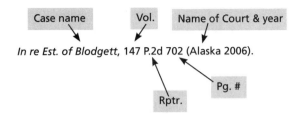

In re Est. of Blodgett, 147 P.2d 702 (Alaska 2006).

The reference to Alaska is necessary to show that the case was decided by the Alaska Supreme Court.

The heading may also include the page number on which the case is found in the casebook, for quick reference to the case if needed later on. *↑ ≠*   *substantive facts: before entering the judicial system*   *↳ cause of action (C/A)*

b. Facts (F)

procedural facts: once ---

This section provides the story. An appellate court opinion contains two types of facts: substantive and procedural.

(1) Substantive facts

These facts explain what happened before the case entered the judicial system, that is, before the plaintiff files a complaint in the court. Your challenge is to determine which of the facts contained in the court opinion are legally significant to the issues addressed in the case. The ability to target the legally significant facts comes more easily with experience. You cannot know which facts are legally significant without first understanding the issues raised by the court, how the court resolved the issues, and why the court resolved the issues as it did. You must, therefore, read the case thoroughly before completing the substantive facts. This section is usually one of the last sections of the brief you finish. The substantive facts in *Blodgett* follow.

> Facts:
>
> • Son Blodgett convicted of the criminally negligent homicide of his father.
> • Father had executed a Last Will and Testament.

When noting the key facts of the story, write the summary in your own words rather than word for word from the court's opinion. Using your own words will help you understand the story and the relationship of the key facts once you get to class and later, when reviewing the cases while preparing for exams.

(2) Procedural facts

This is the part of the story that takes place once the case enters the judicial system, when the plaintiff files the complaint in court. The procedural facts include the cause of action (C/A) that was the subject of the plaintiff's complaint in a civil trial or the prosecution's charge in a criminal trial, and any defenses to the claim raised by the defendant. The procedural facts in *Blodgett* follow.

> C/A: Son requested that the superior (trial) court award him his share of his father's estate as designated in his father's Will.

Since case briefs are for your personal use, you do not need to write the story in paragraph form or even in complete sentences. A list of facts, as in the above examples, is fine, as long as you can understand your notes later on. You may also decide to abbreviate words, discussed in the note-taking section found in section H of this chapter.

c. Procedural history (PH)

This section states what the court below decided. If more than one lower court decision exists, separate the decisions in a manner that helps you to quickly distinguish between the decisions of each court.[15] For example, if you are reading a California Supreme Court decision, you may use *TC* to refer to the trial court and *AC* or *MC* to refer to the middle appellate court. State the judgment in each court below, the basis for the judgment, and the party appealing. The procedural history in *Blodgett* is as follows.

> PH:
>   TC: Court applied Alaska's slayer statute and denied the son's request because (1) he was convicted for his father's death, and (2) no "manifest injustice" would occur by denying the son's request.

d. Statement of the issue

This section focuses on the specific legal issue discussed in the case. (Section E below discusses cases that have more than one issue.) The issue statement is usually written using neutral, generic terms rather than using the personal names of the parties involved in the specific case. If the case involves a contract dispute, for example, instead of referring to the parties as *Smith* and *Jones*, refer to them by their relationship, *buyer* and *seller*. If the case involves a medical malpractice claim, instead of referring to the parties as *Dr. Joe Brown* and *Cindy Carson*, refer to them as *doctor* and *patient*. When

---

15. In most states there are three levels of courts: the trial court, the middle or intermediate appellate court, and the highest appellate court. In smaller states, however, there may be only two court levels: the trial court level and a single appellate court level.

first learning about the sections of a case, you may want to write out separately the substantive issue (SI) raised in the case and the procedural issue (PI) raised in the case.

The substantive issue states the issue based on the legal cause of action. Ideally, the substantive issue statement contains two parts:

(1) the relevant legal question, and
(2) (a) if writing a law-based question,[16] just enough of the facts to put the legal question in the proper factual context; or
    (b) if writing a fact-based question, just enough of the important facts to explain why the issue is in dispute. This will likely require you to include facts supporting both parties.

The substantive issue in *Blodgett* (addressing a fact-based issue) would be as follows.

SI: Under Alaska's slayer statute, which precludes certain killers from receiving the assets of their victims, can a son benefit from his father's Will when the son was convicted of the criminally negligent homicide of his father?

← The first section provides the legal question; what follows are the legally significant facts.

By separating the procedural issue from the substantive issue, you focus on whether the case went to the jury and was decided on the merits[17] or whether the case was dismissed by the judge before it went to the jury based on a procedural motion by one of the parties, such as a motion to dismiss or a motion for summary judgment. The probate court in *Blodgett* decided the case on the merits, so the procedural issue would read like this.

PI: Did the trial court abuse its discretion when it denied a son's request for his father's assets under his father's will?

← The procedural issue addresses the abuse of discretion.

If you prefer not to separate the substantive and procedural issues, a single statement of the issue in *Blodgett* would read like this.

Under Alaska's slayer statute, which precludes some killers from receiving the assets of their victims, did the trial court abuse its discretion when it denied a son's request for his father's assets designated for the son in the father's Will when the son was convicted of the criminally negligent homicide of his father?

← Legal question first; procedural posture second; legally significant facts third.

---

16. A law-based question, for example, would be whether the court adopted the fault or no-fault rule when deciding who pays for damages in an automobile accident.

17. A case decided on the merits is one that was reached at trial.

e. Holding (H)

The holding or *ratio decidendi* of the case is the court's answer to the issue. The holding is the "legal principle to be drawn from the opinion (decision) of the court."[18] If properly stated, the holding is the positive or negative response to the statement of the issue. The holding in *Blodgett*, then, would read like this.

> H: SI: Under Alaska's slayer statute, a son can be precluded from benefiting from his father's Will when he is convicted of criminally negligent homicide of his father.
> *or*
> No.

> H: PI: The trial court did not abuse its discretion when it denied the son's request to benefit from his father's Will.
> *or*
> No.

f. Judgment (J)

The judgment is the final decision of the appellate court after reviewing the lower court's decision. The judgment is usually found at the end of the court's opinion and may state, for example, that the lower court's decision was affirmed, reversed, affirmed in part and reversed in part, reversed and remanded,[19] or modified. In *Blodgett*, the court upheld the lower court's decision, so the judgment would be stated as follows.

> J: Affirmed.

g. Relevant rules or legal principles applied in the case

By separating into their own section the rules or legal principles the court applied in reaching its decision, you emphasize the more general principles that a court is likely to apply when analyzing future cases. By isolating the rules and legal principles, you

---

18. Bryan A. Garner, *Black's Law Dictionary* 552 (West Group 1996).
19. To remand a case is to send it back to the lower court, with specific instructions about how to proceed.

can more easily access this information later on when preparing an outline and study-ing for examinations.

You may find that you are repeating the relevant rules or legal principles in the section of the case brief explaining the court's reasoning (see below), which is not unusual. The part of the case brief that reports rules or legal principles applied in *Blodgett* might read as follows.

> Relevant Rule:
>
> Alaska's Slayer Statute:
>   (a) An individual who feloniously kills the decedent forfeits all benefits . . . with respect to the decedent's estate. . . .
>   (k) In the case of an unintentional felonious killing, a court may set aside the application of (a) . . . of this section if the court makes special findings of fact and conclusions of law that the application of the subsection would result in a manifest injustice and that the subsection should not be applied.
>   Alaska Stat. § 13.12.803.

This statement of the slayer statute omits all unimportant language, to save space.

h. Court's reasoning

The reasoning section represents the heart of the court's opinion. A court that thoroughly explains why it decided the case as it did creates useful precedent for later cases that involve the same legal issue. If a court omits the reasoning section of the opinion, as it sometimes does, the case is often not as useful as precedent.

In the reasoning section, the court may address why it rejected the losing party's arguments or why certain rules, principles, and policies were not applied, or why other rules, principles, and policies were applied. A good explanation includes references to both the key language of the rules or legal principles and references to those facts important to the court's reasoning. In *Blodgett*, the court's reasoning might be reported like this.

> Court's Reasoning:
>
> 1. The court did not err in ruling that the son did not prove that a manifest injustice would occur if he was prevented from acquiring the assets of his father.
> 2. The Alaska Supreme Court had not previously defined "manifest injustice." In this case the court adopted the Alaska Court of Appeals' approach, con-sidering manifest injustice as "plainly unfair" and more than a general finding. Now the court must find special circumstances to consider the defendant something other than a "regular" offender.

3. Here the TC imposed a three-year sentence, not the minimal sentence possible. This sentence suggests that the court considered the son more than minimally responsible. This finding alone supports the conclusion that the son's situation is no different from other regular offenders.

4. The lower court also found that it didn't matter that the son was physically disabled, requiring more finances and arguably more in need of his father's assets. The son could still operate heavy equipment and could work as a mechanic. He still had the potential of making $40,000-50,000 per year.

The Alaska Supreme Court was concerned, however, that future courts might think that a decision on manifest injustice could depend on the defendant's future financial health. The court made clear that this consideration was not the intent of the legislature.

i. Concurrence and dissent

In addition to the sections listed above, in some court opinions one or more judges other than the judge writing the majority opinion may choose to write an opinion. This opinion may be either (1) a concurring opinion or (2) a dissenting opinion.

Always include a section that notes the concurring or dissenting opinion, if included in the court's opinion in the casebook. Many concurrences and dissents are the focus of classroom discussion and may be adopted in later majority decisions. Be careful, however, to keep your notes on the concurrence and the dissent separate from the other sections of your case brief. These opinions are not part of the majority's decision.

Judges write concurrences when they agree with the outcome of the case as decided by the majority of the court but do not agree with all or part of the majority's reasoning. The concurrence allows a judge to explain what is wrong with the majority court's reasoning and how the same result can be reached in a different way.

A dissenting judge does not agree with the decision by the majority of the court. The judge may simply say, "I dissent," or the judge may explain why the majority opinion is wrong. Dissenting opinions are especially important when the vote by the members of a court is close, such as a 5-4 decision by the members of the United States Supreme Court. The wise attorney knows that a single change in the membership of an appellate court may affect the outcome in a future case.

j. Personal comments and reactions

This is the one section of the case brief that does not come directly from the court opinion. In this section, state your own thoughts about the case. You may comment on (1) the validity of the decision, (2) the court's reasoning, (3) how this decision fits with other cases studied in class that address the same legal questions, and (4) anything else that might come to mind when thinking about the case. This section of the case brief is also a good place to note why you believe the author chose to include this case in the book. For example, you may find that the author included the case (1) because it helps explain the law you are studying, (2) because it is an example of poor or mistaken reasoning by the court, or (3) because it suggests an alternative approach to analyzing a particular legal issue. These notes can be especially helpful when preparing for class discussion and later when studying for exams.

An example of the full case brief for *Blodgett* follows.

In re Est. of Blodgett, 147 P.2d 702 (Alaska 2006).
Facts:

- Son Blodgett convicted of the criminally negligent homicide of his father.
- Father had executed a Will.

C/A: Son asked the trial court to award to him his share of his father's estate as stated in his father's Will.
PH: TC: Court applied Alaska's slayer statute and denied son's request because (1) he was convicted for his father's death, and (2) no "manifest injustice" would occur by denying his request.
SI: Under Alaska's slayer statute, which precludes certain killers from receiving the assets of their victims, can a son benefit from his father's Will when the son was convicted of the criminally negligent homicide of his father?
PI: Did the trial court abuse its discretion by denying a son's request for his father's assets under his father's Will?
H: SI: Under Alaska's slayer statute, a son can be precluded from benefiting from his father's Will when he is convicted of criminally negligent homicide of his father.
   PI: The trial court did not abuse its discretion by denying the son's request to benefit from his father's Will after the son's conviction for the criminally negligent homicide of his father.
J: Affirmed.

Relevant Rules:

Alaska's Slayer Statute (Alaska Stat. § 13.12.803)
   (a) An individual who feloniously kills the decedent forfeits all benefits under this chapter with respect to the decedent's estate. . . .
   (k) In the case of an unintentional felonious killing, a court may set aside the application of (a) . . . of this section if the court makes special findings of fact and conclusions of law that the application of the subsection would result in a manifest injustice and that the subsection should not be applied.

Court's Reasoning:

1. The court did not err in ruling that the son did not prove that a manifest injustice would occur if he was prevented from acquiring the assets of his father.
2. The Alaska Supreme Court had not previously defined "manifest injustice." In this case the court adopted the Alaska Court of Appeals' approach,

considering manifest injustice as "plainly unfair" and more than a general finding. Now the court must find special circumstances to consider the defendant something other than a "regular" offender.

3. Here the TC imposed a three-year sentence, not the minimal sentence possible. This sentence suggests that the court considered the son more than minimally responsible. This finding alone supports the conclusion that the son's situation is no different from that of other regular offenders.

4. The lower court also found that it didn't make a difference that the son was physically disabled, requiring more finances and arguably more in need of his father's assets. The son could still operate heavy equipment and could work as a mechanic; he still had the potential of making $40,000-50,000 per year.

The Alaska Supreme Court was concerned, however, that future courts might think that a decision on manifest injustice could depend on the defendant's future financial health. The court made clear that this consideration was not the intent of the legislature.

Personal Comments:

Although initially you may follow this outline of the case brief sections, you may change how you prepare briefs for your individual classes. Different professors may expect a different type of brief. When first learning how to brief, however, it is better to include rather than exclude information. Once you understand the different sections of a brief and also know what you need for each class, you may adjust your briefs accordingly.

E. Briefing a Case with Multiple Issues

When a court addresses more than one issue, separate those issues throughout your case brief. If there are two issues, for example, provide two separate sections for the statement of the issue, the holding, the relevant rules/legal principles applied, and the court's reasoning. For an example of a case brief with multiple issues, see *Shrader v. Equitable Life Assurance Society*, 485 N.E.2d 1031 (Ohio 1985), found in the appendices.

F. Holding v. Dicta

A court must decide the issue raised by the parties in the case before the court. Any comment addressing the specific issue before the court is part of the court's holding. Sometimes, however, a court will make statements beyond what is necessary to resolve the specific issue before the court. A court may comment, for example, on the likely outcome of a case with different facts than the case presently before the court. These comments are not binding on future cases, have persuasive value only, and are known as obiter dicta. Obiter dicta is an assertion "which a party is not bound to make."[20] In *Blodgett*, for example, the court finished its opinion by suggesting that the legislature's purpose was not to focus on a slayer's personal wealth in deciding whether the manifest injustice exception applied. This statement was not necessary to the court's holding because the Alaska Supreme Court relied on the "more than minimal length" of the son's sentence in upholding the superior court's ruling. Thus, while the court's comment on the weight of a slayer's financial security in finding manifest injustice may be predictive of the court's rulings in future cases, it was not a part of the holding in *Blodgett*.

As with the concurrence and the dissent, if you include dicta in a case brief separate it from the main rulings in the case and specifically label it as dicta.

 ## G. Class Participation: The Socratic Method

You must prepare for class in a U.S. law school. Many international classroom professors teach through lecture only, with little or no participation by the students. In many U.S. law classrooms, however, and especially in first-year courses, professors engage students in a dialogue known as the Socratic method.[21] The Socratic method is a way to promote a student's ability to think analytically and to create arguments in support of a party's position. The Socratic method is a method where a professor teaches by asking questions rather than just lecturing. The Socratic method may be the only teaching method used in a law school classroom or it may be combined with other teaching methods, such as a lecture format or the use of in-class exercises. When a professor explores the issues raised in the cases and other material read for class with students through the Socratic method, the classroom becomes a cooperative environment where both professor and student work to help all students understand how to analyze and understand an issue more completely.

The Socratic dialogue requires students to develop, state, and defend their positions. Lawyers are problem solvers, and the primary task in a U.S. law school is to learn the tools needed to solve problems. Laws will change, as will legal problems. Law professors don't have the answers to every legal situation, but they do try to help students develop reasoning skills that can be applied to any legal situation.

Consider a discussion between a professor and student about the court's decision in *Blodgett*:

Professor: Do you agree with the opinion in *Blodgett*?
Student: Yes, it doesn't seem fair that a son who kills his father could actually profit from his act.
Professor: But the statute does allow an exception — the manifest injustice exception. The legislature must have thought that a killer should be able to take assets under

---

20. Bryan A. Garner, *Black's Law Dictionary* 449 (West Group 1996).
21. Socrates (469-399 B.C.) was a famous Greek philosopher.

some circumstances. How could you argue that the facts in *Blodgett* support applying the exception?

Student: Well, a family relationship is special, different from the person on the street who kills another. Also, the son was convicted of criminal negligence rather than murder, so there was no evil intent. Usually, parents want to provide for their children, and the father might have still wanted his son to receive some of his assets.

Professor: As you know, that's not what the court decided. Why did the court refuse to grant the exception to the son?

Student: The court relied on the sentencing more than anything else. The lower court's sentence was more than the minimal sentence that could be imposed. This sentence suggested that the court viewed the son like anyone else, someone who did not deserve any kind of special consideration.

Professor: Did the trial court mention any other reasons for its decision?

Student: Yes, the court said the father-son relationship was a typical relationship, which neither supported granting the exception nor not granting the exception. The court also addressed the son's need for the father's assets, finding that despite the son's physical handicaps he was able to take care of himself financially.

Professor: Were all these reasons part of the court's holding in the case?

Student: Not according to the reviewing court. The court in its opinion made a point to emphasize that it would be wrong to decide the manifest injustice exception based on an individual's income. The appellate court was able to affirm the lower court's opinion because other valid reasons existed for not granting the exception.

Professor: So what if in the next case the sentence was the minimal sentence — could the lower court decide the manifest injustice question based on the financial need of the killer?

Student: Yes. *Blodgett* says the issue shouldn't be decided based on financial need, but the court also said that wasn't at issue in that case. So the comments are only dicta and not part of the holding in the case.

 ## H. Abbreviations in Note Taking

Remember that case briefs are used to help your own study and for use later when studying for examinations. Your goal is to write a brief that is as complete as is necessary but is also as concise as possible. Creating a list of abbreviations for commonly used terms will shorten your time briefing cases and will also help when you take notes in class. Create your own list. Some suggestions are:

K	Contract
P	Plaintiff
D	Defendant
App'ant	Appellant
App'ee	Appellee

Pet.	Petitioner
Resp.	Respondent
BFP	Bona Fide Purchaser
C/A	Cause of Action

 ## I. Legal Terminology

You will find many new words and phrases when studying the law in the United States. Many of the new words and phrases will be legal terms that have special meaning in U.S. law. For this reason, you will need access to a legal dictionary. You may choose to buy a paperback dictionary that is small enough to keep with you whenever you are in class or are studying. In the alternative, there are many legal dictionaries online.[22] When you keep a single list of definitions, separate from individual class notes, you can always check this list first when you read a word or phrase you don't know. If the word or phrase is on the list, you don't need to look further; if not, you can then add the new definition to your master list. By taking the time to learn these terms as you progress through your studies, you should find that eventually you will remember the definition and can then eliminate that word or phrase from your master list. We've also provided a glossary of terms at the end of this book.

● **Exercise 4-A**

Read and brief *Everett v. Rogers*, found in Appendix C.

---

22. See, e.g., FindLaw Law Dictionary, http://dictionary.lp.findlaw.com; Gerald & Kathleen Hill, *The People's Law* (Publisher Fine Communications 2007), http://dictionary.law.com; Merriam-Webster Dictionary of Law (Merriam-Webster 1996) (available at http://dictionary.reference.com/legal).

PART TWO

An Introduction to Writing in the U.S. Legal System

CHAPTER

5

The Legal Writing Process

HIGHLIGHTS

- Writing about the law involves several stages that are necessary to achieve a complete, accurate, and professional document.
- Proper structure, content, and form are essential in a predictive legal analysis.
- Lawyers and judges must use the laws set down by the state—the legislature and the courts—when analyzing a legal issue.
- When writing about the law, the process requires both prewriting steps and redrafting and revising to ensure readability.

 ## A. Introduction: Dispelling Some Myths

As a law student in a U.S. law school, you may be told different stories by other law students about the law school experience, and you must decide what to believe and what not to believe. One myth you may hear is that past writing experiences aren't helpful when writing about the law. This is simply not the case. As with other forms of writing, careful attention to structure, content, and form are essential when you write a professional legal document. The same basic rules of grammar anyone who studies English learns also apply to writing a U.S. legal document; the same guidelines covering the structure of a paragraph apply; and the same guidelines addressing the use of topic, thesis, and transitional sentences all apply. The main difference when analyzing the law based on the facts of a client's case is that the legal rules and principles established by legislatures and courts often dictate the structure of a legal document. (This structuring concept is addressed in more detail in Chapter 11.)

Another myth worth dispelling is that some people simply can write and others cannot. All of us can become solid, professional writers by choosing to learn and apply the basic rules of grammar and style to our own writing. Anyone in the United States who practices law must write; therefore, any U.S. lawyer must develop the skills necessary to become a professional writer. Professional writers produce quality documents in both substance and form.

If you are one who typically delays writing as long as possible (that is, a procrastinator), try to change your writing process. Pay careful attention not only to *what* you write but also to *how* you write. Any good lawyer's written document must withstand careful scrutiny. Your choices about overall paragraph structure, sentence structure, words, and punctuation all count.

A prime example of the need to pay attention to the details is found in the case *Rogers Communications v. Bell Aliant.*[1] In this case, Rogers signed a contract to string cable lines across Aliant's telephone poles in the Canadian Maritime provinces. The language establishing the time frame for the contract was as follows.

> This agreement shall be effective from the date it is made and shall continue in force for a period of five years from the date that it is made, and thereafter for successive five year terms, unless and until terminated by one year prior notice in writing by either party.

A few years after Rogers began installing the lines, and prior to the end of the first five-year period, Aliant canceled the contract and increased the amount Rogers would have to pay to use its telephone poles. The overall increase imposed by Aliant would cost Rogers more than $2 million (Canadian dollars).

Rogers Communications filed suit, and the decision by the Canadian Radio-Television and Telecommunications Commission (Commission) was based on the language of the contract. Rogers argued that the contract could not be terminated within the first five years. The termination clause modified only the clause immediately preceding it — the clause covering the renewal of the contract for successive five-year terms. Aliant argued that the termination clause applied to all the language preceding it, so the contract could be terminated at any time, even in the first five years, provided Aliant gave one year's notice.

The decision turned on the placement of the comma, boldfaced below, and the rules covering punctuation.

---

1. *Telecom Decision CRTC 2007-75*, http://www.crtc.gc.ca/archive/ENG/Decisions/2007/dt2007-75.htm (modified Aug. 17, 2007).

> This agreement shall be effective from the date it is made and shall continue in force for a period of five years from the date that it is **made, and** thereafter for successive five year terms, unless and until terminated by one year prior notice in writing by either party.

The Commission found that the termination clause applied to all five-year terms, including the initial term. Careful drafting, of course, could have prevented this problem. The drafter could have either (1) inserted a semicolon after *made*, eliminated the conjunction *and*, and added "the contract shall continue" or (2) turned the provision into two sentences. If two sentences, the provision would read:[2]

> This agreement shall be effective from the date it is made and shall continue in force for a period of five years from the date that it is made. Thereafter, the contract shall continue for successive five year terms, unless and until terminated by one year prior notice in writing by either party.

Beyond the obvious problem with ambiguous language in contract provisions, because it leaves the interpretation of language to a judicial body, the reasons below also emphasize the need to pay careful attention to your choices about language.[3]

1. *Others may read your documents in bad faith rather than in good faith*

In the U.S. adversary legal system,[4] lawyers read opposing party documents in hopes of finding mistakes that can be challenged. These mistakes may be flaws in reasoning or gaps in arguments. You must be sure that your position and the support for your position are both complete and clear.

---

2. Rogers appealed the Commission's decision, arguing that the French version of the contract had not been considered, but under that version the intent to disallow cancellation during the first five years of the contract was clear. In August 2007 the Commission overturned its decision and ruled for Rogers. *Id.*

3. These suggestions about language matters are based on a talk in the 1980s by Lauren Robel, now dean at the Indiana University School of Law–Bloomington.

4. Adversary systems involve parties who oppose each other. Lawyers representing the parties argue their clients' cases using evidence, witness testimony, legal arguments, and the like before an independent decision maker. At trial, the lawyer for the opposing party may ask questions to challenge the strength of the other side's case.

2. Your readers may be impatient

United States judges and their law clerks[5] may read your document, and both judges and law clerks often feel overworked and underpaid. If your brief to the court is difficult to understand, the judge or law clerk may put down your document and refer to opposing counsel's brief in hopes of understanding the case. If the opposing counsel's brief is clear and complete, it will be more effective; as a result, you may put your client's case at risk. You want judges and their law clerks to understand your story and the legal issues you are explaining the first time they read the information. Your job is to write a clean and clear document.

3. Legal writers must write about complex issues

Lawyers in the United States, like all lawyers, write oftentimes about complex and difficult legal issues. As a U.S. lawyer, the challenge is to write so that even the most complex legal issues can be understood by a reader who is not familiar with your case. If you write your document at the last minute, you may (1) discover that the message is not as complete and logical as you originally thought, and (2) find you don't have the time needed to revise your document so your unfamiliar reader can easily understand it. To avoid this last-minute discovery, draft early, and allow additional time to revise and edit.

4. Your words are powerful and may have far-reaching effects

As a lawyer, your words likely mean more than they have ever meant before. Lawyers are in a position to exercise power, and much of that power is exercised through words. As a result of your words in a criminal case, for example, individuals may lose their freedom. As a result of your words in a custody dispute, parents may lose rights and access to their child. And as a result of your words, you may influence the chief executive officer of a company as to whether a product should be manufactured and introduced into the market, even though the new product carries a potential risk of harm. When you receive this power, you must also accept the responsibility that comes with it. That responsibility includes making careful choices about the substance of your message and the way in which you present your message to your reader.

---

5. Law clerks are lawyers hired to work for judges, sometimes permanently and sometimes for a limited period of time, such as two years.

B. *The Writing Process from Task to Deadline*

You have likely developed a model for your own writing process. You may have developed your own pattern carefully and consciously, or your pattern may have developed without your thinking about it at all. As a U.S. legal writer, you may find it necessary to begin early and redraft more. Consider the various steps that legal writers oftentimes move through when researching and writing legal documents:

Task   ————————————————————▶   Deadline

Steps:

- Determining whether the question has already been answered
- Considering the question on your own and then talking with others
- Taking notes
- Researching
- Predrafting
- Drafting
- Redrafting
- Revising
- Editing

Finding the correct balance between preparing to write and actually writing is challenging for most writers. Consider writing your first draft no later than halfway through the task-to-deadline time period. Writing early in the process gives you sufficient time to make sure your message is complete, accurate, and easy to understand. Writing early is especially helpful when you speak English as your second language. If you tend to procrastinate, consider applying one or both of the following steps.

1. Divide the steps of your process and set your own deadlines for each stage. For example, you may set deadlines for when you will complete the research, the drafting, and the revising. You may also want to set deadlines for different sections of the document, depending on its length and complexity.
2. Commit the deadlines you set to someone else, for example, a supervising attorney, another attorney working on the same project, or an assistant.

What follows is a suggested step-by-step approach to legal writing. The actual process, however, does not usually follow a step-by-step process as what is presented below. You are likely to find that your list of issues and legally significant facts changes as you research and learn more about the law relevant to the case. When you read the law, you may discover more questions to ask your client. When you learn these new facts and do additional research, you may find that new legal issues are raised that require additional, different research, which then requires even more new questions for the client. So while the legal process is set out below using a step-by-step, straightforward process, in reality the process involves repeating steps when necessary and is, therefore, quite recursive in nature.

Here are six steps in the legal writing process, when writing an objective analysis.

1. Collect the facts.
2. Analyze the facts.
3. Collect the law.
4. Analyze the law.
5. Organize the law.
6. Apply the law to the client's facts to analyze and predict the likely outcome regarding each legal issue in dispute.

1. Collect the facts

You must talk with your potential client to learn what happened. You collect the facts by asking careful, probing questions during the client interview. As a good interviewer, you are an active listener, asking questions to acquire the important facts and to make sure that when the interview ends you understand the client's story. Only then can you decide whether to serve as the individual's lawyer, whether there is even a potential legal issue to explore, or how to best respond to the opposing party's claim, in the case where a lawsuit has already been filed in court.

2. Analyze the facts

Once you collect the client's facts, you are ready to analyze the facts by turning the simple language of the story into legal categories. For example, in Exercise 2-B, where Nicholas's wife Selena killed Nicholas and his mistress after Nicholas returned from the war, Selena can be labeled as the wife/killer/potential beneficiary, and Nicholas can be labeled as the husband/victim/decedent. Typical categories in analyzing the facts and preparing to research include the following.[6]

> **T**hings
> **A**ctions
> **R**elief requested
> **P**arties

Think back to the exercises in Chapter 2 that address the evolving nature of the law. In Exercise 2-C, the Assembly passed a law providing that "[n]o person who intentionally causes the death of another shall in any way benefit by the death." In that

---

6. J. Myron Jacobstein & Roy M. Mersky, *Fundamentals of Legal Research* 16 (7th ed., Foundation Press 1998).

exercise, Stephen organized a boar hunt. After Stephen killed the boar, he gave the tusks to Diana, a beautiful huntress and princess who Stephen loved. Stephen's uncles also attended the hunt and also loved Diana. The uncles attacked Stephen with their spears, and one uncle's spear cut Stephen's shoulder. Fearing for his life, Stephen killed both uncles. Both uncles had a Last Will and Testament naming Stephen as a beneficiary.

When determining whether Stephen would be prevented under the law from receiving benefits under each uncle's Last Will and Testament, you might analyze the facts in the following way.

THINGS	ACTIONS	RELIEF REQUESTED	PARTIES
Boar hunt	Killing	Stephen to be denied benefits of uncle's death through inheritance	Nephew
Spears	Self-defense		Nephew's mother
Last Will & Testament			

After analyzing the facts, you may find that some of the words and phrases are more helpful than others. For example, *nephew* and *nephew's mother* are not all that helpful; however, if the parties were *buyer* and *seller*, those neutral, generic references would be extremely helpful when researching. Other terms, such as *killing, self-defense,* and *Last Will and Testament,* are key words to use when researching the law relevant to this case.

3. Collect the law

After analyzing the facts and considering the potential legal issues raised by the facts, you will likely need to research the legal issues. Using the list of words and phrases you generated in step two, create a plan for your research before going to the library or sitting down to research online.

a. Creating an issue statement

Consider drafting a preliminary issue statement[7] using the format discussed in Chapter 4 on briefing cases. The preliminary issue statement reflects both the law and the facts. The legal question identifies (1) the broad area of law at issue, and (2) the specific legal issue you are addressing. This helps you to know where in the library

---

7. Mary Barnard Ray & Jill J. Ramsfield, *Getting It Write and Getting It Written* 311 (West Group 2000).

(whether in an actual library or the library online) to research. It also helps you focus further on the specific legal question within the broad area of law you will need to research. A list of the facts that help explain why the legal issue is in dispute is also helpful. This list of facts will include both facts that help your client's position and facts that help the opposing party's position. You need both to understand the dispute. The more similar your client's facts are to the facts in the cases you find in your research, the better the case will be in your analysis.

The exercises in Chapter 2 address whether a killer could receive a benefit, such as money or property, from a deceased victim. The preliminary issue statement for Exercise 2-C might look like this.

> *Legal Question:* Under the East Carolina statute that precludes one who caused the death of another from benefiting from the victim's death, will a nephew receive the assets of his two uncles following their deaths
> *Facts:* when the nephew, in fear for his life, killed his uncles after they started a fight with the nephew and one uncle cut the nephew's shoulder with a spear?

If you already know about this area of law and understand the importance of self-defense in analyzing the specific legal question, above, you would likely include self-defense in your legal question.

For example:

> *Legal Question:* Under the East Carolina statute that precludes one who caused the death of another from benefiting from the victim's death, can Stephen prove he acted in self-defense and therefore still receive the assets of his two uncles when . . .

When you combine the relevant law and your client's facts, you can then focus on the legal issues that must be addressed in analyzing your client's case. In Exercise 2-C, the outcome of the case depends on whether the nephew, Stephen, can avoid the slayer statute by showing he acted in self-defense. The statute referred to earlier in the first example above ("slayer statute") does not address what might happen when a killer acts in self-defense. Through the merger of the law and facts, you would realize that the court's decision will depend more on how the statute is interpreted, which is a law-based rather than a fact-based question.[8] The court could decide that the words only of the statute are what matters, so acting in self-defense is not an excuse since it's not mentioned in the statute; alternatively, the court might recognize self-defense as

---

8. The analysis of a law-based issue is discussed in detail in Chapter 14.

a way to avoid the slayer statute and still take the assets of the victim. This focus on how to interpret the statutory language would change the legal question.

For example:

> **Legal Question:** Is a court likely to create an exception to the statutory provision that prevents anyone who intentionally causes the death of another from benefiting by that death when the killer acts in self-defense?

b. Researching the legal issue

Your goal when researching is always to access the relevant primary authority. Primary sources of authority include constitutions, statutes, cases, and administrative regulations authorized through a statute. Binding primary authority includes constitutional provisions, statutes, and court decisions from higher courts addressing the same legal issues in the controlling jurisdiction.

If you do not know anything about the legal issue, you may choose to research secondary sources first. Secondary sources are not binding authority. These sources are best used to become more familiar with an area of law so your research for primary authority is more focused. Secondary sources will also refer you to useful primary authority. Typical examples of secondary sources include restatements of law, law review articles, encyclopedias, and treatises.

This book does not include research instruction. Numerous books explain all the research sources available to those researching law in the United States.[9]

As an effective researcher, you will want to keep careful notes of your research. By taking careful notes, you avoid looking unnecessarily at the same materials again. Even when researching carefully, however, you may be uncertain when you have researched thoroughly and can stop with confidence. Consider the "backwards and forwards" method. When you have read all the relevant cases cited in the key cases, the "backwards" research, or historical perspective, is likely complete. And when you find that your key cases are the only ones continually cited in the more recent cases, the "forwards" research is likely also complete.[10]

4. Analyze the law

The first step in analyzing the law is to brief the relevant cases. You don't need to fully brief the entire case in detail, only that portion of the case relevant to the

---

9. Examples of good research texts include Christina Kunz et al., *The Process of Legal Research* (6th ed., Aspen Publishers 2004), and Amy Sloan, *Basic Legal Research* (3d ed., Aspen Publishers 2006).

10. Credit for the "backwards and forwards" method goes to Andrew Solomon, Associate Professor, South Texas College of Law.

legal issue you are researching. A case may address both procedural issues and multiple substantive issues, for example, but you will note only the key facts, the court's holding, and the court's reasoning regarding the issues involved in your client's case. (Chapter 4 provides instruction on finding these parts of a court opinion.)

5. Organize the law

As you brief the relevant cases you plan to use in your analysis, note the relevant legal test courts use to analyze each legal issue. This legal test will create the basic structure for the analysis of your client's case. The structure of the legal test may comprise requirements (or elements), a rule with one or more exceptions, the weighing of factors, and so on. (The structure of these legal tests is discussed in detail in Chapter 11.)

By organizing the law, you can better understand which legal points are truly in dispute. For example, after researching whether Stephen could benefit from his uncles' deaths after killing them, though arguably in self-defense, you may find that different courts focused on the legal issue in different ways. Court A might have focused on whether the killer was convicted of first or second degree murder, or voluntary or involuntary manslaughter; based on the severity of the conviction, the court would or would not allow the killer to benefit from the victim's death. Court B, however, might have focused on the Assembly's intent in enacting the slayer statute, trying to reach a decision consistent with that intent.

The basic structure of a legal test, particularly one developed through the common law, may be introduced in one case and remain constant throughout later cases applying the same test. More likely, however, the legal test is introduced in one case and then further refined in subsequent cases, so the final test is based on synthesizing many court holdings into one legal test. (Chapter 10 specifically addresses how to synthesize case holdings to create a single common law rule.) When you organize the law, separate the parts of the legal test. You can separate the parts of the test either by outlining or perhaps by charting the law and cases. (For more on charting, refer to Chapter 12 on analyzing multiple issues using multiple cases.)

6. Apply the law to the client's facts to analyze and predict the likely outcome regarding each legal issue in dispute

At this point, you have thoroughly collected and analyzed the facts, and have collected, analyzed, and organized the law. Now you want to apply the relevant law to the specific facts of your client's case. In this step, you must determine finally what legal points are in dispute and what legal points, if any, are legally relevant but are not in dispute. You will be able to determine disputable and indisputable points by adding the client's facts to the outline or chart you created previously and noting the potential support that exists for each party regarding each legal point. (Most of the chapters in Part Three of this book address in great detail how to organize and analyze legal issues.)

 ## C. The Writing Process

1. Considerations when beginning to write

As with any piece of writing, you must always consider (a) why a document is being written (purpose), (b) the appropriate tone of the document, (c) the potential audience for the document, and (d) any constraints that may exist with respect to the document.

a. Purpose

You must understand *why* you are writing each document. You may be writing a legal document to create a specific outcome (as in a contract or Last Will and Testament), to objectively analyze and predict the strength of your client's position (as in an office memorandum), or to persuade (as in a document to the court or a demand letter). You may write other correspondence, such as letters to clients or to opposing counsel, simply to inform, to make a recommendation, or to seek additional information.

b. Tone

The type of document you are writing dictates the appropriate tone. Documents to a court are always written in formal language. Office memoranda may or may not be written as formally, depending on how well you know your reader. However, even if you know your immediate reader, an office memorandum may be filed away and eventually read by different parties. If you are not sure what tone is appropriate, choose a more formal one. And all legal documents, regardless of how formally written, should conform to standard rules of grammar and style.

c. Audience

Always consider your reader, or audience. You may be writing to someone who has a law degree, for example, a lawyer or a judge, but who knows little about the specific law and nothing about the specific facts of the client's case. You may be writing to a nonlawyer who knows little if anything about the law *and* little or nothing about the facts of the client's case. Your reader may be highly educated or have very little education, requiring you to choose your language more carefully and explain more terms. You want to pay particular attention to your audience during the later stages of your process, when you rewrite, revise, and edit.

d. Constraints

U.S. lawyers are often constrained by specific deadlines, page or word limits set down by a court, and other rules such as those for properly formatting a document. Always allow yourself sufficient time to check that you are abiding by these rules.

2. The creative and critical stages in the writing process

Your goal is a written document, but writing also influences your thinking process. If you understand that writing promotes thinking, you will understand why drafting early and allowing time to redraft is so important to a clear message. Put another way, "Easy reading is damn hard writing."[11] If you are a procrastinator, however, you don't use writing as a means to heighten your analytical thinking. In the end, you may have an analysis that is not as in-depth and well reasoned as it could be.

In the list of the steps from task to deadline, many of the actions occur prior to writing the first draft. If you write earlier rather than later in the process, your focus can be on the content of the message rather than on the presentation of the message. Once you are confident that the message is complete and accurate, you may then focus on ensuring that your message is easy to read and understand. The task-to-deadline process, therefore, includes both a writer-based focus and a reader-based focus.

a. Writer-based (creative) focus

When first drafting, focus on the substance of your message. Early writing allows you to determine whether your message contains the correct substance and is structured appropriately. During this stage of the writing process, you need not worry about details such as using proper grammar or clear topic, thesis, and transitional sentences. If you do concern yourself with the smaller details, you may overlook important substance. By drafting and redrafting early, your own writing helps you to think.

Ernest Hemingway[12] was asked once whether he always thought about how he could use what he observed in his daily life in one of his novels. He responded that he did not need to live his life that way because he knew he could retrieve what he observed later from his memory, if necessary. Hemingway compared the writing process to an iceberg. "The dignity of movement of an iceberg is due to only one-tenth of it being above water."[13] In other words, for every one-tenth of an iceberg that is actually seen above the water, nine-tenths creates the foundation below.

---

11. Nathaniel Hawthorne (1804-1864), as quoted in Terri Guillemets, *The Quote Garden*, http://www.quotegarden.com/writing.html (last updated Nov. 25, 2007).

12. Ernest Hemingway (1899-1961) was one of the greatest U.S. fiction writers of the twentieth century, writing great works such as *A Farewell to Arms, For Whom the Bell Tolls*, and *The Old Man and the Sea*.

13. Angelfire, *The Write Quote*, http://www.angelfire.com/al/thewritesite/quotes.html (last accessed Feb. 16, 2008).

Similarly, a well-written document typically reflects perhaps one-tenth of what you as a writer know and have considered through the writing process. Writing itself creates new thoughts that may be brought up from the far reaches of your memory. And when you reject a word or a thought in a draft, the rejection of those thoughts will often bring forth new thoughts. In the end, just as the tip of the iceberg above water rests on the solid foundation underneath the water, the final written legal document rests on the solid foundation of the writing and rewriting process.

b. Reader-based (critical) focus

Once you have completed drafting your message, you are ready to move to the critical, reader-based stage of the writing process. This stage requires you to revise and edit so your message can not only be read but also be understood by your reader. Explaining the law can be a challenge. Consider the following story.

You own a lovely rose garden. You are feeding your flowers with a liquid fertilizer. The fertilizer spills on ornamental stones in the garden, and you do not have enough fertilizer for the remaining roses. Is your job finished just because you emptied the watering can? When writing, if you simply "pour out" the information on paper and do not pay attention to whether that information can be understood easily by your reader, you have not finished your job. You have potentially wasted your message on the barren stones.

c. Steps to move through in a task-to-deadline time line

WRITER-BASED STEPS	READER-BASED STEPS
• Determining whether the question has already been answered	• Redrafting
• Thinking about the question and talking with others	• Revising
• Taking notes	• Editing
• Researching	
• Predrafting	
• Drafting	
• Redrafting	

In the best writings, your reader can read straight from the beginning of the document to the end. This straightforward reading can occur only when information is located where most appropriate and when the language used is easy to understand. As an effective writer, you do not want to force your reader to read one reference and then search through the document for information to clarify the reference. You also do not want to force your reader to a dictionary in order to understand what you are trying to say. You must also present a legal document that is professional, free of errors in grammar and style. If your presentation is sloppy, your reader may question whether the sloppy, unprofessional presentation carries through to your analysis.

As you rewrite and revise, consider working on different sections of your document each time you work on it. This allows you to revise in short periods of time rather than in one long sitting. Most of us are more fresh and alert when we first begin working, so the beginning is when we can usually do our best work. Consider also starting at a different place in your document each time you revise. If you always begin at the beginning of the document, you may find that while the early portions are well written, the writing becomes more sloppy and disorganized towards the end. When this happens, it's often because you did not spend as much time as needed on the later portions.

This is the stage where you must pay careful attention to detail — to clear topic, thesis, and transitional sentences; to the content and placement of each word, sentence, and paragraph; to citation rules; and to proper grammar, punctuation, and spelling.[14] Some writers find they can identify errors more easily if they read the paper aloud. And if you are looking only for grammatical errors, consider reading your paper sentence by sentence, beginning at the end of the document. That way you will isolate each sentence and read it out of context. This technique often helps you find small errors that you may otherwise overlook.

---

14. Excellent texts addressing grammar and style include Anne Enquist & Laurel Currie Oates, *Just Writing: Grammar, Punctuation, and Style for the Legal Writer* (2d ed., Aspen Publishers 2005), and Mary Bernard Ray & Jill Ramsfield, *Legal Writing: Getting It Right and Getting It Written* (West 2005).

CHAPTER

6

The U.S. Concept of Plagiarism and the Proper Attribution to Authority

---

HIGHLIGHTS

- Plagiarism is the use of someone else's words or ideas without properly attributing the source of those ideas.
- Words or ideas taken from published or unpublished sources, including written text and Web sites; live, recorded, or broadcast speeches, debates, or conversations; or graphs, charts, illustrations, photographs, and images must be given proper attribution to the original source.
- Matters of common knowledge to the writer's target audience do not need to be attributed to a source.
- Steps to avoid intentional or unintentional plagiarism include taking accurate notes when researching, keeping track of passages copied and pasted from online sources, and allowing sufficient time for the writing process.
- Proper attribution includes (1) accurately reporting the borrowed words or ideas; (2) placing quotation marks around the quoted text or, if the quotation is 50 or more words, placing the quoted text in block format, and (3) accurately citing to the original source.
- All quoted, summarized, and paraphrased information must be properly attributed.

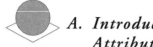

A. Introduction: The U.S. View of Proper Attribution of Sources

1. The importance of avoiding plagiarism

Plagiarism is considered a serious moral and ethical transgression in U.S. culture.[1] A student who plagiarizes can be subject to penalties under an educational institution's student code. Penalties range from failing a paper containing the plagiarized material or failing a course, to suspension or expulsion from school, to withholding a degree.[2] If employed, plagiarists risk losing respect among their colleagues and peers, and even risk losing their jobs.[3]

Software and online services aimed at detecting plagiarism are widely available. Many instructors regularly use these aids to detect plagiarism in student papers. It is far easier today to spot plagiarized passages than in previous years.

Furthermore, giving attribution to respected authorities to support points or ideas in your writing significantly strengthens the likelihood that your reader will accept your argument. Giving appropriate and frequent attribution results in a more persuasive paper.

2. Plagiarism defined

Plagiarism is the use of someone else's words or ideas, whether expressed in writing or orally, without proper attribution to the source.

Written words or ideas found in any public or private document, whether or not published, must be attributed to the source. Even words or ideas taken from a Web site must be given proper attribution. Borrowed words or ideas originally expressed in a live, recorded, or broadcast speech, debate, or conversation must be attributed to the speaker. Charts, graphs, illustrations, photographs, and images, or information found in these sources, if borrowed by a writer, must also be properly attributed to the original source.

---

1. Joseph Gibaldi, *MLA Style Manual and Guide to Scholarly Publishing* 151 (2d ed., Modern Lang. Assn. of Am. 1998).

2. *Napolitano v. Princeton Univ. Trustees*, 453 A.2d 263 (N.J. Super. App. Div. 1982) (the court upheld the university's sanction of withholding a student's degree for a period of one year because the student had quoted and paraphrased passages from a book in a class paper and failed to properly attribute these passages to the book's author).

3. *Iowa Sup. Ct. Bd. of Prof. Ethics & Conduct v. Williams*, 642 N.W.2d 296 (Iowa 2002) (the court suspended an attorney's license to practice law for filing a plagiarized brief in a federal district court); *Matikas v. U. of Dayton*, 788 N.E.2d 1108 (Ohio App. 2003) (the court granted a summary judgment in favor of the university, finding the university was within its rights to terminate a researcher's employment because he committed plagiarism in a manuscript submitted for publication).

3. An exception for information of common knowledge

In U.S. culture, matters of common knowledge to the writer's target audience do not require a citation to a source. Unfortunately, what constitutes common knowledge is confusing. This confusion is further compounded by cultural differences. Matters of common knowledge have been defined as "includ[ing] whatever an educated person would be expected to know or could locate in an ordinary encyclopedia."[4] At least one university Web site on plagiarism suggests that a fact or phrase may be of common knowledge if the information can be found undocumented in five different sources.[5] Still other university Web sites on plagiarism are reluctant to be so specific in definition.[6]

The problem is that what someone in the United States considers common knowledge someone from another country may not, and vice versa. For example, the fact that Sandra Day O'Connor was the first woman to serve as a Justice on the United States Supreme Court is common knowledge to most citizens educated in the United States; however, this information may not be common knowledge to people educated outside the United States. Further complicating the situation is that what may be common knowledge to people educated in one particular discipline may not necessarily be common knowledge to people educated in another discipline. For example, it may be common knowledge among U.S. lawyers that there are 13 federal circuits in the United States, but this is likely not common knowledge to U.S. physicians. Therefore, when determining whether information is common knowledge, writers should consider their audience. If in doubt as to whether the information would be common knowledge to the writer's target audience, the writer should always cite to a source for the information.

4. Intentional plagiarism

Intentional plagiarists knowingly use someone else's document, words, or ideas without attribution. Their intent is to deceive readers into thinking that they, the writers, alone conceived and wrote the material used. Another form that intentional

---

4. Robert A. Harris, *The Plagiarism Handbook* 154 (Pyrczak Publishing 2001).

5. Purdue OWL, *Avoiding Plagiarism, Deciding if Something Is "Common Knowledge,"* http://owl.english. purdue.edu/owl/resource/589/02/ (last updated Sept. 18, 2007) (facts may be of common knowledge if a student "find[s] the same information undocumented in at least five other sources. . . .").

6. *See, e.g.,* UC Davis, Div. of Student Affairs, Off. of Student Jud. Affairs, *Avoiding Plagiarism, Guidelines for Avoiding Plagiarism,* http://sja.ucdavis.edu/files/plagiarism.pdf (Sept. 2006) ("[T]he fact must really *be* common. That George Orwell was the author of the anti-totalitarian allegory *Animal Farm* is common knowledge; that Orwell died at 46 in 1951 is not."). *See also* Ind. U. Writing Tutorial Servs., *Plagiarism: What It Is and How to Recognize It and Avoid It,* http://www.indiana.edu/~wts/wts/plagiarism.html (last updated Apr. 27, 2004) (common knowledge includes "facts that can be found in numerous places and are likely to be known by a lot of people.").

plagiarists use is submitting their own material written for other courses. Unless a professor states otherwise, it is assumed that papers submitted in a course are written solely for the particular purpose of that course.

It may be tempting for you, especially if English is your second language, to turn to writing specialists, tutors, friends, or family members proficient in English to help you write your papers. The pressure to receive a good grade and the awareness that writing concise, grammatically correct sentences will likely improve the paper may induce you to permit others to write or rewrite your papers. You may think that because you performed the research and came up with the essential analysis for the paper, it is permissible for another person to finish the paper by revising phrases, sentences, paragraphs, or sections to make it more readable. Nevertheless, anytime you borrow another person's words without making proper attribution, even when the idea behind the material is your own, you have plagiarized. A paper that you've written for an assignment in a course is expected to be the product of your individual effort, unless the professor states otherwise. Therefore, the temptation to use others to write or rewrite papers, even merely for the purpose of correcting grammar or sentence structure problems throughout the paper, must be avoided. Otherwise, you risk incurring serious penalties that could jeopardize your educational pursuits.[7]

5. Unintentional plagiarism

Most people, however, do not intend to plagiarize. Nevertheless, it is just as serious to unintentionally plagiarize as it is to intentionally plagiarize. Even when their plagiarism has been proved, these unintentional plagiarists may still be convinced that they did not commit any wrongdoing because they never intended to plagiarize. The fact remains, though, that unintentional plagiarists still borrowed text and ideas from other sources without giving proper attribution to the original author. Plagiarism "violates the moral code of learning,"[8] regardless of whether the student intentionally committed the plagiarism.

6. Ways to avoid plagiarism

a. Accurate and thorough researching

Plagiarism often results from sloppy or hasty researching. You should give particular attention, therefore, to your note taking while researching. Do not trust that you will remember later which words in your notes are yours and which are an

---

7. *See, e.g., supra* nn. 2 & 3.

8. Edward M. White, *Student Plagiarism as an Institutional and Social Issue in Perspectives on Plagiarism and Intellectual Property in a Postmodern World* 205, 209 (Lise Buranen & Alice M. Roy eds., State U. of N.Y. Press 1999).

author's. As you research, mark the exact words you have copied, as well as those passages you have paraphrased or summarized. Also, do not trust yourself to remember the source or the page number where you found the information that you have marked in your notes. Write down the source where you found the information while you are creating your notes.[9] When recording the source, be sure to include the complete title of the source, the author's name, and the page number where you found the information. If you are researching in multiple places, such as in the law school library, in the local public library, or on the Internet, note in which location you found the source so that you can easily return if you have questions later on.

b. Special consideration for information found on the Internet

If you found information on an Internet site, note the URL[10] address where you found the information. Plagiarism has become especially troublesome with students' easy access to the Internet. The ease in copying online information and pasting it into your own document heightens the risk of plagiarism. Be especially mindful of noting what has been pasted into your paper. When you are finalizing your paper, you can choose to take the highlighted words or passages and either summarize, paraphrase, or quote them, but you must always include a proper attribution to the Web site where you found the information.

Taking the time while you are researching to note whether you have quoted, paraphrased, or summarized information from a source will save time later because you will not need to find the information again. More importantly, careful documentation while researching will prevent you from attributing text or ideas to the wrong source, or failing to give any attribution at all.

c. Appropriate management of time

Rushing to complete your research or to write your paper to meet a deadline can also give rise to incidents of plagiarism. Give yourself plenty of time to research and write a paper. Realize that most students who read and write English with ease spend many, many hours researching, putting the information together, and drafting and revising their writing in an effort to create well-written papers containing strong legal analyses. If you are not fluent in English, this process may take you even longer. Be honest with yourself about your level of skill in researching and your proficiency in writing, and budget your time accordingly. The research and writing process almost always takes longer than originally anticipated, even for native language learners.

---

9. Note taking also is discussed in Chapter 5.
10. Uniform Resource Locator, or the string of letters, words, and numbers that usually begins with *http*.

B. Giving Appropriate Attribution

Proper attribution has three basic requirements: (1) the writer must accurately report the borrowed words or ideas in his writing; (2) the writer must notify the reader about any quoted words, phrases, or passages by either placing quotation marks around the quoted text or, if the quotation is 50 or more words, by placing the quoted text in block format; and (3) the writer must accurately and completely cite to the original source at all necessary points in her paper where she has borrowed text or ideas. The importance of accurate citations to the source cannot be overemphasized. Providing inaccurate or fictitious citations to borrowed text or ideas is plagiarism because the writer has failed to give correct attribution to the original source.

1. Quoting

Any words, phrases, or passages that are not your own must be attributed to the source where you found it. When using quoted text in your writing, make sure you comply with the following criteria.

1. *The quoted material accurately reflects the words in the original text.* If you modify anything within the quotation, such as changing the tense of a verb, replacing a proper noun with a pronoun, or omitting words or punctuation, you must note this using brackets or ellipses, as appropriate.[11]

Example:[12]

> In *In re Estate of Blodgett*, 147 P.3d 702, 707 (Alaska 2006), the court stated, "The legislature clearly decided that [where an heir commits a criminally negligent act accidentally causing the deceased's death,] there should be discretion in the court to consider the specific facts of the homicide and, if denial of the inheritance [from the deceased] would be manifestly unjust, to permit it."

---

11. See ALWD & Darby Dickerson, *ALWD Citation Manual* 348-355 (3d ed., Aspen Publishers 2006), for explanation and examples of the proper use of brackets and ellipses in a quoted passage.

12. The *Blodgett* passages given in this section were taken from the *Blodgett* case discussed in Chapter 4.

2. *If the quotation contains less than 50 words, begin and end the quoted text with quotation marks.*

◆ *Example:*

"[T]he legislature broadened the application of the slayer statute — by extending it to unintentional killings — and created an escape clause — by enacting the manifest injustice exception." *Blodgett*, 147 P.3d at 706 (referring to Alaska Stat. § 13.12.803(k)).

3. *If the quotation contains 50 or more words, place the quoted text in block format.* Indent both the left and right margins and use single spacing. Do not use quotation marks around the block quote. The block format signals to the reader that the text is quoted material.

◆ *Example:*

In the *Blodgett* case, the court reasoned:

The legislature clearly decided that . . . there should be discretion in the court to consider the specific facts of the homicide and, if denial of the inheritance would be manifestly unjust, to permit it. . . . Where the killer's act was not intentional, and especially where the act was not even reckless, and where other circumstances lessen the overall effect of the crime, the application of the slayer statute may lead to unnecessarily harsh results.

147 P.3d at 707.

4. *Place the citation either within the sentence containing the quotation* (as shown in the example under 1 above) *or in a separate sentence* (a "citation sentence") (as shown in the example under 2 above). In the case of a block quote, the citation is not included as part of the block quote; following the quote, space down and place the citation at the original left margin (as shown in the example under 3 above). (See Chapter 15 for proper placement of a citation).

5. *Follow accurately an established legal citation style when writing citations.* (See Chapter 15 for the basic rules of proper citation format.)

Note that if the writers in the examples under 1, 2, and 3 above had included the quotation marks or block format but had omitted the citation, the writers still would have plagiarized the material. Also, if the writers in the same examples included the citation but omitted the quotation marks (in the examples under 1 and 2 above) or omitted the block format (in the example under 3 above), the writers still would have plagiarized the material. You must provide quotation marks around the quoted text or, in the case of a quote of 50 or more words, a block format *and* a citation to the source in order to give proper attribution to the source.

Some students, who don't give themselves enough time to complete a paper or are too uncomfortable to paraphrase or summarize information from a source, tend to string one quotation after another. Stringing one quote after another results in a paper that essentially is not the writer's work product. Also, quotations can take up a lot of space in a paper, especially when extraneous words or information are included in the quoted text. Overquoting leaves little, if any, room for the writer's own ideas, thoughts, and analyses, which are the objectives of most written assignments in law school. It is important to use quotations judiciously and only when using the source's exact words.

2. Summarizing

You may summarize the information contained in the original text. A summary is shorter in length than the passage in the original text, allowing more space for the writer to convey analyses or ideas. But you should also be aware that, by virtue of its brevity, a summary cannot convey all the points made by the author in the original text. Therefore, you should use a summary when (1) it is important to be brief and (2) it is unnecessary to convey all the points made by the author in the original text. A few quoted words or phrases may be included in a summary, in which case you must place quotation marks around the quoted text. When summarizing information from another source, comply with the following criteria.

1. Make sure that the summary accurately reflects information conveyed in the original text.
2. Quote any special words or phrases from the original text used in the summary.
3. Insert a citation to the source where you found the information you are summarizing, if required. (See Chapter 15 for the rules regarding when a citation is required in a legal document.)
4. Follow accurately an established legal citation style when writing citations to the information you are summarizing. (See Chapter 15 for the basic rules of proper citation format.)

Example:

The original text from the *Blodgett* case reads:

> The legislature limited the broad reach of the slayer statute by giving trial court judges the discretion to allow killers to benefit from the victim's assets if manifest injustice would result otherwise. Should an inheritance be denied to the unskilled teenager who drives his car in a criminally negligent manner and accidentally causes the death of his remaining parent? The legislature clearly decided that in such a case there should be discretion in the court to consider

> the specific facts of the homicide and, if denial of the inheritance would be manifestly unjust, to permit it.
>
> A summary of a passage from *Blodgett* might read:
>
>> The Alaska legislature expanded the coverage of the slayer statute to include unintentional killings but also limited its scope by creating an exception when its application would create a "manifest injustice," such as when a child drives recklessly and accidentally kills her only surviving parent. *Blodgett,* 147 P.3d at 707.

not in italics.

Note that even if the summary had not contained quoted phrases, the summary must include a citation to the original text. Failing to cite to a source when required is plagiarism.

3. *Paraphrasing*

Rather than directly quoting or summarizing a passage, you may elect to paraphrase the information from the original text. A paraphrase restates the original text in your own words. If the original text is complex or awkwardly worded, you may paraphrase the text, rather than directly quoting it, to convey the information in wording that is easier for the reader to understand. You may prefer paraphrasing over summarizing the original text when you want to convey all the points made in the original text.[13] One way to draft a paraphrased passage is to read the original text over and over until you understand it, then put the text aside and draft the paraphrase, using your own words and sentence structure. When paraphrasing information from another text, comply with the following criteria.

1. Make sure that the paraphrased language accurately reflects information conveyed in the original text.
2. Alter the structure of each sentence in the paraphrase to be different from the sentence structure contained in the original text. It is plagiarism if you keep the sentence structure of the original text and only replace words from the original text with either synonyms or change the verb tense, or both.
3. If a special word or phrase from the original text is used in the paraphrase, comply with the criteria for direct quotations in section B1 above.
4. Insert a citation to the source where you found the information you are paraphrasing, if required. (There is an exception that paraphrased facts from a case do not need a citation. See Chapter 15 for the rules regarding when a citation is required in legal writing documents.) Failing to cite to a source when required is plagiarism.

---

13. It is suggested, however, that you quote all rules or relevant sections of a statute that are the focus of a legal analyses to avoid inadvertently changing the meaning of the rules or statutes.

5. Follow accurately an established legal citation style when writing citations to the information you are paraphrasing. (See Chapter 15 for the basic rules of proper citation format.)

> An insufficient attempt at paraphrasing the passage from the *Blodgett* case might read as follows.
>
> > The court in the *Blodgett* case noted that the Alaska legislature narrowed the reach of the slayer statute by giving the trial court judges the discretion to allow killers to benefit from the victim's assets if manifest injustice would result otherwise. In creating the exception, the legislature considered those instances such as when a child unintentionally kills his sole parent. Even though this act would fall within the slayer statute, prohibiting that child from receiving the parent's assets would be fundamentally unfair. The legislature decided that in instances such as this, the trial court may consider the specific facts of the homicide to determine whether denying the defendant the victim's assets would be manifestly unjust. *Blodgett*, 147 P.3d at 707.

This particular passage is plagiarized. The writer essentially has retained the sentence structure from the original text and merely replaced the words with synonyms. Also, the phrase "reach of the slayer statute by giving the trial court judges the discretion to allow killers to benefit from the victim's assets if manifest injustice would result otherwise" has been quoted, and the writer failed to place quotation marks around this phrase. Finally, a citation to the case appears only at the end of the passage. This misleads the reader into thinking that the reasoning appears only in the final sentence of the paraphrase, when, in fact, the entire passage represents the court's reasoning. A citation should have appeared at the end of each sentence. Any one of these errors—a failure to paraphrase the passage, a failure to place quotation marks around the quoted text, or a failure to insert a citation at the end of each sentence—constitutes plagiarism.

> A sufficient paraphrase of the passage from the *Blodgett* case might read:
>
> > In the *Blodgett* case, the court stated that at the same time the Alaska legislature expanded the slayer statute to include unintentional killings, it also added an exception to the slayer statute. 147 P.3d at 707. The exception empowers the trial court to prohibit the application of the main provision of the slayer statute when to do so would be manifestly unjust. *Id.* The court considered those instances such as when a child unintentionally kills his only parent. *Id.* Even though the child's actions would be a homicide and fall within the main provision of the slayer statute, prohibiting that child from receiving his parent's assets may be fundamentally

> unfair. *Id.* Thus, the legislature gave the trial court the ability to permit the defendant to take the victim's assets when a "denial of inheritance would be manifestly unjust. . . ." *Id.*

This is an acceptable paraphrase of the original text. No language is taken directly from the original passage, but the message reflects the original message. A cite appears at the end of each sentence because each sentence constitutes a part of the court's reasoning.

● Exercise 6-A

Using the following excerpt from the *Everett v. Rogers* case (which appears in full in Appendix C), write examples of (1) a summarized passage and (2) a paraphrased passage using the concepts learned in this chapter.

> The discovery rule is fact sensitive so as to adjust the level of scrutiny as is appropriate in light of the identity of the parties; what efforts are reasonable for an individual who is relatively unfamiliar with the art world, for example, may not be reasonable for a savvy collector, a gallery, or a museum. While Rogers could certainly have been more aggressive in his search — for example, making inquiries at galleries and museums rather than merely visiting them — Rogers' occasional visits to galleries and museums and his reliance on the services of the F.B.I. constitute a reasonable search effort under the discovery rule. Notably, the standard is not whether Rogers did everything that might have been done with the benefit of hindsight, but whether his efforts were reasonable given the facts of the case.

Everett v. Rogers, 836 F. Supp. 1030, 1033 (S.D.E.C. 1995).

PART THREE

Writing an Objective Analysis

CHAPTER

7

Writing an Objective Analysis Discussion of a Fact-Based Issue: Based on One Issue and One Case

HIGHLIGHTS

- Three sources used to support a legal analysis are (1) the relevant law, (2) the facts of your client's case, and (3) the underlying policy that supports the relevant law.
- An objective analysis of a fact-based issue includes comparing and contrasting the facts in relevant case law to the facts of your client's case to determine whether the outcome in your client's case will be similar to or different than the outcome reached in the case law.
- The purpose of an objective legal analysis is to inform the reader of the law relevant to a legal issue and to predict the issue's probable outcome in your client's case by weighing the legal support for and against the client's position.
- TRAC (Topic or Thesis Sentence, Rule, Analysis, and Conclusion) may be used as a structural checklist when writing a legal analysis.
- A legal analysis includes a discussion of all relevant rules, definitions, and rule explanations.
- A rule explanation includes (1) the relevant facts of a reported case, (2) any additional facts that make the relevant facts understandable, (3) the court's holding on the issue, and (4) the court's reasoning for its holding.
- In a written legal analysis of a single issue, one side of the issue is completely analyzed before beginning the analysis of the other side of the issue.
- The conclusion includes an explanation of the reasons for the conclusion and acknowledges the predictive nature of an objective legal analysis by stating the conclusion using words, such as *likely* or *probably.*

Drafting a legal analysis can be intimidating, especially when you are addressing a complex issue or multiple issues involving many facts and rules. To introduce the writing process for an objective legal analysis, we begin with a single fact-based issue and a single case. As you become more familiar with the process, we will gradually add cases and issues in later chapters.

We follow the step-by-step approach to research and drafting introduced in Chapter 5. Although this is presented as a step-by-step process, in performing these steps you will likely repeat some steps as you become more familiar with the law during the research process and as you give more thought to your client's case in light of the law.

A. Step One: Collect Your Client's Facts

As discussed in Chapters 3 and 5, the first step in resolving a client's legal problem begins in your client interview. Your client comes to you with a question, such as whether a contract is enforceable. Through careful listening and note taking during the client interview, you collect the important facts and identify potential claims or defenses that will help answer your client's question. Let us say that Ana Hart, a client, met with you to discuss a legal problem. The following are your notes from your interview with Ana.

Example of notes from client Ana Hart's interview:

Last month Ana Hart divorced her husband, David Hart. During the divorce proceeding, David petitioned the court to award him ownership of the couple's health and exercise club business. After a hearing on David's petition, the court ordered that (1) David buy Ana's interest in the business by paying Ana an amount equal to one-half the fair market value in the business, and (2) in exchange for this sum, Ana sell to David her interest in the business and sign a covenant not to compete (CNC). In the CNC, Ana must promise "not to engage either directly or indirectly, on her own or in the employ of another, in the health and exercise club business in any form for a period of five years in the counties of Hamilton, Hancock, Boone, Marion, Johnson, and Hendricks, plus the towns of Arcadia and Bloomtown, East Carolina." (See Figure 7-1 for a map of the fictitious state of East Carolina.) Ana does not want to sign the CNC or abide by the terms of the CNC.

Ana and David live in Flora, East Carolina. Flora is located in Marion County. They met while both were competing in weightlifting competitions. Shortly after their marriage, they started a health and exercise club in Flora under the name of their business partnership, "Hart Fitness Center." Both of them are active partners in the business.

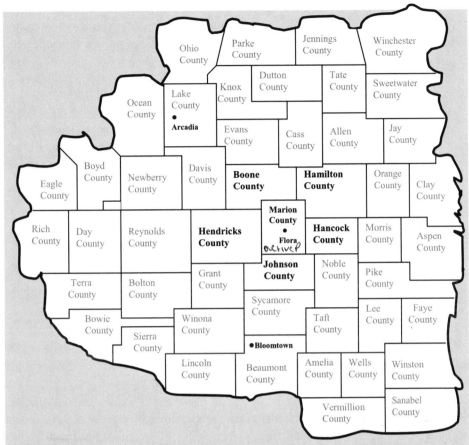

Figure 7-1
East Carolina (a fictitious state)

The business thrived, and the Harts later purchased two other health and exercise clubs, one in Hamilton County and one in Johnson County. The sellers of these clubs did not have any connection with members of Hart Fitness Center prior to the sale. The purchase agreements for these clubs included CNCs that restricted the sellers, for a period of five years, from engaging in the health and exercise club business in the counties where these clubs were located.

Hart Fitness Center does not have any clubs in Boone, Hancock, or Hendricks counties. The business also does not have any clubs in the towns of Arcadia or Bloomtown. The Harts had planned to expand into these areas within the next three years. The counties border Flora. Bloomtown is located approximately 45 miles south of Flora, and Arcadia is located approximately 50 miles northwest of Flora.

At the time of the divorce, the membership in Hart Fitness Center totaled 5,200 clients. A recent survey of club members showed that, although members may use any of the Hart Fitness Center clubs, they usually use the clubs closest to their homes or workplaces.

Ana is concerned about her livelihood if she signs the CNC. Ana is not well known outside the areas where the clubs are located. Except for her athletic career as a weightlifter, Ana's only work experience has been managing the Hart Fitness Center clubs and serving as a personal trainer for some of its members. Ana has dedicated clients who are currently members of Hart Fitness Center and who, because of job and personal restrictions, are unable to travel beyond the CNC restrictions to use her services. Therefore, Ana believes that abiding by the CNC would be an undue burden on her, personally and professionally.

B. Step Two: Analyzing the Facts

When preparing to research the potential issues, you may want to create a list of key words and phrases using the TARP method mentioned in Chapter 5. Using the TARP method, what key words and phrases could be used for Ana's case?

C. Step Three: Collect the Law

Once you have analyzed the facts and identified the potential claims and defenses, you are ready to prepare to research and collect the law relevant to the case. To sharpen the focus of the research, you also may consider combining the potential claims and defenses and your client's facts to draft a preliminary issue statement as discussed in Chapter 5.

After meeting with Ana, you review the facts. In your experience involving divorces, you have never encountered a situation where the court has ordered a spouse to sign a CNC as part of a property settlement. Also, based on the facts in Ana's case, you think the CNC provides more protection for David's business than is necessary. Therefore, you believe the two potential issues are (1) whether the court abused its judicial discretion when it ordered Ana to sign the CNC, and (2) whether the terms of the CNC are unreasonable and thus unenforceable. For purposes of this chapter, we will focus also on the second issue addressing the reasonableness of the CNC.

Example of a preliminary issue statement regarding Ana's CNC:

Under East Carolina law, is a CNC signed in connection with the sale of a health and exercise club unreasonable and thus unenforceable when (1) the CNC prohibits the seller from engaging in the same business in locations where the purchased business is not currently located, and (2) the CNCs required when the club purchased other clubs in the past were limited to the counties in which those businesses were located at the time of the sale?

D. Step Four: Analyze the Law

After you have researched and collected the law related to Ana's case, next brief the relevant cases as discussed in Chapter 4. Let us say that you have researched East Carolina law on CNCs ancillary to or in connection with the sale of a business and found one case in your jurisdiction, *Mats Transport v. ABC Corporation*, dealing specifically with the reasonableness of a CNC. You will want to brief this case on the issue of the reasonableness of the CNC to fully understand the court's decision.

Example of a case brief for **Mats Transport v. ABC Corporation** *relating to the reasonableness of the CNC (The full case appears in Appendix D.)*

Mats Transport v. ABC Corp., 824 S.E.2d 1467 (E.C. App. 1992)

F: The seller sold its trucking business and signed a CNC that restricted the seller from competing, directly or indirectly, for five years with the buyer in the trucking business in the United States. At the time of the purchase, the seller had only one terminal, located in East Carolina, and had hauled freight primarily for a few major clients on routes in East Carolina and adjoining states. The seller had hauled freight elsewhere across the United States on an infrequent basis.

After the sale, the seller leased several trucks to a truck driver who had been seller's employee before the sale of its business to the buyer. The driver began operating a trucking business using the trucks leased from the seller in the territory covered by the CNC.

C/A: The buyer filed a complaint, contending that the seller's leasing of the trucks to the driver violated the CNC signed by the seller.

The seller moved for summary judgment.

PH: The trial court granted the seller's motion for summary judgment. The buyer appealed.

SI: Is a CNC signed as a part of a sale of a trucking business unreasonable when (1) the CNC provides that the seller will not compete, directly or indirectly, with the seller in the business anywhere in the United States, and (2) at the time the seller signed the CNC, the seller's business was limited to several customers in the state or adjoining states, and the seller had only sporadically done business elsewhere in the United States?

PI: Did the trial court correctly grant the seller's motion for summary judgment?

H: SI: Yes.

H: PI: Yes.

J: Affirmed.

Relevant Rules:

1. CNCs are strictly construed against the party seeking enforcement.
2. A CNC will be enforced if it is reasonable.
3. East Carolina courts use a three-pronged test[1] when determining whether a CNC signed in connection with the sale of a business is unreasonable: "(1) the covenant must not be broader than necessary for the protection of the covenantee's[2] legitimate business interest; (2) the covenant cannot have an adverse effect on the covenantor[3]; and (3) the covenant cannot adversely affect the public interest." Quoting *Mats Transport*, 824 S.E.2d at 1468.
4. A CNC is unreasonable "as matter of law" if it fails any of the prongs of the test.
5. When determining whether a CNC is broader than necessary to protect the buyer, the court will consider "the extent of the territory restricted." *Mats Transport*, 824 S.E.2d at 1468.
6. The CNC represents the seller's goodwill, which represents the value of the relationship between the seller and its customers.

Court's Reasoning:

CNCs are strictly construed against the party seeking to enforce them because CNCs restrict trade and undermine the free market system on which the U.S. economy is founded.

Because the CNC failed the first prong of the test — that the covenant was broader than necessary to protect the buyer — the court did not address the other test prongs.

When the seller sold its trucking business to the buyer, the parties knew that the seller's trucking business operated in a limited geographic area, yet the CNC restrained the seller as though its business was a national enterprise with a market, offices, and a fleet of trucks that operated in all states. Because the territorial scope of the CNC exceeded the protection of the buyer's legitimate interests, the CNC was unreasonable as a matter of law.[4]

AMOL

---

1. The terms *legal principle*, *rule*, and *test* are synonymous and used interchangeably in this text.
2. The covenantee is the party for whose benefit the CNC is made.
3. The covenantor is the party who agrees not to compete.
4. Always be aware of the procedural state of the case at the time the court issued its holding. See also Chapter 4, discussing procedural posture in the context of writing a case brief. In this instance, the matter was before the court on a motion for summary judgment by the defendant. Under the East Carolina Rules of Civil Procedure (taken from the Federal Rules of Civil Procedure), summary judgment is proper "if the pleadings, depositions, answers to interrogatories, and admissions on file, together with the affidavits, if any, show that there is no genuine issue of material fact and that the moving party is entitled to a judgment as a matter of law." E.C. R. Civ. Proc. 56(c). In *Mats Transport*, the court found that the CNC was unreasonable as a matter of law; therefore, judgment was entered in favor of the seller.

As you analyze the law found during the research process, you are likely to identify statutes and rules favorably applied by courts in decisions that relate to your client's legal question. You should organize the relevant law and use it to further refine the issue statement for your client.

For instance, in your research of CNCs, you did not find any relevant statutes. The rules applied by the court in *Mats Transport*, however, may lead you to revise your issue statement. After researching, you realize that the territory restricted by the CNC relates to the first prong of the test for reasonableness — whether the CNC is broader than necessary to protect the buyer's interest. Also, the court in *Mats Transport* looked at the size of the business at the time of the sale to determine whether the scope of the restraint in the CNC exceeded the buyer's legitimate business interests. Perhaps other facts that relate to the size of Hart Fitness Center's business may be relevant. Also, the fact that the buyer and seller were partners may be an important factor in determining whether the CNC was broader than necessary for David's protection. Therefore, you may revise the issue statement to more closely reflect what the court in *Mats Transport* focused on when addressing the issue.

Example of a revised issue statement:

> Under East Carolina law, is a CNC, signed by a business partner in connection with the sale of a health and exercise club to a co-partner, broader than necessary to protect the interests of the buyer and thus unreasonable when (1) the CNC prohibits the seller from engaging in the same business in locations where the business being sold is not currently located but where the club had planned to expand in the next three years; (2) club members usually use the clubs closest to their homes or workplaces; and (3) the CNCs required when the club purchased other clubs in the past were limited to the counties in which those businesses were located at the time of the sale?[5]

E. Step Five: Organize the Law

Once you understand the law that is relevant to your client's case, you are in a position to organize the law. Because this chapter addresses a single issue with a single case, there is no need to further organize the law. (How to organize the law

---

5. If an issue statement contains several facts, numbering the different facts can make the statement clearer and easier to read.

is discussed in more detail in Chapters 11 and 12, which address structuring a discussion of and analyzing multiple issues using multiple cases.)

F. Step Six: Apply the Law to Your Client's Facts

Through the application of the law to your client's facts, you are able to determine whether there are legal issues in dispute. As you research and organize the law, identify the disputable issues in your client's case. An issue is considered in dispute if the law and facts support a legitimate argument for each party. In Ana's case, a dispute exists regarding whether the CNC is broader than necessary for the protection of David's legitimate interest.

An objective analysis requires you to consider and present to the reader arguments for both sides of a disputable issue. Use the objective analysis as an opportunity to assess the strengths and weaknesses of your client's case by thoroughly exploring what you will argue on behalf of your client and what the opposing lawyer likely will argue on behalf of his or her client. Through this process you will be able to decide what to recommend to the client, and if litigation is necessary, you eventually will be able to present a complete and accurate argument on behalf of your client.

You have three sources at your disposal to support your client's position: (1) the relevant law, (2) your client's facts, and (3) the underlying policy reasons for the law. You will use facts in relevant court decisions to show how those facts may be similar to[6] or different from[7] your client's facts. If the holding in a court decision reflects what you want the court to find in your client's situation, then you will compare the facts in the court decision favorably to the facts in your client's case.

For instance, the court in *Mats Transport* found that the CNC was overbroad in the protection of the buyer's interest. Thus, you would note any legally significant facts in *Mats Transport* that are similar to the legally significant facts of Ana's case and any reasonable inferences[8] drawn from these analogies to support her position that the CNC she is being ordered to sign is overbroad in its protection of David's legitimate interest. Conversely, David's lawyer would note any legally significant facts in *Mats Transport* that are different from the legally significant facts of Ana's case and any reasonable inferences drawn from these distinctions to support David's position that the CNC is not overbroad. Ultimately, the court will make its decision based in part on

---

6. *Compare, analogy, similarity,* and the various forms of these nouns are synonymous when discussing how facts of a client's case are similar to case facts.

7. *Contrast, distinction, differences,* and the various forms of these nouns are synonymous when discussing how facts of a client's case are different from the case facts.

8. Reasonable inferences are conclusions drawn from the facts of your client's case and from case analogies and distinctions between the facts in your client's case and the facts in a case decision. Reasonable inferences are discussed in section G4d of this chapter.

whether the outcome in Ana's case should be similar to or different from the outcome in the cited case.

You should rely too on other legally significant facts of your client's case that are not directly parallel to case law facts but nevertheless may be used as a basis for reasonable inferences that support your client's position. For example, from the fact that sellers in prior sales of clubs to Hart Fitness Center executed CNCs that restricted competition only in the area where the purchased clubs were already located, you could infer that a reasonable CNC restricts the territory only where the clubs were located at the time the CNC was signed. Although there is no similar fact in *Mats Transport*, you would want to include this fact to support the argument that the CNC that Ana has been ordered to sign is overbroad.

Finally, you may use public policy reasons to further support the argument. (The use of policy in an analysis is discussed in Chapter 8.)

Because U.S. lawyers are interested primarily in advocating their client's position, they sometimes find it difficult to consider the opposing side's position. If you find that you are experiencing the same difficulty, try analyzing the opposing side's position first before considering your client's position. One way to do this is to temporarily adopt the role of the opposing lawyer. In the role of the opposing lawyer, you review the law and facts that may be useful in supporting this lawyer's position. You note any analogies or distinctions between the legally significant facts of a court's prior decision and your client's case. You also note other facts from your client's case that support this lawyer's position. Finally, you draw reasonable inferences, as appropriate, from these facts and factual comparisons. For example, because you represent Ana, you might first think about David's position:

The CNC that Ana has been ordered to sign is not overbroad in its protection of David's interest.

- Unlike the seller in *Mats Transport*, who never expressed to the buyer any intention of expanding the business, David and Ana had agreed to expand the business within the next three years into three counties and two towns where Hart Fitness Center is not presently operating clubs.
- Unlike the CNC in *Mats Transport* that restricted competition in every U.S. state, even though the business operated in only one state and had established trucking routes only in neighboring states, the CNC Ana has been ordered to sign covers a limited geographic area in East Carolina.
- Unlike the previous sellers of clubs who did not have any connection with Hart Fitness Center's members prior to the sale of the clubs, Ana has developed a relationship with Hart Fitness Center's members. Thus, Ana presents a greater threat to David's interest in the business, which relies heavily on the continuing good relationship between the members and the clubs.
- Members usually use the club closest to their homes or workplaces, so if Ana opens a club in the same county or town as Hart Fitness Center, members of the club may join Ana's club if it is closer to their homes or workplaces.

Next, consider your client's position using the same process. For example, consider the following support for Ana's position that the CNC is overbroad for the protection of David's legitimate interest:

> The CNC that Ana has been ordered to sign is overbroad in its protection of David's interest.
>
> - Similar to *Mats Transport*, where the CNC was overbroad for the protection of the buyer's interest when it restricted competition in territory beyond where the seller operated its business, the CNC that Ana has been ordered to sign is overbroad because it restricts Ana from competing in counties and towns where Hart Fitness Center does not operate clubs.
> - CNCs signed by previous sellers of clubs to Hart Fitness Center restricted the sellers from competing in the counties only where the sold clubs were located; thus CNCs limiting the restricted territory to the counties where the clubs are located are sufficient to protect the buyer's interest.
> - Members usually use the club closest to their homes or workplaces, which infers that members will not travel a great distance to go to another club, so it is unnecessary to have a broad territorial restriction.

Note that the facts supporting Ana's position include some of the same facts that appeared when assessing David's position. Sometimes the same facts can be used to support the position for both sides of an issue. In these instances, different inferences can be drawn from the facts, as long as those inferences are reasonable.

While assessing each position, you must be careful not to engage in speculation or otherwise consider situations that are not supported by the facts. Sometimes in an effort to find additional support for your client's case, you might feel tempted to create circumstances that, if they existed, would help your client. You cannot "create" facts through speculation or imagination. The information must be supported by the facts. For example, to state that members of Hart Fitness Center would never travel to neighboring counties to use the clubs is speculative, especially if people lived or worked near the county boundaries and were closer to a club in the neighboring county than to the club located in their county of residence or work. There is nothing in the facts given by Ana that supports this statement.

Now that you have identified the disputable issues and relevant facts that support the parties' respective positions, you are ready to draft a written analysis of the legal issue.

● Exercise 7-A

Review your summary of the interview of Edina Broward from Chapter 3, the *Everett v. Rogers* case in Appendix C, and your brief of *Everett*. Complete the following.

1. Draft an issue statement.
2. List the relevant law and facts that may support Ms. Broward's position that she is not barred by the statute of limitations from bringing an action against Dr. Warren for the return of the painting.
3. List the relevant law and facts that may support Dr. Warren's position that Ms. Broward is barred by the statute of limitations from bringing an action against him for the return of the painting.

When preparing the lists in 2 and 3 above, note any analogies or distinctions between the facts of *Everett* and the facts of Ms. Broward's case. Also note any reasonable inferences that can be drawn from the facts to support each party's position.

G. Structuring an Objective Legal Analysis Based on a Single Issue and a Single Case

When drafting a legal analysis, remember its usual purpose. An objective legal analysis is used to inform the reader of the law on a particular issue and to predict the issue's probable outcome. A strong analysis carefully weighs the parties' respective positions and the support available for each party, such as what a court might rule if it had to decide the legal issue.[9] The reader uses the information provided in an objective legal analysis to make a decision as to what future action to take in the case. The audience for an objective legal analysis, for example, is often another lawyer in your law firm or your client. The choice of words and the information provided to the reader will depend on his or her knowledge of the facts and the law.

In the predrafting process, lawyers often use inductive reasoning by collecting specific information from a variety of sources, including the client's facts and the relevant law, and then use that information to predict a likely conclusion in the client's case. Thus, as Ana's lawyer, you might review the facts of her situation, research the relevant law on enforcing a CNC, and then, based on the facts and the research findings, formulate the probable answer.

While inductive reasoning is effective when identifying the issues and the parties' respective positions, it is not an organized way to present the analysis to a reader. Instead, lawyers often employ deductive reasoning when structuring their written legal analysis. Lawyers often begin with the conclusion and then seek to prove it by presenting the relevant law and applying it to the legally significant facts of the case. For example, you might begin the discussion with a conclusion as to whether the CNC's territorial restriction is overly broad. Next, you would support the conclusion by

---

9. A legal analysis is often written within the procedural context of the case. If the purpose of an analysis is to determine whether the court will likely grant summary judgment because the CNC that Ana has been ordered to sign is unreasonable, you probably will want to focus the analysis on whether there is a genuine issue of material fact that the CNC is unreasonable, thus entitling Ana to a judgment in her favor as a matter of law.

explaining relevant law on this issue and then applying the law to the legally significant facts, as discussed in the remainder of this chapter.

Your goal as a legal writer is to provide a complete, accurate, and concise analysis of the law that is understandable to the reader. You have failed to do this if the analysis is inaccurate or confusing. You also have failed if the analysis is presented in a way that compels the reader to seek outside resources to clarify what is written or to fill in gaps or omissions in the analysis. To avoid these problems, legal writers often use a structural checklist to help organize their analyses. We recommend using "TRAC" as a checklist to help ensure the analysis is structured in a logical manner.[10]

1. TRAC as a structural checklist

A good legal analysis always includes the following components.

T = Topic or thesis sentence introducing the issue
R = Rule(s) and rule explanation(s)
A = Analysis/application of the law to the facts, including support for each position, where it exists
C = Conclusion

2. T = Topic or thesis sentence introducing the issue

The topic or thesis sentence notifies the reader of the issue that is being analyzed. For instance, read the following paragraph.

Your shoulders must be well back but relaxed. Your back must be straight but flexible. Your hips must remain supple. Your upper arms must rest next to your body and your elbows must be slightly bent. Your legs must be relaxed with your knees and toes pointed forward, and your weight must rest in your heels.

The reader would probably not understand what is being discussed. You need to start with a sentence that tells the reader what you are discussing before you begin discussing it. By starting with a topic or thesis sentence, you put what follows into the proper

---

10. Although it is not necessary to always organize your analysis in the exact order as TRAC presents, you are encouraged to follow this order closely until you feel comfortable with structuring a legal analysis. Using TRAC allows you to keep track of the information you are including in your analysis.

TRAC is not the only recommended checklist to use in an objective analysis. Others, for example, include IRAC (Issue/Rule/Analysis/Conclusion), CRAC (Conclusion/Rule/Analysis/Conclusion), and CREAC (Conclusion/Rule/Explanation/Analysis/Conclusion).

context. Using the previous example, you could tell the reader what you are discussing by starting with the following sentence: "The position of your body is a critical factor in becoming an effective horseback rider."

You can introduce the issue in a legal analysis by using a topic sentence, which sets up the issue in a neutral statement, or by using a thesis sentence, which sets up the issue and also provides your conclusion. For example, the analytical discussion of whether the CNC in Ana's case is broader than necessary to protect David's business interest may begin with the following.

◆ *Topic sentence:*

neutral.

> The purpose of this discussion is to determine whether the covenant not to compete (CNC) Ana has been ordered to sign is broader than necessary and thus unreasonable for the protection of David's interest in Hart Fitness Center.

Or, the discussion can introduce the issue by using the following.

◆ *Thesis sentence:*

> The covenant not to compete (CNC) that Ana Hart has been ordered by the court to sign is probably overbroad in its protection of David's business interests and therefore unreasonable.

The advantage to stating the conclusion as a thesis sentence is that the reader knows your ultimate conclusion at the beginning of the discussion and knows how you will end the analysis. Whether you elect to introduce the issue through a topic or thesis sentence may depend in part on such considerations as the likelihood of the reader's accepting the conclusion or the complexity of the issue. If you believe the reader may have difficulty accepting the conclusion, for example, you may consider stating the issue in a neutral manner through the use of a topic sentence and building toward the conclusion through a discussion of the analysis.

● **Exercise 7-B**

Draft one topic sentence and one thesis sentence for the issue that will be discussed in Ms. Broward's case.

3. *Identifying relevant rules, definitions, and rule explanations*

The reader wants to be informed of rules, definitions, and rule explanations as they become relevant in the analytical discussion. Tell the reader what you are talking about (the issue) and then provide the legal basis for each issue as it is raised (the rule). This drafting approach could be compared to building a house. You would never think to build the framework of a house without first laying the foundation on which the framework will rest. The foundation provides a base that lends stability and strength to the framework. In a legal analysis, the relevant rules, definitions, or rule explanations provide a foundation of understanding for the reader on which the analysis will rest.

a. Quoting rules and definitions

When stating relevant rules or definitions, always quote the key words and phrases. By summarizing or paraphrasing a rule or definition, you risk changing the meaning.[11] If you must summarize or paraphrase a rule or definition, make sure that the meaning is not changed. An inaccurately stated rule or definition creates a faulty foundation and leads to a flawed analysis.

Inaccurately stated three-pronged test from **Mats Transport:**

> When determining whether a CNC signed in connection with the sale of a business is reasonable, East Carolina courts look to whether the covenant is broader than necessary to protect the legitimate business interests of the covenantee, and whether the covenant has an adverse effect on the covenantor and the public interest. *Mats Transp. v. ABC Corp.*, 824 S.E.2d 1467, 1468 (E.C. App. 1992).

The above statement inaccurately reports the three-pronged test as stated in *Mats Transport*. First, the rule as written does not state clearly that the court must make three separate and distinct determinations. Second, the statement seems to imply that these criteria are mere factors or considerations the court must weigh when making its determination. For example, under the rule as inaccurately reported above, if a CNC is broader than necessary to protect the covenantee's legitimate business interest, the court seemingly is not necessarily required to find the CNC unreasonable. A review of the three-pronged rule as stated in *Mats Transport* reveals that this is false. An analysis based on the inaccurate statement of the rule would result in an erroneous analysis.

Accurately stated three-pronged test rule from **Mats Transport:**

> In East Carolina, for a CNC related to the sale of a business to be reasonable, "(1) the covenant must not be broader than necessary for the protection of the covenantee's legitimate business interest; (2) the covenant cannot have an adverse effect on the covenantor; and (3) the covenant cannot adversely affect the public interest." *Mats Transp. v. ABC Corp.*, 824 S.E.2d 1467, 1468 (E.C. App. 1992).

---

11. See also Chapter 6 for a discussion on summarizing and paraphrasing.

The above statement accurately reports the three-pronged test. It emphasizes to the reader that the court must make three separate and distinct determinations. The rule also provides that if the court finds that if any of the terms of the CNC does not meet any one of these criteria, then the CNC is unreasonable.

b. Components of a rule explanation

Providing an accurate rule explanation is also critical to a legal analysis. A rule explanation, as used in this book, is a concise description of a court's decision addressing the legal point at issue. The words of a rule may be subject to different interpretations. What is important is how the binding courts have interpreted and applied the rule in earlier cases. The purpose of the rule explanation is to help the reader better understand the rule by showing how a prior court applied the rule in an issue identical to, or similar to, the issue being analyzed. Use a rule explanation to illustrate how a court has applied the rule or definition in other factual situations.

A rule explanation contains at least the following components:

(1) the *facts* of the case relevant to the issue being analyzed;
(2) the *court's holding* on the issue being analyzed; and
(3) the *court's reasoning* for its holding on the issue being analyzed.[12]

In addition to the legally significant facts, court's holding, and court's reasoning, consider including background facts that make the case understandable the first time you give an explanation of the case in the discussion.[13] Background facts, such as the cause of action, show the reader that the same legal issues were being addressed in the court decision as in your client's case. For instance, the first time *Mats Transport* is discussed in a rule explanation, it might be helpful to the reader's understanding of the case to know that (1) the CNC had been executed in connection with the sale of the seller's trucking business to the buyer, and (2) the buyer alleged the seller violated the CNC when the seller leased several trucks to one of the seller's prior employees who used the trucks to operate a trucking business in the area covered by the CNC.

You do not need to set out the components of a rule explanation (facts, court's holding, and court's reasoning) in a particular order. You merely need to ensure that the information is presented in a logical sequence and that all of the parts are present. Include all facts relevant to the court's holding in the issue. Those legally significant facts that may not be comparable to any facts in your client's case should still be included because these facts might be used to support an argument that the case is significantly different from your client's case.

---

12. Sometimes, though, a court does not adequately explain the reasons for its holding. In this instance, the case may not be an ideal one to use. But if the facts of the case are sufficiently similar to the facts of your client's case and you have not found another comparable case that includes an adequate explanation of the court's reasoning, you might consider using the former case so long as the court made a specific ruling on the legal point you are discussing.

13. In later chapters, you will learn that cases can be used for the analysis of more than one issue.

Example of relevant rules from, and a rule explanation of,
Mats Transport v. ABC Corporation

In East Carolina, courts use the following three-pronged test to determine whether a CNC related to the sale of a business is reasonable: "(1) the covenant must not be broader than necessary for the protection of the covenantee's legitimate business interest; (2) the covenant cannot have an adverse effect on the covenantor; and (3) the covenant cannot adversely effect the public interest." *Mats Transp. v. ABC Corp.*, 824 S.E.2d 1467, 1468 (E.C. App. 1992). A CNC is unreasonable "as a matter of law" if it fails any one of the prongs of the test. *Id.*

Rules

In *Mats Transport*, the court held that a CNC related to the sale of a business was unreasonable as a matter of law because it failed the first prong of the three-pronged test and was broader than necessary for the covenantee's legitimate business interest. *Id.* *Mats Transport* involved a dispute as to whether the seller violated the terms of a CNC executed in connection with the sale of its trucking business to the buyer because the seller later leased several trucks to a prior employee who used the trucks to operate a trucking business. The CNC prohibited the seller from competing in the trucking business with the buyer for a period of five years anywhere in the United States. The buyer sued the seller for allegedly violating the CNC. The seller moved for a summary judgment, arguing that the CNC was overbroad in its protection of the buyer's business interest. The trial court granted the seller's motion, and the court on appeal affirmed. *Id.*

Court's holding in the case.

Facts of the case (including key facts and background facts)

tense.

The court noted that when determining whether a CNC is broader than necessary to protect the buyer, the territory restricted is considered. *Id.* The CNC includes the seller's goodwill, which represents the value of the relationship between the seller and its customers. *Id.* (quoting *Matthews v. Acme Tax Consultants*, 470 S.E.2d 756, 763 (E.C. App. 1984)).

The court found that when the seller sold the trucking business to the buyer, the business hauled freight primarily for a few major clients on routes only in East Carolina and adjoining states. *Id.* The parties knew that the seller's trucking business had only one terminal located in East Carolina, yet the CNC restrained the seller as though its business was a national enterprise. Because the territorial scope of the CNC exceeded the protection of the buyer's legitimate interests, the CNC was unreasonable as a matter of law. *Id.* The court did not discuss the other prongs of the test because the CNC failed the first prong of the test. *Id.*

Court's reasoning in the case

c. Use descriptive generic names to identify parties in a reported decision

Note that the parties in the rule explanation of *Mats Transport* are referred to by generic names rather than by their personal names. In the rule explanations and the analysis, do not confuse your reader by using the personal names of the parties in court decisions. Instead, give the parties generic names that identify their respective relationships relevant to the dispute at issue. Use these generic names consistently throughout the rule explanation and analysis whenever referring to that party. Avoid, however, using generic terms such as *plaintiff, defendant, appellant, appellee, petitioner,* or *respondent* because these terms do not adequately identify the parties.

Conversely, you should use personal names only when referring to the parties in your client's case. Referring to the parties in court decisions by generic names and the parties in your client's case by personal names emphasizes the distinction between them. For instance, in the analysis of Ana's case, Ana and David are referenced by their first names, though, alternatively, they could have been referenced by their surnames, Mrs. Hart and Mr. Hart. And the Harts' business is referenced as Hart Fitness Center. But the defendant in *Mats Transport*, ABC Corporation, is referenced as the *seller*, and the plaintiff in that case, Mats Transport, is referenced as the *buyer*.

d. Bring in information as it becomes relevant to the discussion

Also note in the above example that some rules were provided prior to the rule explanation of *Mats Transport*, while other rules were provided in the middle of the rule explanation (the third paragraph of the example). The rules provided in the rule explanation could have been given with the other rules mentioned in the first paragraph, but it was more logical to bring them up later in the explanation of the case. These rules did not become important until that moment and were more understandable to the reader within the context of the rule explanation. Therefore, you do not need to bring up rules until they become relevant in the analysis. Let logic guide you in making this determination.

● Exercise 7-C

1. Write down the relevant rules to the discussion of the issue in Ms. Broward's case. If you are quoting the rules, place the quoted text in quotation marks and note the page in *Everett* where you found the quotation. When summarizing or paraphrasing a rule, make sure that you are not actually quoting the text, confirm that your words accurately reflect the rule, and note the page in *Everett* where you found the rule.
2. Draft a rule explanation of *Everett*.

4. Providing an objective analysis for a disputable fact-based issue

As previously noted, the objective analysis of a disputable fact-based issue must include a *complete* analysis of both parties' positions. One of the common, recurring problems of beginning legal writers is that they give a thorough analysis of the predicted stronger position but do not give sufficient thought or discussion to the predicted weaker position. The hallmark of a good lawyer is the ability to carefully analyze all sides of an issue. A good lawyer knows the opposing party's position as well as the attorney representing that party.

A good legal analysis begins with the analysis of the stronger position, which may not be your client's position. Only after providing a complete analysis of the stronger position should you provide the analysis of the weaker position.

The analysis for *each side* of a fact-based issue that uses only a single case includes

(a) a *topic or thesis sentence* identifying the position being analyzed;

(b) *analogies or distinctions* between the stated facts in the case law and related facts in your client's case, along with any *reasonable inferences* drawn from these comparisons; and

(c) *additional facts* of your client's case, *if any*, that support the position being analyzed, along with the *reasonable inferences* drawn from these facts.

a. Topic or thesis sentence

The topic or thesis sentences at the beginning of the stronger position analysis and at the beginning of the weaker position analysis signal to the reader which party's position is being analyzing. If you are moving from the stronger position analysis to the weaker position analysis, make it clear to the reader that you are beginning a new analysis. An effective way to help the reader understand the change in focus is to provide a transitional word or phrase, such as the following.

alternatively
but
conversely
however
in contrast
nevertheless
notwithstanding
on the contrary
yet

b. Factual comparisons

In an analysis of a fact-based issue, the reader wants to know how the facts of your client's case relate to the facts in the cited case. If a court reached a result that is similar to the desired result of the position being analyzed, then compare directly the relevant case law facts to the related facts in your client's case. Conversely, if a court reached a result that is contrary to the desired result of the position being analyzed, then contrast directly the relevant case law facts to the related facts in your client's case.

In the analysis of Ana's position, for example, you want to show how the facts of *Mats Transport*, where the court found the CNC overbroad and thus unreasonable, are analogous to the facts in Ana's case. She wants the court to find that the CNC she has been ordered to sign is also overbroad and thus unreasonable. Conversely, David wants to distinguish the facts of *Mats Transport* because he wants the court to find that the CNC is reasonable.

The specific facts from the case law must be stated explicitly in the comparison found in the analysis section, even though they are also found in the rule explanation. This is imperative to providing the reader all the information necessary to understand the analysis. If the specific case facts are omitted, then the reader may be unsure about which case facts you are using to compare to the facts of your client's case. Even worse, the reader may stop reading and return to the rule explanation of the case in an attempt to determine which case facts are relevant in making the comparison. In all of these circumstances, you are making the reader do your work. Consider the following examples.

◆ *Poor example of a factual comparison*

> Similar to *Mats Transport*, the CNC that Ana has been ordered to sign restricts Ana from doing business in counties and towns where Hart Fitness Center has no clubs.

A reader reading the above example needs to stop and recollect the facts of *Mats Transport* or return to the rule explanation of the case to ascertain the specific case facts that the writer is comparing to Ana's facts. *One of the goals of every legal writer is not to make the reader do the work that is the job of the writer.*

◆ *A better example of a factual comparison*

> Similar to *Mats Transport*, where the buyer's business did not operate in all the places restricted by the CNC, the CNC that Ana has been ordered to sign restricts Ana from doing business in counties and towns where Hart Fitness Center has no clubs.

This example clearly states the specific facts from the cited case that the writer is comparing to the facts of Ana's case.

Often there are important facts present in the court decision that are not present in the facts of your client's case. In this instance, you must consider whether the lack of these facts in your client's case will change the predicted outcome in your client's case. You must explain to the reader why these facts probably will or will not change the outcome in your client's case.

Finally, do not compare a holding in a court decision to what you hope will be a similar holding in your client's case. For instance, do not write this.

> Similar to the *Mats Transport* case, where the court found the CNC overbroad and unreasonable, the CNC the court has ordered Ana to sign is overbroad and unreasonable.

Making such a comparison is not a legal analysis of a fact issue. Rather, you must *show* the reader why the outcome in Ana's case will be similar to the *Mats Transport* case by explaining the similarities between the legally significant facts of Ana's case and the related facts in the *Mats Transport* case. Also, you have already told the reader the court's holding in the rule explanation, so you do not need to remind the reader of the court's holding in the analysis.

c. Additional facts of your client's case

Your client's case may have additional facts that support the position being analyzed but are not present in the case law facts. Include these facts in the analysis. For instance, in the previous sales of clubs to Hart Fitness Center, the sellers of clubs signed CNCs that restricted competition only to the county in which those clubs were located. In *Mats Transport*, there were no facts like this. Nevertheless, the fact that prior sellers of clubs signed CNCs restricting competition only to the counties in which the clubs were located supports Ana's position that the CNC in her case is overbroad because it restricts competition beyond the places where the current clubs are located. Therefore, you should include this fact in the analysis of Ana's position.

d. Reasonable inferences

Finally, a legal analysis must include reasonable inferences drawn from the facts of your client's case and from case analogies and distinctions. It is not sufficient to provide the reader with a mere laundry list of facts or factual comparisons. Anyone can make such a list and place it in a narrative text for the reader. What separates a lawyer from a person who merely makes lists is the ability to draw reasonable inferences from analogies and distinctions between case law facts and the client's facts and the ability to explain to the reader how these inferences support the position being analyzed. Making reasonable inferences is not a separate part of the analysis. Rather, these inferences are merged into, and become an integral part of, the discussion of the facts or factual comparisons. For instance, when analyzing David's position, it is insufficient to merely state that the CNC to be signed by Ana is reasonable because Hart Fitness Center's members usually use clubs that are closest to their homes or workplaces. At this point, you also need to explain to the reader that, if Ana opened a new club located closer to the homes or workplaces of club members than Hart Fitness Center's clubs, the members may discontinue their memberships with Hart Fitness Center, which, in turn, would lessen the value of David's interest in the business.

e. Internal organization of the analysis

It is more logical to present the analysis of the stronger position first before presenting the weaker position because the stronger position supports the conclusion. In this way, the reader more readily understands the reasons for the conclusion.

While drafting the analysis, you may go back and forth on which position is stronger. The stronger position is not determined by the number of points that can be made to support a position. Rather, you must focus on the *quality* of the support, not the quantity of support, for the position.

Once you have decided which position is stronger, state the analysis of this position before presenting the analysis of the weaker position. In the discussion of an issue, present the *complete discussion* of the analysis of the stronger position before presenting the analysis of the weaker position. Avoid a "back and forth" pattern in your writing, such as stating a point supporting the stronger position, then stating a counter point supporting the weaker position, then stating another point supporting the stronger position, then stating another point supporting the weaker position, and so on. Although you may go through this mental activity while formulating support for each party's position, this wavering back and forth between the stronger and weaker positions in the written analysis confuses the reader and makes it extremely difficult to understand the strength of the arguments for each party.

Example of a "wavering" analysis, which must be avoided:

Similar to *Mats Transport*, where the CNC was overbroad for the protection of the buyer's interest when it restricted competition to territory beyond the location of the business at the time of the sale, the CNC that Ana has been ordered to sign is probably overbroad because it restricts competition in three counties and two towns where Hart Fitness Center has no clubs.	Point supporting Ana's position.
But, unlike the seller in *Mats Transport*, who had no plans to expand beyond where the business was currently located, Hart Fitness Center had plans to start clubs in the restricted areas where no clubs were located.	Point supporting David's position.
This is not persuasive because the CNCs signed by sellers in prior sales of clubs to Hart Fitness Center restricted competition to the counties where the clubs were located.	Point supporting Ana's position.
Even so, David may argue that a larger territorial restriction is needed in Ana's case because she had a relationship with the club's members.	Point supporting David's position.
But Ana can rebut this argument by pointing out that the goodwill represented in the CNC should be limited only to the present club membership and not extend to future members. . . .	Point supporting Ana's position.

In the following example, the analysis of Ana's position is placed in the stronger position and is completely analyzed before the analysis of David's position (the weaker position) is discussed. The presentation of the information in this order is clearer and easier for the reader to understand.

Example of an analysis supporting Ana's position:

The CNC that the court has ordered Ana to sign is likely unreasonable because it is overbroad in its protection of David's interest. The CNC restricts competition in three counties and two towns where Hart Fitness Center has no clubs and so the business has not developed relationships with customers in these areas. This is similar to *Mats Transport*, where the CNC was overbroad because it unreasonably restricted competition in every state and the business operated in only one state with established trucking routes in the surrounding states.

In addition, the CNC is unreasonable because it extends beyond the one-county restriction of the CNCs signed by sellers in prior sales of clubs to Hart Fitness Center. These previous CNCs restricted competition to the county in which the purchased clubs were located. The owners of Hart Fitness Center considered this a reasonable restriction in those prior transactions. Therefore, in Ana's sale of her interest to David, a CNC restricting competition in locations where the clubs are not currently located exceeds what were considered reasonable terms in prior sales transactions.

Further support that the geographic restriction is too broad is that members usually use clubs that are closest to their homes or workplaces. Members probably will not travel great distances to go to another club; thus, it is not necessary to restrict competition over a geographic area that exceeds the present club locations.

Conversely, the CNC the court has ordered Ana to sign may be considered reasonable if more emphasis is placed on the planned expansion of the business, the nature of the business, and the importance of Ana's relationship with members of Hart Fitness Center. Unlike the seller in *Mats Transport*, who never expressed to the buyer any planned expansion into other routes, Ana and David had planned to expand the business in the next three years into the three counties and two towns covered by the CNC. The restriction also covers a limited geographic area in central East Carolina only, unlike the restricted area covered by the CNC in *Mats Transport* that extended to every state, despite the business being located in only one state and operating a limited number of routes in the surrounding states.

Further, although the CNC to be signed by Ana is broader than the one-county restriction contained in the CNCs signed by sellers in prior club purchases, the broader restriction in Ana's case is necessary to adequately protect David's interest in the business. Unlike the previous sellers, who did not have any relationship with members of Hart Fitness Center prior to the purchases, Ana presents a greater threat to the business of Hart Fitness Center because she has developed a relationship with club members. Health and exercise clubs are service-oriented businesses that rely heavily on the good relationship between members and the clubs for the continuing success of the business. Arguably, David

Analysis of Ana's position (shown here as the stronger position analysis)

Analysis of David's position (shown here as the weaker position analysis)

needs to protect his interest in the business, and the CNC would ensure that Ana did not compete with the business and steal away members, which would lessen the value of the business. If Ana has a club in the same county or town where the club members live or work, members may quit Hart Fitness Center, especially if her club is closer to their homes or workplaces, because members use clubs that are close to these places. Ana has developed a relationship with the members; therefore, members may be even more inclined to join Ana's club, rather than continue their memberships with Hart Fitness Center.

● Exercise 7-D

Using the facts of Ms. Broward's stolen painting from Exercise 3-A in Chapter 3 and the *Everett* case (see Appendix C), write an analysis supporting Ms. Broward's position.

● Exercise 7-E

Using the facts of Ms. Broward's stolen painting from the Exercise 3-A in Chapter 3 and the *Everett* case (see Appendix C), write an analysis supporting Dr. Warren's position.

5. Writing the conclusion

After giving a thorough analysis of the stronger position, followed by a thorough analysis of the weaker position, finish the discussion by giving the reader the reasons for your conclusion. The reasons may include a rebuttal of the weaker position and may otherwise explain the pivotal reason(s) why the opposing position is stronger. Any policy that might help support the conclusion may be introduced here, if not already used in the earlier analysis.[14] Otherwise, refrain from adding new information, either law or facts. If important to the outcome of the case, the law or facts should have been previously introduced and discussed in the analysis.

State in your conclusion the predicted outcome of the issue. In instances where the opposing position seems equally strong, you might feel uncomfortable stating a strong conclusion or acknowledging that the arguments are so strong that only the judge or the jury can decide. Leaving the reader with this type of conclusion undermines the predictive nature of an objective legal analysis. Instead, you may acknowledge to the

---

14. Chapter 8 discusses the use of public policy in a legal analysis.

reader that strong arguments support both sides of the issue, but, nevertheless, state the predicted conclusion. The conclusion makes its predictive nature evident by using such qualifying language as *probably* or *likely*. For instance, if you predict that a court would rule in Ana's favor, this conclusion may read, "The court will probably find that the CNC is overbroad for the protection of David's interest and thus is unreasonable."

> *Example of a conclusion paragraph for Ana's issue:*

Nevertheless, the geographic restriction in the CNC extends into   ←   Rebuttal
counties and towns where Hart Fitness Center does not currently
operate health and exercise clubs. This exceeds the value of the   ←   Conclusion
goodwill Ana has in the current membership, which is what the
CNC is meant to protect. Therefore, the CNC is probably overbroad for the protection of David's business interest and is
unreasonable.

● Exercise 7-F

Decide whether Ms. Broward or Dr. Warren has the stronger position. Draft a conclusion.

6. Putting it all together

The complete analytical discussion of whether the CNC Ana has been ordered to sign is overbroad and unreasonable as to David's interest follows. See if you can pick out the TRAC elements, the essential components of the rule explanation for *Mats Transport*, the analysis of the stronger position (Ana's), the analysis of the weaker position (David's), the reasons for the conclusion, and the conclusion statement. Note that the stronger position begins with a thesis sentence, whereas the weaker position begins with a neutral topic sentence. Also, within the analyses of the stronger and weaker positions, note any factual comparisons, additional facts that support Ana's or David's position, and any reasonable inferences.

The covenant not to compete (CNC) that Ana Hart has been   ← *Thesis sentence*
ordered by the court to sign is probably overbroad in its protection of David Hart's business interests and thus unreasonable. In East Carolina, courts use the following three-pronged
test to determine whether a CNC related to the sale of a busi-   ← *rules*
ness is reasonable: "(1) the covenant must not be broader than
necessary for the protection of the covenantee's legitimate
business interest; (2) the covenant cannot have an adverse
effect on the covenantor; and (3) the covenant cannot

adversely affect the public interest." *Mats Transp. v. ABC Corp.*, 824 S.E.2d 1467, 1468 (E.C. App. 1992). A CNC is unreasonable "as a matter of law" if it fails any one of the prongs of the test. *Id.*

In *Mats Transport*, the court held that a CNC related to the sale of a business was unreasonable as a matter of law because it failed the first prong of the three-pronged test and was broader than necessary for the covenantee's legitimate business interest. *Id. Mats Transport* involved a dispute as to whether the seller violated the terms of a CNC executed in connection with the sale of its trucking business to the buyer because the seller later leased several trucks to a prior employee who used the trucks to operate a trucking business. The CNC prohibited the seller from competing in the trucking business with the buyer for a period of five years anywhere in the United States. The buyer sued the seller for allegedly violating the CNC. The seller moved for a summary judgment, arguing that the CNC was overbroad in its protection of the buyer's business interest. The trial court granted the seller's motion, and the court on appeal affirmed. *Id.*

The court noted that when determining whether a CNC is broader than necessary to protect the buyer, the territory restricted is considered. *Id.* The CNC includes the seller's goodwill, which represents the value of the relationship between the seller and its customers. *Id.* (quoting *Matthews v. Acme Tax Consultants*, 470 S.E.2d 756, 763 (E.C. App. 1984)).

The court found that when the seller sold the trucking business to the buyer, the business hauled freight primarily for a few major clients on routes only in East Carolina and adjoining states. *Id.* The parties knew that the seller's trucking business had only one terminal located in East Carolina, yet the CNC restrained the seller as though its business was a national enterprise. Because the territorial scope of the CNC exceeded the protection of the buyer's legitimate interests, the CNC was unreasonable as a matter of law. *Id.* The court did not discuss the other prongs of the test because the CNC failed the first part of the test. *Id.*

The CNC that the court has ordered Ana to sign is likely unreasonable because it is overbroad in its protection of David's interest. The CNC restricts competition in three counties and two towns where Hart Fitness Center has no clubs, and so the business has not developed relationships with customers in these areas. This is similar to *Mats Transport*, where the CNC was overbroad because it unreasonably restricted competition in every state, and the business operated in only one state with established trucking routes in the surrounding states.

In addition, the CNC is unreasonable because it extends beyond the one-county restriction of the CNCs signed by sellers in prior sales of clubs to Hart Fitness Center. These previous CNCs restricted competition to the county in which the purchased clubs were located. The owners of Hart Fitness Center considered this a reasonable restriction in those prior transactions. Therefore, in Ana's sale of her interest to David, a CNC restricting competition in locations where the clubs are not currently located exceeds what were considered reasonable terms in prior sales transactions.

Further support that the geographic restriction is too broad is that members usually use clubs that are closest to their homes or workplaces. Members probably will not travel great distances to go to another club; thus, it is not necessary to restrict competition over a geographic area that exceeds the present club locations.

Conversely, the CNC the court has ordered Ana to sign may be considered reasonable if more emphasis is placed on the planned expansion of the business, the nature of the business, and the importance of Ana's relationship with the members of Hart Fitness Center. Unlike the seller in *Mats Transport*, who never expressed to the buyer any planned expansion into other routes, Ana and David had planned to expand the business in the next three years into the three counties and two towns covered by the CNC. The restriction also covers a limited geographic area in central East Carolina only, unlike the restricted area covered by the CNC in *Mats Transport* that extended to every state, despite the business being located in only one state and operating a limited number of routes in the surrounding states.

Further, although the CNC to be signed by Ana is broader than the one-county restriction contained in the CNCs signed by sellers in prior club purchases, the broader restriction in Ana's case is necessary to adequately protect David's interest in the business. Unlike the previous sellers, who did not have any relationship with members of Hart Fitness Center prior to the purchases, Ana presents a greater threat to the business of Hart Fitness Center because she has developed a relationship with club members. Health and exercise clubs are service-oriented businesses that rely heavily on the good relationship between members and the clubs for the continuing success of the business. Arguably, David needs to protect his interest in the business, and the CNC would ensure that Ana did not compete with the business and steal away members, which would lessen the value of the business. If Ana has a club in

← Analysis of David's position (shown here as the weaker position analysis)

the same county or town where the club members live or work, members may quit Hart Fitness Center, especially if her club is closer to their homes or workplaces, because members use clubs that are close to these places. Ana has developed a relationship with the members; therefore, members may be even more inclined to join Ana's club, rather than continue their memberships with Hart Fitness Center.

Nevertheless, the geographic restriction in the CNC extends into counties and towns where Hart Fitness Center does not currently operate health and exercise clubs. This exceeds the value of the goodwill Ana has in the current membership, ← *Conclusion* which is what the CNC is meant to protect. Therefore, the CNC is probably overbroad for the protection of David's business interest and is unreasonable.

Review

1. Explain the meaning of TARP and its use in the research stage of the writing process.
2. Explain the use of a TRAC checklist when drafting a legal analysis.
3. State the sources of law used to support a legal analysis and explain how they are used in a legal analysis.
4. Explain the difference between inductive reasoning and deductive reasoning and how both might be used in the writing process.
5. Explain the difference between a topic sentence and a thesis sentence.
6. Explain the components of a rule explanation.
7. Explain the information that should be included in the analysis of the stronger position and the analysis of the weaker position.
8. Explain what information should be included in a conclusion statement.

● Exercise 7-G

Using your work from Exercises 7-A to 7-F, draft the complete discussion of whether Ms. Broward will be barred from bringing an action against Dr. Warren for the return of the painting. Include the essential components of the rule explanation from *Everett*, the analysis of the stronger position, the analysis of the weaker position, and the conclusion statement. Within the analyses of the stronger and weaker positions, note the topic sentence, any factual comparisons, additional facts that support the respective position, and any reasonable inferences and deductions. After you have completed a draft, check your work against the checklist in Appendix E.

● Exercise 7-H

This exercise provides you with another opportunity to apply the concepts presented in this chapter by drafting a single fact-based issue discussion using a single case.

Follow the drafting steps explained in this chapter and structure your discussion according to the **TRAC** structural checklist. In the analysis section of your discussion, you must provide not only the support for what you consider the stronger position but also the support for the weaker position. After you have completed a draft, check your work against the checklist in Appendix E.

Whitewater Rafting Accident Involving Mary Ann Moore and Her Son, Jason Moore

Your firm represents Mary Ann Moore and her son, Jason Moore. Jason was severely and permanently injured while vacationing with his mother in Costa Rica in June of this year. Ms. Moore wants to bring a lawsuit against Jungle Rapids Expeditions (JRE), a Costa Rican company, because she claims the negligent acts of the company caused her son's injuries. For many different reasons, including the difficulty of transporting Jason, the costs of traveling to Costa Rica, and the significant time Ms. Moore would have to take off from work without compensation, Ms. Moore does not want to bring a legal action in Costa Rica. Most importantly, though, the amount of damages that might be awarded in a Costa Rican lawsuit will be significantly less than the sizeable amount of damages typically awarded in these types of cases in the United States. Therefore, the law firm wants to file the complaint in the Federal District Court in East Carolina.

A senior attorney in your firm is unsure whether a U.S. federal court can exercise personal jurisdiction over JRE, a foreign corporation. At the attorney's request, you researched the issue and discovered (1) a long-arm statute[15] in East Carolina that the court will use in determining whether it has personal jurisdiction over JRE, and (2) *Loch v. Blue Sail Cayman, Ltd.*, in which a court construed East Carolina's long-arm statute. (The *Loch* case is found in Appendix F, and the relevant section of the long-arm statute is quoted in the case.)

You have been asked to write a legal discussion as to whether the court has jurisdiction over JRE. For this assignment, address *only* whether the requirements of East Carolina's long-arm statute have been satisfied. Do not address the due process question discussed in the case. (The due process issue will be drafted as an exercise in a later chapter.)

The following summarizes the notes from the file. Some of the information is pertinent to drafting the complaint and litigating the claim, but other information is not necessarily relevant to that issue. You must determine which facts in the narrative are relevant to whether JRE has satisfied the requirements of East Carolina's long-arm statute.

---

15. Some states in the United States have so-called long-arm statutes, stating that courts may exercise personal jurisdiction over defendants who are outside the territorial boundaries of the courts' jurisdictions, provided the defendants have certain types of contact with the state, as provided in the statutes.

File Notes on the Moore Case:

In June of this year, Ms. Moore and her 14-year-old son Jason were staying at a hotel located a few hours from San José and just a few miles from the village of El Bajo del Tigre, in the rainforest region of Costa Rica. During their stay, Jason overheard other U.S. tourists talking about an exciting whitewater rafting trip run by JRE. Jason, who always enjoyed new adventures, persuaded his mother to take him whitewater rafting. A display in the hotel lobby offered brochures advertising various tours and services of Costa Rican businesses. In this display, Ms. Moore located a brochure advertising JRE's whitewater rafting trips. Ms. Moore called JRE's telephone number printed on the brochure and made reservations for a two-day tour through the rainforest on the Pacuare River, scheduled to begin the following day.

On June 6, JRE picked up Ms. Moore and Jason in a van and drove them to the rendezvous point at the Pacuare River, where the trip was to begin. They met their guide, Fernando (Ms. Moore couldn't remember his last name), as well as six other adults (two couples from Maryland and a newlywed couple from San José) who would be joining them on the trip.

June is the middle of the rainy season in Costa Rica, and it's typical for a tropical rain storm to occur every afternoon. The rain makes the waters of the Pacuare River rise and move more swiftly downstream. This results in more challenging rapids. On the first day of the trip, there was a short rain storm toward the end of the day. Ms. Moore was amazed at how quickly the waters rose and how the rapids became more unpredictable than those experienced earlier that day. The boat went through only two of these wild rapids before the group arrived at the campsite.

The next morning Ms. Moore, remembering the distressing experience toward the end of the previous run, asked Fernando whether the rapids on the second day of the trip would be as difficult. Fernando assured her that they would be able to easily navigate the rapids. The previous afternoon's shower, he explained, was unusual because of the amount of rain that fell in such a short period of time. The river, he said, was now back to normal levels for that time of year. His encouragement calmed Ms. Moore's anxiety. She climbed back into the boat with Jason and the rest of the group and prepared for another day of rafting.

The rapids in the morning were similar to the intermediate rapids they had experienced the previous day. They stopped and had lunch. Everyone was in good spirits and looking forward to the remainder of the tour. Shortly thereafter, another rain shower swept over them and lasted for 20 or 30 minutes. According to Ms. Moore, the heavy shower had turned the river into a wild, rushing current. No sooner had they climbed back into the boat than the rapids hurled the boat through a narrow channel between sheer rock walls. The boat soared over boulders and narrowly missed overturning several times. The boat bobbed and spun out of control. According to Ms. Moore, the group paddled hard and fast, paddled for their lives, while Fernando called out orders above the loud rush of water.

The boat rounded a sharp bend in the river, and Ms. Moore saw a huge swell of water several feet ahead of them. The current pulled them toward the swell that seemed to throw everything in its path against a large rock. Fernando yelled out more orders, but by this time, the boat had been sucked into the swell. The raft smashed into the rock. The swell pinned Ms. Moore between the boat and the cold, wet stone. The force of the current changed slightly. As instructed by Fernando on the first day, she let her body go limp, allowing her life vest to do its work and allowing the current to carry her through the remainder of the rapid. Minutes later, the two couples from the United States, who had managed to get to shore, pulled her from the river.

Ms. Moore looked for Jason. Downstream she saw Fernando, assisted by the Costa Rican newlyweds (one of whom was a doctor, María Carreira), pulling Jason from the river. Jason was not moving. Ms. Moore became frantic when she saw Dr. Carreira trying to revive Jason.

Fortunately, the boat had overturned not far from the ending point of the trip. Employees of JRE quickly located the group. By this time, Dr. Carreira had revived Jason, but it was clear to Ms. Moore, who could not reach her son on the other side of the river, that he was seriously injured.

Emergency medical help eventually arrived on the scene and took Jason and the others to a local hospital for treatment. Ms. Moore and the others were treated for minor cuts and bruises. Jason, however, had to be flown by helicopter to a hospital in San José. The doctors determined that Jason had fractured and crushed vertebrae in his neck. He spent several weeks in the hospital until his condition had improved sufficiently to return with his mother to the United States.

Once back home, Jason was seen by an orthopedic surgeon and a neurosurgeon. The surgeons agreed with the medical personnel in San José that treated him: Jason's injury was most likely caused by a sharp blow to the neck. A rock in the water could have caused the injury. More surgery was performed on his neck. Unfortunately, Jason's prognosis for recovery is poor.

Jason is a quadriplegic and most likely will remain in this condition the remainder of his life. He requires around-the-clock care. His physical therapy is intensive and will last indefinitely. Because he must use a wheelchair, the Moores will have to move from their two-story home and make renovations to their future home to allow for Jason's mobility and daily care. Transporting Jason is difficult and time-consuming. Ms. Moore has had to purchase a $40,000 van to transport Jason and his wheelchair to and from his physical therapy and the surgeons' offices. Although Ms. Moore has insurance through her employer, there are expenses associated with Jason's injury and care that are not covered by insurance. She cannot afford his long-term care on her public schoolteacher's salary. Jason will never be able to do things that a healthy child his age can do. He will never be able to pursue a career in the police force, which had always been his dream.

The two couples from the United States that had accompanied them on the tour have been contacted. Bradley and Jennifer Long, as well as Paul and Noreen Edmund, live in Baltimore, Maryland. The Longs and Edmunds are friends and vacationed together in Costa Rica. If a lawsuit is filed, all are willing to come to East Carolina to testify. They agree with Ms. Moore's recollections on that day. All admitted to being afraid prior to the accident and would have elected not to continue down the river if Fernando had not persuaded them. The Longs and Edmunds reserved their tour with JRE through their travel agent, who had given them a JRE brochure prior to their vacation in Costa Rica. They have never received promotional information directly from JRE.

The Carreiras, the other passengers on the boat from Costa Rica, live in San José. Dr. María Carreira is a physician in San José but is not associated with the hospital that treated Jason. Although the law firm has left messages for Dr. Carreira to call, the firm has not heard from her.

The firm also has contacted an expert on whitewater rafting, Danny Tong, who lives in East Carolina. Danny has actually rafted the Pacuare River. He said that the rapid on the afternoon of the accident, as described by Ms. Moore, sounded like a dangerous rapid. The boat's guest passengers, none of whom had any previous whitewater experience, should not have been on that rapid run. It is his opinion that Fernando should have stopped the tour, either the previous day when the water reached dangerous levels or after the rainstorm on the day of the accident.

Costa Rica's economy relies on tourism (along with agriculture and electronic exports). More specifically, the region of the country where Jason's accident occurred relies almost exclusively on tourism. Indeed, poverty in this area has been significantly reduced in the last ten years due to the growth of tourism. Although there are no exact figures, the Costa Rican Tourism Agency states that thousands of tourists go on whitewater rafting tours every year. The whitewater rafting business in Costa Rica is not regulated by the government. There are estimated to be about 8 to 10 whitewater rafting companies operating at any given time on the Pacuare River.

An investigation of JRE has turned up the following information:

1. JRE is a corporation formed three years ago under the laws of Costa Rica.
2. JRE does not have a telephone number, employees, mailing address, bank account, or office located in East Carolina or elsewhere in the United States.
3. JRE placed three advertisements over the last 6 months in *Exotic Destinations*, a general travel magazine, and five advertisements over the last 12 months in *Wild Waters*, a magazine written for readers who are serious whitewater rafters. Both magazines are distributed nationally in the United States and available in East Carolina.
4. JRE mails brochures advertising its services to travel agents in the United States, including agents in East Carolina. Of the 25 travel agents in East Carolina contacted by this firm, 15 had copies of the company's brochures.
5. Based on the information given from the 25 travel agents, approximately 100 East Carolinians in the past three years have made reservations with JRE to take whitewater rafting tours.
6. JRE has a Web site on which it provides general information about whitewater rafting; posts a photo gallery; provides information about tours and costs; offers to send through the mail a 12-page brochure that includes a reservation form if the requesting party completes an online form stating his or her name, address, tours of interest, and time of interest; posts Costa Rican telephone numbers and fax numbers; provides an e-mail address to contact JRE for more information; and provides the address of a mail forwarding service in Miami, Florida. JRE's Web site states that the mail forwarding service provides a

quicker means of sending information via postal mail to JRE than if regular postal mail delivery is used (one business day, as opposed to two weeks by regular mail delivery). The Miami service does not provide any other services for JRE. There is no form on the Web site for making reservations with JRE.

7. JRE maintains customer lists. To date, JRE has not sent promotional material to people on this list.

CHAPTER
8

Writing a Discussion of a Fact-Based Issue:
Using Policy to Support a Legal Analysis

HIGHLIGHTS

- Public policy is a principle of law that promotes the protection of the public's well-being.
- Public policy can change over time as legislators or judges perceive a change in the general public's ideas and attitudes.
- When enacting statutes, legislators are guided by public policy reflected in relevant constitutional provisions.
- When deciding issues of law, judges are guided by public policy reflected in relevant constitutional provisions and relevant statutes.
- If the constitution or statutory law is silent on public policy as it relates to certain issues, judges may articulate public policy to support the common law for these issues.
- Judges, usually bound to follow mandatory precedent by the doctrine of stare decisis, may depart from precedent if they are persuaded that public policy no longer supports the precedent.
- Public policy is an important source of law and should be used, where appropriate, in the legal analysis of an issue and to support a client's position in an argument before the court.
- When reaching a decision, a court is able sometimes to "balance the equities" in a case by considering what is fair in light of the particular circumstances of the parties.

134

 ## A. Public Policy Generally

Public policy underlies the creation or application of most U.S. law, whether it is constitutional law, common law, or statutory law. Public policy has been defined as "that principle of the law which holds that no [citizen] can lawfully do that which has a tendency to be injurious to the public, or against the public good. . . ."[1] A more precise definition of public policy, however, is (at least by most courts' account) difficult or impossible to formulate.[2] This is because what one individual or group considers injurious to the public or against the public good may not necessarily be considered so by another individual or group. Furthermore, public policy can change over time as the general public's attitudes and ideas change.

Although it is called public policy, the term should not be interpreted to mean that this policy reflects an agreement among the populace or even a majority opinion as to what is injurious to the public or against the public good. Those who make the laws — legislators and judges — determine public policy. In their effort to remedy what they identify as social evils or to promote what they think is good for the public, legislators create the law, and judges create or apply the law.

 ## B. Sources of Public Policy

The primary source of public policy is reflected in federal and state constitutions. Amendments to the constitutions can be made, though changes are infrequent, to reflect perceived changes in public policy.[3] For example, the 1919 ratification of the Nineteenth Amendment to the U.S. Constitution gave women the right to vote, changing the nation's prior public policy that allowing women to vote would potentially harm the public good or the democratic process because women were considered less knowledgeable in national affairs.

---

1. *Porterfield v. Mascari II, Inc.*, 823 A.2d 590, 602 (Md. 2003) (quoting *Eagerton v. Brownlow*, 4 H.L. (House of Lords) Cas. 1, 196 (1853)).

2. *See, e.g., Twin City Pipe Line Co. v. Harding Glass Co.*, 283 U.S. 353, 356 (1931), quoted in *Terrien v. Zwit*, 648 N.W.2d 602, 609 (Mich. 2002); *Green v. Ralee Engr. Co.*, 78 Cal. Rptr. 2d 16, 22 (Cal. 1998); *Palmateer v. Intl. Harvester Co.*, 421 N.E.2d 876, 878-879 (Ill. 1981); *Donegal Mut. Ins. Co. v. Long*, 564 A.2d 937, 942-943 (Pa. Super. 1989); *Berube v. Fashion Centre, Ltd.*, 771 P.2d 1033, 1042-1043 (Utah 1989).

3. Amendments to the U.S. Constitution can be proposed in one of two ways: (1) the proposed amendment must receive a two-thirds majority vote in the U.S. House of Representatives and in the U.S. Senate; or (2) two-thirds of the state legislatures can call for a Constitutional Convention. None of the amendments made to the U.S. Constitution have been proposed by Constitutional Convention. Congress may set a deadline for state ratification of the proposed amendment. Recently, the deadline has been seven years, though Congress may later decide to extend the deadline. If an amendment is passed by two-thirds majorities of the House and Senate, then three-fourths of the states (38 of the 50 states) must agree to ratify the amendment before it can become part of the U.S. Constitution.

Public policy also is reflected in federal and state statutes that protect the public or advance public interests. Legislatures, acting in accord with public policy expressed in constitutional provisions, identify public policy or express public policy reasons for enacting a statute when stating the statute's purpose. For example, many states have slayer statutes that prohibit a murderer from inheriting any portion of his or her victim's estate. The policy behind this statute is that an individual cannot benefit from his or her own wrongdoing.[4] The policy is not always expressly stated in the statute[5] but may be construed through other means, such as reviewing the legislative history (if available)[6] behind the statute's enactment. As is the case with constitutional provisions, statutes may be amended or revoked by legislatures when perceived public policy has changed from the time of the original statute's enactment.

 ## C. How Public Policy Affects Court Decisions

When public policy has been expressed through constitutional provisions and statutes, the courts must adhere to these policies in each case decision. But when constitutions and statutes are silent on an area of law, courts have the power to step in and articulate principles of public policy to support a common law decision. Thus, in a state where there is no slayer statute, a court still may prohibit a beneficiary from inheriting from an estate if he or she killed the deceased. The court bases its decision on policy identical or similar to the policy considerations of legislatures passing slayer statutes — that is, a person should not benefit from his or her own wrongdoing.[7]

Sometimes, though, a court may be reluctant to establish new principles of public policy. The court may prefer the legislature to take the lead role in identifying public policy. Legislatures are composed of members elected by the public to represent the interests of their constituents. Courts may consider legislators to be in a better position to identify public policy because legislators arguably express the will of the people.

---

4. *See Cook v. Grierson*, 845 A.2d 1231, 1233 (Md. 2004).

5. *But see, e.g.*, Idaho's slayer statute, which states, "This section shall not be considered penal in nature, but shall be construed broadly in order to effect the policy of this state that no person shall be allowed to profit by his own wrong, wherever committed." Idaho Code Ann. § 15-2-803(n) (Lexis 2001).

6. Legislative history comprises actions by a legislative body (e.g., hearings and debates) and legislative documents (e.g., committee reports) that relate to a bill (a proposal for a statute), beginning with the bill's introduction to the legislative body and ending with the legislature's enacting the bill into law (as a statute). The federal government publishes legislative histories (such as committee reports, floor debates, and histories of actions taken) for enacted federal statutes, but few states publish legislative histories for enacted state statutes. The Library of Congress provides a free Web site called Thomas for researching federal statutes: http://thomas.loc.gov/. For a discussion on how to use the Thomas Web site to research a federal statute's legislative history (including congressional reports from 1995 and the *Congressional Record* from 1989), see Kurt X. Metzmeier, *Reading the Mind of Congress: Legislative History Research on the Internet* (Louisville B. Assn. Jan. 2007) (available at http://ssrn.com/abstract=965034). *See also* nn. 35-39 and accompanying text in Chapter 13 for further explanation of the legislative process in Congress.

7. *See, e.g., Ford v. Ford*, 512 A.2d 389, 391 (Md. 1986).

For this reason courts sometimes defer to the legislature on matters involving public policy.[8]

Public policy can serve as a powerful tool of the courts. In addition to being constrained by constitutional provisions and statutes, as discussed in Chapter 2, courts are bound by stare decisis to follow their prior decisions and those of higher courts in their jurisdiction in cases addressing the same issues. As long as the public policy underlying these decisions does not change, courts are bound by the precedent and must apply it. If a court perceives that the public policy supporting the precedent has changed, however, a court may depart from outmoded precedent and create new common law that reflects what the court identifies as the current public policy.[9]

D. How Lawyers Use Public Policy

Because courts use public policy to support the continued use of precedent or to support a break from precedent,[10] lawyers rely on public policy to advance a client's position. A court will sometimes explicitly mention in a decision the public policy for creating or applying a rule. Other times the public policy used by a court will merely be implied in the decision. Lawyers find public policy especially effective in support of a client's position when they refer to a favorable case decision where a court explicitly mentioned the public policy behind the common law and applied that public policy to the facts in the cited case to reach an outcome favorable to the client's position.

Public policy arguments can also be advocated by lawyers to persuade a court to depart from precedent because of a perceived change in the concept of what is injurious to the public. In this regard, lawyers may consider using persuasive law, such as scholarly writings or common law or statutory trends from other jurisdictions, to convince a court to adopt a new rule that reflects current public policy. The argument, however, must be strongly persuasive. Courts are reluctant to overturn precedent because "[a]dherence to precedent promotes stability, predictability, and respect for judicial authority."[11]

A legal writer includes public policy in an analysis when public policy supports a party's position. As mentioned in Chapter 7, lawyers typically consider using three sources to support a client's position: (1) the relevant law, (2) the client's facts, and (3) the policy considerations underlying the law. Because it is bound by precedent, a court

---

8. *See, e.g., Est. of Benson*, 548 So. 2d 775, 777 (Fla. App. 1989) (court rejected the argument that the state's public policy would extend the state's slayer statute to children of the murderer who were natural or statutory beneficiaries under the victims' estates, finding that "[i]f there was to be declared in Florida such a public policy . . . , it must be accomplished by a legislative amendment to the slayer statute and not by a pronouncement of this court.").

9. *See, e.g., State v. Valentine*, 935 P.2d 1294 (Wash. 1997) (court relied on a perceived change in public policy to overrule prior common law that permitted citizens to resist unlawful arrests).

10. Courts also use public policy when deciding questions of law. In these instances, the court may rely on public policy as a basis for choosing the application of one law over another. (This topic is discussed further in Chapter 13.)

11. *Hilton v. S.C. Pub. Rys. Commn.*, 502 U.S. 197, 202 (1991).

is most interested in whether precedent applies to the facts before the court. Therefore, you should begin a fact-based analysis of a party's position by presenting any factual similarities[12] and distinctions[13] between prior case decisions and the facts of your client's case, as well as any additional facts of your client's case that support the party's position but are not comparable to facts in prior case decisions. Public policy may be inserted, where logical, to give additional support to the reasonable inferences drawn from the factual comparisons and the other facts of your client's case.

Remember in Chapter 7 the analysis of Ana's case discussing the reasonableness of a covenant not to compete (CNC). The public policy expressed in the *Mats Transport* case may be added to the rebuttal of David's position that the CNC is not broader than necessary to protect his interests. The last paragraph of that discussion has been revised to reflect the added policy considerations, which are highlighted in boldface:

> Nevertheless, **courts do not favor CNCs and strictly construe CNCs against the party seeking to enforce them because "they impede trade and distort the market mechanism which allows our economy to function."** *Mats Transport*, 824 S.E.2d at 1467. Here, the CNC will be strictly construed against David. The geographic restriction in the CNC extends into counties and towns where Hart Fitness Center does not currently operate health and exercise clubs. **Allowing the CNC to extend beyond the present locations of the clubs will limit the availability of health and exercise clubs to the public and limit competition, which encourages better service and value to the public.** Further, the geographic area exceeds the value of the goodwill Ana has in the current membership, which is what the CNC is meant to protect. Therefore, the CNC is probably overbroad for the protection of David's business interest and is unreasonable.

E. Note: The Differences Between Equity and Law, and Equity and Public Policy

Do not confuse a court's use of law or public policy with a court's balancing of equities between the parties. Unlike law, which is based on "the ideal of rules,"[14] or public policy, which is grounded in the ideal of preserving the well-being of the entire

---

12. *Compare, analogy, similarity,* and the various forms of these nouns are synonymous when discussing how facts of a client's case are similar to case facts.

13. *Contrast, distinction, differences,* and the various forms of these nouns are synonymous when discussing how facts of a client's case are different from the case facts.

14. Ashutosh Bhagwat, *Hard Cases and the (D)evolution of Constitutional Doctrine,* 30 Conn. L. Rev. 961, 1007 (1998).

populace, equity relates to "the ideal of individual justice."[15] A court uses law and public policy to reach a decision, but in some individual cases, the application of law and public policy may result in an unfair result to a party. In these instances, a court, when determining whether to grant a remedy, may "balance the equities" by considering notions of fairness as they relate to the particular circumstances of the parties in the case presently before the court. For instance, in the case of *Everett v. Rogers* from Chapter 4, the court mentioned the public policy served by imposing the statute of limitations rule on causes of action.[16] Nearing the end of its opinion, however, the *Everett* court balanced the equities between the original owner of the painting and the current possessor of the painting to add support to its holding in the case that the painting should be returned to the original owner.[17]

An argument based on law and public policy is far more persuasive than an argument based solely on equity. Nevertheless, you might consider using equity considerations to strengthen a position already supported by law and public policy.

● Exercise 8-A

Add to your analysis of Ms. Broward's case from the exercises in Chapter 7 the public policy expressed in the *Everett* case to support one or both parties' positions.

---

15. *Id.*
16. *Everett v. Rogers*, 836 F. Supp. 1030, 1031-1032 (S.D.E.C. 1995).
17. *Id.* at 1033.

CHAPTER

9

Analyzing the Law: Using Multiple Cases in Analyzing a Single Issue

HIGHLIGHTS

- When using multiple cases in the analysis of a single issue, the structure of the analysis will depend on whether the cases are helpful only in explaining the law, only in applying the law to the client's facts, or both.
- Choosing the best cases to *explain* the law will depend on each court's focus on the law and the court's explanation of any underlying policy that supports the law.
- Choosing the best cases to use *to apply to* the law to the client's facts in the analysis depends on considerations such as the hierarchy and binding nature of the authority, the similarity of the facts to the client's facts, the extent of the court's reasoning about the same legal issue, and the year the case was decided.
- The placement of relevant case law in the analysis will depend on where the information is most relevant and helpful to the legal reader.

 ## A. Introduction

In Chapter 5 we provide a process for moving from the assigned task to the final written document. Step One is to interview the client to acquire the facts; Step Two is to analyze the facts; and Step Three is to collect the law relevant to the client's case. Consider the case introduced in Chapter 7, addressing whether Ana Hart could be forced to sign a covenant not to compete (CNC) as part of her divorce agreement with her husband David. In that chapter, only one case, *Mats Transport v. ABC Corporation*, was used to analyze whether the CNC was overbroad and therefore unreasonable. Usually, you will find more than one case that is relevant to the issue you are analyzing. Using multiple cases creates new decisions. Determining how and where to use multiple cases is an important step in the analytical process. To explain the use of multiple cases in analyzing a single issue, we've added *Hanson v. Albright*, 539 S.E.2d 500 (E.C. App. 1989), another case from the fictitious East Carolina addressing the reasonableness of a CNC. The full case opinion is found in Appendix H.

B. Analyzing the Law

After collecting the relevant law (Step Three in the researching and drafting approach discussed in Chapter 5), Step Four is to analyze the law. A full case brief of *Mats Transport* is set out in Chapter 7. Below is a brief of *Hanson*.

Hanson v. Albright (H&A), 539 S.E.2d 500 (E.C. App. 1989)

F: H&A, a pension consulting firm, was owned by a husband and wife. The buyer negotiated to take over the consulting firm to merge with other consulting firms and paid for the business and a covenant not to compete (CNC).

Under the purchase agreement, the sellers were to remain employees of the new company. The CNC covered twelve states and was to last three years, the length of the seller wife's employment contract with the buyer. The CNC restricted the sellers from directly or indirectly soliciting or accepting any business competing with the new company.

Approximately one year after the sale, the seller wife was fired, and her husband resigned. They began a different pension consulting firm, competing with the buyer by contacting their former clients.

C/A: Sellers filed suit alleging breach of the purchase agreement because the wife was fired. The sellers also argued that the twelve-state restriction in the CNC was broader geographically than necessary to protect the buyer's interests, especially since the buyer had only four customers in seven of the states and no customers in one state.

The buyer filed a counterclaim, requesting injunctive relief by ordering the sellers to abide by the CNC. The buyer noted that he had been engaged in negotiations with a prospective client in one of the new states, and the sellers knew this when the buyer purchased the business.

PH: TC granted a permanent injunction against the sellers, finding the CNC reasonable.

SI: Was the CNC between the buyer and sellers of a consulting firm overbroad and therefore unreasonable when (1) the CNC prohibited the sellers from conducting any direct or indirect business in competition with the new consulting firm for three years in twelve states, (2) there were few or no clients located in some of the restricted states, and (3) the sellers knew the buyer had plans to expand in all states and had engaged in active negotiations to expand the business in one state where at the time of the purchase there were no clients?

PI: Was the trial court's decision in finding the CNC reasonable and issuing a permanent injunction supported by a sufficiency of the evidence?

H: SI: No. CNC reasonable.

PI: Yes. Trial court decision supported by the evidence.

J: Affirmed.

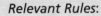

Relevant Rules:

1. Public policy supports every individual's right to work; however, policy also supports allowing any individual the option to sell anything he wants, including that right to work. *Day Cos. v. Patat*, 403 F.2d 792, 796 (5th Cir. 1969).
2. "The goodwill of a business is an intangible asset which may be transferred from seller to buyer, and it becomes the buyer's right to expect that the firm's established customers will continue to patronize the purchased business." *Snider's Agency, Inc. v. Dixon*, 494 S.E.2d 77, 80-81 (E.C. 1985).
3. First, determine whether a protectable interest has been purchased. If so, apply a three-pronged test to determine if the CNC is reasonable:
   a. Is the CNC broader than necessary for the protection of the covenantee in some legitimate interest?
   b. Does the CNC have an adverse effect on the covenantor? and
   c. Does the CNC have an adverse effect on the public interest?

Court's Reasoning:

1. A CNC related to service businesses will be localized because services are usually performed in a small geographic area, though due to the nature of the business some may extend over many states. Here, the consulting firm was dependent on the business representatives' familiarity with the clients. Many contacts occurred between the owner and the clients. Evidence supported that both sellers had good relationships with their clients; if allowed to solicit former clients, the goodwill the buyer purchased would be destroyed.
2. Evidence existed to support that in the states included in the CNC where the seller did not have a business the buyer was in active negotiations with at least one prospective client to expand in those areas, and the seller husband knew this and agreed to include the other states as part of the CNC's restriction.
3. The sellers were employed by the new company and had contact with many of the new company's clients, so the new owner had a protectable interest in those clients in addition to the goodwill purchased in the agreement.

C. Organizing the Law and Applying It to the Client's Case (Steps Five and Six)

Once you have analyzed the relevant law, you are ready to organize and apply the law to the facts of your client's case. First, understand that there is no one way to use the relevant case law. Let your sense of logic guide your decisions every step of the way. You will need to make four decisions:

(1) which cases provide the relevant rules at issue in your client's case;
(2) which cases are needed to explain how the relevant rules have been applied to facts in prior cases (rule explanations);
(3) which cases are most helpful in supporting each party's position when applying the law to the facts of your client's case (the analysis); and
(4) based on your choice of cases in 1, 2, and 3, where is the best place to explain the cases so they will be most helpful to your reader.

1. Choosing which cases provide the relevant rules at issue in the case

In deciding from which cases you will draw the relevant legal principles or rules of law, consider the following.

a. Is the case binding or persuasive precedent?

Address binding authority first, where it exists. As discussed in Chapter 2, binding authority includes (1) any relevant constitutional provision in your case's jurisdiction, (2) any relevant statutory law from your case's jurisdiction, and (3) any case law that is relevant and was decided by the same court or by a higher court within the controlling jurisdiction.[1]

In contrast, persuasive authority includes (1) any primary authority originating from another jurisdiction; (2) any nonbinding case from your own jurisdiction, including a case decided by a lower court within your own jurisdiction or a decision by another intermediate appellate court decision in your own jurisdiction, such as a state court decision from another intermediate appellate court in the state; and (3) any secondary authority that may be helpful, such as a restatement provision or a law review article.

If persuasive authority is helpful, introduce it only after discussing the binding authority. In the CNC case, both *Mats Transport* and *Hanson* were decided by a court in the controlling jurisdiction, East Carolina. Therefore, both are binding, primary authority.

---

1. In a few states, such as Indiana, there are no defined regions for each immediate appellate court, so all intermediate appellate court decisions are binding on all intermediate appellate courts in Indiana.

b. Is the case from an intermediate appeals court or from the highest court within the controlling jurisdiction?

Prefer a decision from a state's highest court over an intermediate level appellate court, a United States Supreme Court case over a federal court of appeals case, and both state and federal intermediate appellate court cases over a federal or state trial court case. In the CNC case, both *Mats Transport* and *Hanson* were decided by the intermediate court of appeals. This may happen when the highest court of the jurisdiction has not yet considered this issue. Therefore, these two cases are from the same level court.

c. What is the age of each case?

Consider the date of each court's decision. If two cases provide the same information and are from the same level court (for example, both are from the intermediate appellate court or both are from the highest appellate court), the more recent case is likely to be more helpful. Some cases, however, are considered landmark cases[2] and are often cited for that reason. Landmark cases are important and should probably either be included or at least mentioned in a footnote.

Consider also whether the legal issue you are addressing has been treated differently over time or is one where the law is changing. If you identify a trend where the law is changing, the more recent cases will likely better reflect that trend.

In the CNC case, *Mats Transport* was decided in 1992; *Hanson* was decided in 1989. Since the two cases were decided three years apart, neither would be more important than the other based solely on age. Presuming *Mats Transport* represents the most recent case from the highest court in East Carolina that has addressed this issue, you would cite to *Mats Transport* for the three-pronged test used to determine the reasonableness of CNCs in East Carolina.

d. Are the general explanations and definitions of the relevant rules different among the various cases?

Rules change as rules are applied.[3] Thus, as courts apply case precedent to a new set of facts, the court may further define what the former common law rule means in light of the facts in the new case. The synthesis of the prior rule with the holding in the new case becomes a part of the new common law rule to be applied in future cases. Sometimes you may find it necessary to synthesize the rules from multiple cases into a single rule, as discussed in Chapter 10.

For example, the court in *Mats Transport* describes the goodwill of a business as that "which represents the value of the relationship between the seller and its customers." *Mats Transport v. ABC corp.*, 824 S.E.2d 1467, 1468 (E.C. App. 1992). *Hanson* provides a bit more information by adding, "The goodwill of a business is

---

2. Landmark cases are those in which a court creates new law, such as when the United States Supreme Court decided that legislative decisions were supreme over all court decisions except those deciding the constitutionality of legislative enactments. *See Marbury v. Madison*, 5 U.S. (1 Cranch) 137 (1803).

3. Edward H. Levi. *An Introduction to Legal Reasoning* (U. of Chicago P. 1948).

an intangible asset which may be transferred from seller to buyer, and it becomes the buyer's right to expect that the firm's established customers will continue to patronize the purchased business." *Hanson*, 539 S.E.2d at 501.

2. Choosing which cases are needed to explain how the relevant rules have been applied to facts in prior cases (*rule explanations*)

This choice depends on the complexity of the law. If, for example, the test is a straightforward one, you may either not need a case at all or need only a single case to explain how the court has interpreted and applied the relevant rule to a set of facts in a case. For example, in many common law burglary cases, the law requires that the crime take place during the nighttime. The common law also may have provided a definition of nighttime, such as that time occurring one hour after the sun sets (dusk) and one hour before the sun rises (dawn). If in your case the alleged crime took place at 2:00 A.M., and the common rule applies, you need only provide the definition to establish that the nighttime requirement is satisfied.

If the test requires assessing a more vague term, such as whether a CNC is broader than necessary and therefore unreasonable based on its geographical restrictions, more case law is likely needed to provide a thorough explanation of how the court has interpreted and applied the legal concept of reasonableness in the past. Some considerations include the following.

a. Whether two or more cases decide the same legal issue but reach different outcomes

If your cases include at least one case where the court applied the rule of law at issue to a set of similar facts and concluded one way, and at least one other case where the court applied the rule of law at issue to a set of similar facts and concluded the opposite way, explaining the first case and then immediately explaining the second case may help your reader better understand the boundaries of the rule.

For example, in *Mats Transport* the court found the CNC too broad and thus unreasonable in protecting the covenantee buyer's legitimate business interest. In *Hanson*, however, the court addressed the same legal question but found the CNC was not too broad in protecting the covenantee buyer's legitimate business interest. When explaining the requirement that a CNC be reasonable and not overbroad, your explanation will likely be most helpful by providing a rule explanation (facts, court's holding, and court's reasoning) of both cases, so your reader will understand how the rule is applied to different factual situations to reach opposite results. The rule explanations regarding reasonableness may look like the following.

Mats Transport *(CNC found unreasonable):*

Facts:
    A seller sold a trucking business and signed a CNC restricting the seller from competing for five years with the buyer in the trucking business anywhere in the

United States. When the business sold, the seller had one trucking terminal in East Carolina and hauled freight elsewhere in the United States only periodically.

After the sale, the seller leased trucks to a driver who had worked for the seller's employee before the sale of the business. The driver began operating a trucking business in the territory covered by the CNC. The buyer filed a complaint, alleging a CNC violation. The seller moved for summary judgment (SJ).

Holding:

SJ affirmed. CNC unreasonable.

Court's Reasoning:

The CNC was broader than necessary since all the parties knew the seller's trucking business was limited to a smaller geographic area. The limitation throughout the United States was geographically overbroad and therefore unreasonable.

Hanson *(CNC found reasonable)*:

Facts:

Sellers husband and wife sold their pension consulting firm to a buyer and signed a CNC. The sellers became the buyer's employees; the CNC covered twelve states and was to last three years, the length of the wife's employment contract with the buyer. One year later the wife was fired, and her husband quit. The sellers began a new pension consulting firm and solicited former clients. The sellers also sued the buyer, arguing that the wife's termination was unlawful and the twelve-state restriction in the CNC was too broad. The buyer filed a counterclaim, requesting an injunction that ordered sellers to refrain from competing and to abide by the CNC.

Holding:

CNC reasonable and not overbroad; the injunction was properly awarded.

Court's Reasoning:

The buyer paid for the goodwill of the purchased business, which is highly dependent on good client relationships. Allowing the sellers to solicit former clients would destroy the goodwill the buyer purchased. The sellers knew of the buyer's plans to expand in areas covered by the CNC and agreed to the restricted states as part of the CNC. The sellers received payment for this restriction and could not then avoid it.

b. Whether different cases provide different helpful information based on each case's facts

Sometimes cases provide different helpful information. For example, two or more cases may describe and emphasize different types of facts in analyzing the same legal issue, and both types of facts are relevant to the client's case. Thus, different cases may be chosen to help explain and support a different aspect of the client's case.

In *Mats Transport,* for example, the buyer of the trucking company did not employ the seller in the new business. In *Hanson,* however, the buyer did employ the sellers in his new business. If your client's case involved the former owners working with the new owner, the familiarity of the sellers with the business and the business's clients may have an effect on whether the CNC is found reasonable. When analyzing this issue in your client's case, therefore, you would want to use the more recent case, *Mats Transport* (1992), but also the older *Hanson* case (1989), because it has important similar facts in determining whether the CNC is reasonable.

c. Whether some cases provide useful public policy explanations

You may find different cases helpful for different reasons. For example, one or more cases may be useful to draw factual analogies and distinctions to support each party's position, while other cases are useful because they provide policy support for the legal arguments raised by the parties.

Continuing with the CNC example, let's say you have read *Hanson* and know how important it is that the buyer is able to rely on the former business relationships and keep the former clients involved with the new business. In deciding whether a CNC is too broad to protect the seller's interest, a second court in its opinion refers to the importance of former business relationships but never really explains why this new fact is relevant. The underlying reason may be based on public policy. If that public policy is found in yet a third case, that third case would be helpful for this particular point. You would want to include a reference to the third case, if for no other reason than to provide the relevant public policy.

For example, in *Hanson,* the court set out policy not set out in *Mats Transport:* "Policy supports every individual's right to work; however, policy also supports allowing any individual the option to sell anything he wants, including that right to work." *Hanson,* 539 S.E.2d at 502.

Applying all these guidelines to the CNC case, you would want to explain both cases. In *Mats Transport,* the court found the CNC unreasonable, while in *Hanson* the court found the CNC reasonable. Because together the two cases help explain the parameters of what constitutes reasonableness in a CNC, and because both are useful in analyzing both parties' positions, the best approach is to provide an explanation of each case, one right after the other. The older case, *Hanson,* also provides information not found in *Mats Transport* regarding additional, similar facts as well as public policy.

3. Choosing which cases are most helpful in supporting each party's position when applying the law to the facts of the case in the analysis

After you have assessed the value of each case, determine which cases are helpful when drawing factual analogies and distinctions to the facts of the client's case to support each party's position in the analysis. Consider the suggested factors below. Balance these guidelines with your own judgment and common sense.

a. *Prefer a case with facts similar to your client's facts over a case with facts dissimilar to your client's case*

When analyzing a fact-based issue, the closer the facts in a case are to your client's facts, the more persuasive your analysis. This is because you are better able to draw reasonable factual analogies between the facts of the cited case and the facts of your client's case. Of course, this factor must be weighed against the other factors in this list. For example, as discussed in b., below, even though the facts may be similar, the case may not be helpful if the court didn't explain in its reasoning *why* the facts were significant.

b. *Prefer a case where the court gave a well-reasoned basis for its decision over one where the court's reasoning is superficial or nonexistent*

Some courts in their opinions omit the reasoning entirely or provide only a superficial explanation for their holdings. The more thorough the court's reasoning, the more helpful the case will be when drawing factual analogies and distinctions in your analysis. Be careful to avoid using a case just because the facts sound strikingly similar to your client's facts. If the court never explained why it concluded as it did — or even worse, never actually addressed the legal issue for which the similar facts are relevant — that case will not be helpful to you. Pay careful attention to each court's reasoning, and use a case only when analyzing the same legal point the court analyzed in reaching its decision.

Further, pay careful attention to what the court *says* it will address in its opinion and what the court *actually does* address in the opinion. Sometimes the court sets out an issue raised on appeal but never actually addresses the issue in deciding the case.

c. *Prefer cases from the highest binding court in the controlling jurisdiction*

As discussed in C.1 on organizing the law and choosing cases to cite and explain rules, draw your factual analogies and distinctions with a case decided by the highest court in the jurisdiction controlling your client's case, where possible. If not, refer to a controlling intermediate appellate court, where possible.

Sometimes you will need to use cases outside your controlling jurisdiction. When addressing a state law question, state court opinions from other jurisdictions are usually more helpful than federal court opinions where the federal court applied state law. This is because state courts outside the controlling jurisdiction address the same state issues more frequently than federal courts. For this reason, state courts have a greater ability than federal courts to reason through these state issues.[4]

---

4. This relationship between the federal and state courts is discussed more thoroughly in Chapter 2.

Any decision that does not originate in the controlling state jurisdiction is persuasive authority only. Further, any decision about a state law issue from a federal court, even a federal decision where the court applied the controlling state's law, is persuasive authority only. Based on the same logic, when your client's issue involves a federal question, decisions by federal courts are more useful than decisions by state courts.[5] Any state court decision is not binding on a federal court resolving federal issues. (Chapter 2 discusses the dual state and federal court systems in detail.)

d. Prefer cases where the support is found in the majority opinion

Prefer cases where the court's discussion of the issue is found in the majority opinion rather than in a concurring or dissenting opinion.[6] Also note whether the discussion is part of the actual holding in the case or is merely dicta (extraneous to the holding). The persuasive value of the discussion is greater if it is part of the court's binding decision. If dicta, the information may still be useful, but it must be identified as dicta in your own discussion.

4. Choosing where best to place information from the cases

Determining where to place information from the case law depends on how you plan to use each case. The following are sample outlines of different ways a discussion of one legal issue may be structured.

a. Using two cases to support both parties' positions

Consider using the following structure where you have two cases and both can be used to support each party's position.

> - **Topic/thesis** (identifying the legal issue)
> - **Rule** (and, where available, general explanations of the rule, such as definitions)
> - **Rule explanations** (case facts, holding, and reasoning) provided one case at a time)
> - **Analysis/application** of the law to the client's case

---

5. This choice of state versus federal court may arise, for example, when your client's case involves a constitutional question, such as whether your client's rights were violated under the Fourth Amendment to the U.S. Constitution, which protects citizens from unreasonable searches and seizures by the government. State opinions exist where the court addresses the U.S. Constitution's Fourth Amendment since all states are bound to the federal constitutional provision as well as a state's own constitutional provision, if raised.

6. Concurring and dissenting opinions are discussed more thoroughly in Chapter 4.

In the CNC case, both *Mats Transport* and *Hanson* can be used to support both parties' position. The best pattern to follow in this discussion, therefore, is the above pattern, where both cases are explained together and then used to support each party's position. When providing support for why the CNC is reasonable, compare favorably the facts in *Hanson* with the facts in the client's case, and contrast the facts from *Mats Transport* with those from the client's case. When providing support for why the CNC is unreasonable, compare favorably the facts from *Mats Transport* to the client's case, and contrast the facts from *Hanson* with the facts from the client's case. Figure 9-1 below illustrates this process.

To Support a Finding of Reasonableness:

←——→

Hanson (CNC reasonable)   *Mats Transport* (CNC not reasonable)
Analogize client's facts with   Distinguish client's facts from facts in
facts in *Hanson*   *Mats Transport*

To Support a Finding of Unreasonableness:

←——→

Hanson (CNC reasonable)   *Mats Transport* (CNC not reasonable)
Distinguish client's facts from   Analogize client's facts with
facts in *Hanson*   facts in *Mats Transport*

Figure 9-1

b. Using one or more cases to support the stronger position and one or more additional cases to support the weaker position

More often than not, you will find more than two cases that are helpful in your analysis of the client's case. While there is no single template for structuring a legal analysis with multiple cases, your goals are (1) to ensure that your reader has a clear understanding of what the law says and how it has been interpreted and applied by the courts, and (2) to provide a complete and accurate analysis of the issue in the client's case by thoroughly exploring how to best support each party's position on each legal issue.

When you use too few cases, you run the risk of not being thorough; when you use too many cases, you run the risk of not being clear. For example, if you begin your discussion of an issue by explaining five cases in a row, your reader may have difficulty distinguishing among the cases in the analysis. To better ensure you do not lose your reader, you may choose to discuss some cases when supporting the stronger position (which may also be used to support the weaker position), and then introduce and use additional cases when supporting the weaker position. Introducing new cases within the analysis of the weaker position works only if those cases are more helpful in the analysis for the weaker position. The structure might look like this.

- *Thesis* (identifying the legal issue and conclusion)
- *Rule* (and, where available, general explanations of the rule, such as definitions)
- *Rule explanations* (explanations of the cases—key facts, holding, and reasoning—provided one case at a time)
- *Analysis/application* of the law to the client's case
  - *Assertion and support for the stronger position*
  - *Inferences from client's facts and from case analogies and distinctions to support the stronger position*
  - *Transition to the weaker position*
  - *Rule explanation(s) of additional case(s) used only to support the weaker position*
  - *Inferences from client's facts, and case analogies and distinctions from newly introduced as well as previously introduced cases to support the weaker position*
- *Conclusion,* including a rebuttal of the weaker position and/or a statement why the first position is stronger

You also may choose to limit the number of full rule explanations and provide references to other cases through the use of a parenthetical, which usually provides only the court's factual holding in parentheses following the citation to the case. Using all the cases you find addressing a single issue is not necessary. You want to provide just enough information to give your reader a solid understanding of the relevant law and arguments that can and likely will be made on behalf of both sides.

c. Considering *public policy cited in the relevant cases and where to include that policy in your discussion*

The final consideration is how to use court statements of public policy, as discussed in Chapter 8, and where to place that policy. When addressing a fact-based issue such as the CNC issue, statements of policy are used primarily to educate the reader as to why a rule exists and to provide additional support for the legal arguments based on the relevant law and the facts of the case. When addressing law-based questions, as discussed in Chapter 14, statements of public policy serve as the primary basis of the analysis because what is relevant are those underlying reasons why a rule exists, why a rule should be interpreted a certain way, or why one rule should be applied over a different rule. Statements of public policy are usually included in one or more of the following places:

(1) With the explanation of the rule.
(2) With the explanation of the case.

(3) In the analysis.

(4) As part of the conclusion, to support why the first position discussed in the analysis was stronger than the second, weaker position.

Examples of public policy in the CNC cases include the following.

Mats Transport:

Nevertheless, courts do not favor CNCs and strictly construe CNCs against the party seeking to enforce them because "they impede trade and distort the market mechanism which allows our economy to function." *Mats Trans. v. ABC Corp.*, 824 S.E.2d 1467, 1467 (E.C. Ct. App. 1992).

Hanson:

Policy supports every individual's right to work; however, policy also supports allowing any individual the option to sell anything he wants, including that right to work. *Hanson v. Albright*, 539 S.E.2d 500, 502 (E.C. App. 1989).

---

d. Considering *how to use* those cases that are decided *favorably for the opposing party*

Do not weaken the persuasive value of your client's position by avoiding cases that provide the strongest support for the opposing party's position. If opposing counsel is competent, those cases will be introduced. By ignoring these cases, you run the risk of losing your client's case. Instead, carefully consider how to support each party's position using those cases that provide the strongest support for each respective position.[7]

As previously discussed, the placement of the case explanations may vary, depending on the relevant information provided in the case and how that information fits into your analysis. The key guideline, as stated throughout Part Three of this book, is to provide the relevant information from the case at that point where it is most relevant to your reader.

The sample discussion found in Chapter 7, with the addition of *Hanson* and the policy discussed in Chapter 8, might read like the following. As you read this example, identify the different parts of the discussion, such as the topic or thesis sentences, rules, rule explanations (case facts, holdings, and reasonings), factual analogies and distinctions and the inferences drawn from those analogies and distinctions, additional facts

---

7. In fact, in the United States Model Rules of Professional Conduct Rule 3.3(2) mandates that an attorney inform the court of any binding authority that is relevant to the legal issue being addressed.

152

and inferences from the client's case, policy statements, transitional words and phrases, and conclusions.

Thesis sentence

T

The covenant not to compete (CNC) that Ana Hart has been ordered by the court to sign is probably overbroad in its protection of David Hart's business interests and thus unreasonable. In East Carolina, courts use the following three-pronged test to determine whether a CNC related to the sale of a business is reasonable: "(1) the covenant must not be broader than necessary for the protection of the covenantee's legitimate business interest; (2) the covenant cannot have an adverse effect on the covenantor; and (3) the covenant cannot adversely affect the public interest." *Mats Transp. v. ABC Corp.*, 824 S.E.2d 1467, 1468 (E.C. App. 1992). A CNC is unreasonable "as a matter of law" if it fails any one of the prongs of the test. *Id.*

Rules

Rule Explanation

RE explanation 1

reason 1

In *Mats Transport*, the court held that a CNC related to the sale of a business was unreasonable as a matter of law because it failed the first prong of the three-prong test and was broader than necessary for the covenantee's legitimate business interest. *Id.* *Mats Transport* involved a dispute as to whether the seller violated the terms of a CNC executed in connection with the sale of its trucking business to the buyer because the seller later leased several trucks to a prior employee who used the trucks to operate a trucking business. The CNC prohibited the seller from competing in the trucking business with the buyer for a period of five years anywhere in the United States. The buyer sued the seller for allegedly violating the CNC. The seller moved for a summary judgment, arguing that the CNC was overbroad in its protection of the buyer's business interest. The trial court granted the seller's motion, and the court on appeal affirmed. *Id.*

Facts

The court noted that when determining whether a CNC is broader than necessary to protect the buyer, the territory restricted is considered. *Id.* The CNC includes the seller's goodwill, which represents the value of the relationship between the seller and its customers. *Id.* (quoting *Matthews v. Acme Tax Consultants*, 470 S.E.2d 756, 763 (E.C. App. 1984)).

reason

The court found that when the seller sold the trucking business to the buyer, the business hauled freight primarily for a few major clients on routes only in East Carolina and adjoining states. *Id.* The parties knew that the seller's trucking business had only one terminal located in East Carolina, yet the CNC restrained the seller as though its business was a national enterprise. Because the territorial scope of the CNC exceeded the protection of the buyer's legitimate interests, the CNC was unreasonable as a matter of law. *Id.* The court did not discuss the other prongs of the test because the CNC failed the first part of the test.

unreasonableness

Rule Explanation by cases 2 holding:

In contrast, the court in *Hanson v. Albright*, 539 S.E.2d 500, 502 (E.C. App. 1989), found a CNC reasonable and enforceable. The husband and wife sellers owned a pension consulting firm that they sold to the buyer, who then merged that company with the buyer's other firms. As part of the sale, the buyer hired the sellers as employees of the new company. The CNC was to last for a three-year term, which was the length of the wife's employment contract. The CNC

Rule Explanation 2

restricted the sellers from directly or indirectly soliciting or attempting to solicit any business that was competing with the purchased company covering twelve states.

Approximately one year later, the wife was fired from the new company, and soon afterwards her husband resigned. They began a new pension consulting firm, competing with the buyer by contacting their former clients. The sellers filed a lawsuit, alleging a breach of the agreement because the wife was fired. They also argued that the CNC was broader than necessary to protect the buyer's interest, since it extended to a twelve-state area. The sellers argued that the buyer had only four customers in seven of the states and no customers in one state. The buyer was engaged in negotiations with a prospective client, however, and the sellers were aware of this when the buyer purchased the business from the sellers.

The appellate court affirmed the trial court's ruling that under the three-pronged test set down in *Mats Transport* the CNC was reasonable and granted the buyer's request for a permanent injunction against the sellers. *Id.* The court found the first prong was met because, as a service business, familiarity with the clients is essential. If competition were allowed by the sellers the new owner's business could be destroyed. *Id.* at 501. The court found further that under the second prong, even though the buyer did not have ongoing businesses in all twelve states covered in the CNC, the buyer had been working to expand the business into these states, and the buyer's active negotiations with potential customers was known by the seller at the time of the bargain. *Id.* at 502. Finally, the court found prong three met because under the arrangement as employees of the new business, both former owners would have access to the old clients. *Id.* This contact supported the new owner's position that he purchased a protectable interest as well as the goodwill in the sales agreement. *Id.* "The goodwill of a business is an intangible asset which may be transferred from seller to purchaser, and it becomes the buyer's right to expect that the firm's established customers will continue to patronize the purchased business." *Id.* at 502.

The CNC that the court has ordered Ana to sign is likely unreasonable because it is overbroad in its protection of David's interest. The CNC restricts competition in three counties and two towns where Hart Fitness Center has no clubs, and so the business has not developed relationships with customers in these areas. This is similar to *Mats Transport*, where the CNC was overbroad because it unreasonably restricted competition in every state, and the business operated in only one state with established trucking routes in the surrounding states. Unlike in *Hanson*, where there were at least some clients in each area restricted by the CNC, or there were active negotiations to expand into those areas, Hart Fitness Center has neither any clubs in these other areas nor any ongoing negotiations to establish clubs in those areas.

Further, the sellers in *Hanson* knew that the buyers intended to expand to new areas where there were no clients at the time of the sale. More importantly, at least one of the sellers agreed to include in the CNC the state with no clients at that time. This is different from Ana's situation. Unlike in *Hanson* where the sellers voluntarily agreed to include the new state in the CNC, Ana made no such agreement and, in fact, is being forced to sign the CNC as part of her divorce settlement.

In addition, the CNC is unreasonable because it extends beyond the one-county restriction of the CNCs signed by sellers in prior sales of clubs to Hart Fitness Center. These previous CNCs restricted competition to the county in which the purchased clubs were located. The owners of Hart Fitness Center considered this a reasonable restriction in those prior transactions. Therefore, in Ana's sale of her interest to David, a CNC restricting competition in locations where the clubs are not currently located exceeds what were considered reasonable terms in prior sales transactions.

Further support that the geographic restriction is too broad is that members usually use clubs that are closest to their homes or workplaces. Members probably will not travel great distances to go to another club; thus, it is not necessary to restrict competition over a geographic area that exceeds the present club locations.

Conversely, the CNC the court has ordered Ana to sign may be considered reasonable if more emphasis is placed on the planned expansion of the business, the nature of the business, and the importance of Ana's relationship with the members of Hart Fitness Center. Unlike the seller in *Mats Transport*, who never expressed to the buyer any planned expansion into other routes, Ana and David had planned to expand the business in the next three years into the three counties and two towns covered by the CNC. The restriction also covers a limited geographic area in central East Carolina only, unlike the restricted area covered by the CNC in *Mats Transport* that extended to every state, even though the business was located in only one state and operated only a limited number of routes in the surrounding states. The Harts' planned expansion is similar to the buyer's expansion in *Hanson*, who had already taken steps to expand the business at the time of the purchase. David's planned expansion would also cover only a limited geographic area in central East Carolina, similar to the restricted area in *Hanson* and unlike the expanded restricted area covered by the CNC in *Mats Transport*.

Further, although the CNC to be signed by Ana is broader than the one-county restriction contained in the CNCs signed by sellers in prior club purchases, the broader restriction in Ana's case is necessary to adequately protect David's interest in the business. Unlike the previous sellers, who did not have any relationship with the members of Hart Fitness Center prior to the purchases, Ana presents a greater threat to the business of Hart Fitness Center because she has developed a relationship with club members. This is similar to the sellers in *Hanson*, who had good relationships with their former clients and could threaten the goodwill the buyer purchased if they tried to compete with the buyer. In addition, just as in *Hanson*, where the pension consulting firm was a service-oriented business, health and exercise clubs are service-oriented businesses that rely heavily on the good relationship between members and the clubs for the continuing success of the business. Arguably, David needs to protect his interest in the business, and the CNC would ensure that Ana did not compete with the business and steal away members, which would lessen the value of the business. If Ana has a club in the same county or town where the club members live or work, members may quit Hart Fitness Center, especially if her club is closer to their homes or workplaces, because members use clubs that are close to these places. Ana has developed a relationship with the members; therefore, members may be even more inclined to join Ana's club, rather than continue their memberships with Hart Fitness Center.

Nevertheless, courts do not favor CNCs and strictly construe CNCs against the party seeking to enforce them because "they impede trade and distort the market mechanism which allows our economy to function." *Mats Transport*, 824 S.E.2d at 1467. Here, the CNC will be strictly construed against David. The geographic restriction in the CNC extends into counties and towns where Hart Fitness Center does not currently operate health and exercise clubs. Allowing the CNC to extend beyond the present locations of the clubs will limit the availability of health and exercise clubs to the public. The CNC extension would also limit competition, which encourages better service and value to the public. Further, the geographic area exceeds the value of the goodwill Ana has in the current membership, which is what the CNC is meant to protect. Therefore, the CNC is probably overbroad for the protection of David's business interest and is unreasonable.

A sample checklist for a discussion of an objective discussion is found in Appendix J.

● Exercise 9-A

Read and brief *Schuler v. Baldwin*, found in Appendix I. Revise your previous discussion drafted in Exercise 7-G by incorporating *Schuler* into the discussion of whether Ms. Broward will be barred from bringing an action against Dr. Warren for the return of the painting. This exercise provides you with an opportunity to apply the concepts presented in this chapter by drafting a single fact-based issue discussion using two cases.

● Exercise 9-B

Read and brief *Langford v. Emerald Beach Resort & Marina*, found in Appendix G. Revise your previous discussion drafted in Exercise 7-H by incorporating the *Langford* case into the discussion of whether the requirements of East Carolina's long-arm statute has been satisfied. This exercise provides you with an opportunity to apply the concepts presented in this chapter by drafting a single fact-based issue discussion using two cases.

CHAPTER
10

*Taking the Objective Analysis to a
Higher Level:*

*Synthesizing a Single Rule from
Multiple Cases*

HIGHLIGHTS

- Common law rules are developed when courts apply legal principles set down in earlier cases that are binding on a new case addressing the same legal issue found in the earlier case.
- Dicta, or nonbinding language found in an earlier court opinion, may become part of a common law rule and therefore become binding, when a court specifically adopts a legal point that an earlier court included as dicta in its opinion.

Common law rules are developed over a period of time and through numerous court decisions. It is the common thread existing in multiple cases where the same legal issue is being addressed that eventually develops into a common law rule. When a court is faced with a legal issue, it must review the relevant law in the controlling jurisdiction and decide the case in a way that is consistent with the binding case precedent. The facts of the current case before the court, however, are virtually never identical to the facts of the prior binding cases; it is because of the factual differences that common law rules often change as the rule developed in prior cases is applied to the facts in the new case. As one legal scholar wrote, "Rules change as rules are applied."[1]

Recall the exercises in Chapter 2, where the courts had to determine whether someone who killed another could still take the assets of the victim. This question was raised by U.S. courts in the twentieth century. In some states, such as Maryland, the

---

1. Levi, *supra* n.3, at 143.

rules were developed through a series of cases, creating a common law rule. Consider the following three cases from the fictitious jurisdiction of East Carolina.[2]

Sellers v. Johnson, 165 S.E. 470 (E.C. 1933)[3]

James Osgood shot and killed his wife after she divorced him. Almost immediately thereafter James Osgood committed suicide. The record contained evidence that the husband had threatened to kill his wife. The wife died without a Last Will and Testament (Will), so the court applied the statute of descent and distribution. The statute designates who takes the assets of a person who dies without a Will. The special probate court[4] held that because James Osgood killed his wife, the husband's relatives, or heirs, and personal representatives could not share in the wife's estate. The court reached this result even though under the statute of descent and distribution the husband's relatives would be able to take one-half of the assets. This decision was affirmed on appeal, and the losing parties have now appealed to this court.

The East Carolina Legislature has not enacted a slayer statute[5] in this state, and this factual question has never been addressed before in this jurisdiction. In reviewing court decisions in other jurisdictions, we find two differing approaches in resolving this issue. The first approach applies the common law principle of equity, providing that "no one shall be permitted to profit by his own fraud, to take advantage of his own wrong, to found any claim upon his own evil, or to acquire property by his own crime." *Madsen v. Jones*, 140 S.E. 23, 25 (E.C. 1920). Under this approach courts will interpret a Will, a life insurance policy, and the statute of descent and distribution to prevent a killer from benefiting from the death of the victim. In reaching this decision, the court focuses on the universally recognized principles of justice and morality.

The second approach recognizes the public policy of the common law but determines that this policy is outweighed by a new and different public policy, which was the basis for the Legislature's enacting one or more statutes. Thus, the Legislature declared its public policy when it enacted the statute to govern how property is disposed when a Will is properly executed, and the common law should not take priority over legislative intent.

We choose to follow the first approach, which prevents one who kills another from benefiting through the estate of the killer's victim. A person cannot lose what he never had; because of the husband's murderous act, he never gained a beneficial interest in

---

2. The three cases from Maryland that have been summarized for purposes of this example are *Shifanellia v. Wallace*, 315 A.2d 513 (Md. App. 1974); *Cordell v. Jenifer*, 150 A.2d 251 (Md. App. 1959); and *Sellers v. Hitaffer*, 165 A. 470 (Md. App. 1933). The internal case citations in each case have been omitted.

3. The information in this parenthetical reveals that this opinion was written by the highest court of our fictitious jurisdiction, East Carolina.

4. A probate court is a special court that rules on matters related to a deceased's estate.

5. A slayer statute prevents a person who kills another to benefit from the victim's death. The specific requirements vary from state to state.

any part of his wife's estate. This court will abide by the rule that no one should be permitted to profit by his own fraud, to take advantage of his own wrong, to found any claim upon his own evil, or to acquire property by his own crime.

The court's decision in *Sellers* sets down the court's first ruling on this legal issue: "No one shall be permitted to profit by his own fraud, to take advantage of his own wrong, to found any claim upon his own evil, or to acquire property by his own crime." Specific to this case, a killer who would otherwise profit under the statute of descent and distribution from the estate of the killer's victim cannot take. Another court addressed the same issue 26 years later.

Cordell v. Roberts, *150 S.E.2d 251 (E.C. 1959)*

This case presents the court with the question whether a wife can recover the proceeds of her husband's life insurance policy when she caused the husband's death. The relationship between this husband and wife had been unstable. The husband at times would drink too much alcohol, become intoxicated, and beat his wife with a weapon. At other times he would become intoxicated but not become violent. On this particular occasion, no evidence was introduced to show that the husband possessed a weapon, although he did slap his wife and make threatening motions. In response, the wife picked up a knife and stabbed her husband to death. The wife was found guilty of manslaughter, not murder, and the judge in the criminal court did not state whether the conviction was for voluntary or involuntary manslaughter.

Manslaughter is different from murder, only because murder requires that the killer plan the killing (premeditation); voluntary manslaughter is intentional, while involuntary manslaughter is not. The wife's representatives contend in this civil suit that her killing was unintentional and, though unlawful and felonious, does not bar her from recovering her husband's insurance proceeds. We find that this killing was intentional, however, so the wife cannot receive the life insurance proceeds.

The court in *Sellers v. Johnson* sets out the basic rule in this state, which is that one who kills ordinarily may not profit by taking any portion of the estate of the one murdered 165 S.E. 470, 470 (E.C. 1933). The court in *Sellers* stated in dicta[6] that this common law principle would apply not only in the case of intestacy, where the victim died without a Last Will and Testament ("Will"), but also to benefits that the killer may receive when the victim had a Will or life insurance policy. *Id.*

This court does not distinguish between murder and manslaughter, because both are felonies and distinguished only by the presence or absence of malice aforethought.[7] Other courts have drawn a line, not between murder and manslaughter but between voluntary and involuntary manslaughter. We need not decide whether to draw the

---

6. Dicta includes statements by a court in its opinion that are not part of the direct holding in the case.
7. Malice aforethought occurs when one plans in advance to do something wrong.

same line here because it is clear that the killing in this case was intentional. The wife did not act in self-defense, nor did she strike her husband by accident. She reacted to her husband's slap on the face with an excessive degree of force; she did not just act negligently or unintentionally. Where the killing is both felonious *and* intentional, the killer cannot benefit, and the lower court's ruling must be affirmed.

The court in *Cordell* expanded the rule set down in *Sellers*: First, the court found that, when determining whether a slayer can take assets from the victim, the same result should occur whether the assets are part of an estate where the deceased victim had no Will (the facts in *Sellers*) or are part of the proceeds of the deceased victim's insurance policy (the facts in *Cordell*). Second, the court found that a slayer can be prohibited from acquiring the assets of the deceased regardless of whether the deceased was convicted of murder or voluntary manslaughter. Both convictions require that the acts be felonious and intentional. This adds to the East Carolina common law rule, since in *Sellers* there was no conviction because the husband committed suicide.

Finally, here is the most recent decision of the three Supreme Court of East Carolina cases addressing the same issue.

Turner v. Heinz, *315 S.E.2d 513 (E.C. 1974)*

This appeal arises out of a dispute over the proceeds of a life insurance policy issued upon the life of Susan A. Heinz, now deceased. Susan was shot by her husband, George Heinz, who was the named beneficiary of Susan's life insurance policy. John Turner, the attorney for Susan's estate, filed a suit in probate court on behalf of Susan's two minor children by prior marriages. Turner argued that the proceeds of Susan's insurance policy should be paid to Susan's estate and not to George. The probate court disagreed and ruled that the proceeds be paid to the named beneficiary, George. We affirm.

The husband George in this case unintentionally killed his wife and was found guilty of gross negligence. In *Cordell v. Roberts*, 150 S.E.2d 251, 252 (E.C. 1959), we found that "[w]here the killing is both felonious and intentional, . . . the beneficiary cannot prevail. . . ." In *Cordell*, a wife was convicted of manslaughter for killing her husband. When someone kills another unintentionally, however, the majority of jurisdictions allow recovery from the deceased. Where there is no intent, the rule that no one should profit by his felony does not apply. Where the death is the result of an accident or even caused by such gross negligence[8] on the part of the beneficiary that he is guilty of involuntary manslaughter, the killer/beneficiary may still recover.

---

8. Gross negligence is when an actor either does something in a conscious, voluntary manner or omits to do something in reckless disregard of a legal duty and the consequences to another party.

In *Turner* the court makes certain what could have been inferred from the reasoning in the former cases: that if a killing is unintentional, the killer may still benefit from the victim's assets.

This synthesis of multiple court holdings into one single common law rule is a prime example of inductive reasoning. Inductive reasoning occurs when you reason from many specific ideas to one general principle. In contrast, deductive reasoning occurs when you reason from one general principle and apply it to a specific situation (such as applying a

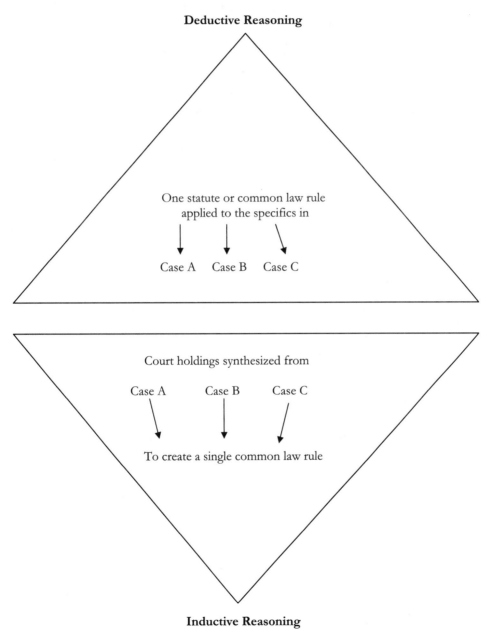

Figure 10-1

statute to individual cases). Figure 10-1 illustrates inductive and deductive reasoning based on the three cases in this chapter.

The resulting common law rule in this example, as developed through the three cases, becomes the following.[9]

A person who kills another

a. *may not* share in the distribution of the decedent's estate as an heir by way of the statute of descent and distribution or as the beneficiary who collects the proceeds under a policy of insurance on the decedent's life when the homicide is felonious and intentional;

b. *may* share in the distribution of the decedent's estate as an heir by way of the statute of descent and distribution, or as one who would otherwise take under the decedent's will, and *may* collect the proceeds as a beneficiary under a policy of insurance on the decedent's life when the homicide is unintentional, even though it is the result of such gross negligence as would render the killer criminally guilty of involuntary manslaughter.

● Exercise 10-A

Read the following case excerpts and write the common law rule applied in each case. Then write the common law rule that would apply in a future case in determining whether a landowner could be liable in negligence for injuries to a trespasser on the landowner's property. To complete this exercise, the rules applied in the cases must be synthesized into one single common law rule.

Case One: **McClain v. Painter,** *439 S.E.2d 555 (E.C. 1976)*

On October 15, 1974, Sarah McClain was walking to school when she saw an apple tree on her neighbor's property, full of apples ready to be eaten. Since she had not eaten breakfast, she went through the neighbor's gate, climbed the tree, and began shaking the limbs so apples would fall to the ground. As she was stretching out for some apples above her, the dead limb she was sitting on gave way, causing Sarah to fall to the ground with the apples, breaking her arm. Sarah's parents brought a negligence claim on behalf of Sarah against Jack Painter, owner of the property with the apple tree. Painter moved to dismiss the case, which was granted by the trial court and affirmed on appeal. The McClains have appealed, and we affirm.

It has been a long-standing rule that landowners owe no duty to trespassers. In this case there is no doubt that Sarah was not invited through the gate, up the tree, and onto the ground where she eventually landed.

Case Two: **Sanders v. Kona Exports, Inc.,** *452 S.E.2d 1040 (E.C. 1978)*

Kona Exports owns a coal mine in Salem, East Carolina. Seven-year-old Johnny Sanders lived in a housing development situated near the coal mine. Kona Exports left

---

9. *Ford v. Ford*, 512 A.2d 389 (Md. 1986).

on its property equipment that was necessary to the mining business, including mining cars used to bring the coal out from the depths of the mine. The cars had brakes and locks that would disable the cars, preventing them from being moved. Unfortunately, the coal mine workers set the brakes but habitually failed to lock the cars at the end of each day.

Johnny and his friend, Tim Rider, would often go over to the mine and play on the equipment left on the property. When the cars were locked the boys would get inside the car and play around; on a couple of occasions, however, the children were there when the cars were unlocked, and they would take off the brake and push one another around. Mine supervisors saw children trespassing near the cars and other equipment; sometimes they told the children to leave, and other times they did not.

On April 24, 1980, Johnny and his friends went onto the property and found the cars unlocked. Johnny climbed into one of the cars, and his friends rolled him around and into the mine. While they were inside a mine wall collapsed, and Johnny died. Johnny's parents, Jim and Cady Sanders, filed a negligent wrongful death claim against the mine owners. The trial court dismissed the case, relying on the general rule that landowners owe no duty to trespassers. After the court of appeals affirmed the trial court's decision, the Sanders appealed.

Courts have long held that landowners are not liable to trespassers on their land. *McClain v. Painter*, 439 S.E.2d 555, 555 (E.C. 1976). However, Kona Exports keeps on its land machinery that is known to be dangerous, machinery that could be safeguarded. The landowner was also aware that children trespassed onto the land. Due to the nature of the condition and the knowledge by the landowner that children trespass on the land, a jury may find the landowner liable in negligence. The trial court's dismissal of this case is reversed, and the case is remanded for trial.

Case Three: Vinson v. Hirokawa Imports, *530 S.E.2d 12 (E.C. 1980)*

Susie Vinson is 14 years old. She and her friends rode their skateboards onto a construction site of Hirokawa Imports, located in Spring Valley, East Carolina. Hirokawa was building a warehouse to hold its goods. Workers neatly stacked the construction materials for the warehouse. Because some of the workers had seen children in the area before, the supervisor placed signs at multiple locations, instructing trespassers to stay off the construction site.

Susie decided to try and ride her skateboard across the top of the stacked construction materials. The construction materials were steel beams that were being used to build the main structure of the warehouse. The top of the stacked beams was approximately ten feet from the ground. Susie began climbing up the side of the stacked beams when they broke loose, falling down on top of Susie, who was seriously injured.

At trial the jury found for the plaintiff and awarded the Vinsons $100,000, which was affirmed by the court of appeals. We granted the appeal of Hirokawa Exports, Inc., and now reverse.

In this case the general rule that landowners owe no duty to those trespassing on their land applies. *McClain v. Painter*, 439 S.E.2d 555, 555 (E.C. 1976). A 14-year-old teenager who is of normal or above intelligence has the capacity to understand the danger that exists in going onto construction sites and playing on the materials left by the workers. These workers had no choice but to leave the materials on site, and they apparently tried to keep the materials stacked in an orderly manner. The supervisor also posted multiple "No trespassing" signs, which a 14-year-old of normal intelligence could easily read and understand. When a child is old enough and has sufficient intelligence to appreciate the danger on another's property, the landowner will not be held liable for the child trespasser's injuries. Reversed.

Case Four: Jackson v. Wayne, *570 S.E.2d 1224 (E.C. 1982)*

Kenny Jackson, a five-year-old, often went to a neighbor's swimming pool with his parents to swim. On June 23, 1997, Kenny was at home with his mother, Sylvia Jackson. Mrs. Jackson put Kenny down for a nap and went into another room to watch television. When Mrs. Jackson went into the bedroom to check on Kenny, she found the bedroom window open and Kenny missing. Mrs. Jackson could see the swimming pool in the neighbor's yard from the open window; at the same time she heard a neighbor screaming. She ran next door and found the neighbor struggling to pull Kenny out of the pool. Kenny was rushed to the hospital for care. He survived but now suffers from brain damage.

In an affidavit, a neighbor stated that she saw Kenny walk into the neighbors', the Waynes', open gate and toward the pool. Apparently he started to walk down the pool steps but then slipped, according to the neighbor, because he fell and slid into the water. She thought he hit his head on the concrete steps. Upon inspection, the emergency workers and the neighbor found a slippery substance, later determined to be sun tanning oil, at the top of the steps.

The judge granted defendant Wayne's motion for summary judgment and dismissed the case, and the court of appeals affirmed. The Jacksons have appealed.

There are conflicting policy reasons for allowing this case to go to trial. Courts used to hold that water was an open, apparent danger for which a landowner could not be held responsible. As the law has evolved, the rules have become less exact. Further, courts have held that even if an injury occurs due to a water-related accident, if the landowner negligently maintains the water or the areas surrounding the water, the landowner may be held liable for the dangerous condition.

However, courts also recognize the need for parents to supervise their children, particularly those children of an age where they are unable to appreciate the danger before them or the potential dangerous consequences of their acts. At those times courts have found the parents and not the landowner responsible for the unfortunate injuries of their very young child. Parents have the responsibility to guide and protect their children, especially those children such as this five-year-old child who are too young to take care of themselves.

In this case the facts were not clear as to whether the child's injuries were due to the water or the fall on the pool steps. There is also some question about whether the landowner negligently maintained the pool and whether the landowner knew or should have known about the dangerous condition near the pool. A landowner cannot be held liable for something of which he does not or should not know. Further, a jury must determine whether the parents' lack of supervision over their child prevents them from recovering from the landowner or at least reduces the damages awarded to the parents.

These cases must be decided on a case-by-case basis, assessing carefully the individual facts before the court. There are sufficient factual disputes in this case to warrant sending the case to trial.

Reversed and remanded for trial.

● Exercise 10-B

In the United States, a man who wants to marry a woman (the prospective groom) often gives the woman (the prospective bride) a special ring when he asks her to marry him. Read the following excerpts and write the common law rule applied in each case. Then write the common law rule that would apply in a future case in determining whether a prospective groom could recover an engagement ring he gave to his prospective bride after the engagement is broken. To complete this exercise all the rules applied in the cases must be synthesized into one single common law rule.

Case One: Smith v. Keener, 754 S.E.2d 43 (E.C. App. 1998)

John Smith proposed to Sandy Keener and gave her an engagement ring. John and Sandy agreed that if something happened and they did not get married, Sandy would return the ring to John. Four months later, Sandy learned that John had been seeing another woman. Sandy broke their engagement, and John then asked for the engagement ring back. Sandy refused to return the ring, and John brought a lawsuit to order its return. The trial court found that Sandy could keep the ring. John has appealed.

After a broken engagement, an explicit agreement made between the parties as to who will keep the ring should the engagement be broken will dictate ownership of the ring. It doesn't matter that John was unfaithful; Sandy must return the ring.

Reversed and remanded with instructions. *ring goes to bought*

Case Two: Jones v. Beck, 782 S.E.2d 113 (E.C. App. 2001)

Sam Jones and Cathy Clauson became engaged on February 14, 1998. They planned to be married on March 23, 1999; four weeks before the wedding Sam broke their engagement. After multiple efforts to get Cathy to return the engagement ring, Sam sued. The lower court found for Sam and ordered Cathy to return to Sam either the ring or its value. Cathy now appeals.

Though jurisdictions address this issue in different ways, this court considers an engagement ring to be a conditional gift. When the condition — the engagement to be married — is broken, the ring must be returned to the donor, the prospective groom.

Reversed. *ring goes to donor, conditional gift →*

Case Three: Singer v. Lansing, 880 S.E.2d 409 (E.C. App. 2003)

Laura Lansing, a single 25-year-old woman, began to date Jim Singer in the spring of 2001. At the time, Jim Singer was married to Nancy Singer. Jim promised Laura that he would get a divorce from his wife and marry Laura. To prove his commitment to Laura, he bought her an engagement ring. No wedding date was set, and while Jim continued to express his love for Laura he never took any steps toward leaving his wife.

After six months, Laura broke up with Jim, who then demanded that Laura return the engagement ring. When Laura refused, Jim sued. After Jim presented his case, the trial judge awarded Laura's motion for a directed verdict.[10] Jim has appealed the trial court's decision.

Notions of equity dictate that the party seeking equitable relief (in this case the return of a ring) must come to court with "clean hands"; here the party seeking relief, Jim Singer, violated the bonds of marriage by engaging in an affair outside his own marriage. He did not, therefore, come to court with clean hands and is not in a position to ask a court to grant him any equitable relief.

Affirmed.

---

10. A party moving for a directed verdict (or JMOL) claims that the opposing party has not sufficiently proved his or her case, justifying the judge's dismissal of the case.

CHAPTER

11

Beyond the Single TRAC: Structuring an Analysis of Multiple Fact-Based Issues

HIGHLIGHTS

- The structure of a legal analysis when addressing multiple legal questions depends on the legal test used to resolve each legal issue.
- A legal test that requires an analysis of multiple elements, or requirements, is usually structured element by element.
- A legal test that requires an analysis of various factors, or considerations, is usually structured factor by factor, with the analyzed factors weighed together at the end.
- A legal test that requires a balancing of the merits of each party's position is usually structured by first setting out the relevant law for each party and then weighing one party's argument against the other to determine which position is stronger.
- Some legal tests require different parties to meet certain burdens of proof; once met, the burden then shifts to the opposing party to prove the next part of the legal test, and the analysis tracks the shifting burdens of proof.

 ## A. Introduction

Analyzing legal issues would be easier if each analysis involved only one single question based on one simple organizational structure; this, however, is not the case. Legal tests may be created by a legislature in a statute or by an administrative agency required to establish rules based on a statute; the tests may also be created judicially through the common law. A legal test that contains multiple requirements, all which must be met to establish the test, is called an elements analysis. Another legal test, known as a factors analysis, has no requirements but weighs the strength of different factors to determine the outcome. These are just two of the types of legal tests applied to determine the outcome of a legal issue.

Understanding the law and the tests the legislature or the courts have created is vital to an effective analysis and may create a different structure than in non-legal documents. This difference is due to how lawyers and judges solve problems when faced with litigation. In the broadest sense, lawyers and judges strive to resolve conflicts between parties. This definition is itself broad, however, because it includes non-lawyer problem solving such as what psychiatrists and marriage counselors do. The more accurate definition of what lawyers and judges do is to try and solve conflicts between parties using the rules set by the government and the judiciary as their starting point.

This last definition of problem solving provides the key difference between the structure of nonlegal and many legal documents. Understanding the law and the tests the legislature or courts have created in order to analyze the law is vital to a good analysis, since the legal test creates the basic structure of the analysis.

Your goal is to structure your legal analysis to reflect the approach courts in prior binding decisions have used in analyzing and answering a legal issue. If you are not sure how to structure a legal analysis, use the relevant court opinions as your guide. If the court separates its discussion of a legal test by elements or factors, for example, consider doing the same.

As stated in earlier chapters, one of the best guidelines to keep in mind is that as a legal writer you bring in information only when it becomes most relevant to your legal reader. This is why TRAC serves as a logical checklist for your analysis. For example, when analyzing a rule of law that has both a general rule and one or more exceptions to the rule, logic dictates that you would address the general rule before analyzing the exceptions. Or, when analyzing a rule of law with its own multipart test, use the multipart test to create the overall basic structure of your analysis. What follows are suggestions for the basic structure of a discussion, depending on the legal test raised. As discussed in Chapter 9, on using multiple cases in a single analysis, and in Chapter 12, on addressing legal issues that are not in dispute, the final structure may change depending on the specifics of a case.

B. Alternative Ways to Structure a Discussion of a Single Legal Issue

1. Elements analysis

An elements analysis sets out specific requirements that must be met in order to prove a legal test. In the covenant not to compete (CNC) example provided throughout this text, the reasonableness of a CNC is based on three elements: (1) the covenant cannot be broader than necessary for the protection of the buyer/covenantee in some legitimate interest, (2) the covenant cannot have an adverse effect on the seller, and (3) the covenant cannot have an adverse effect on the public interest. The overall basic structure of these elements might look like the following.

Topic/thesis   Legal issue being addressed

Rule   Statement of the elements that must be met in order to satisfy the legal issue

[*Note*: At this point you have identified multiple requirements that must be analyzed in order to answer the legal issue. If you continue by explaining the definitions and explanations of all the cases relevant to the requirements, you may confuse your reader because you are providing more information than your legal reader can grasp or remember. You are not bringing in information where it is most helpful to your reader. Further, because the court must find that all the requirements have been met in order to find the legal issue satisfied or, alternatively, must find that one of the requirements has *not* been met in order to find the legal issue is not satisfied, an element-by-element analysis is the most logical way to begin structuring this objective analysis. You may decide later to move various sections around, but it is the most logical way to begin. The overall analysis of this legal issue with multiple requirements, therefore, is composed of the analysis of each legal requirement, each with its own TRAC checklist:]

Analysis/Application of the Law to the Facts

Topic/thesis:	Element #1
Rule:	Any definition or explanation of element #1
Rule explanation:	Any case law relevant to explain how the courts have analyzed the element in different factual situations
Analysis:	Application of the law to the client's facts to assess the strengths and weaknesses in determining whether the element has been met
Conclusion:	Regarding element #1 only

Topic/thesis:	Element #2
Rule:	Any definition and explanation of element #2
Rule explanation:	Any case law relevant to explain how the courts have analyzed the element in different factual situations
Analysis:	Application of the law to the client's facts to assess the strengths and weaknesses in determining whether the element has been met
Conclusion:	Regarding element #2 only

Topic/thesis:	Element #3
Rule:	Any definition or explanation of element #3
Rule explanation:	Any case law relevant to explain how the courts have analyzed the element in different factual situations
Analysis:	Application of the case law to the client's facts to assess the strengths and weaknesses in determining whether the element has been met
Conclusion:	Regarding element #3 only

Conclusion: Regarding the main legal issue

Sub-elements :

What if one of the three elements in the example above has its own elements analysis? As you may guess, this requires a further breakdown in the structure.

Topic/thesis:	Element #3
Rule:	To satisfy element #3, two sub-elements must be met (and state the two elements)

Analysis/application of the law to the facts:

Topic/thesis:	Re: sub-element #1
Rule:	Definition and explanation of sub-element #1
Rule explanation:	Regarding sub-element #1
Analysis:	Application of law to facts to analyze sub-element #1
Conclusion:	Re: sub-element #1

Topic/thesis:	Re: sub-element #2
Rule:	Definition and explanation of sub-element #2
Rule explanation:	Regarding sub-element #2
Analysis:	Application of law to facts to analyze sub-element #2
Conclusion:	Re: sub-element #2

Conclusion: Regarding element #3

Since finding that any one of the elements or <u>sub-elements</u> will defeat a claim that the legal test has been met, the most logical structure is to analyze each requirement separately from all other requirements. By following this structure, you make it easier for your reader to understand the legal significance of your analysis. One word of caution, however: If an element is obviously in dispute and you conclude that the element is likely not met, you should not stop your analysis there. You need to complete your analysis of the remaining required elements because a court might find that, in contrast to your conclusion, the first element has, in fact, been satisfied.

2. Factors analysis

The structure of a factors analysis often depends on the numbers and complexity of the factors used in determining a legal issue. If a further breakdown of the factors is warranted, the structure of the factors analysis looks much like that of the elements analysis, with one additional component. After assessing the strengths and weaknesses of each factor, it is necessary to weigh the factors together to predict a likely outcome regarding the legal issue. For example, many statutes covering residential burglary require that a burglary takes place in a dwelling. To determine whether a structure legally is a dwelling, courts look at factors such as (1) the composition or nature of the structure, (2) the use of the structure, and (3) the frequency of the use of the structure. These factors do not all need to be met in order to satisfy the dwelling requirement; they are only considerations courts use to determine whether the building is a dwelling. One basic way to structure a factors analysis is as follows.

Topic/thesis: Legal issue being addressed
Rule: List of factors a court uses to determine the legal issue raised in this example (here based on two factors)
Analysis:

Topic/thesis:	Factor #1
Rule:	Any definition and explanation of factor #1
Rule explanation:	Any case law relevant to explain how the courts have analyzed factor #1 in different factual situations
Analysis:	Application of the law to the client's facts to assess the strengths and weaknesses of factor #1
Conclusion:	Regarding factor #1 only

[*Note*: There may be times when a conclusion at this point is not appropriate; rather, a single conclusion after discussing and weighing all the factors together may work best.]

Topic/thesis:	Factor #2
Rule:	Any definition and explanation of factor #2
Rule explanation:	Any case law relevant to explain how the courts have analyzed factor #2 in different factual situations
Analysis:	Application of the law to the client's facts to assess the strengths and weaknesses of factor #2
Conclusion:	Regarding factor #2 only

Weighing/balancing factors #1 and #2 to determine whether, collectively, they support finding that the legal issue had been met.

Conclusion: Regarding the legal issue

Again, remember that the suggested organizational scheme above is not an absolute formula that you must follow in all cases. You may decide, for example, to combine factors, or, if the number of factors is small and the analysis is straightforward, to address all factors together.

Determining the most logical structure is best achieved by reviewing the document from the reader's viewpoint. If you find that the draft is difficult to follow because you have combined factors, rewrite it, separating one or more factors. If, conversely, you find that the factors are introduced separately in a way that makes the final weighing of the factors difficult to follow, rewrite it, combining one or more factors.

A good source in determining this structure is, again, the relevant court opinions. If you find that binding courts tend to separate the factors, do that as well. If, however, binding court opinions tend to group factors together, this is likely the best approach in your own discussion. The final decision may also depend on whether the factor is or is not disputable.

3. Balancing test

Some legal issues involve balancing the opposing parties' positions to determine which is stronger. This test is often used when assessing the validity of a constitutional claim. For example, let's say that a citizen is prohibited from protesting on a courthouse lawn. To determine whether the citizen's First Amendment right to free speech under the U.S. Constitution has been violated, a court must weigh the government's interest in maintaining a peaceful environment on public, governmental property against an individual's right to speak her own political thoughts. An example of the need to balance interests in a criminal case may occur when a police officer stops a suspect, searches him, and finds drugs in his pocket. Since the police officer does not have a warrant, the defendant might move to suppress introducing the evidence of drugs in court. The court must balance the governmental interest in bringing to justice criminals against the individual's right under the Fourth Amendment to be free from unwarranted governmental intrusions.

Balancing tests exist in state law issues as well. In a state nuisance action, for example, the court must weigh a plaintiff homeowner's complaint that the defendant neighbor's actions are intruding on the homeowner's right to the peaceful enjoyment of his property against the neighbor's right to use and enjoy her own property.

The structure of a balancing test might look like the following.

Topic/thesis:	Legal question (such as nuisance) that is based on a balancing test
Rule:	Statement of the balancing test
Rule explanation:	Description of relevant case law where courts applied the same balancing test in a similar factual situation (case law may also be introduced when the weaker position is introduced)
Analysis:	Application of the law to the facts
	Support for the stronger position
	Support for the weaker position
Conclusion:	Why, when weighing one party's interest against the other, the first position is stronger.

4. *Shifting burdens of proof test*

Sometimes deciding a legal issue includes both procedural and substantive components. For example, in a lawsuit where a female plaintiff is fired and sues her former employer for sexual discrimination the plaintiff employee bears the initial burden to show that the employer fired her for a discriminatory reason based on her gender. If the employee meets this initial burden, the burden shifts to the defendant employer to prove a nondiscriminatory reason for firing the employee. If the employer is able to meet its burden, the burden shifts again back to the employee, who then has an opportunity to prove that the employer's stated reason for firing the employee is really a pretext (or false reason) for the actual, discriminatory reason.[1] The structure of the analysis would follow the structure of the shifting burdens test, as follows.

Topic/thesis:	Re: legal issue being addressed
Rule:	Statement of the shifting burdens of proof test
Rule explanation (optional):	Any case law descriptions where courts have applied the same test to similar factual situations
Analysis:	

---

1. The burdens of proof for indirect employment discrimination claims have been established in *McDonnell Douglas Corp. v. Green*, 411 U.S. 792 (1973), and later clarified in *Tex. Dept. of Community Affairs v. Burdine*, 450 U.S. 248 (1981).

Topic/thesis:	Re: first test (plaintiff's burden)
Rule:	Any explanation/definition of the first test
Rule explanation:	Case law descriptions where courts have applied the same test to similar factual situations
Analysis:	Application of the law to the client's facts (stronger then weaker position)
Conclusion:	Regarding first test

Topic/thesis:	Re: second test (defendant's burden)
Rule:	Any explanation/definition of second test
Rule explanation:	Case law descriptions where courts have applied the same test to similar factual situations
Analysis:	Application of law to the client's facts (stronger then weaker position)
Conclusion:	Regarding second test

Topic/thesis:	Re: third test (plaintiff's burden)
Rule:	Any explanation/definition of third test
Rule explanation:	Case law descriptions where courts have applied the same test to similar factual situations
Analysis:	Application of law to the client's facts (stronger then weaker position)
Conclusion:	Regarding third test

Conclusion:	Regarding legal issue

Again, notice in the above examples that the outlines refer only generally to the structure of the objective analysis. The examples do not include where to place specific information such as case explanations, relevant public policy considerations, and the like. Placement of specific information depends on the specific questions raised and the extent of the relevant case law.

C. Tell the Reader What Is to Come: Providing a Framework Section for the Discussion

Again, strive to provide information when it becomes most relevant to the legal reader. This guideline is essential when determining what to provide in the first section of an objective discussion. What to include depends on the result of the merger of the law with the client's facts.

1. A topic or thesis sentence

You always want to tell the reader your purpose in writing a document. The purpose usually originates in the supervising attorney's instructions to an associate in a law firm. It is quite likely, however, that someone other than the supervising attorney ultimately will read the document. Setting out the purpose of the document at the beginning tells the reader the scope of the analysis and helps any reader who is not familiar with the case.

Let's return to the covenant not to compete (CNC) example used in prior chapters. A topic sentence might read as follows.

> The issue is whether the CNC that Ana Hart has been ordered by the court to sign is overbroad in its protection of David Hart's business interests and is therefore unreasonable.

If you wanted to change the topic sentence into a thesis sentence and also include your conclusion on the legal issue, you might write this.

> The CNC that Ana Hart has been ordered by the court to sign is likely overbroad in its protection of David Hart's business interests and is therefore unreasonable.

Include also in the framework paragraph some factual context for the legal issue being addressed. You need provide only enough of the client's story to enable the reader to understand why the legal issue is in dispute. This factual context may be included with the main issue statement or it may follow in a sentence or two.

In the CNC example, a thesis provided within the factual context might read as follows.

> The CNC that Ana Hart has been ordered by the court to sign as part of her divorce settlement is likely overbroad in its protection of David Hart's business interests and is therefore unreasonable. David and Ana Hart owned a health and exercise club business; David petitioned for and the court ordered that David buy Ana's interest for fair market value and Ana sell her interest and sign a covenant not to compete.

2. Any relevant rules

This framework or introductory section, sometimes also called a roadmap, usually contains the main rule you are applying to resolve the legal issue. This may be a constitutional provision, a statute, or a common law rule. If the main rule used to determine the legal issue has its own constituent parts, as with an elements or factors analysis, setting out the main rule means setting out those elements or factors used to determine the outcome of the legal issue.

An example of a framework section in Ana Hart's CNC case is as follows.

> The covenant not to compete that Ana Hart has been ordered by the court to sign as part of her divorce settlement is likely overbroad in its protection of David Hart's business interests and is therefore unreasonable. David and Ana Hart owned a health and exercise club business; David petitioned for and the court ordered that David buy Ana's interest at fair market value and Ana sell her interest and sign a covenant not to compete (CNC).
>
> East Carolina courts use the following three-pronged test to determine whether a CNC signed as part of the sale of a business is unreasonable: "(1) the covenant must not be broader than necessary for the protection of the [buyer] covenantee's legitimate business interest; (2) the covenant cannot have an adverse effect on the [seller] covenantor; and (3) the covenant cannot adversely effect the public interest." *Mats Transp. v. ABC Corp.*, 824 S.E.2d 1467, 1468 (E.C. App. 1992).
>
> [As discussed earlier, what follows would be a discussion, using the TRAC checklist of each of the three requirements, concluding at the end whether the CNC was or was not reasonable.]

3. Stipulations

Stipulations occur when opposing parties agree on the outcome of a legal issue or point, thus eliminating the need to argue the issue or point during the pretrial stage or at trial. Once you set out the main rule, it is appropriate to set out any stipulations agreed to by the parties. If you provide a stipulation *before* explaining the law, however, you are not providing the legal context that your reader needs to understand why the stipulation is legally relevant. For example, consider the following framework section.

> The covenant not to compete that Ana Hart has been ordered by the court to sign as part of her divorce settlement is likely overbroad in its protection of David Hart's business interests and is therefore unreasonable. David and Ana Hart owned a health and exercise club business; David petitioned for and the court ordered that David buy Ana's interest at fair market value and Ana sell her interest and sign a covenant not to compete (CNC). Both parties agree that the sale of this health club does not affect the public interest.
>
> East Carolina courts use the following three-pronged test to determine whether a CNC signed as part of the sale of a business is unreasonable: "(1) the

covenant must not be broader than necessary for the protection of the [buyer] covenantee's legitimate business interest; (2) the covenant cannot have an adverse affect on the [seller] covenantor; and (3) the covenant cannot adversely affect the public interest." *Mats Transport v. ABC Corp.*, 824 S.E.2d 1467, 1468 (E.C. App. 1992).

If your reader does not know the law governing CNCs, the legal significance of your stipulation at the end of the first paragraph, "Both parties agree that the sale of the health club does not affect the public interest," will likely be confusing until your reader gets to the definition that includes the requirement that the covenant not "adversely affect the public interest." And because you have not placed the information in the appropriate order, your reader likely will have to go back and reread the earlier reference, so the facts are tied to the appropriate legal point. The better structure is to provide the stipulation immediately after the three-pronged test. Because the parties have stipulated that requirement number three of the legal test has been met, you don't need to provide an analysis of this requirement and can focus on the remaining two requirements.

● Exercise 11-A

Your professor will provide you with the case excerpts to use for this exercise. Read the case excerpts and determine (1) what legal test the court applied in reaching its decision, and (2) how to set out the basic structure of the legal test.

CHAPTER

12

Analyzing the Law: Using Multiple Cases in Analyzing Multiple Issues

HIGHLIGHTS

- When writing a structured discussion with multiple issues or sub-issues, address each legal point separately.
- When a single case is relevant to more than one legal point, explain the key facts, the court's holding, and the court's reasoning as it becomes relevant to each legal point.
- Separate the parts of a legal test, and create a chart or outline of the legal test as soon as possible, placing relevant information from the case law where appropriate in your chart or outline.
- When addressing a fact-based issue, creating a chart of each legal point that includes both the client's facts and the facts from the relevant cases better ensures that your analysis is accurate and complete.
- When analyzing a rule with elements, or requirements, you must address all the elements, even those not in dispute in your client's case.
- When writing an objective discussion, let logic guide your choices about the order in which to place the multiple issues.

A. Introduction

Chapter 7 addresses how to analyze a single issue using a single case; Chapter 9 addresses how to analyze a single issue using multiple cases; and Chapter 11 addresses the various legal tests and the basic outlines for each. This chapter adds to the guidance from those chapters and focuses on how to analyze a client's case when it involves multiple issues and multiple cases.

As discussed in Chapter 11, the law usually creates the basic structure of the analysis. For example, the law may require an elements analysis, a factors analysis, a rule with one or more exceptions, or a balancing test. In many instances, the analysis of a client's case requires a combination of these legal tests.

To illustrate how to analyze a client's case when multiple issues and cases are involved, consider this example: In *Excel, Inc. v. Milton Hotels*, a buyer in East Carolina, the president of Milton Hotels, ordered special towels for his chain of hotel spas. He placed this order with a seller in East Carolina, Excel, Inc. Excel manufactures and sells towels, specifically focusing its business on the manufacture and sale of large quantities of towels to hotel chains. The buyer ordered 50,000 light pink and purple towels, which were the colors used in the hotel spas. The towels were to cost $500,000. The agreement was finalized through a series of e-mail exchanges. One e-mail followed a phone conversation and verified that Excel would add a logo of a jogger on the lower left-hand corner of the towels. Some of the e-mails had a signature block (a place for the sender's signature), but some, including the one verifying the addition of the logo to the towels, did not. The president of Milton Hotels was later terminated for mismanagement of company funds. The new president sent a fax to Excel, canceling the contract. Excel is suing Milton Hotels for breach of contract.

This contract would be covered by East Carolina state law and specifically the statute of frauds, which provides that any contract (1) for the sale of goods that (2) exceeds $500 must (3) be in writing and (4) be signed by the party against whom enforcement is sought. This statute creates an elements analysis. If any one of the four elements of the statute of frauds is not met, however, another section of the statute of frauds states that the contract may still be enforced if the seller can prove that the goods were specially manufactured for the buyer. This is an exception to the general rule that a contract such as this must be in writing.

The East Carolina statute of frauds states that, to determine whether the goods are "specially manufactured," the seller must prove three elements, that is, that "(1) the goods are to be manufactured specially for the buyer, (2) the goods are not suitable for sale to others in the ordinary course of the seller's business, and (3) the seller has made a substantial beginning of their manufacture prior to repudiation by the buyer. . . ."[1]

Thus, in *Excel*, the logical structure is to first analyze whether the main provision of the statute of frauds has been met, which is an elements analysis, and then analyze whether, if the statute has not been met, the contract can still be enforced under the specially manufactured goods exception to the statute of frauds requirement. This analysis of the exception is based on yet another elements analysis.

In analyzing the specially manufactured goods exception to the statute of frauds, you would follow the same basic legal analysis structure discussed in previous chapters and address each of the three requirements separately. Even if you conclude that one of the requirements is likely not met, you should still address all three requirements. If the requirement is disputable, that is, that reasonable arguments can be made to support

---

1. E.C. Stat. § 26-1-2-201(3)(a) (2007).

each party's position, your conclusion may be wrong, so you must analyze the other requirements as well.

B. Using Multiple Cases When the Client's Case Involves Multiple Fact-Based Legal Issues

This section discusses how to use case law that addresses more than one of the legal points being analyzed. For example, let's say you have found four cases (A, B, C, and D) that are helpful in analyzing whether the client's case meets the statutory exception to the statute of frauds. Each of the courts in these cases, however, did not rule on all three requirements. This might happen when a court finds that one of the elements is not met in the case, so the court does not address the remaining elements. Alternatively, when certain points are obviously met in a case, a court may not provide any reasoning when establishing the element.

Keeping in mind that you want to bring in information only when it is most relevant to your reader, you may chart the law. This chart will help you understand the overall structure of the law you are analyzing and which cases are relevant to each legal point you are addressing. The following is a chart of Cases A, B, C, and D, showing which legal requirements of the specially manufactured goods exception were addressed by the courts.

ELEMENTS → AUTHORITY ↓	1. SPECIALLY MANUFACTURED FOR BUYER	2. NOT SUITABLE FOR SALE IN THE ORDINARY COURSE OF BUSINESS	3. SUBSTANTIAL BEGINNING ON MANUFACTURE PRIOR TO REPUDIATION
Case A	X		X
Case B	X		
Case C		X	X
Case D		X	

Figure 12-1

When analyzing the first requirement, you will refer only to Cases A and B; when analyzing the second requirement, you will refer only to Cases C and D; and when analyzing the third requirement, you will refer only to Cases A and C.

C. Deciding Where to Place the Rule Explanations

When a single case is relevant to more than one legal requirement, as in this example, you must decide where to place the rule explanations. If you provide a rule explanation only once, at the beginning of the discussion of the issue, and include all the information from the case that is relevant to *all* the legal requirements the court addressed, two things are likely to happen:

(1) your reader must read more than is necessary to acquire the key facts, the court's holding, and the court's reasoning as it relates to each legal requirement; and

(2) your reader likely will have to return to the single case explanation at the beginning of the discussion when reading about a later requirement discussed in the same case, to determine which facts, and which parts of the court's holding and reasoning are relevant to the later legal requirement or where the same case applies.

Keeping in mind that you want to bring in information when it is most relevant to your reader, the preferred method is to explain the case twice, within the TRAC of each legal requirement. The key facts, the court's holding, and the court's reasoning (F/H/R) relevant to one requirement will be different from the key facts, the court's holding, and the court's reasoning for a different requirement.

Thus, an explanation of Case A would be found twice: when addressing requirement 1, you would provide the *key facts* the court relied on to determine whether the goods were "specially manufactured for the buyer," whether the court did, in fact, find the goods specially manufactured (*court's holding*), and why the court did or did not find the goods specially manufactured (*court's reasoning*). When addressing requirement 3, you would provide the *key facts* the court in Case A relied on to determine whether there had been a "substantial beginning of their manufacture prior to repudiation by the buyer," whether the court did, in fact, find there had been a substantial beginning (*court's holding*), and why the court did or did not find there had been a substantial beginning of their manufacture (*court's reasoning*). The chart of Cases A, B, C, and D would look like the following.

ELEMENTS ⟶ AUTHORITY ↓	1. GOODS MUST HAVE BEEN SPECIALLY MANUFACTURED FOR BUYER	2. GOODS ARE NOT SUITABLE FOR SALE IN THE ORDINARY COURSE OF BUSINESS	3. SELLER UNDERWENT SUBSTANTIAL BEGINNING ON MANUFACTURE PRIOR TO REPUDIATION
Case A	F/H/R Re: whether the goods were specially manufactured for the buyer		F/H/R Re: whether the seller made a substantial beginning prior to the buyer's repudiation
Case B	F/H/R Re: whether the goods were specially manufactured for the buyer		

ELEMENTS ⟶ AUTHORITY ↓	1. GOODS MUST HAVE BEEN SPECIALLY MANUFACTURED FOR BUYER	2. GOODS ARE NOT SUITABLE FOR SALE IN THE ORDINARY COURSE OF BUSINESS	3. SELLER UNDERWENT SUBSTANTIAL BEGINNING ON MANUFACTURE PRIOR TO REPUDIATION
Case C		F/H/R Re: whether goods were suitable for sale to others in seller's ordinary course of business	F/H/R Re: whether seller made a substantial beginning on the manufacture prior to the buyer's repudiation
Case D		F/H/R Re: whether goods were suitable for sale to others in seller's ordinary course of business	

F = Facts relevant to the legal point being addressed
H = Holding by the court regarding the legal point
R = Reasoning by the court regarding the legal point

Figure 12-2

The first time you explain a case, provide not only the key facts, the court's holding, and the court's reasoning regarding the specific legal point you are addressing but also the overall holding in the case. For example, if you first explain Case A when providing the TRAC for the requirement that the goods be "specially manufactured for the buyer," you would also include whether the court found that the specially manufactured goods exception to the statute of frauds was met. In addition, when first explaining a case, provide any background information necessary to put the case in the proper context so your reader understands why the dispute arose.

 ## D. Creating a Chart of the Facts for the Analysis of a Fact-Based Issue

Creating a chart can also be helpful when determining how to use the facts of your client's case as well as the facts of the cited cases in the analysis. For example, let's say that in *Excel*, the court found that the e-mails did not satisfy the signature requirement of the statute of frauds. The issue then becomes whether the goods fall within the specially manufactured goods exception to the statute of frauds. You remember that prior to Excel's beginning the manufacture of the towels, Milton Hotels' president had altered the spa towel order to include a jogger in the lower left-hand corner of each towel. After the order was canceled, Excel could sell only 1,000 of the 5,000 towels manufactured after trying for three months, by adding stitching to the jogger so it looked like a flower. In assessing requirement 2 of the exception, which addresses whether the goods would be suitable for sale to others in the ordinary course of business, you have found the two following cases.[2]

Case One: Savilla Manufacturing v. American Crate Co., 778 S.E.2d 1045 (E.C. 1995)

Seller Savilla Manufacturing agreed to set up a cleat manufacturing plant in Honduras, to sell cleats to a crate manufacturer, American Crate Company. Cleats are the pieces of wood placed on the bottom of crates to raise the crate off the ground. American Crate agreed to purchase all the cleats Savilla could produce. The only evidence of this oral agreement was a vague letter written by Juan Carlos, president of Savilla, and signed by American Crate's president, Dave Dormand. About one year after Savilla began production, Dormand refused to purchase Savilla's entire output of cleats. Savilla, after failing to find other purchasers, went out of business.

The lower court appropriately ruled that the signed letter was not a "contract for sale" and was, therefore, insufficient to satisfy the writing requirement of the statute of frauds. The only relevant exception to the writing requirement would be that relating to specially manufactured goods. However, the cleats were not so unusual as to qualify for this exception. The cleats are merely wooden sticks that form the frame of a crate; they were not so unusual or special that the very fact of their manufacture can testify to the existence of a contract for their sale to a particular buyer without written proof as required by the statute of frauds. The lower court also noted that the cleats were not manufactured specifically for American Crate, as evidenced by the fact that Savilla was able to sell one container of the 100 containers of cleats to a different crate company. Affirmed.

Case Two: By Special Order, Inc. v. Hayakawa, Inc., 998 S.E.2d 587 (E.C. 2003) (BSO)

This case involves the application of the specially manufactured goods exception to the statute of frauds. Apparently the seller, By Special Order, Inc. (BSO), entered into an oral agreement with the buyer, Hayakawa, Inc. (Hayakawa), to design, construct, and mass-produce custom candle-rack fixtures. BSO manufactures custom designed retail store fixtures of all kinds. On three occasions, the president of BSO, James Olsen, informed Hayakawa that the construction of the prototype racks would be expensive and that if the company decided not to purchase a substantial number of the racks after the prototypes had been constructed, then Hayakawa would have to reimburse BSO for the cost of their construction. Prototypes are original models designed and created prior to the mass production of the goods. Hayakawa specified the desired dimensions of the racks to Olsen, and Olsen had sketches drafted of the prototypes, which were approved by Hayakawa's agent. Hayakawa then instructed Olsen to continue with the construction of the prototypes, which cost $2,750. The completed prototypes were also approved by Hayakawa's representatives. After several

---

2. The two hypothetical cases from East Carolina are based on *Maderas Tropicales v. S. Crate & Veneer*, 588 F.2d 971 (5th Cir. 1979), and *Bloom & Son, Inc. v. Kameyama, U.S.A., Inc.*, 1984 WL 560329 (R.I. Super. Dec. 4, 1984).

weeks Olsen had received no order, so he mailed a bill to Hayakawa for $2,750. Hayakawa refused to pay.

The lower court found that the specially manufactured goods exception was met in this case, and we agree. BSO would be unable to sell the prototypes to another purchaser in the ordinary course of its business. The crucial inquiry is whether the manufacturer could sell the goods in the ordinary course of its business to someone other than the original buyer. If with slight alterations the goods could be sold, then they are not considered specially manufactured. If, however, the goods could be sold only after the seller makes essential changes to them, then the goods are specially manufactured and fall within the statute's exception. The evidence suggests that Olsen could not have resold the prototypes to any of its customers, and any change necessary to sell the models would require significant alterations. Affirmed.

When analyzing whether the goods could be resold in the ordinary course of business (one of the requirements to prove the goods were specially manufactured), you could chart the facts of the client's case and the facts of the two relevant cases as follows.

Requirement 2: Whether the goods could be resold in the ordinary course of business

SAVILLA	EXCEL	BSO
• Wooden cleats for crates	• **Pink & purple towels with jogger logo**	• Prototypes of candle racks
• Cleats not unusual or special as to support the existence of a contract without a writing	• **Oral evidence that buyer specifically requested colors to match spa décor**	• Evidence that prototype designed to buyer's specification
	• **Jogger added by verbal request at a later date**	• Evidence that seller told buyer prototypes expensive & seller would pay for them if substantial amount of racks weren't purchased
• Parties never met personally	• **Parties met only once**	• Parties met at least three times
• Seller was able to sell one container of cleats out of 100 to different crate company	• **Excel sold 1,000 of 5,000 towels after changing jogger logo to a flower**	• Seller unable to sell prototypes in ordinary course of business without making significant changes

E. Preparing to Write the Support for Each Side

In the section of your analysis that provides support for why the spa towels could be resold in the ordinary course of business, compare favorably the relevant facts of the client's case to the relevant facts in *Savilla*, and contrast or distinguish the relevant facts of the client's case from the relevant facts in *SBO*. By doing so, you are aligning the relevant facts of your client's case with the relevant facts in *Savilla* to support the argument that the client's case should be decided the same way.

To Support Why the Towels Could Be Resold in the Ordinary Course of Business:

◄──►

Savilla (court found goods   *BSO* (court found goods
could be resold)   could not be resold)

Compare the client's   Contrast the
facts to the facts   client's facts
in *Savilla* to support   from the facts in
why the goods could   *BSO* to support
be resold in the ordinary   why the goods could
course of business   be resold in the
                                      ordinary course of
                                      business

Figure 12-3

Conversely, when you provide support for why the spa towels could *not* be resold in the ordinary course of business, compare favorably the relevant facts of your client's case to the relevant facts in *BSO*, and contrast or distinguish the relevant facts of your client's case from the relevant facts in *Savilla*, to support the argument that your client's case should be decided the same way as *BSO*.

To Support Why the Towels Could Not Be Resold in the Ordinary Course of Business

◄──►

Savilla (court found goods   *BSO* (court found goods
could be resold)   could not be resold)

Contrast the client's   Compare the
facts from the facts   client's facts to
in *Savilla* to support   the facts in
why the goods could not   *BSO* to support
be resold in the ordinary   why the goods could not
course of business   be resold in the
                                      ordinary course of
                                      business

Figure 12-4

F. Establishing the Large-Scale Organization

When researching and drafting an objective discussion you want to think about the logical structure of the document. When doing so, consider the following.

1. Organizing as you research

You do not need to wait until you have compiled all the relevant authority before organizing the relevant law. As soon as you determine the legal structure, or test, used by the court in resolving a legal issue, you may begin to separate the legal points and incorporate the relevant law where appropriate. This helps in two different ways:

1. By organizing as you research the relevant law, you may determine earlier than you would otherwise when you have sufficient case law to analyze a legal point and can stop researching; and
2. By organizing as you research the relevant law, you combine two steps (researching and organizing) into one, allowing you to write your first draft earlier than you might otherwise, which will give you additional time for redrafting, revising, and editing.

2. Dividing into logical sections

You may have noticed that each legal requirement is analyzed in its totality before moving to the next legal requirement. As discussed in Chapters 9 and 11, when each legal point at issue requires a separate analysis, you help your reader most by keeping the issues separate in your objective analysis.

When discussing whether the requirements of the specially manufactured goods exception have been met, for example, the requirements would be introduced in an introductory or framework paragraph, followed by a separate discussion (TRAC) of each of the three requirements. You can predict the conclusion regarding the exception only after analyzing whether each of the requirements is likely to be met.

● **Exercise 12-A**

Create the large-scale structure for the issues raised in *Excel, Inc. v. Milton Hotels.*

G. Providing Framework Paragraphs When Addressing Multiple Issues

Chapters 7, 9, and 11 discuss what to provide in a framework paragraph. The decision about where to provide information in your document becomes more complex when you are addressing multiple legal points. As discussed previously, the best strategy is to use information when it becomes most relevant to your reader. Wait until the TRAC of each requirement to explain that part of the case relevant to that requirement. If you are addressing more than one issue, and each issue has its own sub-issues, include multiple framework paragraphs: one in the main introduction and additional framework paragraphs at the beginning of each issue.

● **Exercise 12-B**

Draft the appropriate framework paragraphs for the discussion of *Excel, Inc. v. Milton Hotels.*

H. Addressing Legal Requirements (Elements) That Are Not in Dispute But Must Nonetheless Be Established

You may find that not all parts of the legal test you are analyzing are in dispute. However, if the indisputable point is a requirement that must be satisfied to prove the legal test, you cannot omit a discussion of that requirement. You must still establish the requirement as part of your discussion. The general guideline is to provide as much of the TRAC checklist as is necessary. That is, tell the reader which requirement you are addressing (**T**); if applicable and necessary, provide the relevant rule, including any relevant definition, and any relevant rule explanations, if necessary (**R**); apply the rule to the facts in the client's case to support what you believe is the obvious outcome (**A**); and write a conclusion (**C**). If you change the topic sentence to a thesis statement that states your conclusion, you likely do not need to repeat the conclusion at the end.

For example, the main provision of the statute of frauds requires that (1) the agreement involve a sale of goods, (2) the goods cost more than $500, (3) the agreement include a writing sufficient to indicate that a contract for sale has been made between the parties, and (4) the writing be signed by the party against whom enforcement is sought. Establishing that the agreement involves (1) a sale of goods that (2) exceeds $500 is usually quite easy. Since they are both requirements, however, each requirement must be established as part of the analysis. In the contract dispute over the sale of spa towels, you would need only to set out the statute of frauds language and then match the legal requirement (e.g., sale of goods/over $500) with the facts of the client's case (spa towels/$500,000).

Some indisputable legal points require a more extensive discussion. The extent of the discussion of an indisputable issue depends on the legal point being addressed. For example, let's say that the agreement at issue in a contract dispute involves not only the sale of goods but also the performance of services. You have found a supreme court case in your jurisdiction stating that when both sales and services are involved in a contract dispute, the agreement falls within the statute of frauds, and the statute of frauds must be satisfied as though the agreement involved only a sale of goods.[3] The requirement that the agreement in dispute involves a sale of goods is now not so clear but is still not in dispute. To establish this indisputable issue, you must do more than just match the fact with the requirement. You need to explain the supreme court case in a way that proves that an agreement involving both sales and services falls within the statute of frauds.

To do this, after explaining when the statute of frauds applies, write a TRAC checklist for the sale of goods requirement, as follows.

T—Does a contract involving both sales of goods and services fall within the statute of frauds requirement that the contract involve the sale of goods?

R—Rule explanation of the supreme court case establishing that an agreement that involves both a sale of goods and a sale of service falls within the statute of frauds.

A—The client's case also involves a combination of a sale of goods and a sale of service.

C—Therefore, the requirement is met, and the entire contract must meet the statute of frauds as a sale of goods.

I. Determining the Overall Structure of the Objective Analysis with Multiple Issues

First and foremost, if the law dictates a certain structure, you must follow it. A classic example of this is the shifting burdens test, as the former employee's sexual discrimination case described in Chapter 11. When applying this test, the plaintiff has the initial burden of proof in the case. If the plaintiff fails to meet the initial burden, the case does not move forward, and the plaintiff loses. If, however, the plaintiff meets the burden, the burden of proof then shifts to the defendant. This test requires the legal writer to follow the logic of the law and address the plaintiff's burden first, before moving to the defendant's burden.

If, however, the law does not dictate a particular order in presenting information, let logic be your guide. Logic dictates, for example, that you address all threshold issues first. A threshold issue is the logical beginning point. In *Excel*, the logical beginning point is to address whether the main provision of the statute of frauds has been met before addressing whether the specially manufactured goods exception to the statute of frauds has been met. In another example, let's say you are analyzing a contracts case, and one of the questions is whether the claim has been brought within the statute of

---

3. *See Colo. Carpet Installation, Inc. v. Palermo*, 668 P.2d 1384 (Colo. 1983).

limitations period.[4] If a judge determines that the statute of limitations has passed, the case will not proceed, the contract dispute is irrelevant, and the judge will dismiss the case. Logically, therefore, you would address the procedural statute of limitations question before analyzing the substantive issues in the contracts claim.

Should you prevail on the statute of limitations question, however, and proceed to the breach of contract claim, you would need to address whether the contract is enforceable. An enforceable contract has three requirements: (1) a valid offer, (2) a valid acceptance, and (3) consideration.[5] Again, logic dictates that you address whether the buyer made a valid offer before addressing whether the seller validly accepted the offer since the legal questions are raised in this order chronologically. The placement of the consideration requirement, however, is not dictated by logic and may be introduced either before or after the analysis of the offer and acceptance requirements.

An outline of the contracts issue analysis might look like the following.

I. Was the lawsuit filed within the statute of limitations period?
II. If the lawsuit was filed within statute of limitations period, did the parties create an enforceable contract?
   A. Was there a valid offer?
   B. If there was a valid offer, was there a valid acceptance?
   C. Did the agreement include consideration?

One last question that may logically dictate an order for your analysis occurs when the law in the jurisdiction is not settled. The initial question the court must answer, therefore, is which rule of law to apply; only after that decision is made can the court apply the correct rule of law to the particular facts of the client's case to determine the outcome.

For example, in the state of Ohio as of this writing, the intermediate appellate courts have applied two different rules when determining whether a man who gave a woman an engagement ring in contemplation of their pending marriage can recover the ring once the engagement is broken.[6] One Ohio court follows the "fault" rule, deciding who gets the ring based on who was to blame for the breakup of the engagement.[7] Another Ohio court follows the "no-fault" rule, where the court does not determine whether the man or woman was at fault but just orders that the ring be returned to the man.[8] If a case addressing the same issue was decided by the Ohio Supreme Court, the court would first need to decide whether to apply the fault or no-fault rule. Once decided, lower courts would then rule on who would retain the ring by applying the adopted rule to the facts of the specific case.

---

4. The statute of limitations period for most contract actions is two years.
5. Consideration is an agreement to exchange performances or promises between two or more parties that requires the parties to act, forbear from acting, or give up a present or future right.
6. This hypothetical case was first introduced in Chapter 10.
7. See *Coconis v. Christakis*, 435 N.E.2d 100 (Ohio County Ct. 1981).
8. See *Lyle v. Durham*, 585 N.E.2d 456 (Ohio 1984).

If the structure of your analysis is not dictated by the law or by obvious logic, consider using one of the following organizational patterns.

1. Present the indisputable points first, followed by the disputable points; or
2. Present the legal points in the order in which they are provided in the law, regardless of whether they are disputable or indisputable.

Appendix J provides a general checklist when analyzing multiple issues using multiple cases.

● Exercise 12-C

Based on *Excel, Inc. v. Milton Hotels* and the cases included in this chapter, draft a discussion addressing whether the specially manufactured goods exception to the statute of frauds can be proved where the only issue in dispute is whether the goods could be resold in the ordinary course of business. This exercise requires you to structure the discussion of a multi-part test, provide a framework or roadmap, and determine how to include discussions of both disputable and indisputable requirements of a legal test.

● Exercise 12-D

Recall the story of the Moores from Chapter 7 and the revised draft of the discussion you wrote in Exercise 9-B. You will now address the second step of the two-step analysis of whether East Carolina's long-arm statute comports with federal due process requirements and then conclude whether the court will be able to assert personal jurisdiction over Jungle Rapids Expedition (JRE) in light of the two-step analysis.

The purpose of this exercise is to provide you with experience in all of the following:

1. Using a case (*Loch*) in the analysis of more than one fact-based issue.
2. Determining where to place the discussion that you drafted in Chapter 9 in this new document (whether it is better placed before or after the discussion of the federal due process issue).
3. Writing the federal due process issue analysis that
   (a) uses one case (*Loch*),
   (b) is a factors analysis,
   (c) that may include some sub-issues not in dispute, and
   (d) includes balancing tests.
4. Writing a framework paragraph and a conclusion paragraph to the discussion of whether the court may exercise personal jurisdiction over JRE.

CHAPTER

13

An Overview of Statutory Interpretation in the U.S. Courts

HIGHLIGHTS

- U.S. courts interpret and apply statutes to legal disputes.
- When interpreting ambiguous statutes, courts use such tools of statutory interpretation as codified statutory rules of interpretation, the plain meaning rule, canons of construction, and legislative histories.
- When using tools of statutory interpretation, courts may use different approaches.
  - A textualist approach focuses on the meaning of the statute's words and phrases.
  - An intentionalist approach focuses on ascertaining the legislative intent of the statute.
  - A purposivist approach focuses on the purpose served by the statute.
- When a statute no longer reflects current policies or societal or legal norms, some scholars support a court's use of dynamic statutory interpretation, which reviews the statute in light of current policies or norms.

 ## A. Introduction

One of the most important roles of U.S. courts is to act as interpreters and enforcers of statutory law. This chapter introduces the interpretation tools and theories of statutory interpretation most commonly used by U.S. courts. You may find that some of these tools and theories of interpretation are similar to those used by courts in other legal systems.[1]

B. The U.S. Court's Role in Statutory Interpretation

When a case involves the interpretation of a statute, a court's role is to interpret and to apply the statute in a correct manner for the situation. The court's task is made easy if the legislators have created a statute expressing a clear meaning. Even after diligent effort, however, legislators occasionally create an unclear statute. For example, legislation that by its wording appears to be clear might actually be unclear under the intense scrutiny of interested parties and lawyers. Furthermore, legislators can't foresee every instance where a statute might apply and thus may fail to address the statute's applicability to an unanticipated situation. Aside from this, clerical errors in the drafting of the legislation can create ambiguity. Ambiguity means that a provision is capable of at least two mutually conflicting meanings. When a statute is ambiguous, a court must determine the statute's true meaning.

Besides interpreting ambiguous statutes, a court may interpret statutes that are incomplete. Sometimes legislatures enact laws that intentionally leave gaps in the law. For example, legislators may leave gaps in the law for political convenience. They may be rushed to pass legislation before the ending of a legislative session and, perhaps because of disagreement among the law makers, they are unable to fill in the details of the legislation before enactment.

Whenever a legislature intentionally or unintentionally leaves gaps in a statute, a court as part of its policy-making duties must fill in the gaps. By using tools of statutory interpretation, a court strives to give full voice to the true meaning of a statute. Commenting on a federal court's important gap-filling duties, Justice Stevens of the United States Supreme Court wrote:

> For example, [w]hen a federal statute creates a new right but fails to specify whether plaintiffs may or may not recover damages or attorney's fees, we must fill the gap in the statute's text by examining all relevant evidence that sheds light on the intent of the enacting Congress. The inquiry varies from statute to statute. Sometimes the question is whether, despite its silence, Congress intended us to recognize an implied cause of action. . . . Sometimes we ask whether, despite its silence, Congress intended us to enforce the pre-existing remedy provided in [the statute]. . . . And still other times, despite Congress'

---

1. *See generally, e.g., Interpreting Statutes: A Comparative Study* 464 (D. Neil MacCormick & Robert S. Summers eds., Dartmouth Publishing Co. 1991) (discussing the similarities in statutory interpretation rationale used by courts in Argentina, Finland, France, Germany, Italy, Poland, Sweden, the United Kingdom, and the United States); Claire M. Germain, *Approaches to Statutory Interpretation and Legislative History in France*, 13 Duke J. Comp. & Intl. L. 195 (2003) (focusing on the statutory interpretation in France).

inclusion of specific clauses designed specifically to preserve the pre-existing remedies, we have nevertheless concluded that Congress impliedly foreclosed the [statute's] remedy. . . . Whenever we perform this gap-filling task, it is appropriate not only to study the text and structure of the statutory scheme, but also to examine its legislative history.[2]

Legislatures also may leave gaps in a statute intending a government administrative agency with expertise or knowledge in the subject of the statute to fill the gaps with regulations. In this instance, the legislature usually includes language in the statute designating a specific administrative agency to create regulations that further define the law.[3] All general and permanent regulations created by federal agencies appear in a multivolume codification, entitled the *Code of Federal Regulations*.

When interpreting an ambiguous statute, courts usually defer to agency regulations created in response to that statute if (1) Congress *explicitly* intended for the agency to fill in the gap and (2) the agency's regulations are not "arbitrary, capricious, or manifestly contrary to statute."[4] Courts defer to an agency administrator's interpretation of a statute if (1) Congress *implicitly* intended for the agency to fill in the gap and (2) the agency administrator's interpretation is reasonable.[5] If the test for an agency regulation fails, the test for an agency administrator's interpretation of a statute fails, or there are no regulations to fill in a gap or otherwise clarify an ambiguous statute, a court will use tools of statutory interpretation to fill in the gap or to clarify the meaning of an ambiguous statute.

 ## C. The Tools of Statutory Interpretation

This section describes the tools commonly used by U.S. courts when interpreting a statute. A court usually begins by reviewing the statute's text to determine its plain meaning. If the statute's meaning still remains ambiguous, courts may review outside sources to determine either the legislature's intent in enacting the statute or the statute's purpose.

---

2. *City of Rancho Palos Verdes v. Abrams*, 544 U.S. 113, 129 (2005) (Stevens, J., concurring) (citations omitted). Not all scholars agree that courts should so quickly use legislative history as a tool in interpreting an ambiguous statute. See the discussion on textualism in section D1 of this chapter.

"Legislative history" comprises actions by a legislative body (e.g., hearings and debates) and legislative documents (e.g., committee reports) that relate to a "bill" (a proposal for a statute), beginning with the bill's introduction to the legislative body and ending with the legislature enacting the bill into law. The federal government publishes legislative histories (such as committee reports, floor debates, and histories of actions taken) for enacted federal statutes; but few states publish legislative histories for enacted state statutes. *See also* nn. 35-39 and accompanying text in this chapter for further explanations of the legislative process in Congress.

3. *See, e.g.*, 47 U.S.C. § 227(b)(2) (2000) (stating that the Federal Communications Commission shall create regulations to give effect to the Telephone Consumer Protection Act).

4. *Chevron U.S.A., Inc. v. Nat. Resources Def. Council, Inc.*, 467 U.S. 837, 843-844 (1984).

5. *Id.* at 844.

Usually, it is left to the court's sole discretion to determine whether it should refer to outside sources and whether, when reviewing these sources, its goal should be to uncover the legislature's intent, the statute's purpose, or merely the meaning of the words. (See the discussion in section D of this chapter.) How broadly or narrowly a court interprets a statute depends on the statutory interpretation tools employed and the court's goal for using them.

1. Codified statutory rules of interpretation

The statutory codes of all states, the District of Columbia, and the United States include statutes providing general rules of interpretation for reading their statutes.[6] These interpretive rules usually appear at the beginning of the statutory code. Few courts, though, seem to cite and thus directly rely on these rules when interpreting statutes, even though it is assumed that legislatures enact the statutes with these interpretive rules in mind.

2. Plain meaning

When interpreting a statute, a court begins by looking at the language of the statute to determine its plain meaning. For example, the Federal Arbitration Act (the "Arbitration Act")[7] requires courts to enforce written arbitration agreements. Section 1 of the Arbitration Act excludes from coverage under the Arbitration Act "contracts of employment of seamen, railroad employees, or any other class of workers engaged in foreign or interstate commerce."[8] Let's say an employee working in a retail store brings an employment discrimination action against his employer in court. When the retail employee was hired, however, he signed an agreement to settle all disputes arising out of his employment by arbitration. Because of this agreement, the employer responds to

---

6. *See, e.g.*, Nicholas Quinn Rosenkranz, *Federal Rules of Statutory Interpretation*, 115 Harv. L. Rev. 2085, 2089 n. 10 (2002). For example, § 311.023 of the Texas Code provides:

In construing a statute, whether or not the statute is considered ambiguous on its face, a court may consider among other matters the:

(1) object sought to be attained;
(2) circumstances under which the statute was enacted;
(3) legislative history;
(4) common law or former statutory provisions, including laws on the same or similar subjects;
(5) consequences of a particular construction;
(6) administrative construction of the statute; and
(7) title (caption), preamble, and emergency provision.

Tex. Govt. Code Ann. § 311.023 (1999).

7. 9 U.S.C. §§ 1-16 (2000 & Supp. 2005).
8. *Id.* § 1 (2000).

the employee's complaint by seeking to dismiss the action and compel arbitration of the employee's claims as required under the Arbitration Act.[9]

Typically, a court first considers commonly accepted English principles of grammar, syntax, and punctuation to determine the meaning of a statute's words as understood by a reasonable person.[10] Here, the court does not refer to outside sources, not even a dictionary, to help ascertain the meaning of the words. Such a restrictive approach to statutory interpretation, however, rarely yields the meaning of an ambiguous statute.

A court attempting to determine whether the plain language of section 1 of the Arbitration Act applies to the retail employee's dispute could construe the provision to exclude all "contracts of employment of . . . any other class of workers engaged in foreign or interstate commerce." This reading would exclude the retail employee's agreement with his employer. On the other hand, the statute makes an explicit reference to "seamen" and "railroad employees" directly preceding what may be considered the residual clause, "any other class of workers." Arguably, if Congress had intended to exclude all employment agreements from the Arbitration Act, it would not have specifically included employment agreements of seamen and railroad employees before the residual clause in section 1. Because both arguments present reasonable but conflicting interpretations of the statute's plain meaning, a court might use selected canons of construction, discussed next, to help with its interpretation of the statute.

3. Canons of construction

At any stage in interpreting a statute, a court may use a variety of canons of construction to help determine the meaning of a statute. Canons of construction

---

9. This problem is based on the facts of *Circuit City Stores, Inc. v. Adams*, 532 U.S. 105 (2001).

10. William N. Eskridge Jr., *Dynamic Statutory Interpretation* 38 (Harv. U. Press 1994).

See, e.g., Tenn. Valley Auth. v. Hill, 437 U.S. 153 (1978) (Court used the plain meaning rule when interpreting the Endangered Species Act of 1973 to uphold the U.S. Secretary of Interior's decision to stop construction of a dam, almost completed at an expense of $100 million, because it would destroy the only known habitat of the snail darter, a species of perch):

> One would be hard pressed to find a statutory provision whose terms were any plainer than those in § 7 of the Endangered Species Act. Its very words affirmatively command all federal agencies "*to insure* that actions *authorized, funded*, or *carried out* by them do not *jeopardize* the continued existence" of an endangered species or "*result* in the destruction or modification of habitat of such species. . . ." 16 U.S.C. § 1536 (1976 ed.) (Emphasis added.) This language admits of no exception. Nonetheless, petitioner urges, as do the dissenters, that the Act cannot reasonably be interpreted as applying to a federal project which was well under way when Congress passed the Endangered Species Act of 1973. To sustain that position, however, we would be forced to ignore the ordinary meaning of plain language.

Tenn. Valley Auth., 437 U.S. at 173 (citations omitted).

are persuasive rules or principles used by courts to help give meaning to ambiguous statutory language.[11] These canons, however, do not necessarily take the place of other tools of statutory construction. As noted by the United States Supreme Court, "canons of construction are no more than rules of thumb that help courts determine the meaning of legislation, and . . . interpret[] statutes. . . ."[12]

Because canons are persuasive, a court may pick and choose which ones to use in interpreting a statute. Indeed, sometimes canons contradict other canons.[13] It remains in the wise discretion of the interpreting court to decide which canons are appropriate to apply to the statute in question. A reviewing court abuses this discretion if it selects a canon to support a predetermined end rather than to correctly interpret a statute.[14]

As previously noted, an interpreting court uses canons when the plain meaning of the statute cannot be determined.[15] A scholar of U.S. statutory interpretation, William N. Eskridge, Jr., has divided canons of construction into three categories:

(1) *textual canons* that focus on interpreting the words of the statute,
(2) *extrinsic source canons* that "direct the [interpreting court] to an authoritative source of meaning," and
(3) *substantive policy canons* that focus on prudential considerations or "public policies drawn from the Constitution, . . . statutes, or the common law."[16]

a. Textual canons

Textual canons guide the interpreting court in finding the meaning of statutory words or phrases. These canons focus on the legislature's choice of words in the statute, the syntax used, or the relationship of the words or phrases in question to words or phrases found in other provisions of the same statute or in those found in similar statutes.[17] For example, textual canons can direct a court to use

---

11. "Canons are not mandatory rules. They are guides 'that need not be conclusive.'" *Chickasaw Nation v. United States*, 534 U.S. 84, 94 (2001) (quoting *Circuit City Stores*, 532 U.S. at 115).

12. *Conn. Natl. Bank v. Germain*, 503 U.S. 249, 253 (1992).

13. *Circuit City Stores, Inc.*, 532 U.S. at 115. "The canon requiring a court to give effect to each word '*if possible*' is sometimes offset by the canon that permits a court to reject words 'as surplusage' if 'inadvertently inserted or if repugnant to the rest of the statute. . . .'" *Chickasaw Nation*, 534 U.S. at 94 (quoting Karl N. Llewellyn, *The Common Law Tradition* 525 (Little, Brown 1960)).

14. Cass R. Sunstein, *Interpreting Statutes in the Regulatory State*, 103 Harv. L. Rev. 405, 452 (1989).

15. In *Connecticut National Bank*, the United Supreme Court stated:

[I]n interpreting a statute a court should always turn first to one, cardinal canon before all others. We have stated time again that courts must presume that a legislature says in a statute what it means and means in a statute what it says there. [Citations omitted.] When the words of a statute are unambiguous, then, this first canon is also the last: "judicial inquiry is complete."

503 U.S. at 253-254 (quoting *Rubin v. United States*, 449 U.S. 424, 430 (1981)).

16. Eskridge, *supra* n. 10, at 323. Eskridge lists more than 100 canons of construction used by the United States Supreme Court from 1986 through 1991. *Id.* at 323-328.

17. *See* James J. Brudney & Corey Ditslear, *Canons of Construction and the Elusive Quest for Neutral Reasoning*, 58 Vand. L. Rev. 1, 12-13 (2005).

dictionaries.[18] Textual canons also may direct a court to review the "statutory scheme" of the statute in question. The statutory scheme of a statute may include (1) statutory definitions of terms used in the statute in question, (2) other statutory provisions related to the statute in question, (3) any codified preamble that pertains to the statute in question,[19] and (4) the title of a "legislative act"[20] that includes the statute in question.

Textual canons include the following.

- "[T]erms connected by a disjunctive [word must] be given separate meanings, unless the context dictates otherwise."[21]
- Words shall be given "their ordinary, contemporary common meaning," unless otherwise specifically defined.[22]
- *Shall* imposes a mandatory duty; *may* is permissive.[23]
- Words shall be read so that their meaning is consistent with other provisions of the same statute or other statutes.[24]
- *Ejusdem generis*: General words following specifically listed words include only those items "similar in nature" to the listed words.
- *Expressio unius est exclusio alterius*: Mentioning one or more items of a class implies the exclusion of other items.[25]
- *Noscitur a sociis*: The meaning of a word or phrase may be known from "the words immediately surrounding it."[26]

For an example applying a textual canon of construction, let's return to the problem of whether a retail employee's agreement to arbitrate disputes with his employer is excluded from the Arbitration Act by section 1 of that act. The court may use the canon of *ejusdem generis* to help uncover the statute's meaning. Applying this canon,

---

18. *See* Eskridge, *supra* n. 10, at 323 (listing as a textual canon "[f]ollow dictionary definitions of terms unless Congress has provided a specific definition"). *See also generally* Note, *Looking It Up: Dictionaries and Statutory Interpretation*, 107 Harv. L. Rev. 1437 (1994).

19. A codified preamble usually states the legislature's purpose for a series of statutes. *See, e.g.*, 42 U.S.C. § 7401 (2000) (stating the congressional purpose of the Clean Air Act, 42 U.S.C. § 7401 *et seq.* (2000 & Supp. 2004)).

20. "When introduced into the first house of the legislature, a piece of proposed legislation is known as a bill. When passed to the next house, it may then be referred to as an act. . . . After enactment the terms 'law' and 'act' may be used interchangeably." *Black's Law Dictionary* 13 (Henry Campbell Black ed., abr. 5th ed., West 1983).

21. *Reiter v. Sonotone Corp.*, 442 U.S. 330, 339 (1979).

22. *Perrin v. U.S.*, 444 U.S. 37, 42 (1979).

23. *See, e.g., Weinstein v. Albright*, 261 F.3d 127, 137 (2d Cir. 2001).

24. *See U.S. v. Jones*, 527 F.2d 817, 829 n. 13 (D.C. Cir. 1975).

25. *See, e.g., Barnhart v. Peabody Coal Co.*, 537 U.S. 149, 168 (2003) (quoting *United States v. Vonn*, 535 U.S. 55, 65 (2002)) ("the canon *expressio unius est exclusio alterius* does not apply to every statutory listing or grouping; it has force only when the items expressed are members of an 'associated group or series,' justifying the inference that items not mentioned were excluded by deliberate choice, not inadvertence.")

26. *Black's Law Dictionary* 1084 (Bryan A. Garner & Henry Campbell Black eds., 7th ed., West 1999). *See, e.g., Gutierrez v. Ada*, 528 U.S. 250, 255 (2000) (quoting *Jarecki v. G.D. Searle & Co.*, 367 U.S. 303, 307 (1961)) ("The maxim *noscitur a sociis*, . . . while not an inescapable rule, is often wisely applied where a word is capable of many meanings in order to avoid the giving of unintended breadth to the Acts of Congress.")

the meaning of the general phrase in section 1, "any other class of workers engaged in . . . commerce," includes "only objects similar in nature to those objects enumerated by the preceding specific words."[27] In section 1, "seamen" and "railroad workers" preceded the general phrase. These types of workers have transportation jobs. Therefore, by applying the canon of *ejusdem generis*, the phrase "any other class of workers engaged in . . . commerce" refers only to employment agreements of transportation workers. The employee in our problem worked in a retail store; therefore, under this interpretation, the employee's agreement would be subject to the Arbitration Act.

b. Extrinsic source canons

In addition to using textual canons, a court also may use extrinsic source canons. These canons rely on any available agency interpretations of the statute in question, legislative histories of the statute in question, or common law rules of other courts that have interpreted the statute in question or a similar statute. The following are examples of extrinsic source rules.

- Legislative history should be reviewed to interpret the meaning of an ambiguous statute.[28]
- Statutes that affect prior common law rules should be narrowly construed.[29]
- "[W]here [the legislature] borrows language from another statute when enacting a statute, the meaning accorded to the source statute can be taken [to prove] the meaning of the borrowing statute."[30]
- It is presumed that Congress did not create a law that interferes with other nations' sovereign authority.[31]

One of the most often used extrinsic source canons is the review of a statute's legislative history. If the logical meaning of a statute is clearly determined by reviewing the words of the statute and its statutory scheme, an interpreting court usually will stop there.[32] But in instances where the logical meaning remains ambiguous even after a plain reading of the statute, a court may review legislative history to determine:

(1) the meaning of words or phrases to avoid an absurd result under a plain reading of text;

---

27. *Circuit City*, 532 U.S. at 114-115 (quoting 2A N. Singer, *Sutherland on Statutes and Statutory Construction* § 47.17 (5th ed., Clark Boardman Callaghan 1991)). Using the canon of *ejusdem generis*, the Supreme Court found that the phrase excluding "contracts of employment of seaman, railroad workers, or any other class of workers engaged in foreign or interstate commerce" from the coverage of the Federal Arbitration Act, 9 U.S.C. § 1, was limited to workers engaged in enterprises similar to "seamen" and "railroad workers." *Id.*

28. Eskridge, *supra* n. 10, at 325 (citing *Wis. Pub. Intervenor v. Mortier*, 501 U.S. 597, 610 n. 4 (1991)).

29. [S]tatutes which invade the common law . . . are to be read with a presumption favoring the retention of long-established and familiar principles, except when a statutory purpose to the contrary is evident." *U.S. v. Tex.*, 507 U.S. 529, 534 (1993).

30. *See Zoltek Corp. v. U.S.*, 442 F.3d 1345, 1361 (Fed. Cir. 2006).

31. *See, e.g., F. Hoffmann-LaRoche Ltd. v. Empagram S.A.*, 524 U.S. 155, 164 (2004).

32. *See, e.g., Circuit City Stores*, 532 U.S. at 119 (Court did not review legislative history because the meaning of the statute could be determined from the text of the statute.)

(2) whether clerical errors occurred in the text, and if so, how to fix the errors;

(3) whether certain words or phrases in the text have special meaning;

(4) whether the words or phrases serve a reasonable purpose; or

(5) which among several "reasonable interpretations of a politically controversial issue" is the correct interpretation to apply.[33]

The first three purposes are not controversial because they focus on the meaning of the words. But purposes (4) and (5) on the list are considered controversial because the focus is on legislative purpose or legislative intent, which critics argue may lead to an interpretation that is not expressed in the text.[34]

For instance, in determining whether the retail employee's agreement with his employer is subject to the Arbitration Act, a court may review the legislative history of section 1 to find out whether Congress intended to exclude only the employment agreements of transportation employees from the Arbitration Act.[35] This may include reviewing published House and/or Senate committee reports,[36] congressional hearings,[37] conference reports,[38] bills,[39] and floor debates.[40]

---

33. Stephen Breyer, *On the Uses of Legislative History in Interpreting Statutes*, 65 S. Cal. L. Rev. 845, 861 (1992). In 1994, Justice Breyer became an Associate Justice to the United States Supreme Court.

34. *See id.* at 861.

35. The majority in *Circuit City* did not resort to legislative history, noting that available history on section 1 was "sparse," because the meaning of the statute was made clear by interpreting the statute using the canon of *ejusdem generis. Circuit City*, 532 U.S. at 119. Even so, the dissenting opinion criticized the majority for overlooking abundant legislative history that supported Congress's intent to exclude all employment agreements from the Arbitration Act. *Id.* at 123-128 (Stevens, Ginsburg, and Breyer, JJ., dissenting).

36. *See, e.g., Sutton v. United Air Lines*, 527 U.S. 471, 499 (1999) (quoting *Garcia v. United States*, 469 U.S. 70, 76 (1984), and *Zuber v. Allen*, 396 U.S. 168, 186 (1969)):

In surveying legislative history we have repeatedly stated that the authoritative source for finding the Legislature's intent lies in the Committee Reports on the bill, which "represen[t] the considered and collective understanding of those Congressmen involved in drafting and studying proposed legislation." . . . We have eschewed reliance on the passing comments of one Member, [citation omitted], and casual statements from the floor debates, [citations omitted]. . . . Committee reports are "more authoritative" than comments from the floor. . . .

After a bill is formally presented in either the U.S. House of Representatives or U.S. Senate, the bill is reviewed by an appropriate committee of that house. For example, a bill relating to protecting the environment introduced in the Senate would be reviewed by the Senate Committee on Environment and Public Works. When Congress is ready to act on a bill, the committee members issue a report stating their findings, which may include the perceived intent of the legislation, as well as the committee's recommendations and reasons for the recommendations.

37. A congressional committee reviewing a bill often holds hearings, calling witnesses who are experts or interested parties to speak to the committee members in order to gather information and gain further understanding about the bill and its possible ramifications should the bill ultimately be enacted into law.

38. When two different versions of a bill have been passed in the House of Representatives and the Senate, a conference committee, consisting of representative members of each house, will meet to settle their differences. Although there are no transcripts of these meetings, the conference committee will issue a report explaining the compromise reached.

39. A bill usually goes through amendments before reaching its final form that is enacted by the Congress into law. Sometimes a court will look at the evolution of the legislation, reviewing the bill in its earlier forms, noting words or phrases added or deleted that may signal the meaning of the final legislation.

40. Transcripts of debates among the members on the floor of Congress are included in the *Congressional Record*, a government publication issued daily when Congress is in session.

Most states do not offer published legislative histories. Courts interpreting statutes in these states are left to plain meaning interpretations and other canons of construction tools. Even in those states that do offer published legislative histories, most do not have extensive legislative histories, such as transcripts of floor debates. A state's legislative history also may be unreliable,[41] or the history may not be easily accessible.[42] On the federal level, however, Congress provides published, extensive legislative histories of statutes that are readily accessible. A court may use legislative history to interpret an ambiguous federal statute.[43]

c. Substantive policy canons

If the meaning of a statute cannot be determined using textual canons or extrinsic source canons, a court may turn to substantive policy canons. These canons do not focus on the meaning of the text or what the legislature intended when it drafted the text. Rather, substantive canons relate to matters such as constitutional concerns, the common law prior to the statute's enactment, and specific statutory policies.[44]

Prudential considerations seeking to ensure accurate, consistent, and efficient judicial decision making also influence a court when interpreting a statute. For instance, the legal tests regarding a court's deference to agency regulations or an agency administrator's interpretation of a statute, as described in section B of this chapter, are considered substantive canons.[45] Another substantive canon arising out of prudential considerations is the presumption that federal law does not preempt matters traditionally within the realm of state governance.

There are many substantive canons. In addition to the substantive canons previously mentioned, a sampling of the more commonly used substantive canons include the following.

- An ambiguous criminal statute is interpreted in favor of the defendant.

---

41. *See, e.g.*, Eric Lane, *How to Read a Statute in New York: A Response to Judge Kay and Some More*, 28 Hofstra L. Rev. 85, 113-114 (1999) (noting that the history of statutes in New York are presented in a bill jacket along with the bill and mainly consist of "executively generated post passage documents" (as opposed to institutionally or legislatively generated materials) that are essentially comments on the bill gathered by the counsel for the governor "from executive agencies and groups affected by the legislation.")

42. *See, e.g.*, Georgia (where the *Georgia State Law Review* publishes state legislative history in "Peach Sheets"); Illinois (where the Legislative Research Bureau publishes state legislative histories in "Legislative Synopsis and Digest"). *See generally* Michael B. Slade, *Democracy in the Details: A Plea of Substance over Form in Statutory Interpretation*, 37 Harv. J. Legis. 187, 202-203 nn. 70-71 (2000).

43. The Library of Congress provides a free Web site called "Thomas" for researching federal statutes: http://thomas.loc.gov/. For a discussion on how to use "Thomas" to research a federal statute's legislative history (including congressional reports from 1995 and the *Congressional Record* from 1989), see Kurt X. Metzmeier, *Reading the Mind of Congress: Legislative History Research on the Internet* (Louisville B. Assn. Jan. 2007) (available at http://ssrn.com/abstract=965034).

44. *See, e.g.*, Eskridge, *supra* n. 10, at 325-328.

45. *See generally* Charles Tiefer, *The Reconceptualization of Legislative History in the Supreme Court*, 2000 Wis. L. Rev. 205, 246-249.

- *In pari materia:* Statutes relating to the same subject matter should be interpreted similarly to avoid inconsistencies.
- A statute is interpreted to avoid unconstitutional results.

D. *Theories of Statutory Interpretation*

"The hard truth of the matter is that American courts have no intelligible, generally accepted, and consistently applied theory of statutory interpretation."[46] Such was the situation when these words were first written, and such is still the situation today.

Courts may use any or all of the tools of statutory interpretation mentioned in section C of this chapter, but the focus of a court when employing these tools will vary. Some courts, pointing to the supremacy of the legislature, exercise judicial restraint when interpreting statutes by focusing on the meaning of the statute's words. Other courts are more interested in the meaning of the statute as intended by the legislature or the meaning of the statute in furthering the purpose of the legislation.

The four basic theories of statutory interpretation — textualism, intentionalism, purposivism, and dynamic statutory interpretation — are presented on a continuum in Figure 13-1. Depending on what theory of statutory interpretation the court embraces, it may move away from acting as an agent of the legislature by merely applying a statute as written toward becoming a partner with the legislature by assigning meanings that go beyond a statute's plain words. The further a court moves away from the plain meaning of a statute, the greater the danger the court will be influenced by personal views or opinions.

Figure 13-1
Four Theories of Statutory Interpretation

Agent of the Legislature			Partner with the Legislature
Textualism	Intentionalism	Purposivism	Dynamic Statutory Interpretation

1. *Textualism*

Justices Scalia and Thomas of the United States Supreme Court promote a conservative position that many scholars have labeled "textualism."[47] Those who

---

46. Henry M. Hart Jr. & Albert M. Sacks, *The Legal Process: Basic Problems in the Making and Application of Law* 1201 (tentative ed. 1958) (reprinted in Henry M. Hart Jr., Albert M. Sacks, William N. Eskridge Jr. & Phillip P. Frickey, *The Legal Process: Basic Problems in the Making and Application of Law* 1169 (Found. Press 1994)).
47. *See generally* Caleb Nelson, *What Is Textualism?* 91 Va. L. Rev. 347 (2005).

support this approach to statutory interpretation discourage rushing to legislative history and other sources to decipher the meaning of a statute, insisting that courts should make great efforts to interpret a statute by closely reviewing the statute's plain language. Justice Scalia has written extensively about the perils of moving too hastily to sources beyond a statute's plain meaning:

> The . . . threat is that, under the guise or even the self-delusion of pursuing unexpressed legislative intents, . . . judges will in fact pursue their own objectives and desires. . . . When you are told to decide, not on the basis of what the legislature said, but on the basis of what it meant, and are assured that there is no necessary connection between the two, your best shot at figuring out what the legislature meant is to ask yourself what a wise and intelligent person should have meant; and that will surely bring you to the conclusion that the law means what you think it ought to mean.[48]

Essentially, Justice Scalia echoed one of the major criticisms of turning to legislative history for help in interpreting a statute: Legislative history eclipses "the voice of the statute,"[49] which should speak for itself.

Textualists embrace plain meaning and textual canons of construction. Unlike those who champion intentionalism or purposivism, textualists are reluctant to turn to legislative history to determine the meaning of a statute. Even so, textualists may look at legislative history to determine the meaning of the statutory words when there is "genuine ambiguity in the statute"[50] or when reading the statute according to its plain meaning causes an absurd or unconstitutional outcome.[51]

2. Intentionalism

Although there are various schools of thought on intentionalism, the common goal is to determine the "collective intent of the enacting legislature."[52] Unlike the textualist, who prefers to embrace the plain meaning of a statute and employs other interpretation tools only if to do otherwise would produce an absurd result or unconstitutional outcome, the intentionalist looks to the words of a statute as an expression of the legislature's intent that can be clarified through the use of outside sources.[53]

---

48. Antonin Scalia, *Common-Law Courts in a Civil-Law System: The Role of United States Federal Courts in Interpreting the Constitution and Laws*, in *Matter of Interpretation: Federal Courts and the Law* 17-18 (Amy Gutmann ed., Princeton U. Press 1997), as cited and quoted in David A. Strauss, *Why Plain Meaning?* 72 Notre Dame L. Rev. 1565, 1577 (1997).

49. Kenneth W. Starr, *Observations About the Use of Legislative History*, 1987 Duke L. J. 371, 375, quoted in Michael H. Kolby, *The Supreme Court's Declining Reliance on Legislative History: The Impact of Justice Scalia's Critique*, 36 Harv. J. on Legis. 369, 377 (1999).

50. *See, e.g., Bd. of Trade v. SEC*, 187 F.3d 713, 720 (7th Cir. 1999) (Easterbrook, J.).

51. *See, e.g., Green v. Bock Laundry Mach. Co.*, 490 U.S. 504, 527 (1989) (Scalia, J., dissenting).

52. David A. Forkner & Kent M. Koska, *Unanimously Weaving a Tangled Web: Walters, Robinson, Title VII, and the Need for Holistic Statutory Interpretation*, 36 Harv. J. on Legis. 161, 178 (1999).

53. Carlos E. González, *Reinterpreting Statutory Interpretation*, 74 N.C. L. Rev. 585, 606 (1996).

The intentionalist may refer to legislative history, agency determinations, previous cases determining legislative intent, and legislatively created purpose statements. If the discovered legislative intent conflicts with the plain meaning of the statute, the intentionalist's paramount concern is giving effect to the intent of the legislators who passed the statute as opposed to a plain reading of the text, which might create a result not intended by the legislature.[54] Critics of this theory argue that the intent of the legislature simply cannot be determined[55] and that the intentionalist may be influenced by personal policy preferences.

3. Purposivism

The purposivist gives paramount consideration to the purpose of the statute.[56] Purposivists employ some of the same interpretation tools[57] as textualists[58] and intentionalists, but they focus on discovering the purpose or goal of a statute. Purposivism is arguably less subjective than intentionalism. Rather than "delving into the mind of legislators or their draftsmen, or committee members," the purposivist looks to the aim of the legislation, such as "obviat[ing] some mischief, [supplying] an inadequacy, [affecting] a change of policy, [or formulating] a plan of government."[59] Once the purpose or goal of a statute is determined, the purposivist interprets the statute in a light consistent with that identified purpose or goal.[60] Critics of purposivism argue that determining the chief purpose for a statute may be impossible because oftentimes many conflicting interest groups influence the legislative process or the legislation may have been the result of compromise among these interest groups.[61] Critics further argue that even if there is a clear purpose behind the statute, purposivists run the danger of usurping the power of the legislature by interpreting a statute in such a way that its application goes beyond the original intent of the legislators.[62]

---

54. Forkner & Koska, *supra* n. 52, at 179. *See, e.g., Pub. Citizen v. U.S. Dept. of Just.*, 491 U.S. 440 (1989).

55. Michael H. Kolby, *The Supreme Court's Declining Reliance on Legislative History: The Impact of Justice Scalia's Critique*, 36 Harv. J. on Legis. 369, 377-380 (1999).

56. *See, e.g., Bob Jones v. U.S.*, 461 U.S. 574 (1983); *United Steel Workers of Am. v. Weber*, 443 U.S. 193 (1979).

57. *See generally* Michael Rosensaft, *The Role of Purposivism in the Delegation of the Rulemaking Power to the Courts*, 29 Vt. L. Rev. 611, 622-630 (2005) (discussing the methods for determining purpose that include reviewing the text of the section at issue, the entire statute, any legislatively created purpose statement relating to the statute, other statutes that are similarly worded and address similar concerns, legislative history, and case law).

58. *See generally* John F. Manning, *What Divides Textualists from Purposivists?* 106 Colum. L. Rev. 70 (2006).

59. Felix Frankfurter, *Some Reflections on the Reading of Statutes*, 47 Colum. L. Rev. 527, 538-539 (1947).

60. Eskridge, *supra* n. 10, at 26 (citing Henry M. Hart Jr. & Albert M. Sacks, *The Legal Process: Basic Problems in the Making and Application of Law* 166-167, 1148-1179, 1200 (tentative ed. 1958)).

61. *See generally* Rosensaft, *supra* n. 57, at 630-634 (responding to criticisms).

62. *Id.* at 634-636 (responding to criticisms).

4. Dynamic statutory interpretation

This theory of statutory interpretation condones the more traditional tools of statutory construction unless the text of the statute is ambiguous "and the original legislative expectations have been overtaken by subsequent changes in society and law. In such cases, the pull of text and history will be slight, and the interpreter will find current policies and societal conditions most important."[63] Essentially, if a court is faced with a statute that does not reflect current political, legal, or societal norms, the interpreting court should consider what the statute ought to mean in the context of present norms.[64] Critics of this theory are concerned that a court will use perceived changes in public policy to "openly rewrite" statutes, thus preempting the legislature's power.[65] While many scholars heatedly debate the virtues and shortcomings of dynamic statutory interpretation, courts have not explicitly embraced this theory. Some scholars, however, suggest that courts have applied its principles in interpreting "outdated" statutes.[66]

● Exercise 13-A

A Russian brewer (a manufacturer of beer) and a New York beer wholesaler entered into a written agreement in which the brewer agreed to supply the wholesaler with beer. Under the terms of the agreement, the brewer transferred the beer to the wholesaler's possession at the Russian brewer's place of business. There is no indication that there was an "offer to sell" the beer in New York.

The agreement permitted either party to unilaterally terminate the agreement. On January 1 of this year, the brewer refused to fill the wholesaler's most recent order and advised that it would not fill any future orders. The wholesaler claims that New York law, which governs the agreement between the parties, prohibits brewers from terminating agreements with wholesalers unless the termination occurs for "good cause." New York Alcoholic Beverage Control Law § 55-c(4)(a) states: "No brewer may cancel, fail to renew, or terminate an agreement unless the party intending such action has good cause for such cancellation, failure to renew, or termination. . . ." N.Y. Alcoh. Bev. Control L. § 55-c(4)(a) (McKinney Supp. 2008).

The brewer does not contend that it terminated the agreement for "good cause." Rather, the brewer argues that the New York statute applies only to sales or offers to sell

---

63. William N. Eskridge Jr., *Dynamic Statutory Interpretation*, 135 U. Pa. L. Rev. 1479, 1484 (1987). *See also* Eskridge, *supra* n. 10 (a book expanding on Eskridge's ideas initially discussed in his University of Pennsylvania law review article).

64. *See generally* Eskridge, *supra* n. 63.

65. R. Shep Melnick, *Statutory Reconstruction: The Politics of Eskridge's Interpretation*, 84 Geo. L.J. 91, 98 (1995).

66. *See, e.g.*, Chai R. Feldblum & Lisa Mottet, *Gay People, Trans People, Women: Is It All About Gender?* 17 N.Y. L. Sch. J. Hum. Rights 623, 657 n. 89 (2000) (citing *United Steel Workers of Am. v. Weber*, 443 U.S. 193, 209 (1979) (Blackmum, J., concurring); *Shine v. Shine*, 802 F.2d 583 (1st Cir. 1986); *Li v. Yellow Cab of Cal.*, 532 P.2d 1226 (Cal. 1975)); Eskridge, *supra* n. 63, at 1547-1548 (citing *Bob Jones v. U.S.*, 461 U.S. 574, 606 (1983) (Powell, J., concurring)).

that occur in New York. The brewer contends further that the business deal between the wholesaler and brewer occurred outside of New York.

The wholesaler contends that the statute applies to any transaction entered into with a New York wholesaler no matter where the deal took place.

Both parties base their arguments on New York Alcoholic Beverage Control Law § 55-c(2)(b), which states:

> "Brewer" means any person or entity engaged primarily in business as a brewer, manufacturer of alcoholic beverages, importer, marketer, broker or agent of any of the foregoing who sells or offers to sell beer to a beer wholesaler *in this state* or any successor to a brewer.

N.Y. Alcoh. Bev. Control L. § 55-c(2)(b) (McKinney Supp. 2008).

There is no published legislative history for this statute. However, the policy statement specifically addressing agreements between brewers and beer wholesalers states:

> It is hereby declared to be the policy of this state, that the sale and delivery of beer by brewers to beer wholesalers shall be pursuant to a written agreement. That further, the regulation of business relations between brewers and beer wholesalers is necessary and appropriate to the general economy and tax base of this state and in the public interest.

New York Alcoholic Beverage Control law § 55-c(1) (McKinney Supp. 2008).

Other sections of the New York Alcoholic Beverage Control Law also may assist in determining the application of section 55-c(4)(a). The general policy statement for all sections of the New York Alcoholic Beverage Control Law provides:

> It is hereby declared as the policy of the state that it is necessary to regulate and control the manufacture, sale and distribution within the state of alcoholic beverages for the purpose of fostering and promoting temperance in their consumption and respect for an obedience to law.

N.Y. Alcoh. Bev. Control L. § 2 (McKinney 2000).

Section 3(28) of the New York Alcoholic Beverage Control Law provides:

> "To sell" includes to solicit or receive an order for, to keep or expose for sale, and to keep with intent to sell and shall include the delivery of any alcoholic beverage in the state.

N.Y. Alcoh. Bev. Control L. § 3(28) (McKinney Supp. 2008).

Using the statutory interpretation tools discussed in this chapter, draft an argument that supports the brewer's position that the statute applies only to sales or offers to sell in New York. Then, draft an argument that supports the wholesaler's position that the statute applies to any transaction entered into with a New York wholesaler no matter where the deal took place.

● Exercise 13-B

Read the United States Supreme Court decision *Small v. United States*, which is reprinted in Appendix K.

1. For the *majority decision*, answer the following.
   a. Identify the statutory interpretation tools used. Did the court consider legislative history or particular canons of construction, including case law, other extrinsic sources, public policy, and/or prudential considerations?
   b. In what order were the statutory interpretation tools used?
   c. Did the court use these tools effectively? How?
   d. What overriding theory of statutory interpretation may have been used by the majority in this decision? Identify the passages in the majority decision that support your answer.
2. For the *dissenting opinion*, answer the following.
   a. Identify the statutory interpretation tools used. Did the dissent consider legislative history or particular canons of construction, including case law, other extrinsic sources, public policy, and/or prudential considerations?
   b. In what order were the statutory interpretation tools used?
   c. Did the dissent use these tools effectively? How?
   d. What criticisms did the dissent offer of the majority's approach? Were these criticisms valid? Why or why not?
   e. What overriding theory of statutory interpretation did the dissent embrace? Identify the passages in the dissenting decision that support your answer.

CHAPTER

14

Introduction to an Objective Legal Analysis of a Law-Based Issue

---

HIGHLIGHTS

- A law-based issue analysis determines whether a statute, rule, or principle applies to a dispute or, if competing rules exist that may apply to a dispute, determines which rule should apply.
- Most law-based analyses involve an issue of first impression.
- An objective discussion of an issue involving statutory interpretation informs the reader of the law and legislative history surrounding the statute in question and, using the tools of statutory interpretation, predicts how the court will likely interpret the statute.
- An objective discussion of <u>competing</u> rules or principles includes a thorough <u>discussion</u> of the rules and <u>whether</u> the law and policies in the reviewing court's jurisdiction <u>favor</u> the adoption of one rule over another.

 ## A. Introduction

Previous legal writing chapters have focused on drafting fact-based issue discussions. This chapter turns to drafting a law-based issue analysis. Under a fact-based issue, the parties are not disputing which statute, rule, or principle is applicable to the legal issue raised and are not disputing the facts of the case. Rather, the focus is on whether the facts of the case satisfy the accepted statute, rule, or principle. Under a law-based issue, the parties are disputing either (1) whether a statute, rule, or principle applies to the case; or (2) in the case of alternative rules or principles, which rule or principle should apply. This chapter addresses both situations.

Unless a party to the action is attempting to persuade the court to overturn mandatory precedent, the reviewing court is deciding an issue of *first impression*, that is, an issue that has never been addressed by the reviewing court.

B. Drafting an Objective Discussion of a Statutory Interpretation Issue

An issue requiring the interpretation of a statute may not be evident until the attorney researches the issue. Recall the divorce of Ana and David Hart introduced in Chapter 7. Let's say Ana has told a senior attorney in your firm that during the marriage David became suspicious that Ana was having an extramarital affair. To find evidence of this, David purchased a telephone recording device at a local electronics store and secretly attached the device to a telephone in the couple's home. Without Ana's knowledge, David taped several conversations between Ana and her friend, John. Ana is outraged that her soon-to-be ex-husband taped her telephone conversations with John without her knowledge or consent. She wonders whether she has a cause of action against David for his actions. The senior partner in your firm has assigned you, as a junior attorney, to look into the matter and write an objective discussion of the issue.

1. The predrafting process

You begin the pre-drafting process by following the steps introduced in Chapter 5 and further discussed in Chapter 7. After collecting and analyzing the facts (Steps One and Two), you collect the relevant law (Step Three) and analyze it (Step Four). In your research of federal statutory law, you discover 18 U.S.C. §§ 2510-2522 (2000 & Supp. III 2003) (the "Wiretap Act"). Section 2511(a) of the Wiretap Act generally prohibits interceptions of telephone conversations without the knowledge or consent of the parties talking on the telephone:

> Except as otherwise specifically provided in this chapter any person who — (a) intentionally intercepts, endeavors to intercept, or procures any other person to intercept or endeavor to intercept any wire, oral, or electronic communication . . . shall be punished . . . or shall be subject to suit. . . .

David intercepted Ana and John's conversations by making recordings of their conversations without their knowledge or consent. Although the Wiretap Act doesn't explicitly state that it prohibits a spouse's wiretapping of a partner's conversation with a third party ("interspousal wiretapping"), the Wiretap Act's broad, general prohibition language seems to include this situation.

In your research, you also discover that section 2511 and section 2520 of the Wiretap Act permit a lawsuit against those who violate the act and allow for the recovery of damages. If Ana can show that the Wiretap Act prohibits interspousal wiretapping, she may bring a legal action against David.

When analyzing a statutory interpretation issue, you must be mindful of the interpreting court's role and be able to respond to the court's concerns. As noted in Chapter 13, some courts take a strict view of statutory interpretation, focusing on the plain meaning of a statute and using textual canons of construction, turning to extrinsic sources, only if the statute's meaning remains ambiguous, or if applying the plain meaning of the statute would create an absurd result. Other courts, however, are quick to refer to extrinsic sources to determine the legislative intent or the legislative purpose behind a statute.

You can never be sure what tools of statutory interpretation the court will use when construing a statute or how the court will use these tools in reaching its decision. Therefore, you should perform diligent research beyond the mere text of the statute. For instance, explore the legislative history of the statute, the statutory scheme surrounding the statute, any related statutes in the code, and any administrative regulations that may have been promulgated under the statute. Your goal is not only to determine the plain meaning of the statute but also to move beyond the statute's plain meaning to determine, if possible, the legislative intent and legislative purpose for the statute. Consider too what other canons of construction might be helpful or relevant to uncovering the meaning of the statute.

Returning to Ana's case, you note that section 2511(a) states that there are exceptions to the Wiretap Act's prohibition. Your review of the Wiretap Act's exception provision discloses that none of the exceptions expressly apply to Ana's case. So far, this is good for Ana.

The plain meaning of section 2511(1)(a) apparently prohibits interspousal wiretapping, such as that conducted by David, because it applies to all persons except those specifically exempt from the statute's reach. But you anticipate that David's attorney will argue that section 2511(1)(a) is ambiguous and that the Wiretap Act impliedly excepts interspousal wiretapping. David's attorney may try to persuade the court that the statutory scheme of the Wiretap Act supports his argument. Therefore, you decide to look at all parts of the Wiretap Act, as well as sections surrounding the Wiretap Act, to see if anything might support David's position. You become a little concerned when you discover that the Wiretap Act is part of an act entitled the "Omnibus Crime Control and Safe Streets Act of 1968." This title might suggest that the purpose of the Wiretap Act is to focus solely on serious crimes, as opposed to a mere domestic dispute between a married couple. Moreover, a prudential consideration comes to mind, that federal courts are reluctant to address matters that are typically addressed in state courts, such as domestic disputes. Congress may not have intended the Wiretap Act, a federal law, to govern domestic wiretapping issues. Although the language of section 2511(1)(a) seems clear as written, an interpreting court might find it ambiguous as applied to Ana's case.

You anticipate that a court might look beyond a plain reading of the Wiretap Act to the legislative intent or the legislative purpose to clarify the scope of section 2511(1)(a)'s prohibition. Therefore, you research the legislative history of the Wiretap Act to ensure that the legislative intent and the legislative purpose support a plain reading that section 2511(1)(a) prohibits interspousal wiretapping. Because the federal government publishes legislative history for its federal legislation, you are able to locate committee reports, transcripts of legislative hearings, and debates on the Wiretap Act. You find that some of the legislative history seems to support Ana's position that the congressional intent and statutory purpose of the Wiretap Act were to prohibit inter-spousal wiretapping. Still other excerpts from legislative history seem to support David's position that interspousal wiretapping is an implied exception to the Wiretap Act.

In an effort to obtain more clarification, you research case law in the federal jurisdiction of the Thirteenth Circuit (which includes East Carolina)[1] to determine how prior courts have construed section 2511(1)(a). Your research reveals that no court in this jurisdiction has addressed the issue of whether interspousal wiretapping is prohibited by section 2511(1)(a). You decide to expand your research of case law to cases decided by courts outside the Thirteenth Circuit. You discover that courts in other jurisdictions are divided on the issue of whether interspousal wiretapping is prohibited under the Wiretap Act.

After you finish researching and analyzing the law (Steps Three and Four), you organize the law (Step Five). In this step, you may choose to organize the law by charting the law, as generally discussed in Chapter 12. You organize the law according to whether the law supports Ana's position or David's position. While you are organizing the law, you note whether a court used a plain reading interpretation of the statute or looked at extrinsic sources such as legislative intent, the purpose of the statute, public policy concerns, or prudential considerations. At this point, think about any additional canons of construction, public policy, or prudential considerations that courts have not yet used. Consider which arguments provide the most persuasive support for each position. And, applying the guidelines provided in Chapter 9, make choices about which sources to use in the discussion. Now you are ready to begin drafting the law-based issue analysis.

2. *Structuring an objective legal analysis of a statutory interpretation issue*

Just as in a fact-based issue discussion, you must keep in mind the purpose of the writing and the audience. In an objective analysis of a statutory interpretation issue, you are informing the reader of the law and legislative history surrounding the statute in question and predicting how the court will interpret the statute. If there is more than one reasonable interpretation of the statute, you must inform the reader of the different interpretations and explain the support for these positions. Then you must carefully weigh the respective interpretations of the statute to decide which interpretation the court will likely adopt. As is the case in any writing, your goal is to provide a complete, accurate, and concise analysis of the law that is understandable to the reader.

---

1. The Thirteenth Circuit is a fictitious federal jurisdiction, and East Carolina is a fictitious state created solely for purposes of this case problem.

a. The framework paragraph

Begin your objective discussion with a framework paragraph. The framework paragraph for a statutory interpretation issue that raises two different interpretations of a statute usually includes

(1) a topic or thesis sentence introducing the issue,
(2) a quote of the pertinent language of the statute in question,
(3) a statement that the issue is one of first impression in the jurisdiction (so that the reader will understand why you are not using authority from the governing jurisdiction), and
(4) a statement that courts outside the governing jurisdiction are divided on the issue (if this is, indeed, the case).

b. The analysis of a statutory interpretation issue

Similar to the basic organizational structure of a fact-based issue analysis, begin a statutory interpretation issue discussion with your analysis supporting the stronger position. The stronger position is the interpretation of the statute that you've concluded the court will likely adopt. After you complete your stronger position analysis, present your analysis of the weaker position. The weaker position is the interpretation of the statute that the court will less likely adopt. Finish the analysis with a conclusion that includes an explanation of your reasons for the conclusion.

While the basic organizational structure of a statutory interpretation analysis is similar to the organizational structure of a fact-based issue analysis, the substantive focus of the discussion is different. Recall that in a fact-based issue analysis, the substantive focus is on the facts of the client's case. Such an analysis shows the analogies and distinctions between the client's case facts and the facts in the case law. But the substantive focus in a statutory interpretation analysis is on the text of the statute and interpreting that statute with the tools of statutory interpretation discussed in Chapter 13. The law used in the stronger and weaker position analyses of a statutory interpretation issue may include any or all of the following:

- the language of the statute in question;
- the statutory scheme of the statute in question (including statutory definitions of terms used in the statute in question, preambles, other statutory sections related to the statute in question, and titles);
- any administrative regulations that may have been created under the statute in question;
- canons of construction;
- legislative history of the statute in question (including committee reports, hearings, bills, and floor debates);
- case decisions of courts that have interpreted the statute in question or a similar statute;
- scholarly treatises or articles that have discussed possible interpretations of the statute in question;

214

- public policy concerns;
- prudential considerations.

Case decisions, as noted above, are persuasive to show that other courts have adopted a similar view. When using a case in a statutory interpretation analysis, the rule explanation of the case takes a slightly different focus than in a fact-based issue analysis, where the facts of the cited case are of great importance. In a rule explanation for a statutory interpretation analysis, you include only enough facts to show that the situation in the cited case raised an interpretation issue similar to the one addressed in your client's case. Your primary focus is on the cited court's holding and reasoning, including its use of legislative tools and its goal in using these tools. These aspects of the cited case are discussed in great detail in the rule explanation.

An annotated sample of an objective statutory interpretation analysis of Ana's issue regarding whether interspousal wiretapping is exempt from the Wiretap Act follows.

The purpose of this discussion is to address whether David Hart's recording of several telephone conversations between his wife and our client, Ana Hart, and her friend John Sweeney without their knowledge or consent is prohibited under Title III of the Omnibus Crime Control and Safe Streets Act of 1968 (the "Wiretap Act"). 18 U.S.C. §§ 2510-2522 (2000 & Supp. III 2003). If David's recordings violate the Wiretap Act, then he will be subject to civil remedies authorized under 18 U.S.C. § 2520 (2000 & Supp. III 2003). This is a case of first impression in the Thirteenth Circuit.

Courts in other federal circuits have considered whether interspousal wiretapping is within the scope of the Wiretap Act and are divided on the issue. Several courts have found that interspousal wiretapping is prohibited by the Wiretap Act. *See, e.g., Glazner v. Glazner,* 347 F.3d 1212, 1215-1216 (11th Cir. 2003); *Heggy v. Heggy,* 944 F.2d 1537, 1541 (10th Cir. 1991); *Kempf v. Kempf,* 868 F.2d 970, 973 (8th Cir. 1989); *Pritchard v. Pritchard,* 732 F.2d 372, 374 (4th Cir. 1984); *U.S. v. Jones,* 542 F.2d 661, 673 (6th Cir. 1976); *Kratz v. Kratz,* 477 F. Supp. 463, 472 (E.D. Pa. 1979); *People v. Otto,* 831 P.2d 1178, 1190 (Cal. 1992). Other courts, however, have found that interspousal wiretapping is impliedly exempt from the Wiretap Act. *See Anonymous v. Anonymous,* 558 F.2d 677, 679 (2d Cir. 1977); *Simpson v. Simpson,* 490 F.2d 803, 810 (5th Cir. 1974); *Lizza v. Lizza,* 631 F. Supp. 529, 532-533 (E.D.N.Y. 1986); *Stewart v. Stewart,* 645 So. 2d 1319,

Statement introducing the purpose of the discussion.

Statement advising reader that this is a case of first impression in the reviewing court's jurisdiction.

Statement advising that courts are divided on the issue.

1321 (Miss. 1994); *Baumrind v. Ewing*, 279 S.E.2d 359, 353 (S.C. 1981).

A court in the Thirteenth Circuit will probably find that the Wiretap Act applies to interspousal wiretapping. The Wiretap Act mandates that "[e]xcept as otherwise specifically provided in this chapter *any person* who — (a) intentionally intercepts, endeavors to intercept, or procures any other person to intercept or endeavor to intercept *any wire, oral, or electronic communication* . . . shall be punished . . . or shall be subject to suit. . . ." 18 U.S.C. § 2511(1)(a) (2000) (emphasis added). David is "any person" within the meaning of section 2511(1)(a). *Id.* Also, his recording of telephone conversations between Ana and John using a device he purchased and attached to a telephone within the Harts' home fits the description of "intentionally intercept[ing] . . . any wire, oral, or electronic communication. . . ." *Id.* Therefore, under the plain meaning of section 2511(1)(a), David's recording of Ana and John's conversations violated the Wiretap Act. "The language of [the Wiretap Act] demonstrates that Congress decided that one spouse should not be permitted to record, without consent, electronically transmitted conversations between the other spouse and third parties." *Glazner*, 347 F.3d at 1215 (overruling the decision of *Simpson* as precedent in the Eleventh Circuit[2] and holding that interspousal wiretapping is not an exception to the Wiretap Act). The meaning of the statute is unambiguous. *See id.* Furthermore, the application of the Wiretap Act to David and his recordings is clear and does not lead to an absurd result. *See id.*

Although a court usually will not refer to legislative history when a statute is "clear on its face," legislative history nevertheless reveals that Congress intended the Wiretap Act to apply to interspousal wiretapping. *Jones*, 542 F.2d at 667. Professor Robert Blakey, the author of

---

Thesis statement beginning the analysis of the stronger position supporting the conclusion

The writer quotes the relevant language of the statute.

Writer applies the plain meaning of the statute to the facts of the client's case.

---

2. In 1981, the Fifth Circuit Court of Appeals split into two circuits. The states of Louisiana, Mississippi, and Texas remained in the Fifth Circuit; Alabama, Florida, and Georgia formed the new Eleventh Circuit Court of Appeals. Although the Eleventh Circuit was not required to follow previous decisions of the Fifth Circuit Court of Appeals, it was thought that starting anew, with no binding precedent, was too daunting for the courts. Consequently, the Eleventh Circuit Court of Appeals in *Bonner v. City of Pritchard*, 661 F.2d 1207, 1209 (11th Cir. 1981) (en banc), decided to "adopt" the Fifth Circuit Court of Appeals' decisions existing on September 30, 1981, as precedent for the Eleventh Circuit.

Although the Eleventh Circuit Court of Appeals in *Glazner* overruled *Simpson*, the holding in *Simpson* that interspousal wiretapping is an implied exception from the Wiretap Act is still binding precedent in the Fifth Circuit.

the Wiretap Act, testified before the Subcommittee on Administrative Practice and Procedure of the Senate Judiciary Committee. In his testimony, Professor Blakey stated that wiretapping in a marital dispute was one of the two main reasons for the Wiretap Act: "[P]rivate bugging in this country can be divided into two broad categories, commercial espionage and marital litigation." Sen. Subcomm. on Admin. Prac. & Proc. of the Sen. Jud. Comm., *The Right to Privacy Act of 1967*, 90th Cong. 413 (1967) *quoted in Jones*, 542 F.2d at 669.

A co-sponsor of the Wiretap Act, Senator Hruska, joined by Senators Dirksen, Scott, and Thurmond, stated: "A broad prohibition is imposed on private use of electronic surveillance, particularly in domestic relations and industrial espionage situations." Sen. Rpt. 90-1097 (Apr. 29, 1968) (reprinted in 1968 U.S.C.C.A.N. 2112, 2274). Additionally, the chairman of the Subcommittee on Administrative Practice and Procedure, Senator Long, identified divorce cases as one of three areas "where private electronic surveillance was widespread." *Jones*, 542 F.2d at 668 n. 12. The Sixth Circuit Court of Appeals relied, in part, on these comments to conclude that section 2511(1)(a) "establishes a broad prohibition on all private electronic surveillance and that a principal area of congressional concern was electronic surveillance for the purposes of marital litigation." *Id.* at 669 (reversing a district court's dismissal of a criminal indictment of a husband for recording telephone conversations between his estranged wife and a third party in the estranged wife's home in violation of the Wiretap Act).

Furthermore, the legislative purpose of the Wiretap Act supports the conclusion that interspousal wiretapping is prohibited. The Senate Report on the Wiretap Act stated:

> [The Wiretap Act] has a dual purpose (1) protecting the privacy of wire and oral communications, and (2) delineating on a uniform basis the circumstances and conditions under which the interception of wire and oral communications may be authorized. To assure the privacy of oral and wire communications, [the Wiretap Act] prohibits all wiretapping and electronic surveillance by persons other than duly authorized law enforcement officers. . . ."

Sen. Rpt. 90-1097 (reprinted in 1968 U.S.C.C.A.N. at 2153). Reviewing this passage from the Senate Report,

Passages from legislative history showing legislative intent.

Parenthetical explanation briefly stating court's holding under the case facts.

Legislative purpose supporting the plain meaning of the statute.

the Sixth Circuit Court of Appeals concluded, "[T]he Senate Report makes it clear that the purpose of the bill was to establish an across-the-board prohibition on all unauthorized electronic surveillance." *Jones,* 542 F.2d at 668.

Finally, an individual's right to privacy is a fundamental right in our society. A spouse's taping of a telephone conversation between the targeted spouse and a third party, without either party's knowledge or consent, is a violation not only of the spouse's privacy but also the third party's privacy. *See id.* at 670.

Although the majority of federal and state courts have concluded that the Wiretap Act is applicable to interspousal wiretapping, *see Glazner,* 347 F.3d at 1215, a minority of federal courts and two state courts have found that interspousal wiretapping is impliedly excepted from the Wiretap Act. *Anonymous v. Anonymous,* 558 F.2d at 679; *Simpson v. Simpson,* 490 F.2d 810; *Lizza v. Lizza*, 631 F. Supp. at 532-533; *Stewart v. Stewart*, 645 So. 2d 1321; *Baumrind v. Ewing*, 279 S.E.2d 353. In the leading case for this position, the Fifth Circuit Court of Appeals found that, although "the naked language" of the Wiretap Act seemingly applies to interspousal wiretapping, "Congress did not intend such a [far-reaching] result." *Simpson,* 490 F.2d at 805.

In the *Simpson* case, the court concluded that a husband's actions were impliedly excepted from the Wiretap Act when he purchased a recording device and attached it to a telephone within the marital home to record conversations between his wife and a third party. *Id.* at 810. Reviewing Senate Report 90-1097, the court found that most of the report focused on "electric surveillance by law enforcement officials" and "contain[ed] no clear indication that Congress intended to intrude into the marital relation within the marital home." *Id.* at 807. Reviewing transcripts of several congressional hearings on the Wiretap Act, the court found sparse references to private surveillance within the marital home, most of which were "directed towards the involvement of private investigators in marital conflicts." *Id.* at 807-809. Based on the court's findings, it would seem that the Wiretap Act would apply only to those domestic situations where a third party, such as a private investigator, was responsible for attaching a recording device and recording the telephone conversations.

Reporting the Sixth Circuit court's reliance on the statute's purpose to support its holding.

Public policy supporting the plain meaning of the statute.

Transition to the weaker position analysis.

Reporting the Fifth Circuit court's reasoning for its interpretation of the statute, which focuses on its review of legislative history to ascertain legislative intent.

Lending further support to the assertion that there is an implied exception in the Wiretap Act for interspousal wiretapping, at least one court has pointed to the comment of Professor Herman Schwartz, who appeared at a hearing before the House Judiciary Committee: "I take it nobody wants to make it a crime for a father to listen in on his teenage daughter or some such related problem." H.R. Jud. Comm., *The Anti-Crime Program Before Subcom. 5*, 90th Cong. 901 (1967), (quoted in *Lizza*, 631 F. Supp. at 532). In *Lizza*, the District Court for the Eastern District of New York deduced that "if nobody wants to make it a crime for a husband to record conversations between his wife and his daughter . . . , a husband's recording of conversations between his wife and a third party should [not] be viewed any differently." *Lizza*, 631 F. Supp. at 533 (citing *Anonymous*, 558 F.2d at 679). In *Lizza*, the court held that interspousal wiretapping is impliedly excepted by the Wiretap Act, dismissing a complaint filed by a wife and third party against her husband for recording conversations on the telephone within the marital home without the parties' knowledge or consent.

Courts finding an implied exception for interspousal wiretapping also have noted that the Wiretap Act is a part of the Omnibus Crime Control and Safe Streets Act of 1968, which is a crime control act. *See Simpson*, 490 F.2d at 806. According to Senate Report 90-1097, "The major purpose of [the Wiretap Act] is to combat organized crime." Sen. Rpt. 90-1097 (reprinted in 1968 U.S.C.C.A.N. at 2157). Consequently, in addition to providing civil remedies, the Wiretap Act "prescribes criminal sanctions for its violators." *Simpson*, 490 F.2d at 809. Thus, if spouses violate the Wiretap Act for taping conversations between their partners and third parties, the spouses will be "subject to severe criminal penalties, assuming of course that the prosecution could meet the higher standards of proof required for criminal convictions." *Id*. Because of this possibility, the court in the *Simpson* case stated that a court construing the Wiretap Act should be "bound by the principle that criminal statutes must be strictly construed." *Id*.

Further, if the Wiretap Act were to apply to interspousal wiretapping, it arguably "would have serious ramifications as to the degree of federal control over actions by family members within their own homes." *Lizza*, 631

Additional legislative history that a district court used to concur with the Fifth Circuit in its interpretation of the statute.

Brief explanation of the facts and holding in the district court case.

Purpose of the statute based on the statutory scheme.

Substantive canon of construction.

Prudential considerations.

F. Supp. at 533. Domestic conflict within a marital home is an area "normally left to states" to handle. *Simpson*, 490 F.2d at 805. The court in *Simpson* noted that finding interspousal wiretapping subject to the prohibition of the Wiretap Act would "override the interspousal immunity for personal torts accorded by the majority of states." *Id.* at 805 n. 7. "Given the novelty of a federal remedy for persons aggrieved by the personal acts of their spouses within the marital home, and given the severity of the remedy seemingly provided by [the Wiretap Act]," *id.* at 805 (footnote omitted), and absent a clear indication from the statute's language or the legislative history, the courts in the *Simpson* and *Lizza* cases refused to find that the Wiretap Act applied to interspousal wiretapping. *Simpson*, 490 F.2d at 10; *Lizza*, 631 F. Supp. at 533.

Nevertheless, although Congress amended the Wiretap Act in 1986 extensively by the Electronics Communications Privacy Act, 18 U.S.C. §§ 2510-3127 (2000 & Supp. III 2003), it did not revise the language of section 2511(1)(a) or other sections of the Wiretap Act to provide an express exception for interspousal tapping. Since the *Simpson* decision, the "overwhelming majority of federal circuit and district courts, as well as state courts, addressing the issue have refused to imply an exception to [the Wiretap Act] liability for interspousal wiretapping." *Glazner*, 347 F.3d at 1215. In light of this strong trend in the courts, it would seem that if Congress had intended to provide an interspousal exception to the Wiretap Act it would have expressly done so when amending the Wiretap Act for other reasons. The Wiretap Act prohibits interspousal wiretapping. Therefore, David is subject to civil penalties, as well as criminal sanctions, for his recording of the telephone conversations between Ana and John. *See* 18 U.S.C. §§ 2511, 2520 (2000 & Supp. III 2003).

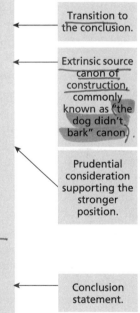

Transition to the conclusion.

Extrinsic source canon of construction, commonly known as ('the dog didn't bark" canon).

Prudential consideration supporting the stronger position.

Conclusion statement.

C. *Drafting an Objective Analysis of an Issue Addressing Alternative Rules or Principles*

In addition to a statutory interpretation issue, another type of purely legal question arises when a court must determine which of several competing rules or principles should govern the resolution of a dispute. The result will vary depending on which rules or principles are ultimately applied.

Sometimes districts or circuits within a jurisdiction may be divided as to which rules or principles should apply. For example, there might be a split within a state's intermediate appellate courts as to which rules or principles are appropriate to apply to resolve an issue. Let's say, as an attorney in East Carolina, you represent a man who has recently broken an engagement for marriage with a woman. Your client had given his ex-fiancée an expensive ring, symbolizing their commitment to each other (commonly referred to as an engagement ring), at the beginning of the engagement. In light of the broken engagement, your client wants his ex-fiancée to return the ring, but she refuses. While researching the issue of whether the ex-fiancée must return the ring, you find that the appellate courts in East Carolina are divided as to which rule to apply when determining whether an engagement ring should be returned. Of the three state districts, the First Circuit Court of Appeals for East Carolina has applied a "fault" rule, mandating that unless the parties mutually agree to end the engagement, the party who unjustifiably broke the engagement should not receive the ring. Conversely, the Third Circuit Court of Appeals for East Carolina has applied the "no fault" rule, providing that the ring should be returned to the man, regardless of who is at fault. Because your client and his ex-fiancée reside in the jurisdiction of the Second Circuit Court of Appeals, you will need to determine whether the Second Circuit court will apply the "fault" rule or the "no fault" rule.

Another situation where a court must choose between competing rules is when the controlling jurisdiction has not addressed the issue but courts in other jurisdictions have. In this instance, the reviewing court may look to jurisdictions outside the reviewing court's jurisdiction ("foreign courts") that have addressed the issue to determine how those jurisdictions resolved the issue. Sometimes the foreign courts are divided on how to resolve the issue, and the reviewing court must determine what rules or principles it will adopt to resolve the present dispute.

To illustrate, recall again the divorce of Ana and David Hart introduced in Chapter 7. The trial court in that scenario ordered as part of the property settlement that Ana sell her interest in a health club business owned by the couple and sign a covenant not to compete (CNC) with the business in exchange for David's payment of the fair market value of Ana's interest in the business. The fact-based issue in Chapter 7 focused on whether the terms of the CNC imposed by the trial court were reasonable. You have been asked by a senior attorney in the firm to research this issue and report back to her. While researching this issue, you discover there may be an additional issue, whether the trial court exceeded its judicial power when ordering Ana to enter into the CNC. Although no East Carolina court and no East Carolina statute has addressed this issue, you have found that foreign state courts have considered the issue and are divided on whether a trial court has exceeded its judicial authority by ordering a spouse to enter into a CNC as part of a divorce property settlement. After you report this finding to your senior attorney, she asks you to look further into this issue.

When an issue is one of first impression, as in Ana's case, you will research the law outside the jurisdiction of the reviewing court. Upon determining how other foreign jurisdictions have resolved the issue, you will research the law in the jurisdiction of the reviewing court to determine whether the existing law and public policies in the reviewing court's jurisdiction would support the adoption of the new rules or principles.

After thoroughly researching the issue, analyzing the law, and organizing the law, you are ready to begin drafting an objective discussion of the issue that will explain these alternative rules or principles embraced by foreign jurisdictions. In your analysis, you will discuss these alternative rules or principles in light of existing laws and policies in the reviewing court's jurisdiction to determine whether the reviewing court is likely to adopt any of the new rules or principles. In Ana's case, if she appeals the trial court's order requiring her to sign a CNC and the appeals court finds that the trial court abused its judicial power, then the trial court's order would be reversed. If this occurs, Ana would not be forced to sign the CNC, regardless of whether the terms of the CNC are reasonable.

1. The framework paragraph

An objective analysis of a law-based issue addressing alternative rules or principles begins with a framework paragraph that usually includes

(1) topic or thesis sentence,
(2) a statement that the issue is one of first impression within the jurisdiction of the deciding court, and
(3) a brief introduction to the alternative rules or principles that may be adopted by the deciding court. Using the law-based issue raised in Ana's case as an example, begin the discussion as follows.

Thesis statement and introduction to alternative rules

The trial court probably abused its judicial discretion when it ordered Ana to execute the CNC in return for David's payment of one-half of the fair market value of her interest in Hart Fitness Center. Whether a court can order a spouse to sign a CNC as part of a property settlement in a divorce proceeding is a case of first impression in East Carolina. Jurisdictions, including Oklahoma and Texas, have ruled that it is an abuse of the trial court's discretion to order a spouse to sign a CNC as part of a property settlement because the interest protected by

Thesis statement.

Statement advising this is an issue of first impression so that the reader understands why decisions of foreign courts are being used.

222

> the CNC is an involuntary agreement that restricts trade and represents the spouse's future earning capacity, which is not marital property subject to division upon divorce. *Favell v. Favell*, 957 P.2d 556, 561 (Okla. Civ. App. 1997); *Ulmer v. Ulmer*, 717 S.W.2d 665, 667-668 (Tex. App. 1986). Other jurisdictions, such as Idaho and Maine, permit courts to order a spouse to sign a CNC as part of a property settlement, identifying the interest protected by the CNC as the goodwill of the business, which is subject to division upon divorce. *Carr v. Carr*, 701 P.2d 304, 309-310 (Idaho App. 1985); *Lord v. Lord*, 454 A.2d 830, 834-835 (Me. 1983).

2. *The analysis*

Next, the analysis would include a discussion of each rule or principle. If logical, you should begin with the analysis of the rules or principles that you predict the reviewing court will ultimately adopt (the stronger position). Open with a topic or thesis sentence that signals the beginning of the analysis of the stronger position. If necessary, define the rules or principles supported by the stronger position, and then follow with an explanation of the primary decision(s) where the foreign court(s) adopted the rules or principles. Similar to a rule explanation for a fact-based issue discussion, the rule explanation for a law-based issue discussion contains

(1) the facts of the case relevant to the issue being analyzed,
(2) the foreign court's holding on the issue being analyzed, and
(3) the foreign court's reasoning for its holding on the issue being analyzed.

The rule explanation in a law-based issue discussion, however, does not emphasize the case facts as in a fact-based issue discussion; rather, the rule explanation in a law-based issue discussion emphasizes the court's reasoning for adopting the rule or principle and shows how the rule was applied in that case. The court's reasoning is of utmost importance because the law and policies relied on by that court will be used as a basis to determine whether the reviewing court in the present instance will adopt that rule.

◆ *Example of a rule explanation supporting the stronger position in Ana's case*

> An East Carolina appeals court will most likely follow the court in the *Favell* case and find that the trial court abused its discretion when it ordered Ana to sign

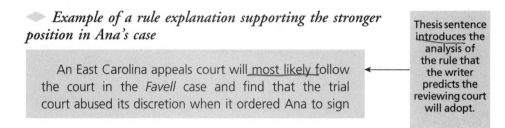

the CNC. In the *Favell* case, the husband and wife were majority stockholders in nine corporations created or acquired after the couple's marriage. In return for awarding the husband a portion of the corporate assets, the trial court imposed a CNC on the husband, preventing him from competing with the corporations awarded to the wife. The appellate court reversed the trial court's decision, holding that the court could not impose a CNC upon the husband. *Favell*, 957 P.2d at 561. *See also Ulmer*, 717 S.W.2d at 667 (trial court erred in ordering a husband not to compete with the janitorial business awarded to the wife because an individual's ability to practice his profession is not property subject to division in a divorce proceeding). The court in the *Favell* case reasoned that the imposition of the CNC was contrary to Oklahoma policy expressed in statutory law, which limited restraints on trade to specific situations where the seller of the goodwill of a business or where the parties dissolving a business agree to "refrain from carrying on a business within geographically specified (and statutorily limited) parameters." *Favell*, 957 P.2d at 560-561 (citing Okla. Stat. tit. 15, §§ 217-219 (1989)). The court in *Favell* also reasoned that the CNC "violated another general principle" that future earning capacity is not recognized in Oklahoma as marital property subject to division upon divorce. *Id.* at 561 (citing *Mocnik v. Mocnik*, 838 P.2d 500 (Okla. 1992)). The CNC infringed on the "[h]usband's right to pursue his chosen line of work, i.e., his future earning capacity." *Id.* at 561. "By including in the marital estate the value directly attributable to a restriction on [the h]usband's future earning ability, the trial court [impermissibly] treated at least a portion of [the h]usband's future earning capacity as marital property and awarded a portion of the value of that capacity to [the w]ife." *Id.*

The writer *briefly* states the facts so that the reader understands the situation is similar to the client's issue. The holding follows.

Because *Ulmer* does not add anything helpful to the analysis, the writer does not provide a rule explanation but only cites it with a parenthetical explanation showing that the *Ulmer* court ruled similarly.

Because the writer provides a rule explanation only of *Favell*, the analysis focuses only on that decision.

The court's reasoning focused on public policy as reflected in Oklahoma statutes.

The second part of the court's reasoning relied on another general principle applicable to divorces in Oklahoma as expressed in the state's common law.

After you explain the foreign court's reasons for adopting the rule, the reader begins to understand what laws and policies may persuade a reviewing court to adopt certain rules or principles over others. Now that you have set out this basic foundation, next analyze the likelihood that the reviewing court will adopt the rules or principles followed by the foreign court. To do this, focus on current law and public policy in the reviewing court's jurisdiction that may support that court's adoption of these new rules or principles. Where necessary, use analogy or distinction to compare these laws and policies in the reviewing court's jurisdiction to the laws and policies existing in the foreign court's jurisdiction at the time that court made its decision. By making these comparisons, you determine whether the two jurisdictions have similar laws and public policy interests. If appropriate, you also apply the rules or principles to the facts of your client's case.

◆ *Example of the analysis of the stronger position in Ana's case*

An East Carolina appeals court is likely to concur with the court's decision in *Favell* that Ana's CNC is against public policy because the CNCs in *Favell* and in Ana's case were court ordered. Similar to Oklahoma statutes on restrictions of trade, the public policy reflected in East Carolina statutes also disfavor agreements restricting competition. *Compare* E.C. Code §§ 24-1-1-1, 24-1-2-1 (1999) (contracts in restraint of trade are not favored by law and are void if they lessen competition) *with* Okla. Stat. tit. 15, §§ 217-219 (1989) (agreements between buyers and sellers of a business that restrain trade are void if the terms exceed statutorily imposed territorial limits). Therefore, an East Carolina appeals court will probably be reluctant to enforce the trial court's order forcing Ana to sign a CNC that restricts her right to compete against the health club business.

An analogy between Oklahoma statutory law and East Carolina statutory law.

Furthermore, similar to Oklahoma law, East Carolina law does not consider a spouse's future earning capacity as part of the marital property, subject to property division upon divorce. *Young v. Young*, 711 S.E.2d 1265, 1269 (E.C. 1999). The outcome of the issue depends primarily on whether the East Carolina appeals court will find (as did the court in the *Favell* case) that a spouse's interest in the business, which the other spouse is purchasing in return for the court-ordered CNC, actually represents the selling of a spouse's future earning capacity.

An analogy between Oklahoma common law and East Carolina common law.

In East Carolina, CNCs executed in connection with the sale of a business protect "the value of the business's goodwill, which represents the value of the customers'

Further explanation of the state of the common law in East Carolina.

relationship with the business at the time of the sale." *Mats Transport v. ABC Corp.*, 824 S.E.2d 1467, 1468 (E.C. App. 1992) (quoting *Matthews v. Acme Tax Consultants*, 470 S.E.2d 756, 763 (E.C. App. 1984)) (emphasis added). There are two types of goodwill that East Carolina courts have identified: "enterprise goodwill," which is subject to division upon divorce; and "professional goodwill," which represents future earning capacity and is not subject to division. *Young*, 711 S.E.2d at 1268-1269. It must be determined, then, whether the goodwill value represented by the court-ordered CNC to be signed by Ana represents enterprise goodwill or professional goodwill.

This paragraph and the following paragraph describe an East Carolina decision that explains two different types of goodwill and whether they are subject to property division upon divorce. Note that the rule explanation briefly states the facts and court holding. The bulk of the rule explanation focuses on the court's reasoning.

In the *Young* case, the court addressed the issue of whether a spouse's goodwill value in a business was divisible property in a divorce based on its status as enterprise or professional good will. *Id.* at 1268. Enterprise goodwill consists of those factors that may "contribute to the anticipated future profitability of the business . . . ," such as the business location, name recognition, and business reputation. *Id.* Enterprise goodwill is a business asset and "is property that is divisible in a dissolution to the extent that it inheres in the business, independent of any single individual's personal efforts and will outlast any person's involvement in the business." *Id.* at 1268-1269.

Conversely, professional goodwill "depends on the continued presence of a particular individual." *Id.* at 1269. As such, it is considered a personal asset and "[a]ny value that attaches to a business as a result of this 'personal goodwill' represents nothing more than the future earning capacity of the individual and is not divisible." *Id.* The court noted that E.C. Code § 31-15-7-5(5) (1998), mandating that the "relative earning power" of the husband or wife is not divisible property, reflects the policy in the state that future earning capacity should not be considered divisible property. *Young*, 711 S.E.2d at 1269. The court in *Young* remanded the case for a determination of whether the goodwill of the husband was enterprise goodwill or personal goodwill. *Id.* at 1272.

In light of the personal and professional nature of Ana's work at the health club, including personal coaching, name recognition, and a dedicated clientele, an East Carolina court would likely find that there was professional goodwill directly attributable to Ana. Because there was professional goodwill involved and

The rules applied to the facts of Ana's case.

East Carolina case law demonstrates that such goodwill, which represents future earning capacity, is not marital property, East Carolina is likely to determine that the court abused its discretion in ordering Ana to sign the CNC.

After you complete the analysis of the stronger position, you present the rules or principles that the court will be less likely to adopt (the weaker position). Similar to the analysis of the stronger position, the analysis of the weaker position usually includes

- any necessary definitions of the rules or principles supported by the weaker position;
- an explanation of the primary decision(s) in which foreign court(s) adopted the rules or principles;
- an analysis of the likelihood that the rules or principles followed by the foreign court will be adopted by the reviewing court, which may include
  - current law and public policy in the reviewing court's jurisdiction that may support the reviewing court's adoption of these new rules or principles;
  - where necessary, analogies or distinctions between the current laws and/or policies in the reviewing court's jurisdiction and the laws and policies existing at the time of the foreign court's decision to determine whether the two jurisdictions have similar law and public policy interests; and
  - if appropriate, an application of the rules or principles to the facts of the client's case.

Example of the analysis of the weaker position in Ana's case

Alternatively, an East Carolina appeals court might find that the trial court did not abuse its discretion in ordering Ana to execute the CNC. In the *Lord* case, the husband and wife owned an insurance agency, and the trial court ordered that the wife execute a CNC with her husband in their insurance business in order to receive her one-half value of the agency. The Supreme Judicial Court of Maine held that the trial court did not exceed its judicial powers in requiring the wife to execute a CNC. *Lord*, 454 A.2d at 834.

> The transitional word *alternatively* followed by a topic sentence signals the beginning of the weaker position analysis.

The court distinguished a professional practice (a doctor's business), where goodwill is dependent on that person's continued employment at the professional practice he helped create, from an insurance agency, where goodwill was not dependent on the continued employment of the insurance agent who created the business. *Id.* at 833. *See also Carr*, 701 P.2d at 309-310 (ordering a spouse

> The rule explanation of the Maine case briefly states the facts and holding. The remainder of the explanation focuses on the court's reasoning.

to execute a CNC in connection with the sale of a truck stop business owned by a husband and a wife was not an abuse of discretion because the business had only business goodwill and was not a professional practice). Thus, the goodwill of the couple's insurance agency was marital property because it comprised business goodwill, as opposed to personal goodwill. *Lord*, 454 A.2d at 833. Additionally, the court reasoned that the judicial power to order a CNC when awarding the business to the other spouse was comparable to the court ordering specific terms for payment of a sum representing one spouse's share in a business subject to division. *Id.* at 834 (construing 19 Me. Rev. Stat. Ann. § 722-A to grant the court the power necessary to render effective property division). Finally, the court reasoned that the CNC was necessary for a fair and just division of the marital business and to protect the value of the goodwill. *Id.* at 834.

> Analogies are made between the common law existing in Maine at the time of the *Lord* decision and the common law presently existing in East Carolina.

An East Carolina court may find there was no abuse of judicial discretion in ordering the CNC. Just as Maine allows business goodwill to be divided in a divorce decree because it is marital property, East Carolina recognizes enterprise goodwill as divisible property. *Young*, 711 S.E.2d at 1267. Ana and David's business might have only enterprise goodwill. The goodwill in a health club business is not dependent on the individuals who owned the business because health club members arguably belong to the club to use its facilities; this would not necessarily cease if Ana was no longer an owner.

> The rule is applied to the facts of Ana's case.

Additionally, similar to Maine courts that have the power to order specific terms for payment of a sum representing one spouse's share in a business subject to division, 19 Me. Rev. Stat. Ann. § 722-A, East Carolina courts have the power to award the property to one of the spouses and require the other "spouse to pay an amount, either in gross or in installments, that is just and proper." E.C. Code § 31-15-7-4(b)(2)(1997).

> Analogies are made between the statutory law existing in Maine at the time of the *Lord* decision and the statutory law presently existing in East Carolina.

East Carolina courts also are given broad discretionary powers by statute to divide the marital property in a "just and reasonable manner." *Id.* § 1-15-7-4(b). Therefore, East Carolina may concur with the court's reasoning in the *Lord* case that a CNC was necessary in order to protect the value of the business that one spouse was awarded. Otherwise, the spouse who sold his or her share of the business could open a rival business, depriving the other spouse of the full value of the business awarded in the divorce decree.

> Additional statutory law in East Carolina supports the weaker position analysis.

3. The conclusion

After a thorough analysis of both the stronger and weaker positions, you must state the conclusion and the reasons for the conclusion. As is the case with a fact-based issue discussion, the reasons in a law-based issue discussion may include a rebuttal of the weaker position and may otherwise explain the pivotal reason why the opposing position is stronger.

> #### Example of a conclusion paragraph for Ana's issue

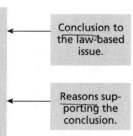

Nevertheless, East Carolina is more likely to find that it was an abuse of discretion for the trial court to order Ana to sign the CNC. East Carolina is careful to separate professional goodwill from enterprise goodwill, and an East Carolina court would probably find that there was professional goodwill directly attributable to Ana in the valuation of the business because of her name recognition and dedicated clientele. Because there was professional goodwill, which represents future earning capacity that is not marital property, and because public policy in East Carolina does not favor agreements in restraint of trade, an East Carolina appeals court is likely to determine that the trial court abused its discretion in ordering Ana to sign the CNC.

Conclusion to the law-based issue.

Reasons supporting the conclusion.

 ## D. Organizing a Document Containing a Law-Based Issue Analysis and a Fact-Based Issue Analysis

If you were to address the law-based issue analysis for Ana's case (whether the trial court exceeded its judicial powers in ordering Ana to sign the CNC) in the same document as the fact-based issue analysis for Ana's case (whether the terms of the court-ordered CNC are reasonable), you would need to determine whether the law-based issue or fact-based issue should be presented first. (See Chapter 12 for a discussion of threshold issues.) In Ana's case, the threshold issue is the law-based issue. If the trial court exceeded its judicial powers in ordering Ana to sign the CNC (as was the conclusion in the foregoing discussion), then the appellate court would not need to address whether the terms of the CNC are reasonable. But because you are only *predicting* what a court is likely to conclude and your goal is to inform the reader on all the issues relevant to the case, you also should provide a complete discussion of whether the terms of the CNC were reasonable.

A document containing both issue discussions should begin with an overall introduction presenting the two issues to be addressed, followed by the entire law-based discussion. An example of an overall introduction in Ana's case might look like the following paragraph.

> This discussion will address whether the trial court abused its judicial discretion when it ordered Ana to execute a CNC in return for David's paying her one-half of the fair market value of their health club business. This discussion will further address whether, if the trial court did not abuse its discretion, the CNC is unenforceable because it is overbroad in its protection of David's business interests.
>
> [The law-based issue discussion of whether the trial court exceeded its judicial powers when it ordered Ana to execute the CNC would be inserted here.]

Immediately following the law-based issue discussion in the document discussing Ana's case would be the fact-based issue discussion of whether the terms of the CNC are reasonable, as found in Chapter 9. The second issue would begin with an appropriate transitional statement:

> In the event the appeals court should find that the trial court did not exceed its authority when it ordered Ana to sign the CNC, the appeals court will probably find that the CNC that Ana has been ordered to sign is overbroad in its protection of David's business interests and is therefore unreasonable.
>
> [The fact-based discussion of whether the provisions of the CNC are reasonable would be inserted here.]

The document would end with an overall conclusion that summarizes the conclusions reached under the law-based issue and fact-based issue:

> The appeals court will probably find that the trial court exceeded its discretion when it ordered Ana to sign the CNC because the CNC represents a protection against the professional goodwill of Ana. The value of professional goodwill is tied to future earning capacity, which is not an asset subject to division upon divorce. Even if the court should find that the trial court did not abuse its discretion, the court will probably find the CNC unenforceable because the territorial restriction is overbroad for the protection of David's business interests.

● Exercise 14-A

The purpose of this exercise is to provide you with an experience in (1) drafting a legal discussion of a law-based issue addressing alternative rules and (2) choosing the law to use in a legal discussion. Your professor will give you the cases and statutes that may be helpful in writing the discussion. You will need to make choices about which cases and/or statutes to use in your discussion in order to present a *fair and balanced objective* discussion.

Whitewater Rafting Accident Involving Mary Ann Moore and her Son, Jason Moore

Recall the story of the Moores from Chapter 7. A senior attorney in your law firm has discovered an issue that might block the Moores' pursuit of a negligence action against Jungle River Expeditions (JRE), even if the court finds that the two-part test for personal jurisdiction has been satisfied.

The senior attorney recently learned that before the rafting trip Ms. Moore signed on behalf of Jason a release of JRE's liability in the event of an accident. If the release is enforceable against Jason, the Moores will be unable to bring an action on behalf of Jason against JRE in the court. The release did not specify the law governing the interpretation of the release. A federal court may look to the law of East Carolina to determine whether Ms. Moore's signing of the release on behalf of Jason is enforceable. At the senior attorney's request, you researched East Carolina law and found no East Carolina decision addressing the issue of whether a release is enforceable against a minor child's claim when the parent signed a pre-injury release. Therefore, this is an issue of first impression in your jurisdiction.

You have been able to locate, however, several cases from other states that have addressed the issue. The courts deciding those cases disagree on whether a pre-injury release signed by a parent bars a child's injury claim. In your reading of the cases, you found that many of the courts looked to statutes in their respective states existing at the time of the respective court's decisions to help determine the state's policy on whether parents have the power to sign a pre-injury release on behalf of their children. You have found some East Carolina statutes that speak to parental control over a minor child or the minor child's independent power in various circumstances. Perhaps these statutes (in addition to the cases from outside jurisdictions) will assist you in determining which position East Carolina may adopt.

Read the relevant cases and East Carolina statutes that your professor supplies, and then brief the cases. Decide which law you will use for your discussion. Then, following the drafting concepts learned in this chapter, write a discussion addressing the issue of whether an East Carolina court would enforce a pre-injury release signed by a parent, thus preventing a minor child from bringing a negligence claim against the released party.

CHAPTER

15

Citing to Authority

HIGHLIGHTS

- Never assume that a citation as provided in another source is proper; always check one of the citation manuals that contains the rules for proper citation form.
- Omitting information that tells your reader where information originates and how to access that source creates serious problems.
- Following the guidelines for how to provide information in a proper form gives your reader what is expected; failing to follow the guidelines may lead to questions of credibility that may affect the reader's perception of your substance.

Entire books are written about proper U.S. legal citation form. The two best known books are the *ALWD Citation Manual: A Professional System of Citation* (3d ed., Aspen Publishers 2006), and *The Bluebook: A Uniform System of Citation* (18th ed., Harv. L. Rev. Assn. 2005).[1] Because those books give extensive details, this chapter provides only a broad overview of correct citation form to help you better understand its role in writing legal documents. Particular attention is paid to using proper citation form when writing office memoranda and documents directed to the court.[2]

---

1. Books exist even to explain the citation manuals. *See, e.g.*, Maria L. Ciampi, Rivka Widerman & Vicki Lutz, *The Citation Workbook: How to Beat the Citation Blues* (2d ed., Anderson Publishing Co. 1997); Larry L. Tepley, *Legal Writing Citation* (ThomsonWest 2008).

2. Unless explicitly stated otherwise, the examples in this chapter, as throughout the book, follow the rules found in the *ALWD Citation Manual.*

Note that each U.S. state may have its own officially recognized rules for proper citation form or may adopt a commercial rule book as its official source for proper citation form. As always, check the local rules of the court for guidance on proper citation form before submitting any court document.

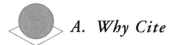

A. Why Cite

The U.S. legal system's reliance on primary authority (constitutional and statutory provisions, case law, and administrative regulations) requires you to refer to the source of the information you include in a legal document. This is especially important when that information comes from a source that is binding on your case and is included in an office memorandum or a brief to the court. Even when the source is not from your jurisdiction and, therefore, is not binding, you must cite any information that either originates in a persuasive primary source, such as a statute, case, or constitutional provision from outside the jurisdiction of your case, or any secondary source, such as a law review article written by a scholar in the field, a provision of the relevant Restatement of the Law, a book, or a treatise.

If you do not cite where required, you give the impression that your ideas or words form the basis for the information. This is a mistake for two reasons. First, relevant material that comes from a primary source of law offers the most persuasive and effective support for your argument. Second, conveying the incorrect impression that the ideas or words are yours and not another source's is plagiarism,[3] which can affect adversely your credibility and ultimately the strength of your client's case.

Citing to sources also allows your reader to access the information provided in your written document. Your reader can then (1) check the accuracy of your reference, (2) read further information found in the cited source, or (3) use that source to locate further sources. A law clerk working for the judge in your case, for example, will likely check your sources for accuracy. Your reader may want to read the entire case or statutory language to which you have cited. Your reader may want to look at more sections of a cited law review article. Finally, your reader may find your document during the research process and use your document as a resource for accessing further helpful authority to which you have cited.

The same guidelines apply when you are writing a scholarly article, such as a paper for a class or a law review article. Although you do not have to worry about binding case law, you still must carefully document where the information included in your paper originated; to do otherwise is to commit plagiarism. In addition, scholarly papers are particularly useful because authors provide extensive information on the legal resources available on the topic of the paper. This information is oftentimes found in the footnotes or endnotes of the paper.[4]

---

3. Chapter 6 addresses plagiarism in detail.

4. Footnotes are found at the bottom of each page on which a source is mentioned; endnotes are found at the end of the document in a numbered series. This book includes footnotes rather than endnotes.

B. When to Cite

Knowing when to cite is difficult for everyone. A general guideline to follow is that when in doubt provide a citation. Providing a citation when one is not needed is never wrong; omitting a citation where one is required, however, creates problems.

1. Cite quoted language originating in another source

Cite anytime you quote directly the language of a source. For example, in Chapter 7 the court in *Mats Transport v. ABC Corporation* sets out a three-pronged test used to determine the reasonability of a covenant not to compete. If writing a document that referred to *Mats Transport* and the three-pronged test, using the same words found in the opinion, you would quote the test as follows:

> To prove reasonability, "(1) the covenant must not be broader than necessary for the protection of the covenantee's legitimate business interest; (2) the covenant cannot have an adverse effect on the covenantor; and (3) the covenant cannot adversely affect the public interest." *Mats Transp. v. ABC Corp.*, 824 S.E.2d 1467, 1468 (E.C. App. 1992).

Once you have quoted and cited a source, however, you do not need to continue to quote that language when referring to it later in your document. In the quote above, for example, after you provide the direct quotation, should you later refer to a covenant that does not adversely affect the public interest, you do not need to include quotation marks around the legal phrase "adversely affect the public interest."

2. Cite anytime you paraphrase information found in another source

Even when you paraphrase or summarize information found in another source, as discussed in Chapter 6, the idea still belongs to the original author of the source. Since the idea was not yours originally, you must provide a citation.

Example of the original quoted language:

> In *Mats Transport*, the court wrote, "Whether a covenant [not to compete] is overly broad depends, in part, on the extent of the territory restricted." *Mats Transp. v. ABC Corp.*, 824 S.E.2d 1467, 1468 (E.C. App. 1992).

The term "not to compete" appears in brackets in the above example. This indicates to the reader that the writer has added this language to the quoted language; this phrase is not part of the original quotation.

▸ *Example of the writer's paraphrase of the original language:*

> In determining whether a covenant not to compete is too broad, courts will consider the geographic distance of the territory being restricted. *Mats Transp. v. ABC Corp.*, 824 S.E.2d 1467, 1468 (E.C. App. 1992).

Notice that in both of the above examples, the writer still cites to the location in the opinion where the reference is located.

3. Cite to one source that refers and cites to a different source

In some instances, you may be reading one source that includes a reference and citation to a different source. For example, when citing the three-pronged test above, the court in *Mats Transport* cited to *Hanson v. Albright*, 539 S.E.2d 500, 500 (E.C. App. 1989). In deciding whether you cite only to *Mats Transport* or also to *Hanson*, consider the following choices.

(a) You may choose to find and read *Hanson* and cite directly to *Hanson* for the reference, without any reference to *Mats Transport*; or

(b) You may choose to cite both *Mats Transport* and *Hanson*, showing that *Hanson* was cited in *Mats Transport*.

If you choose the second approach, assuming that this is the first time you refer to both cases, you would cite to these sources in one of the two following ways.

▸ *Alternative 1:*

> *Mats Transport v. ABC Corp.*, 824 S.E.2d 1467, 1468 (E.C. App. 1992) (citing *Hanson v. Albright*, 539 S.E.2d 500, 500 (E.C. App. 1989)).

▸ *Alternative 2:*

> *Hanson v. Albright*, 539 S.E.2d 500, 500 (E.C. App. 1989) (cited in *Mats Transport v. ABC Corp.*, 824 S.E.2d 1467, 1468 (E.C. App. 1992)).

In determining whether to cite to the second source (the source contained in the main source to which you are referring), follow these guidelines.

(a) If the source to which you are referring *directly quoted* the language from a second source, and you are also quoting the language, you *must* cite to the original source of the quoted language. You may do this one of two ways:

◆ *Alternative 1:*

Mats Transport v. ABC Corp., 824 S.E.2d 1467, 1468 (E.C. App. 1992) (quoting *Hanson v. Albright*, 539 S.E.2d 500, 500 (E.C. App. 1989)).

◆ *Alternative 2:*

Hanson v. Albright, 539 S.E.2d 500, 500 (E.C. App. 1989) (quoted in *Mats Transport v. ABC Corp.*, 824 S.E.2d 1467, 1468 (E.C. App. 1992)).

(b) If the source to which you are referring did *not* directly *quote* language from a second source but only *cited* to that source for the idea, you are not required to cite to the second source. However, you may choose to cite to both sources if you have a substantive reason to do so, such as when the main source to which you are referring is a state intermediate appellate court decision and that court cites to a decision by the same state's highest court. You could obtain the highest court's opinion and cite directly to that source, or you could cite to both the intermediate appellate court decision and the highest court's decision. This is especially appropriate when the decisions are separated by many years. For example, if the highest court's decision was issued in 1975 and was then cited in an intermediate appellate court case decided six months prior to when you are researching, you would likely want to cite to both cases, to show that the language cited was originally set down by the highest court in 1975 and was still being followed in the more recent case.

4. When it is not necessary to provide a citation

Another way to consider when to cite is to think about when it is not necessary to cite. Consider the following guidelines.

(a) ***Substantive facts.*** You do not need to cite when providing the substantive facts, or story, from a court opinion, unless you are quoting directly from the facts found in that opinion. Quoting the facts is usually not necessary unless the court has included quoted testimony from the trial court case and that quotation is important to the legal issue you are addressing. For example, in a case involving a contract dispute, the testimony of the parties may be significant in deciding whether an enforceable contract existed. If the parties' testimony is quoted in the court opinion, you will likely want to provide the direct quote in your document as well. In this instance, you must provide quotation marks and a citation to where those facts are located in the court's opinion.

(b) ***Procedural facts.*** You do not need to cite to the procedural facts from a court opinion. As discussed in Chapter 4, the procedural facts include the procedural history of the case or the actions taken by the courts below. The procedural facts include a statement of the cause of action (e.g., an action for breach of contract or negligence) and the judgment in the lower court case (e.g., affirmed, reversed, etc.).

(c) You do not need to cite information that is considered common knowledge, as discussed in Chapter 6 on plagiarism. This determination is often difficult for those living both inside and outside the United States. The best solution to this dilemma is to follow the guideline given at the beginning of the chapter: When in doubt, provide a citation. Anytime you find information in another source and are not sure whether that information is considered common knowledge, provide a citation.

● **Exercise 15-A**

Read the following passage and place checkmarks where citations are needed.

We are required to balance the right of the defendant to confront his accuser with the competing interest of the state in protecting child witnesses from the trauma of giving testimony before a court and the person whom they allege brought them to harm. (An Indiana appellate court considered whether a child's videotaped testimony was properly admitted in the prosecution of a defendant for child abuse. "When a hearsay declarant is unavailable, his statement may not be admissible unless it bears adequate indicia of reliability." There is no ambiguity in the constitutional provision. Face to face confrontation must surely mean "face to face" confrontation. The right granted by Article I Section 13 [of the Indiana Constitution] is violated when a defendant is placed at a location where he or she cannot be seen or heard by the witness, even though the defendant is permitted to observe the witness and listen to the witness's testimony. In *Coy v. Iowa* the United States Supreme Court stated that the United States Constitution guarantees defendants the right of confrontation and ruled that the Iowa statute violated that right and was, therefore, unconstitutional. The Iowa statute in *Coy* was deficient because it did not require individualized findings of need for special protection. Based on this, the Court stated that "something more than the type of generalized finding underlying such a statute is needed when the exception is not 'firmly rooted in our jurisprudence.'"

C. How to Cite

Legal citation rules ensure that readers receive the information they need to find an original source. They also promote consistency of form so that readers know what to expect. Citation rules explain (1) what to include in a citation (the substance), and (2) how to structure the citation (the form). The first instruction — what to provide in a proper citation — is of the utmost importance.

1. What to include in a citation (the substance)

a. Primary authority

Including the recommended information ensures that your reader can (1) understand the source of the information and (2) access that source. The information required in the citation varies depending on the source itself. Again, always refer to a legal citation manual, such as the *ALWD Citation Manual* or the *Bluebook*, for the specific rules relevant to each source. The basic substance to include when citing to primary authority follows. In the examples below, the part of the cite being emphasized is shown in boldface type. In a regular citation, no bold typeface would be used.

(i) Constitutional provisions[5]

When referring to a constitutional provision, provide the following basic information.

- The source of the provision, that is, whether it is the U.S. Constitution or a state constitution.

Examples:

> **U.S. Const**. amend. IV.
> **N.Y. Const**. art. IV, § 7.

- The section, article, or clause.

Examples:

> U.S. Const. **amend. IV**.
> N.Y. Const. **art. IV, § 7**.

(ii) Statutory provisions[6]

- The volume of the book where the statute is found.

Examples:

> **23** U.S.C. § 1331 (2005).
> **810** Ill. Comp. Stat. § 5/2-314 (1) (2001).

---

5. Specific rules on constitutions are found in Rule 13.0 of the *ALWD Citation Manual* and Rule 11 of the *Bluebook*.

6. Specific rules covering statutes are found in Rule 14.0 of the *ALWD Citation Manual* and Rule 12 of the *Bluebook*. Guidelines for citing statutes found online or on the Internet appear in Rule 14.5 of the *ALWD Citation Manual*.

- The abbreviation for the code or statute. Cite to the official code if possible. The official federal code is the United States Code, cited as "U.S.C." Official state code or statute names vary from state to state; they are listed in Appendix 1 of the *ALWD Citation Manual* and Table 1 of the *Bluebook*.

Examples:

> 23 **U.S.C.** § 1331 (2005).
> 810 Ill. **Comp. Stat**. § 5/2-314 (2001).

- The specific section that references the statute.

Examples:

> 23 U.S.C. § **1331** (2005).
> 810 Ill. Comp. Stat. § **5/2-314** (2001)

- If citing an unofficial code (one that has not been adopted by a court), indicate within parentheses which company publishes it. The unofficial sources for federal statutes are the United States Code Annotated (U.S.C.A.), published by West Publishing Company, and the United States Code Service (U.S.C.S.), published by LexisNexis. The state unofficial sources vary state by state and are listed in Appendix 1 of the *ALWD Citation Manual* and Table 1 of the *Bluebook*.

Examples:

> 23 U.S.C.A. § 1331 (**West** 2005).
> 23 U.S.C.S. § 1331 (**Lexis** 2005).
> 810 Ill. Comp. Stat. Ann. § 5/2-314 (**West** 2001).

- The year of the publication of the book in which the statute is located, placed in parentheses.

Examples:

> 23 U.S.C. § 1331 **(2005)**.
> 810 Ill. Comp. Stat. § 5/2-314 **(2001)**

- Books including statutes also have supplements. Supplements are published periodically and added to the hard volumes, usually at the back of the book. The supplements contain new statutes and amendments to statutes that were enacted since the date of the publication of the book. If the reference in your text is found in the supplement, indicate that in parentheses.

> *Example:*

> 23 U.S.C. § 1331 (**Supp. 2007**).

- If the main volume contains a statute that is still valid, and the supplement contains an amendment to that statute, both are shown in the parenthetical.

> *Example:*

> 23 U.S.C. § 1331 (**2005 & Supp. 2007**).

If researching online, the updated information is automatically integrated with the previous provisions already online, so a reference to a supplement is not needed.

Individual statutory references may include additional information, such as the subject matter or topic of the statute or its title, for example. Check your citation manual for specific guidelines.

(iii) Court opinions

- Case names: Providing a proper case name requires checking multiple rules found in a citation manual. The basic rules for citing case names are found in Rule 12.2 of the *ALWD Citation Manual* and Rules 10.2 and B5.1.1 of the blue practitioners' pages of the *Bluebook*.[7] A general approach to providing proper case names is to assume nothing and check for a rule about everything. Never assume, for example, that the citation found on the top of the court opinion is written in proper citation form. In fact, the reported case name usually contains more information than is necessary for a proper citation. When referring to a case, provide the following basic information.

> *Examples:*

> (federal) ***Bush v. Gore***, 531 U.S. 98 (2000).
> (state) ***Trossman v. Phillipsborn***, 869 N.E.2d 1147 (Ill. App. 1st Dist. 2007).

- The volume of the reporter where the opinion is located. In a written text, the volume number is found on the spine of the book.

> *Examples:*

> (federal) *Bush v. Gore,* **531** U.S. 98 (2000).
> (state) *Trossman v. Phillipsborn,* **869** N.E.2d 1147 (Ill. App. 1st Dist. 2007).

---

7. General rules covering case citations are found in Rule 12 of the *ALWD Citation Manual* and Rule 10 of the *Bluebook*. Guidelines for citing cases found online or on the Internet appear in Rules 12.12 and 12.15 of the *ALWD Citation Manual*.

- The abbreviated name of the reporter where the opinion is located.

Examples:

> (federal)   *Bush v. Gore*, 531 **U.S.** 98 (2000).
> (state)   *Trossman v. Phillipsborn*, 869 **N.E.2d** 1147 (Ill. App. 1st Dist. 2007).

In the two above examples, "U.S." is the abbreviation for "United States Reports," and "N.E.2d" is the abbreviation for "North Eastern Reporter, Second Series." The North Eastern Reporter is one of West's regional reporters, which are the official reporters in most U.S. states. Each regional reporter contains cases from multiple state courts, primarily appellate courts. The abbreviations for most reporters are found in Chart 12.1 of the *ALWD Citation Manual.* Also refer to Appendix 1 in the *ALWD Citation Manual* or Table 1 in the *Bluebook.*

- The page of the reporter where the first page of the opinion is located.

Examples:

> (federal)   *Bush v. Gore*, 531 U.S. **98** (2000).
> (state)   *Trossman v. Phillipsborn*, 869 N.E.2d **1147** (Ill. App. 1st Dist. 2007).

- Subsequent page where the relevant information in the case is found, if applicable.

Examples:

> (federal)   *Bush v. Gore*, 531 U.S. **98, 99** (2000).
> (state)   *Trossman v. Phillipsborn*, 869 N.E.2d 1147, **1150** (Ill. App. 1st Dist. 2007).

- The year when the case was decided (provided in parentheses).

Examples:

> (federal)   *Bush v. Gore*, 531 U.S. 98 **(2000)**.
> (state)   *Trossman v. Phillipsborn*, 869 N.E.2d 1147 (Ill. App. 1st Dist. **2007**).

- Any other necessary identifying information (see below).

When citing to a federal decision:

- If the U.S. Supreme Court decided the case, no other information is necessary.

- If a federal circuit (intermediate appellate) court decided the case, include the specific circuit. In the next example, the court opinion originated in the Ninth Circuit of the United States Court of Appeals.

Example:

> *Smith v. Jones,* 232 F.3d 547 (**9th Cir.** 2004).

- If a federal district (trial) court decided the case, include a specific reference to the trial court. In the next example, the court opinion originated in the United States District Court for the Northern District of Ohio.

Example:

> *Brown v. White,* 450 F. Supp. 1250 (**N.D. Ohio** 1997).

When citing to a state decision:

- If the highest court of the state decided the case, and you are citing to a regional reporter, such as the Pacific Reporter, Second Series, listed in the citation below, include a reference to the state along with the year the case was decided in parentheses. A U.S. legal reader will know the case comes from the highest state court when the citation includes only an abbreviation of the state and no other identifying court information.

Example:

> *Simmons v. Hershey,* 75 P.2d 698 (**Ariz.** 1978).

- If an intermediate appellate state court decided the case, and you are citing to a regional reporter, such as the North Eastern Reporter, Second Series, listed in the citation below, include a reference to the specific appellate court in parentheses. The reference to the appellate court is indicated by "App." if following the *ALWD Citation Manual.* If following the *Bluebook,* the appellate court is indicated by "App." or "Ct. App." The state-by-state tables in the citation manuals provide the guidelines for each state.

- The *ALWD Citation Manual* also requires any citation to a state case to refer not only to which level of court decided the case but also to the specific state court that decided the case, where applicable. Again, the state-by-state table found in the *ALWD Citation Manual* is the best resource for these references.

Example:

> *Morrow v. Mills*, 666 N.E.2d 872 (Ind. App. 1st Dist. 2004).

- Sometimes you will find that the state case is found in more than one reporter. This happens when both an official and one or more unofficial reporters publish the same court opinion. If it is necessary to cite to multiple reporters,[8] always cite to the official reporter first and to any unofficial reporter(s) thereafter. Use Appendix 1 of the *ALWD Citation Manual* and Table 1 of the *Bluebook* to determine where parallel citations are needed.

Example:

> *Simmons v. Hershey*, 645 Ariz. 1245, 75 P.2d 698 (1978).

The above example reveals that the highest court in Arizona decided the case (Ariz.) and that the case is found in both the Arizona Reports (the official reporter) and the Pacific Reporter, Second Series (the unofficial reporter). Unlike prior examples, there is no state abbreviation in the parentheses. This omission is because the state and level of court (the highest court in Arizona) is indicated in the official citation to the Arizona Reports.

Rules that set out what to include on a state-by-state basis are found in Appendix 1 of the *ALWD Citation Manual* and Table 1 of the *Bluebook*.

b. Secondary sources

(i) Law review articles (periodicals)[9]

When referring to a law review article, provide the following basic information:

- The author of the article.

> **Nicholas Quinn Rosenkranz**, *Federal Rules of Statutory Interpretation*, 115 Harv. L. Rev. 2085 (2002).

---

8. Court rules often require writers submitting documents to the court to include references to both the official and unofficial reporters. Most states no longer have official reporters. However, states likely had official reporters in the past; if you are citing to a case when both official and unofficial reporters existed you must cite to both. As always, it's essential that when submitting a document to the court you check the appropriate court rules.

9. Guidelines for citing to periodicals are found in Rule 23 of the *ALWD Citation Manual* and Rule 16 of the *Bluebook*.

- The title of the article.

> Nicholas Quinn Rosenkranz, *Federal Rules of Statutory Interpretation*, 115 Harv. L. Rev. 2085 (2002).

- The volume (if applicable) in which the article is located.

> Nicholas Quinn Rosenkranz, *Federal Rules of Statutory Interpretation*, **115** Harv. L. Rev. 2085 (2002).

- The abbreviated name of the periodical where the article is located. The law review below is the Harvard Law Review. The list of abbreviations for periodicals are found in Appendix 5 of the *ALWD Citation Manual* and Table 13 of the *Bluebook*.

> Nicholas Quinn Rosenkranz, *Federal Rules of Statutory Interpretation*, 115 **Harv. L. Rev.** 2085 (2002).

- The first page on which the article begins.

> Nicholas Quinn Rosenkranz, *Federal Rules of Statutory Interpretation*, 115 Harv. L. Rev. **2085** (2002).

- Subsequent pages where the relevant material in the article is found, if applicable.

> Nicholas Quinn Rosenkranz, *Federal Rules of Statutory Interpretation*, 115 Harv. L. Rev. 2085, **2090** (2002).

- The year of the publication of the periodical in which the information is located (placed in parentheses).

> Nicholas Quinn Rosenkranz, *Federal Rules of Statutory Interpretation*, 115 Harv. L. Rev. 2085 **(2002).**

Other information may be required. To ensure completeness, refer to your citation manual.

(ii) Restatements of law

The American Law Institute (ALI) brings together judges, professors, and legal scholars who document in the Restatements the relevant common law rules developed throughout the country in a particular legal area.[10] In addition, the Restatement authors provide commentary to those common law rules, helping to clarify how the rules have been interpreted and applied. The commentary may include criticism of the rules and any minority viewpoints regarding the relevant rules. When citing to a Restatement, include the following basic information.

- The name of the Restatement.

> *Restatement (Second) of Torts* § 402A (1995).

- The relevant section of the Restatement.

> *Restatement (Second) of Torts* **§ 402A** (1995).

- A comment reference ("cmt."), if applicable.

> *Restatement (Second) of Torts* § 402A **cmt. i** (1995).

- The year of publication of the Restatement.

> *Restatement (Second) of Torts* § 402A **(1995)**.

(iii) Books[11]

When citing to books, provide the following basic information.

- The name of the author of the book.

---

10. As of 2007, published Restatements cover the following legal doctrine: Agency, Business Associations, Conflict of Laws, Contracts, Foreign Relations Law of the United States, Judgments, The Law Governing Lawyers, Property, Restitution and Unjust Enrichment, Security, Suretyship and Guaranty, Torts, Trusts, and Unfair Competition. Guidelines for citing to Restatements are found in Rule 27.1 of the *ALWD Citation Manual* and Rule 12.8.5 of the *Bluebook*.

11. Rules addressing citations to books are found in Rule 22 of the *ALWD Citation Manual* and Rule 15 of the *Bluebook*.

> **William N. Eskridge Jr.,** *Dynamic Statutory Interpretation* 323 (Harv. U. Press 1994).

- The title of the book.

> William N. Eskridge Jr., ***Dynamic Statutory Interpretation*** 323 (Harv. U. Press 1994).

- The page in the book where the information to which you are referring is located.

> William N. Eskridge Jr., *Dynamic Statutory Interpretation* **323** (Harv. U. Press 1994).

- If following a citation format that requires it, the identity of the publisher (provided in parentheses). The publisher in the example is Harvard University Press.

> William N. Eskridge Jr., *Dynamic Statutory Interpretation* 323 (**Harv. U. Press** 1994).

- The year of publication of the book (provided in parentheses).

> William N. Eskridge Jr., *Dynamic Statutory Interpretation* 323 (Harvard U. Press **1994**).

Rules also exist for additional information that may be necessary when citing to secondary authority. Always check your citation manual.

(iv) International materials

Coverage of international materials in the *ALWD Citation Manual* and the *Bluebook* is not extensive. However, Aspen Publishers will be publishing a new text, *ALWD Citation Manual: International Sources*, in the near future. Rules for international materials are covered in Rule 21 of the *ALWD Citation Manual* and Rules 20 and 21 of the *Bluebook*. You must refer to your citation manual for the specific rules and guidance.

International treaties: When citing to an international treaty, include the following basic information.

- The name of the treaty.

> ***Treaty on European Union*** (July 29, 1992), Off. J.C. 191.

- The date the treaty was signed, in parentheses.

> *Treaty on European Union* **(July 29, 1992)**, Off. J.C. 191.

- One source for locating the treaty.

> *Treaty on European Union* (July 29, 1992), **Off. J.C. 191**.

- The Internet is becoming a main source for international agreements and may also be used. The URL is provided as the source for locating the treaty.

> *Treaty on European Union* (July 29, 1992),
> **http://europa.eu.int/eurlex/lex/en/treaties/dat/11992M/htm/**
> **11992M.html.**

- In addition, if referring to a specific subdivision of the treaty, include a reference to that subdivision.

> *Treaty on European Union* (July 29, 1992), **Title III**, Off. J.C. 191.

International case law: When citing to an international case, include the following basic information.

- As with all cases, begin this citation with the case name.

> ***Craig v. South Australia***, 184 CLR 163 (1995).

- Follow with the volume and abbreviated name of the publication where the case can be located. In the example below, "CLR" documents court decisions from the High Court of Australia.

> *Craig v. South Australia*, **184 CLR** 163 (1995).

- Follow with the page on which the case begins (or the number of the case):

> *Craig v. South Australia*, 184 CLR **163** (1995).

- End with the date of the case, provided in parentheses.

> *Craig v. South Australia*, 184 CLR 163 (**1995**).

2. How to structure a citation (the form)

Some of the guidelines provided above — those guidelines focusing on the substance of a citation — provide information necessary for the reader to identify the specific source and the specific location of the reference within that source. Omitting the substantive information is a major error.

The chart in Appendix L, however, focuses on the technical form of a citation, based on the rules found in the *ALWD Citation Manual*. Failing to follow these rules on form is less serious than failing to follow the rules on substance. Nevertheless, if you ignore these rules your reader, most likely a judge, may get the impression that detail does not matter to you. This impression may carry over to the substance of your argument, which is something you want to avoid. These guidelines on form include basic rules with examples of proper citations, such as the order in which to provide the information and the abbreviations, spacing, and so on. The citation manuals provide many more rules than the basic ones provided in this chapter and should always be checked when writing proper citations.

● Exercise 15-B

1. Consider again the passage in Exercise 15-A. The relevant portions of that passage are found in the cases below. Incorporate the proper citations into the passage from Exercise 15-A. Use the citation manual assigned to your class. Remember that the citations as provided in the case may not be correct according to the citation manual you are using, so you'll need to check each one for accuracy.

2. Once you have added the proper citations to the passage, edit the passage to conform with the stylistic rules found in your citation manual. Chapter 6 discusses in detail the points raised below. Specifically, consider the following questions:

   a. Are quotations properly integrated into the larger sentence?
   b. Do any quotations exceed 49 words, requiring that they be written in block form (indented and single spaced, with no quotation marks)?
   c. Have you shown omissions of words from quotations through the use of ellipses (three spaced dots, shown as "...")?

Court of Appeals of Indiana, First District.
Berry Altmeyer, Appellant (Defendant Below)
v.
State of Indiana, Appellee (Plaintiff Below).
No. 1-1285A308.
Sept. 2, 1986.

496 N.E.2d 1329

Robertson, Presiding Judge.

Appellant/defendant Berry Altmeyer (Altmeyer) appeals his convictions of three counts of child molesting and one count of attempted child molesting.

We remand.

The facts pertinent to our preliminary disposition of this appeal are summarized as follows: Altmeyer was charged with the child molesting of his nieces J.M. and D.M.,[12] who are sisters, and of A.M., Altmeyer's niece and cousin of J.M. and D.M. The victims were age 12 or under at the time of the offenses in the late summer of 1983.

In October 1984, Charles Perkins, an Indiana state trooper, and Lisa Berry, a caseworker in the county welfare department, questioned A.M. about the incidences of sexual abuse, recording her statements on videocassette tape. On the prosecutor's motion and after a hearing, the trial court ruled that although the three victims were competent witnesses, A.M. was unavailable to testify at trial because her participation would be a traumatic experience for her, and that her videotaped statement was admissible in lieu of her testimony. In so ruling, the court stated on the record that it had found the statements bore sufficient indications of reliability. No transcription of A.M.'s videotaped statement appears in the record. After the State presented evidence corroborating the acts of which Altmeyer

was charged, including testimony of J.M. and D.M., the jury viewed the videotape. Altmeyer was found guilty on all four counts.

On appeal, Altmeyer raises several points of error. Because we remand, we will address only these issues: I. Whether A.M. was unavailable to testify at the trial; and *1330 II. Whether the videotape of A.M.'s statements was admissible hearsay under Ind. Code 35-37-4-6.

****

Issue I

Altmeyer contends that the statute as it applies to him deprived him of his right to cross-examine A.M. He argues that I.C. 35-37-4-6 impermissibly expands the meaning of unavailability because it does not require the State to make a good faith effort to produce the child witness where a psychiatrist certifies that testifying at trial would be a traumatic experience for the child. I.C. 35-37-4-6(c)(2)(i).

****

Altmeyer declares that I.C. 35-37-4-6 is unconstitutional on its face because it denies the defendant his right to confront his accusers. He has failed to persuade us that we decided incorrectly *Hopper v. State*, (1986) Ind.App., 489 N.E.2d 1209 in which we held the child hearsay statute constitutional. In *Hopper*, we determined that I.C. 35-37-4-6 met the requirements of *Ohio v. Roberts*, (1980) 448 U.S. 56, 100 S.Ct. 2531, 65 L.Ed.2d 597 because it provided that the hearsay statement must bear sufficient indications of reliability and that the child declarant must either testify at trial or be found unavailable.

****

*1331 In the instant case, a psychiatrist certified to the court that any participation by A.M. in the trial would be a "severe traumatic experience" for A.M. After hearing the

---

12. To protect the children, the court refers to them using initials rather than their actual names.

psychiatrist's testimony, the court found A.M. unavailable. We hold that Altmeyer has not shown error with respect to the trial court's determination.

Issue II

2

When a hearsay declarant is unavailable, his statement may not be admissible unless it bears adequate indicia of reliability. *Ohio*

v. Roberts, supra, 448 U.S. at 66, 100 S. Ct. at 2539. Where the evidence falls within a firmly rooted hearsay exception, its reliability may be inferred. *Id.* If the evidence cannot be admitted within a hearsay exception, then it may be admitted only upon a showing of "particularized guarantees of trustworthiness." *Id.*

indicia of reliability

****

Court of Appeals of Indiana, Third District.
Michael Brady, Appellant (Defendant Below)
v.
State of Indiana, Appellee (Plaintiff Below).
No. 71A03-8809-CR-266.
June 21, 1989.

540 N.E.2d 59

****

*62 Staton, Judge. Michael Brady was convicted by a jury in the St. Joseph Superior Court of Child Molesting, a class C felony. IC 35-42-4-3(b). He was sentenced to seven years in prison and fined $1,000.00. . . . Brady presents 28 issues for appellate consideration, which we restate as:

I. Whether the statute authorizing and the procedures used to videotape a child witness's testimony violated Brady's right to confront his accusers?

****

Affirmed.

The marriage of Carla Myers and Michael Brady was dissolved in 1983. Carla received custody of their daughter, T.B.[13] (born

June 22, 1982), subject to Brady's visitation rights.

****

The evidence most favorable to the verdict discloses that on Friday night, April 4, 1986, Brady collected T.B., who was now three years of age, for her first weekend visit pursuant to a revised visitation order.

****

As per the visitation order, Brady returned T.B. to Carla at approximately 6:00 p.m. on Sunday, April 6.

On the following morning, April 7, 1986, Mark Myers, Carla's present husband, received a telephone call from a teacher at T.B.'s school informing him that T.B. had been found hiding in the closet of the school's bathroom.

****

*63 During an interview in October of 1986, T.B. demonstrated with "anatomically correct" dolls how "Daddy Mike" (Brady) had hurt her. [This out-of-court testimony was elicited in T.B.'s home by Detective Sergeant Elaine Battles, and Brady's attorney was present. Brady sat in the garage and watched the interview on a television monitor.]

****

---

13. To protect the child, the court refers to the child using initials rather than the actual name.

540 N.E.2d 64

*64 A statute is presumed constitutional until the party challenging it as unconstitutional makes a clear showing to the contrary. *Hopper v. State (1986)*, Ind. App., 489 N.E.2d 1209, 1212, *trans. denied*. When two interpretations of a statute are possible, the courts must adopt the interpretation which upholds the statute. *Eddy v. McGinnis (1988)*, Ind., 523 N.E.2d 737, 738. We conclude that Brady's argument that IC 35-37-4-8 is facially invalid is without merit.

[2] Our supreme court recently examined the constitutionality of West's AIC 35-37-4-6, a statute which allows child hearsay statements to be admitted into evidence upon meeting criteria very similar to those of IC 5-37-4-8(d), and determined that, provided a defendant has the opportunity to cross-examine the child witness at some point, his right to confront his accusers has not been violated. *See Miller v. State*, (1987), Ind., 517 N.E.2d 64. The *Miller* court stated that, although the Indiana Constitution specifically gives criminal defendants the right to face-to-face confrontations of their accusers, cross-examination is the primary right protected under Article 1, Section 13 of the Indiana Constitution. *Id.* at 68. The United States Supreme Court, however, recently addressed the question of whether an Iowa statute, which permitted child witnesses to testify from behind a screen, unconstitutionally violated a defendant's right to confront his accusers. The Supreme Court in *Coy v. Iowa* (1988), 487 U.S. 1012, 108 S.Ct. 2798, 101 L.Ed.2d 857, established that Amendment Six of the United States Constitution does indeed ensure defendants the right to confront their accusers face-to-face, even without specific language to that effect, and proceeded to declare the Iowa statute unconstitutional as a violation of that right.

Brady urges that the *Coy* holding requires in all cases that a defendant must be given the opportunity to face his accusers. We disagree. The specific problem with the Iowa statute struck down in *Coy* was its establishment of a blanket exception to the right of face-to-face confrontation for victims of sexual abuse by presuming trauma to those victims. No individualized findings of need for special protection were required. In regard to this, the Supreme Court stated, ". . . something more than the type of generalized finding underlying such a statute ***65** is needed when the exception is not 'firmly . . . rooted in our jurisprudence.'" *Id.*, 108 S.Ct. at 2803. The Supreme Court went on to acknowledge that the right to confront one's accusers face-to-face is not an absolute, and left open the subject of whether exceptions to that right exist. We conclude that IC 35-37-4-8 creates one such exception without violating Brady's right to confront his accusers.

[3] As with any constitutional analysis, we are required to balance the right of the defendant to confront his accuser with the competing interest of the state in protecting child witnesses from the trauma of giving testimony before a court filled with strangers and the person whom they allege brought them to harm.

We agree with Justice O'Connor's position that the protection of child witnesses in cases such as this is a state interest compelling enough to override a defendant's right to a face-to-face confrontation, provided the procedural safeguard of finding need on a case-by-case basis is required and adhered to. *See* O'Connor, J., concurring opinion, *Coy, supra*, 108 S.Ct. at 2803. (White, J., joining in Justice O'Connor's concurring opinion.)

****

*73 Affirmed.

Conover, P.J., concurs.

Hoffman, J., dissents with separate opinion.

Hoffman, Judge, dissenting.

I respectfully dissent from the majority's disposition of the first appellate contention raised by Brady: whether Ind. Code § 35-37-4-8 (1988 Ed.) and the procedures used to videotape the testimony of the child witness, T.B., violated Brady's right to confront his accusers. Ind. Code § 35-37-4-8 provides in pertinent part:

> (f) If the court makes an order under subsection (c), only the following persons may be in the same room as the child during the child's videotaped testimony: . . .
>
> (3) The defendant's attorney (or the defendant, if the defendant is not represented by an attorney). . . .
>
> (7) The defendant, who can observe and hear the testimony of the child without the child being able to observe or hear the defendant. However, if the defendant is not represented by an attorney, the defendant may question the child.

In the instant case, Brady was represented by an attorney who attended the videotaping session during which T.B.'s testimony was elicited. Pursuant to Ind. Code § 35-37-4-8(f)(7), Brady was placed in the garage of T.B.'s home and watched the proceedings on a television monitor.

Section 35-37-4-8(f) is unconstitutional, as it violates Article I, § 13 of the Indiana Constitution. Article I, § 13 provides criminal defendants in this State with a right of confrontation independent of the right to confront granted by the Sixth Amendment of the federal constitution. Article I, § 13 states: "In all criminal prosecutions, the accused shall have the right . . . to meet the witnesses face to face. . . ."

There is no ambiguity in the constitutional provision. "Face to face" confrontation must surely mean "face to face" confrontation. The right granted by Article I, § 13 is violated when a defendant is placed at a *74 location where he or she cannot be seen or heard by the witness, even though the defendant is permitted to observe the witness and listen to the witness's testimony.

The majority suggests that the right of confrontation is adequately protected so long as there is an opportunity to cross-examine the child witness. *Miller v. State* (1987), Ind., 517 N.E.2d 64, is cited in support of that proposition. The Supreme Court in *Miller* did not hold that cross-examination fully satisfies the constitutional mandate found in Article I, § 13; rather, the Court held that Article I, § 13 includes the right to cross-examine. *Id.* at 69. The right to meet witnesses face to face is in no way undermined by the *Miller* decision. For the foregoing reasons, I dissent.

****

PART FOUR

Expository Writing

CHAPTER

16

Writing Letters

HIGHLIGHTS

- Client letters are written for one or more of the following reasons: (1) to answer specific questions from the client, (2) to update the client about the case, (3) to predict a possible outcome in the case, or (4) to make recommendations as to how to proceed in the case.
- Demand letters make specific requests to either take certain actions or refrain from certain actions.
- Demand letters must include (1) the specific request, (2) the justifications for the request, (3) a clear deadline for compliance with the request, and (4) a clear statement of the consequences should the reader not comply with the request.

 ## A. Introduction

This chapter focuses on expository writings and, specifically, on letters and e-mail communications written by U.S. attorneys. Most of us have experience and are comfortable writing letters, either in handwritten form or in an e-mail. When writing letters or communicating via e-mail about a case or legal issue, however, you must be cautious. In the United States, lawyers are advised to consider any written product as potential evidence to be used in court and to write even e-mail communications with this understanding. If you are considering whether something you want to write will later create a problem, don't write it.

This chapter focuses specifically on two types of letters often written by lawyers: client letters and demand letters. The recommendations we give in this chapter are recommendations U.S. lawyers often learn, either in school or in practice. We realize, however, that cultural differences may be reflected in these types of writings. For example, we discuss some of the techniques to consider when communicating a disappointing message to a client; in other countries, however, the custom may be to be more direct than what we advise here. When writing letters to a party in another country, it is essential to understand the customs lawyers in that country follow. This knowledge can only help you be more effective in international practice. This chapter provides you with an opportunity to see the approach U.S. lawyers take when writing letters.

 ## B. Letters to Clients

1. Consider purpose, tone, and audience

As with any written document, you must first consider (1) why you are writing the letter (purpose); (2) the type of letter you are writing (requiring, for example, a formal or informal tone); and (3) any special considerations based on who will receive the letter (audience).

a. The purpose

We write client letters for any one or more of the following reasons:

- To verify information received from the client.
- To answer questions posed by the client.
- To inform the client of progress in the case.
- To inform the client of your analysis of the legal issues in the case.
- To ask the client further questions.
- To ask the client for additional information.
- To predict how the case might proceed.
- To make recommendations to the client.

It is vital that you understand the purpose of the letter so that you include only the elements that satisfy that purpose. With this clear direction you can better ensure that your letter is complete.

b. The tone and the audience

The appropriate tone of a letter written by a U.S. attorney depends on the person receiving the letter (the audience). If, for example, the client is a friend or someone you know well, you may choose to adopt a more informal, friendly tone in your letter. If, however, you do not know the client or know that the client receiving the letter uses a formal style, you will want the tone of your letter to be more formal.

Consider too the client's background and education. Strive to write a letter that your client can easily understand. If your client is also a lawyer or otherwise has a legal background, you may feel comfortable using legal terminology in the letter and being more specific about the source of the law, the analysis, and so forth. If, however, your client has no advanced education or experience reading legal materials, avoid legal terminology wherever possible and use language that can explain your message and be easily understood. Your job is to satisfy your client's needs; to achieve this goal, you must pay particular attention to your tone.

The guidelines below include examples of a client letter that might have been written to Edina Broward, the client who wants the return of her stolen art painting, which is now in the possession of Dr. Thomas Warren. This exercise was first introduced in Chapter 7.

2. *What to include in the letter*

In the United States, letters from attorneys to clients usually contain the following sections:

- Heading
- Salutation
- Introduction
- Statement of the facts about the case
- Statement of conclusion
- Reasoning behind the conclusion and how it might affect the client's case
- Recommendation
- Offer to meet or talk further
- Closing

a. *Heading*

Begin a client letter with a heading that includes your address, the client's address, and the date. You will likely also want to indicate the case file to which you are referring, using a "Regarding" or "Re:" line.

The heading in our sample letter would look something like this.

Smith, Jones, & Brown, P.C.
Attorneys at Law
532 Main Street
Grantham, East Carolina 53498

April 22, 2008

Edina Broward
303 Forest Drive
Oak Park, Illinois 48723

RE: Recovery of the John Singer Sargent painting

b. Salutation

Next, provide a salutation. In the above example, the salutation would be "Dear Ms. Broward" or "Dear Edina," if you know her well. Alternative ways to formally address the client in this situation would be "Miss Broward," if she is single, or "Mrs. Broward," if she is married. "Ms. Broward" is usually used when the writer is not sure whether the recipient is single or married, or when the recipient has expressed a preference to be referred to as "Ms."

A sample salutation for our sample letter follows.

> Dear Ms. Broward:

c. Introduction

The introduction must state the purpose of the letter and, if answering a specific question or request by the client, an explicit reference to the question or to the request to which you are responding. You might also refer to your last contact with the client, whether that contact was in person, by phone, or through written communication.

The sample letter's introduction might read as follows.

> Thank you for meeting with me on Monday, April 16, regarding your James Singer Sargent painting, missing since you moved in 1975. I understand that you recently learned of its whereabouts and would like it returned. I will be happy to help you in this endeavor. My recommendations provided below are based on the accuracy of the facts as I understand them.

In addition, if the purpose of the letter is to provide good news, you may want to include the conclusion — the good news — in the introduction. If, however, the news is bad, you may want to wait and provide the conclusion later. See section C1 regarding structure. Regardless of when you provide the conclusion, make sure you include a clear statement that your conclusion and its validity are based on the accuracy of the facts provided by the client. This clear statement may serve as an effective transition to the next section.

d. Statement of the facts about the case

Sometimes the story the client meant to convey and the story the lawyer heard in the initial meeting are not the same. In addition, clients may omit facts. These facts may be helpful to the client's position or helpful to the opposing party's position. Of course, your goal is to gather as many legally significant facts as possible when interviewing the client about the case. Even if you repeat the facts to the client orally during the meeting, however, it is always advisable to repeat those facts—especially those legally significant facts on which you are relying—in written form. This gives your client the opportunity to clarify any misunderstanding about what actually took place. Once you have provided the facts as you understand them, ask the client to advise you of any additions or corrections, and stress again that your analysis of the case depends on the accuracy of the facts. You may want to emphasize to the client that facts supporting the opposing client's case are equally important in determining how to proceed with your client's case.

Sample facts for the letter on behalf of Edina Broward follow.

As I understand the facts, your painting was lost in 1975, during the renovation of your home. Your father purchased the painting in 1925, and you inherited it when he died in 1964. You have no records of the original sale. As soon as you discovered that the painting was missing, you and your attorney filed a report with the police. You also hired a private investigator who conducted a private investigation for several weeks. Neither the investigator nor the police were able to locate the painting.

Once the official investigation seemed to slow down, your attorney, William McIntyre, continued to write museums and local art dealers and auction houses in search of the painting. Mr. McIntyre later followed up his written communications with phone calls. You also offered a $25,000 award for any information leading to the painting's location.

Due to an illness, however, you were unable to actively pursue the search beyond the end of 1976, after Mr. McIntyre died. Last year, however, you saw an article in the *Chicago Tribune* about American Impressionist painters such as James Singer Sargent. You then wrote letters to the museums, auction houses, and art dealers Mr. McIntyre had contacted previously, reminding them of the painting. You were contacted subsequently by the curator at the Art Institute of Chicago. The curator did not know anything about your painting but suggested that you file a theft report with the International Foundation for Art Research (IFAR), a global organization that reports stolen art to museums, galleries, auction houses, and other businesses and experts dealing in fine art. You filed your report in July of last year.

You never heard from IFAR; however, your grandniece heard from a friend who attended an art exhibit and thought she saw your painting. The painting was on display with a plaque providing the name of the person who presently possesses the painting, Dr. Thomas Warren, of Flora, East Carolina.

You phoned Dr. Warren and learned that he did, in fact, have your painting, but he refused to return it to you. He claims he bought it from a reputable art gallery in Flora in 1978, paying $200,000. The painting was part of the estate of Jeremy Thorne, a wealthy art collector of American Impressionist paintings. Dr. Warren apparently received no records with the painting and did not look into its history prior to making the purchase. Dr. Warren exhibited the painting several times before, in 1980, 1985, 1990, and 1995.

e. Statement of your conclusion and reasoning behind the conclusion

If your conclusion is not included in the introduction, provide it here. It is essential that you answer explicitly the client's question or request. Once you've provided the conclusion, explain how you reached that conclusion. This requires that you lay out your reasoning step by step, so your reasoning is clear to your client. State completely any advice or recommendations for action. State the facts on which you base your answers and advise. This thoroughness will allow your client to assess whether you are acting on complete and accurate information.

You may need to explain why the client's position is weaker than the opposing party's position. You may need to consider and include arguments for both parties in order to be thorough and to convince the client that your conclusion and recommendation are valid. Be careful, however, about including case analysis or quoted statutory language. Present the information in more general terms, if those general references suffice, or omit this detailed information if it's not necessary to explain your conclusion and recommendation. Further, avoid specific references or citations to cases, statutes, or other sources of authority. Unless your reader is an attorney or business client who wants this information, this level of detail is not necessary and likely only confuses your reader. If you decide to include specific references to the law, consider placing the information in footnotes.

This section of the sample letter about Edina Broward's stolen painting follows.

> The law supports the return of your painting, if we can convince the court that you acted with reasonable or due diligence in trying to recover the painting once you discovered it was gone. Normally the law allows claims for recovery of items like your painting for only a certain period of time, which in your case passed many years ago. There is an exception, however; if we can show that you used due diligence in trying to recover the painting, the court may rule that the time to file a claim with the court did not begin until you discovered the whereabouts of the painting. In your case, that discovery occurred last year, so you would have three years from that date to file an action to recover the painting. The difficulty lies in the thirty years when you took no affirmative action to look for the painting. Your illness coupled with your unfamiliarity with the art world should help you explain your inaction during that time.

f. Recommendation

Based on your prediction, recommend to the client a certain course of action. That recommendation may be to negotiate, settle, or proceed with the claim (or defense of the claim). Remember as you write your recommendation that written communications are sometimes later used as evidence. Strive to fulfill your responsibility to inform your client fully, but do so in a way that avoids as many future problems as possible. This can occur only by thoroughly explaining your reasons for your conclusions as well as any concerns you may have about the case.

Sometimes you must tell a client that she cannot do what she wants. Whenever possible, make this bad news easier for the client to receive by offering alternatives that lead to the same or a similar objective. For example, you may believe that a lawsuit is financially impractical, but a negotiation may bring about some of the client's desired results. When telling clients something they don't want to hear, again, include the key reasons for the conclusion, in case an unhappy or angry client skips reading the section where you explain your reasons for the conclusion.

Where appropriate, provide exact time schedules, costs, or other important information related to the recommendations you make in your client letter. If certain information is not available at the time you write the client letter, inform the client and provide some idea as to when the information will become available.

Often, a the U.S. attorney may want to communicate recommendations more quickly, either in person during a meeting, over the phone, or by e-mail. By conveying the information in a quick meeting or over the phone, you may save the client money and can then proceed more quickly. If the discussion takes place over the phone, however, always document in writing any decisions you and the client make. If you choose to make your recommendations by letter, it may look like the following.

> I recommend that we first act to convince Dr. Warren to return the painting. Before filing a complaint in court, I recommend that I send him a letter and demand the painting's return, set a deadline for its return, and make it clear that if he does not comply we will file a complaint with the court.

g. Offer to meet or talk further

It is essential that you invite the client to contact you. This is especially important when your news is bad; if you omit this invitation, your client may feel as though he is not being treated fairly or is not as important as other clients. It is essential to convey the message that you want to help the client work through the reasons why the case is weak or lacks merit.

The following paragraph from the letter to Ms. Broward makes this offer.

> If you would like to talk further about this matter, please call and set up an appointment with my assistant, Delores Gray, at 587-3544. If you would like me to proceed with the demand letter, please let me know. You may reach me at the same number or you may e-mail me at ssmith@sjb.law. I will proceed as quickly as possible once I hear from you.

h. Closing

Include a respectful closing, such as "Regards," "Sincerely," or "Respectfully."

> Sincerely yours,
> Samuel Smith
> Attorney at Law

The final version of the sample letter appears below.

Smith, Jones, & Brown, P.C.
Attorneys at Law
532 Main Street
Grantham, East Carolina 53498

April 22, 2008

Edina Broward
303 Forest Drive
Oak Park, Illinois 48723

Re: Recovery of the John Singer Sargent Painting

Dear Ms. Broward:

Thank you for meeting with me on Monday, April 16, regarding your James Singer Sargent painting, missing since you moved in 1975. I understand that you recently learned of its whereabouts and would like it returned. I am happy to help you in this endeavor. My recommendations provided below are based on the accuracy of the facts as I understand them.

Your painting was lost in 1975 during the renovation of your home in Illinois. Your father purchased the painting in 1925, and you inherited it when he died in 1964. You have no records of the original sale. As soon as you discovered that the painting was missing, you and your attorney filed a report with the police. You also hired a private investigator who conducted a private investigation for several weeks. Neither the investigator nor the police were able to locate the painting.

Once the official investigation seemed to slow down, your attorney, William McIntyre, continued to write museums and local art dealers and auction houses in search of the painting. Mr. McIntyre later followed up his written communications with phone calls. You also offered a $25,000 award for any information leading to the painting's location.

Due to an illness, however, you were unable to actively pursue the search beyond the end of 1976, after Mr. McIntyre died. Last year, however, you saw an article in the *Chicago Tribune* about American Impressionist painters such as James Singer Sargent. You then wrote letters to the museums, auction houses, and art dealers Mr. McIntyre had contacted previously, reminding them of the painting. You were contacted subsequently by the curator at the Art Institute of Chicago. The curator did not know anything about your painting but suggested that you file a theft report with the International Foundation for Art Research (IFAR), a global organization that reports stolen art to museums, galleries, auction houses, and other businesses and experts dealing in fine art. You filed your report in July of last year.

You never heard from IFAR; however, your grandniece heard from a friend who attended an art exhibit and thought she saw your painting. The painting was on display with a plaque providing the name of the person who presently possesses the painting, Dr. Thomas Warren, of Flora, East Carolina.

You phoned Dr. Warren and learned that he did, in fact, have your painting, but he refused to return it to you. He claims he bought it from a reputable art gallery in Flora in 1978, paying $200,000. The painting was part of the estate of Jeremy Thorne, a wealthy art collector of American Impressionist paintings. Dr. Warren apparently received no records with the painting and did not look into its history prior to making the purchase. Dr. Warren exhibited the painting several times before, in 1980, 1985, 1990, and 1995.

The law supports the return of your painting, if we can convince the court that you acted with reasonable or due diligence in trying to recover the painting once you discovered it was gone. Normally the law allows claims for recovery of items like your painting for only a certain period of time, which in your case passed many years ago. There is an exception, however; if we can show that you used due diligence in trying to recover the painting, the court may rule that the time to file a claim with the court did not begin until you actually discovered the whereabouts of the painting. In your case, that discovery occurred last year, so you would have three years from that date to file an action to recover the painting. The difficulty lies in the thirty years when you took no affirmative action to look for the painting. Your illness coupled with your unfamiliarity with the art world should help you explain your inaction during that time.

I recommend that we first act to convince Dr. Warren to return the painting. Before filing a complaint in court, I recommend that I send him a letter demanding the painting's return, set a deadline for its return, and make it clear that if he does not comply we will file a complaint with the court.

If you would like to talk further about this matter, please call and set up an appointment with my assistant, Delores Gray, at 587-3544. If you would like me to proceed with the demand letter, please let me know. You may reach me at the same number or you may e-mail me at ssmith@sjb.law. I will proceed as quickly as possible once I hear from you.

> Sincerely yours,
> Samuel Smith
> Attorney at Law

 ## C. General Guidelines

1. Considerations about the structure of the document

How you communicate information and where you place that information within the document, paragraph, and sentence influence the way your reader interprets your writing. This is equally true when writing a client letter.

When you have bad news for the client, for example, paying particular attention to the organization of your letter may help to convey the information in a way the client is more likely to accept. One organizational approach is to begin the letter with general information, setting the tone before providing specific negative information. Once the specific negative message is conveyed, reestablish the tone and provide any positive results that you may work on in the alternative before concluding the letter. Again, end by inviting the client to speak with you further about your conclusions and the reasons for those conclusions. See section E at the end of this chapter for suggested techniques to emphasize and deemphasize information.

2. Recommendations of style

a. Be direct

This recommendation may seem to contradict the recommendations made when giving bad news, but that is not the case. The above recommendation refers to the placement of adverse information; this recommendation refers to making your message clear at that point where you choose to convey it to the client. No matter what the conclusion and reasoning, your goal must be to answer directly the question or request posed by the client. If you cannot provide a direct answer, be direct by saying so, and then explain why no direct answer exists.

b. Be clear

Use language that the client can understand and avoid so-called legalese, which is exaggerated legal language, including words such as *aforementioned, hereinafter,* and *heretofore.* (More on legalese is found in Chapter 19 on word choice.) No reason justifies using legalese. In fact, since the goal of all writing is to clearly communicate a message, you must pay particular attention to using language that is easily understood by the reader receiving your letter.

In addition, avoid references to technical terms. After drafting your letter, review it and edit any words that may be unfamiliar to your reader, paying particular attention to your audience. If technical terms, such as legal terms, are necessary in order to be thorough, define those legal terms within the letter, unless you feel confident that the reader will know the definitions. For example, instead of referring only to the "statute of frauds," refer to "a statute that requires some contracts to be written and signed." If referring to the "beneficiary of a will," refer to "a beneficiary, or one who takes under a Last Will and Testament." If the definition alone does not clarify the meaning of a legal term, consider providing an example as a way to make sense of the term. This would require more words and, therefore, make the letter longer. Sometimes brevity, however, must give way to clarity.

c. Be brief whenever possible

While clarity is the overriding goal of any legal writer, be brief and concise wherever possible. You can achieve this goal by eliminating any unnecessary statements or redundancies. Strive to reduce the language without eliminating the substantive message.

d. Finish by considering tone, purpose, and audience

Be considerate of your client. Remember that your client is an individual — even the corporate client who is represented by an individual — with a problem. This individual has turned to you for assistance, and you want to respond to the client in a way that recognizes the client's concerns and needs but still provides the legal information the client must hear.

● **Exercise 16-A**

Consider Ana and David Hart, who were introduced in Chapter 7. Their impending divorce has created a dispute over the covenant not to compete (CNC) related to their health club business. *Presume for purposes of this exercise that Ana contacted you prior to the divorce but after David's proposal to pay Ana one-half the fair market value of the business if Ana signed the CNC.* Draft a client letter to Ana that states your opinion that the CNC is unreasonable and recommends she not sign the CNC based on the facts set out in Chapter 7 and the authority you found (*Mats Transport* and *Hanson,* found in the appendices).

 D. Demand Letters

1. Consider purpose, audience, and tone

This section addresses guidelines U.S. attorneys follow when writing demand letters. A demand letter communicates with your adversary (audience) and makes specific requests to either take certain action or refrain from taking certain action (purpose). To accomplish this purpose, you must be particularly careful about adopting the correct tone. When writing a demand letter, strive to be firm but not belligerent. If your tone is too aggressive, you may not get what you are demanding because of the *way* you make the request rather than because the adversary disagrees with the substance of your demand.

A demand letter is usually directed to opposing counsel, if the opposing party has hired an attorney. If you want to send a letter to the opposing party, and an attorney is representing the other party, you must first get permission from the opposing party's attorney.[1] If the opposing party is not represented, any written communication you send should include a clear statement that you are representing your client in the legal matter.

---

1. Model R. Prof. Conduct 4.2.

Even though you may direct a letter to the attorney, you should write the message so it is also clear to the opposing party, who will likely read the letter. As with all communications, strive to present the information using plain English and clear and simple sentences.

2. Ethical considerations

The American Bar Association, in its 1996 Guidelines for Conduct, urges all lawyers to "treat all other counsel, parties, and witnesses in a civil and courteous manner," both in person and through any written communication.[2] The Guidelines specifically cite as inappropriate any "offensive conduct" and "disparaging personal remarks" toward all other parties involved in a dispute.[3]

As with all actions by attorneys, strive to present your demand in a firm yet respectful manner, to be professional, and to be honest. Your reader is more likely to carefully consider your demand if you adopt a tone that is credible, conveying a message that you are professional and competent. The Model Rules of Professional Conduct make clear that you cannot lie about the facts, the law, or what could happen should the reader not comply with your request.[4]

3. What to include in the letter

Most demand letters contain the following sections:

- Heading
- Salutation
- Introduction
- Statement of the facts and law that support your request
- Statement of the deadline to respond
- What will happen should the reader not comply with your demand
- Closing

a. Heading, salutation, and introduction

A demand letter contains the same heading and salutation as a client letter. The introduction, however, usually includes not only the purpose of the letter

---

2. ABA Section on Litigation Guidelines for Conduct (ABA 1996).
3. *Id.*
4. Model R. Prof. Conduct 4.1.

but also the specific request that the recipient take certain actions or refrain from certain actions.

In the sample letter about the stolen art, these sections might read as follows.

> ### Smith, Jones, & Brown, P.C.
> ### Attorneys at Law
> ### 532 Main Street
> ### Grantham, East Carolina 53498
>
> April 25, 2008
>
> Thomas Warren
> 232 W. Findlay Avenue
> Flora, East Carolina 57468
>
> Dear Dr. Warren:
>
> My client, Ms. Edina Broward, recently learned that her James Singer Sargent painting of the Rialto Bridge, stolen from her home in 1975, is in your possession. She understands that you purchased the painting in 1989, unaware that Ms. Broward was the true owner. Under the law, however, Ms. Broward still retains the legal right to her painting and now wants you to return it to her.

b. Support for your request

As in a letter to a client, follow the request with an explanation of the specific facts and law on which you are relying in making your request.

i. Explanation of the facts

> Ms. Broward's painting was lost in 1975 during the renovation of her home in Illinois. Her father purchased the painting in 1925, and Ms. Broward inherited it when he died in 1964. As soon as Ms. Broward discovered that the painting was missing, she filed a report with the police. She also hired a private investigator, who conducted a private investigation for several weeks. Neither the investigator nor the police were able to locate the painting.
>
> Once the official investigation seemed to slow down, Ms. Broward's attorney continued to write museums and local art dealers and auction houses in search of the painting. Her attorney later followed up his written communications with phone calls. Ms. Broward also offered a $25,000 award for any information leading to the painting's location.

Due to Ms. Broward's illnesses, she was unable to actively pursue the search; however, after seeing an article in the *Chicago Tribune* last year about American Impressionist painters such as James Singer Sargent, she contacted the curator at the Art Institute of Chicago. The curator did not know anything about the painting but suggested that Ms. Broward file a theft report with the International Foundation for Art Research (IFAR). As you may be aware, IFAR is a global organization that reports stolen art to museums, galleries, auction houses, and other businesses and experts that deal in fine art. Ms. Broward filed her report in July of last year.

Ms. Broward did not hear from IFAR; however, a relative heard from a friend who attended an art exhibit and saw Ms. Broward's painting. The painting was on display with a plaque providing your name and location.

ii. *Explanation of the law supporting your client's position*

Ms. Broward did everything required to locate her painting. Her diligent efforts tolled the statute of limitations until the time when she discovered its whereabouts, keeping her ownership of the painting intact. Furthermore, as a purchaser of art you are expected to question the history of the painting prior to purchasing it. Your inaction has put you in this unfortunate position.

c. *A Statement of the deadline*

Do not make an open-ended demand. Once you have stated clearly your request and the justification for the request based on the law and facts, provide a specific timeline of what you expect from the recipient. Consider carefully by what time you want the reader to respond. An unreasonable time limit will more likely result in a negative response. Give the reader sufficient time to comply with your request, and explain why the time frame is fair. Finally, set the time limit knowing that you will be in a position to act should the recipient not comply with your demand.

Here is an example of this section of the demand letter.

Therefore, Ms. Broward requests that you return to me on her behalf the James Singer Sargent painting of the Rialto Bridge no later than 5:00 P.M. on Friday, May 4, 2008. Two weeks should be sufficient time to bring the painting to my office.

d. A Statement of the consequences of noncompliance

Your recipient needs to understand what will happen should your demand be ignored. The consequence of ignoring your demand, for example, may be to proceed to court, request a temporary restraining order requiring that the party not take certain action, or turn over a debt to a collection agency. By making the consequence clear in your demand letter, you demonstrate that you are ready to take action as soon as your deadline has passed, without communicating further with the opposing party. A statement of the consequences in Edina Broward's case follows.

> If I do not receive the painting by that time, Ms. Broward has instructed me to file an action to recover the painting the following week.

e. Closing

Include a respectful closing, such as "Regards" or "Respectfully."

> Regards,
>
> Samuel Smith
> Attorney at Law

A complete demand letter based on Edina Broward's case follows.

> Smith, Jones, & Brown, P.C.
> Attorneys at Law
> 532 Main Street
> Grantham, East Carolina 53498
>
> April 25, 2007
>
> Thomas Warren
> 232 W. Findlay Avenue
> Flora, East Carolina 57468
>
> Dear Dr. Warren:
>   My client, Ms. Edina Broward, recently learned that her James Singer Sargent painting of the Rialto Bridge, stolen from her home in 1975, is in your possession. She understands that you purchased the painting in 1989, unaware that Ms. Broward was the true owner. Under the law, however, Ms. Broward still retains the legal right to her painting and now wants you to return it to her.

Ms. Broward's painting was lost in 1975 during the renovation of her home in Illinois. Her father purchased the painting in 1925, and Ms. Broward inherited it when he died in 1964. As soon as Ms. Broward discovered that the painting was missing, she filed a report with the police. She also hired a private investigator who conducted a private investigation for several weeks. Neither the investigator nor the police were able to locate the painting.

Once the official investigation seemed to slow down, Ms. Broward's attorney continued to write museums and local art dealers and auction houses in search of the painting. Her attorney later followed up his written communications with phone calls. Ms. Broward also offered a $25,000 award for any information leading to the painting's location.

Due to Ms. Broward's illnesses, she was unable to actively pursue the search; however, after seeing an article in the *Chicago Tribune* last year about American impressionist painters such as James Singer Sargent, she contacted the curator at the Art Institute of Chicago. The curator did not know anything about the painting but suggested that Ms. Broward file a theft report with the International Foundation for Art Research (IFAR). As you may be aware, IFAR is a global organization that reports stolen art to museums, galleries, auction houses, and other businesses and experts that deal in fine art. Ms. Broward filed her report in July of last year.

Ms. Broward did not hear from IFAR; however, a relative heard from a friend who attended an art exhibit and saw Ms. Broward's painting. The painting was on display with a plaque providing your name and location.

Ms. Broward did everything required to locate her painting. Her diligent efforts tolled the statute of limitations until the time when she discovered its whereabouts, keeping her ownership of the painting intact. Furthermore, as a purchaser of art you are expected to question the history of the painting prior to purchasing it. Your inaction has put you in this unfortunate position.

Therefore, Ms. Broward requests that you return to me on her behalf the James Singer Sargent painting of the Rialto Bridge no later than 5:00 P.M. on Friday, May 4, 2007. Two weeks should be sufficient time to bring the painting to my office. If I do not receive the painting by that time, Ms. Broward has instructed me to file an action to recover the painting the following week.

Regards,

Samuel Smith
Attorney at Law

● **Exercise 16-B**

Presume for the purposes of this exercise that you have now convinced Ana Hart that it is a mistake to sign the CNC as part of her divorce settlement. Draft a demand letter to David Hart's attorney, James Fielder, (1) setting out the reasons why the CNC as proposed is unenforceable, and (2) stating that for a settlement to be reached, the CNC cannot exceed the geographic boundaries where spas are currently located, in Flora, Hamilton, and Johnson Counties, East Carolina.

E. E-mail Communications

E-mail is a quick method of communicating with clients, colleagues, and other attorneys, but you must be careful when using e-mail communications for business. As with any written communication about a client's case, pay careful attention to what you say, how you say it, and to whom you sent it.

For example, too often an e-mail is sent to the wrong person, often because the wrong person shares the same or similar name with the intended recipient. The consequences of a misdirected e-mail can be drastic. In 2008, for example, an attorney representing a major pharmaceutical company in the United States meant to send an e-mail containing confidential information regarding the law firm's private negotiations with the government on the pharmaceutical company's behalf. The suit involved alleged marketing improprieties involving up to $1 billion, and it was vital to the company that these negotiations remain confidential. Unfortunately, instead of sending the e-mail to *Bradford* Berensen, an attorney in another law firm also working for the pharmaceutical company, the e-mail was sent to a New York Times reporter, *Alex* Berenson.[5]

1. Purpose and tone

Help your reader know immediately what the purpose of the e-mail communication is by providing a helpful reference to the subject of the communication in the subject line. Retain that same reference when sending further e-mail communications on the same topic, again for clarity. For example:

> Subject Line: CNC as part of settlement agreement between Ana and David Hart

Even though e-mail communications are usually informal in tone, remember that your e-mail may be read by anyone. If, for example, you say something negative about a coworker or supervising attorney, your comment may end up on that person's computer screen. Proceed with great caution. In this age of technology, furthermore, an e-mail is never truly deleted; it's out there somewhere forever, because deleted e-mail communications can usually be retrieved.

---

5. Katherine Eban, *Lilly's $1 Billion E-Mailstrom*, Conde Nast Portfolio.com, www.Porfolio.com/news-markets/top-5/2008/02/05/Eli-Lilly-E-Mail-to-New (accessed 3/9/08).

2. Clarity and conciseness

When communicating with others who live in different countries around the world, pay careful attention to the different time zones. When referring to a date or time in an e-mail, make it clear to which time you are referring (for example, Chicago time). References to general times such as "tonight" or "tomorrow" are likely ambiguous and will only confuse your recipient, requiring further clarification. (More on ambiguites about time is found in Chapter 19 on word choice.)

Pay attention to how you present yourself professionally, even in an e-mail communication. Sloppy writing and rambling sentences may affect your credibility. Take the extra time to review and revise your e-mail communication. Write short, simple sentences, and make every word count. Be concise. You may also want to use bulleted lists and other formatting techniques to highlight information. Remember, however, that your formatting may not transfer to the e-mail when received by your reader.

Consider how your recipient will receive the e-mail. In this day and age, for example, your recipient may be receiving your e-mail on a small electronic device, using a small screen. Large e-mails and large attachments may create problems and may take considerable time to download. You may want to ask the recipient, for example, if sending an attachment by fax would be *preferred*.

Finally, remember to think before hitting the *Send* button. If you are not sure whether you want to send the message, save it and give yourself some time to think it over. The worst feeling occurs when you write an e-mail because you are angry or otherwise emotional and then immediately regret sending it. Remember, once it's out there, it's out there forever.

F. Mechanical Considerations

We can all become more effective writers once we understand the mechanical tools available to persuade our readers. Specific writing techniques emphasize certain pieces of information and deemphasize others. These techniques work not only when writing letters but also when writing other documents not covered in this textbook, such as briefs submitted to a court. To apply these techniques, you must first understand why they work.

1. The reader expectation theory[6]

Readers in the United States expect information to be located in certain places within a sentence, a paragraph, and an overall document. This is known as the reader expectation theory. For example, we emphasize information by placing it at the beginning of a

---

6. George D. Gopen, "Let the Buyer in the Ordinary Course of Business Beware: Suggestions for Revising the Prose of the Uniform Commercial Code," 54 U. Chi. L. Rev. 1178, 1185 (1987).

sentence, paragraph, or document. We may also emphasize information by placing it at the end of a sentence or paragraph (and sometimes a document). This is the information that readers will most likely remember. It follows logically that placing information in the middle of the sentence, paragraph, or document deemphasizes that information.

2. Sentence choices

To emphasize information within a sentence, writers in the United States place the information

(1) at the beginning of the sentence;
(2) at the end of the sentence; or
(3) at other points where the reader pauses, such as before a colon, semicolon, or comma.

Readers are therefore more likely to remember information found in these positions. Consider the following examples, based on Sally's tort action against Henry for breaking her vase.

Henry chose to break Sally's **vase**.

In this example, "Henry" and "vase" are emphasized.

Information is also emphasized if placed before other punctuation, such as before the colon, semicolon, or comma. Readers pause for punctuation, which allows readers more time to absorb what they just read, as in the following sentence.

Sally's valuable vase **was broken**; the vase was broken by **Henry**.

3. Emphasize information by using active instead of passive voice

"Active voice" is used when the subject of the sentence reflects the actor in the sentence, the verb of the sentence reflects the action taken by the actor, and the subject and verb may then be followed by the object of the action. The result is a simple sentence, with information placed where the reader expects to read it, as follows.

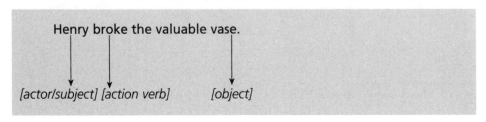

Henry broke the valuable vase.

[actor/subject] [action verb]   [object]

"Passive voice" is used when the subject of the sentence does not reveal the actor in the sentence, and the verb is a form of "to be." The verb shows the subject as acted on rather than as acting. One way to identify passive voice is to look for the word *by* in the sentence, which is often, though not always, used to introduce the actor.[7] For example:

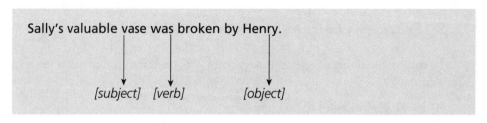

Using a form of "to be," however, does not automatically mean that you are using passive voice. For example, when you are showing a state of existence, you use a form of the verb "to be," but you do not use passive voice. Thus:

> Sally is sad.

In the above sentence, "Sally is sad" reflects her state of existence and is not, therefore, passive voice. Consider the expanded version of the sentence.

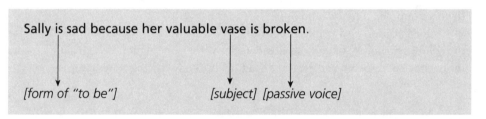

In this example, the second clause, "her valuable vase is broken," is an example of passive voice since the subject of the sentence does not reveal the actor and the verb is a form of "to be."

Active voice is stronger because your readers are able to continue reading without stopping, since information is provided where expected. Sentences written using passive voice, however, must often be reread once the actor is revealed (which is often at the end of the sentence). Many readers will automatically read the sentence again, mentally placing the actor at the beginning of the sentence. The following sentence converts the previous example into active voice.

> Sally is sad because Henry broke her valuable vase.

---

7. The last example in section F2 includes two clauses using passive voice.

Some writers may choose to use passive voice, for one of the following reasons:

1. The actor is unknown.
2. The actor is unimportant.
3. The writer wants to minimize the actor's role.
4. The writer wants to deemphasize certain information.

4. *Emphasize information by including it in a short sentence*

When you write short sentences, every word is emphasized. Short sentences are easier to read; they are, therefore, easier to understand. Writing a sentence using active rather than passive voice will always take fewer words and therefore be shorter and stronger.

Consider the following two sentences:

Example A:
It was decided by Sally that the vase Henry broke was so precious to her that she would sue Henry in tort and at least recover the value of the vase.

Example B:
Sally decided to sue Henry to recover damages for her vase.

Be careful not to write too many short sentences, however. If you string together several short sentences, you will create a choppy writing style, and the short sentences will lose their persuasive value.

5. *Emphasize information by placing it in the main clause of a sentence*

Another way to emphasize information is to include it in the main clause of a sentence (independent clause), rather than in a clause that depends on the main clause to make the overall sentence grammatically correct (dependent clause). If I were Henry and I wanted to deemphasize the value of the vase, for example, I might write the following:

Sally's vase, **known to be valuable**, was broken.

[dependent clause]

As Henry, I might even decide to take all references to ownership and action out of the sentence, in hopes that the reader will not sympathize with Sally. For example:

> The vase, known to be valuable, was broken.

6. Emphasize information by providing more detail

As readers, we tend to remember those stories that give us a mental picture of what happened. By providing more detail we emphasize that information, and the reader is therefore more likely to remember it. By adding detail to the story, you may also be able to evoke a desired emotion from the reader. For example, Henry may choose to refer to what was broken simply as "the vase." Sally, however, may go into more detail about the vase, to give the reader a stronger mental picture. By doing so, the reader is more apt to feel sympathy toward Sally's loss. For example:

> Before she died, Sally's grandmother gave Sally the vase. Sally's grandfather gave her grandmother the handpainted vase on their wedding day. The artist painted a man on his knee, giving flowers to a woman, who was standing before him. Sally's grandmother kept the vase on her dining room table and filled it with fresh flowers every day until she died.

7. Emphasize information through parallel construction

"I came; I saw; I conquered." This quote is known to originate with Julius Caesar. It is the classic example of using parallel construction for emphasis. Each phrase reflects the simple subject/verb order. Consider the alternative:

> The general rode with his troops to the battle. When he arrived, he saw the men fighting in the valley below. He and his troops took charge and eventually won the battle.

The example above may also be effective since it provides more detail. The emphasis through parallel construction, however, is lost.

PART FIVE

Drafting Contracts

17

Overall Contract Structure

HIGHLIGHTS

- Lengthy and complex contracts may begin with a cover page, a table of contents, and a definitions section.
- The introductory statement is the first textual paragraph of the contract; the clause refers to the title of the contract, states the date of the agreement, and identifies the contracting parties.
- Recitals are statements of fact regarding the background of the parties or the subject matter of the contract.
- A transitional clause signals the end of the recitals and the beginning of the body of the contract.
- Terms may be defined in the contract when they are first mentioned (embedded within the sentence), or, if there are many defined terms in the contract, the terms may be listed and defined in a separate section of the contract.
- The body of the contract includes terms of the parties' agreement and specifically addresses the details of the contract relationship or the transaction that is the subject matter of the agreement.
- The concluding statement formally ends the substantive provisions of the contract.
- The signature lines are placed at the end of the agreement and may include blank lines for dates if the parties are signing the contract at different times.
- Schedules and exhibits are attached to the contract.

A. *Introduction*

This part of the book shifts from the writing process used by U.S. lawyers in litigation-related matters to the writing process used by U.S. lawyers in transactional work. In U.S. litigation practice, a lawyer writes legal memoranda using objective analyses that explain the law to the reader. The litigation lawyer also writes briefs to the courts using persuasive techniques and analyses to convince the courts of the proper application or interpretation of the law. A business client usually seeks the help of a U.S. litigation lawyer after a business relationship has failed and a legal dispute has arisen.

In contrast, a business client uses a U.S. transactional lawyer's services when creating a business relationship. Here, the client wants to ensure the business relationship protects his interests. To this end, the transactional lawyer works with the client to accomplish the client's goals, ensuring the client's interests are protected as much as possible along the way.

The extent of the U.S. transactional lawyer's involvement in the client's business deal depends on the client's needs. For instance, a lawyer may only draft the contract that memorializes an agreement that the client and the other parties have previously negotiated. In some situations, however, a client may request services beyond the mere drafting of the contract. For example, the client may ask the lawyer to participate in negotiations of the deal or review supporting documentation to provide advice about the deal. The client may also ask the lawyer to supervise the closing of the transaction or oversee and administer post-closing tasks, such as filing documents with government offices.

When negotiating and drafting a contract, the parties are creating agreed terms that will govern their relationship. Of course, all terms in a contract are subject to overriding state or federal law applicable to the parties or the subject matter of the agreement. Because of this, a U.S. lawyer strives to draft a clearly written testament of the parties' agreement. Ideally, the terms are expressed so precisely that, if a dispute should later arise, a judge reviewing the contract would interpret the contract as the parties originally intended and in a way that protects the client's interests.

Another motivating factor for drafting a thorough, clear, and precise contract is the U.S. courts' adherence to the parol evidence rule when interpreting written contracts governed by U.S. state or federal law.[1] The parol evidence rule addresses whether a court will admit evidence intended to interpret disputed terms in an executed,

---

1. The Restatement (Second) of Contracts § 213 (1981) states the common law parol evidence rule as recognized by many U.S. courts. The Uniform Commercial Code § 2-202 states the parol evidence rule as it applies to transactions involving the sale of goods between U.S. parties. The parol evidence rule is excluded from the UNIDROIT Principles of International Commercial Contracts 2004 (the UNIDROIT Principles) and the 1980 United Nations Convention on Contracts for the International Sale of Goods (the CISG). Therefore, contracts governed by the UNIDROIT Principles or the CISG are not subject to the parol evidence rule.

written contract. Parol evidence includes evidence relating to oral statements or extraneous writings made prior to the execution of a written contract. Parol evidence also includes evidence relating to oral statements and sometimes extraneous writings made contemporaneous with the execution of the written contract. The parol evidence rule prohibits admission of parol evidence to contradict, supplement, or explain disputed terms in a written contract

(1) when the contract is intended by the parties to be and, in fact, is a final and complete expression of their agreement (a "fully integrated agreement"), or

(2) when the contract is not a fully integrated agreement but the disputed contract term is determined by the court to be clear and unambiguous.[2]

Conversely, if the contract is not a fully integrated agreement and the disputed contract term is deemed unclear or ambiguous, the court may admit parol evidence to supplement or explain that term to the extent the evidence is consistent with other terms in the contract. The admitted parol evidence is recognized as part of the contract only if the fact-finder decides that the evidence is credible.

Because of the foregoing concerns, U.S. lawyers are inclined to draft contracts in great detail. But more language does not necessarily result in a contract that is clearly and precisely written.

This chapter provides a brief overview of the basic sections found in many U.S. contracts. In addition to stating the purpose of various sections, the discussion includes some points to consider when drafting these sections.

The following chapters (1) introduce the basic concepts of U.S. contract drafting, (2) provide an overview of fundamental drafting skills, and (3) address some of the drafting concerns that may arise in an international transaction. Chapter 18 looks at basic provisions commonly found in contracts and their purpose in communicating the parties' intent. Chapter 19 further refines how the parties' intent is articulated by concentrating on appropriate word choice. Chapter 20 expands the focus to sentence structure. Finally, Chapter 21 discusses checklists and organizational format.

The examples used throughout the chapters to illustrate various concepts are taken from a distribution contract between a non-U.S. manufacturer (Optex, Inc., a fictitious corporation incorporated under the laws of the fictitious country of Solandia) and a U.S. distributor (Ecklander Distributors, Inc., a fictitious corporation incorporated under the laws of Delaware). The example distribution contract memorializes the agreed terms of Optex's promotion and sale of Ecklander's sunglasses in the United States and Canada. Assume that the agreed language for this contract is English.

---

2. The parol evidence rule does not prohibit admission of parole evidence to invalidate a contract based on such claims as fraud, misrepresentation, mistake, or duress.

B. Preface for a Lengthy Contract

An extremely long and complex contract usually includes a cover page and a table of contents. A definitions section is sometimes also inserted after the table of contents. The cover page, a table of contents, and, if used, a definitions section precede the introductory statement of the contract. (Definitions sections are discussed in section G of this chapter.)

1. Cover page

A cover page formally introduces the contract by stating the title of the contract. (See Section C of this chapter.) The title is usually typed in large, bold letters and centered in the middle of the page. Oftentimes the title page also includes the name of the contracting parties and the date of the agreement.

2. Table of contents

The purpose of a table of contents is to assist the reader in quickly locating specific sections and subsections in a contract. Enumerated headings and subheadings are listed in the table of contents along with the page numbers on which these headings and subheadings appear in the contract. Additionally, all schedules and exhibits attached to the contract are included in the table of contents.

C. Title of the Contract

If the contract does not have a cover page, the title is centered at the top of the first page of the contract. For emphasis, consider presenting the title in all capital letters, using bold type and a slightly larger font than the substantive text of the contract.

The title should adequately identify the contract. Using "Agreement" or "Contract" as the title is too generic and may lead to confusion later on, especially if the parties have entered into more than one contract. Include words that sufficiently convey the business of the contract. For instance, the example contract between Optex and Ecklander might be titled "Distribution Agreement" or "Distributorship Contract."

D. Introductory Statement

The first textual paragraph in a contract is the introductory statement, which formally introduces the name of the contract, gives the date of the contract, and identifies the parties to the contract. It is not unusual to omit the verb from the introductory statement, thus making it an incomplete sentence. But for improved readability, write the introductory statement as a complete sentence. See Figure 17-1 for an example.

Sample Distribution Agreement

DISTRIBUTION AGREEMENT

This Agreement, is dated as of August 1, 20XX, between Optex, Inc., a Solandia corporation ("Manufacturer"), and Ecklander Distributors, Inc., a Delaware corporation ("Distributor").

BACKGROUND

Manufacturer designs and produces the Product (as defined in Section 1) in Solandia and desires to have the Product promoted, sold, and distributed in the Territory (as defined in Section 1).

Distributor promotes, sells, and distributes merchandise in the Territory, including merchandise similar to those of the Product.

The parties desire to enter into this Agreement for the purpose of granting Distributor the exclusive distributorship of the Product in order to promote, sell, and distribute the Product in the Territory.

Therefore, the parties agree as follows:

Figure 17-1

1. Date of the contract

The date of the contract, usually the day on which all the parties sign the document, is stated in the introductory statement. When the date of signing is not known or uncertain, leave the date blank to allow for the parties to fill in the appropriate date.

The words *as of* typically preface the date if the contract will be signed by at least one of the parties after the date of the contract. In this instance, each party should note the date he or she signed the contract in a space provided for this purpose next to that party's signature line at the end of the contract.

The date of the contract is commonly the date when the agreed terms of the contract take effect. If the parties intend the agreed terms to take effect subsequent to the date of the contract, then a provision that states the effective date of the contract should be included in the body of the contract.

2. Identifying the parties

Use the preposition *between* in the introductory statement when referring to the relationship of the contracting parties, even in contracts with more than two contracting parties. Although the phrase *by and between* is often used in the introduction, the words *by and* don't add any legal effect and therefore should be omitted.

Identify the parties by their full legal names and their states or national citizenships. A corporation's citizenship is the place where it is incorporated. If relevant, the state of the corporation's principal place of business or the state where it is doing business can be identified along with its place of incorporation.

Refrain from inserting the parties' addresses in the introductory statement; this is not essential to identifying the parties. If the parties' addresses are necessary to give notice under the contract, then state the addresses in the notice provision in the body of the contract. (See section H of this chapter.)

For conciseness, the parties' names often are shortened when referring to the parties in the contract provisions. Introduce a party's shortened name as a defined term in the introductory statement. After the party has been fully identified, state the shortened name in quotation marks and parentheses. An example of this format is shown in Figure 17-1.

Choosing the shortened name is purely a matter of preference. Using Ecklander Distributors, Inc. as an example, a party's shortened name may be one or two words from the party's proper name ("Ecklander"), the party's initials ("EDI"), or a generic name that succinctly expresses the party's role in the contract ("Distributor"). Be careful, however, in choosing generic names for the parties that are spelled similarly. For instance, the difference between "licensor" and "licensee" is a matter of the *-or* and *-ee* on the endings. If both these names were used to identify the parties in a contract, it would be easy to overlook a typographical error that resulted in the use of *licensor* instead of *licensee*, or vice versa.

The advantage in choosing a generic name over a shortened proper name of a party is that it saves editing time if the contract is used as a model in future deals. The name does not need to be changed throughout the contract to coincide with the new party's proper name. As is the case with any defined term in a contract, refer consistently to the party throughout the contract by the party's defined term. If a generic name is used, ensure that the first letter of the generic name is always capitalized when referring to the party.

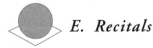

E. Recitals

Recitals are a series of fact statements that set up the circumstances for the agreement. These statements might address the parties' backgrounds, their relationship to each other, or their motives for entering into the contract. Recitals also may state the purpose or the nature of the deal underlying the contract, or identify other documents or transactions related to the contract. Recitals are not a required section in a U.S. contract, but when they are included, recitals may help resolve a later dispute between the parties over the interpretation of unclear or ambiguous substantive terms in the contract. Therefore, ensure that recitals accurately and concisely reflect the facts being reported.

If recitals are provided in a contract, state the recitals after the introductory statement. Do not state the substantive terms of the agreement in the recitals. All agreed terms of the deal belong in the body of the contract.

The archaic format for presenting recitals in U.S. contracts usually opened with the word *witnesseth*, followed by fact clauses beginning with *whereas*. Because these words have no legal effect, omit them from contracts.[3]

Recitals in modern U.S. contracts may include a heading, entitled either "Recitals" or "Background." Each fact statement may be numbered, though this is optional. See Figure 17-1 for an example of a recitals section.

F. Transitional Clause

If recitals are used in the contract, a transitional clause is usually included to signal the end of the recitals section and the beginning of the body of the contract. The transitional clause is a simple statement, such as: "The parties agree as follows:"; "Agreed:"; or "Therefore, the parties agree as follows:". An example of a transitional clause is provided in Figure 17-1.

G. Definitions

Deciding when to use defined terms is discussed in Chapter 18. The method chosen to introduce the defined terms depends on the number of defined terms in the contract and the drafter's preference. In a contract with relatively few defined terms, consider introducing each term in quotation marks and inside parentheses after the word or phrase that is being defined.

> Distributor shall promote, advertise, and distribute Rio sunglasses (the "Product") within Canada and the United States of America (the "Territory").

---

3. *Witnesseth* and *whereas* are forms of legalese and thus should not be used in the contract. (Avoiding the use of legalese in a contract is discussed in Chapter 19.)

If there are numerous defined terms in the contract, then it may be more convenient for a reader's reference to place the defined terms and their corresponding definitions in a separate section. In this instance, list the defined terms alphabetically according to the defined term. Each term and its definition are stated in a sentence.

> "Product" means Rio sunglasses.
> "Territory" means Canada and the United States of America.

The definitions section may be located after the table of contents, if one is included in the contract. Otherwise, most drafters insert the definitions section at the beginning of the body of the contract, though some find this placement disruptive and prefer placing the definitions section toward the end of the contract.

If the definitions section is placed at the beginning of the body of the contract, any defined term mentioned in the recitals should be cross-referenced to the definitions section in the following manner.

> **BACKGROUND**
> Manufacturer designs and produces the Product (as defined in Section 1) in Solandia and desires to have the Product promoted, sold, and distributed in the Territory (as defined in Section 1).

Because cross-referencing definitions can be disruptive to the reader, limit these occurrences by presenting the definitions section as soon as logically possible in the contract. Cross-referencing to the definitions section, however, does not apply to terms defining the contracting parties that are embedded in the introductory statement. Customarily, the parties may be defined in the introductory statement without reference to the definitions section. See Figure 17-1.

When a provision in the contract refers to the contract itself, the term to use is "this agreement" instead of "hereof."[4] The defined term "Agreement" (with the first letter capitalized) may be used to refer to the contract, although prefacing "agreement" with the adjective "this" makes this reference clear.

 ## H. Body of the Contract

The body of the contract contains all the agreed terms of the business deal. The obligations, rights, discretionary powers, representations, exceptions, conditions,

---

4. *Hereof* is a form of legalese and thus should not be used in the contract. (Avoiding the use of legalese in a contract is discussed in Chapter 19.)

and other agreed terms should be drafted using the concepts discussed in Chapters 18-21. If there are numerous provisions, consider organizing the provisions into sections and subsections, as discussed in Chapter 21, thus making the contract more readable and easier to navigate. The provisions in the body of the contract may be classified into four basic groups: (1) the core provisions, (2) the dispute resolution provisions (if any), (3) the exit provisions, and (4) the miscellaneous provisions.

1. Core provisions

The core provisions state the essence of the business deal. Core provisions are typically presented at the front end of the body of the contract. In the distribution agreement, for example, the core provisions might be grouped into sections with the following headings: Exclusive Distributorship, Product Promotion, Product Purchase, Shipment, Acceptance, Payment, Intellectual Property Rights, Product Warranty, Covenant Not to Compete,[5] Indemnification,[6] and Confidentiality.[7] (See the list in section A of Chapter 21.)

The initial core provisions should establish the primary obligations imposed or the primary rights arising from the business deal. In the distribution agreement, for instance, the first substantive section establishes Ecklander's exclusive distributorship. The remaining sections comprising the core provisions provide the details of the distribution deal.

2. Dispute resolution provisions

Because litigation in the courts can be lengthy, expensive, and public, many parties are resorting to alternative methods to resolve disputes. The two most common methods of resolving international commercial disputes are mediation (sometimes referred to as conciliation outside the United States) and arbitration. Both are effective and more private methods for resolving disputes.

---

5. A covenant not to compete restricts a party from competing with the business of the other party; whether a covenant not to compete is enforceable under law may depend on the nature of the business restricted, the duration of the restriction, and the territory covered by the covenant. In the United States, the law governing this relationship is found in a state's statutory or common law. Thus, the law of the state governing the contract determines whether a covenant not to compete in the contract is enforceable. See "Choice of Law" under "Miscellaneous Provisions" in this chapter.

6. An indemnification is an agreement providing that a party who breaches a contract provision agrees to compensate the nonbreaching party for any losses or damages arising out of the breach.

7. A confidentiality covenant provides that a party obtaining private information about the other party by means of the contract relationship may not disclose the information unless specific exceptions are stated.

Every major international arbitration organization[8] offers the services of mediators and arbitral judges, and provides procedural rules for both processes, which the parties may elect to use in the event of a later dispute.

Mediation, a formal negotiation process supervised by a trained expert, is relatively new to the international scene. It is gaining popularity, however, with international parties who have discovered that it can effectively resolve disputes in less time, with less expense, and with more privacy than arbitration or litigation. The objective of mediation is for the parties, under the direction of the mediator, to work toward a resolution to the dispute. There is no guarantee, though, that a resolution will be reached, and even if one is reached, it is not binding on the parties.

Because the nature of the process requires each party to continue communication and to work toward a common goal, the additional benefit of mediation is the preservation of goodwill between the disputing parties. Parties should consider mediation if they want their business relationship to continue beyond the resolution of the dispute.

If a section on mediation is included in a contract, consider including provisions that address the following.

1. Provide a definition of *mediation* because the word means different things in different countries.
2. Establish a time period in which the parties must initiate and complete the mediation process before the parties are able to resort to arbitration or formal litigation.
3. State whether the parties may arbitrate the dispute or resort to another form of dispute resolution if the parties are unable to reach an agreement through mediation.
4. Establish a procedure for selecting a mediator (ideally someone who is familiar with all cultures involved, is fluent in the languages of the disputing parties, and has some knowledge of the respective laws of the disputing parties' countries).
5. Provide the number of mediation sessions in which the parties must participate.
6. Provide for payment of damages by a party who fails to participate in the agreed process.
7. State whether the mediation will be administered under an institution's procedural rules[9] or whether the parties may create their own mediation rules.

Arbitration is a more formal dispute resolution process where parties present their dispute to one or more arbitral judges who then render a final and binding determination on the parties. This process is adversarial, placing the parties more at odds against each other than in mediation. Furthermore, international arbitration can be as

---

8. These organizations include the American Arbitration Association, the International Arbitration Association, the International Center for Settlement of Investment Disputes, the Center for Public Resources, the China International Economic and Trade Arbitration Commission, the World Intellectual Property Organization, and the Commercial Arbitration and Mediation Center of the Americas.

9. In addition to the organizations mentioned in note 8, *supra*, the United Nations Commission on International Trade Law (UNCITRAL) has issued mediation rules.

expensive and as lengthy as transnational litigation, and it offers no guarantee that the parties' private information will remain private. The number of people usually involved in the arbitration process—for instance, the contracting parties, arbitral judges, and witnesses—increases the expense and the privacy risks. Despite these drawbacks, parties may still prefer arbitration to transnational litigation because arbitration allows the parties flexibility and some control over the process, and arbitral judgments may more likely be enforced than judgments made in foreign courts.

Ideally, contract provisions covering arbitration should do the following.

1. State whether arbitration will be limited to certain types of disputes or whether it will apply to all disputes related to the contract. For example, the distribution agreement between Optex and Ecklander may limit arbitration to disputes over rejected product.
2. State whether a mediator in an unsuccessful mediation may also serve as an arbitral judge in the dispute.[10]
3. Establish the selection process for one or more arbitral judges.[11]
4. State whether the parties must use the procedural rules of a particular arbitration organization or submit the process to a particular arbitration organization.[12]
5. State the location of the arbitration.
6. State the law governing the substantive issues of the arbitration.
7. State the language(s) that will be used at the arbitration proceeding.
8. State whether one party will bear the costs of arbitration and payment of attorneys' fees or whether the parties will share this burden.
9. Provide the rights and remedies available to nonbreaching parties in the event a party breaches the terms of the arbitration.

3. Exit provisions

Exit provisions address the parties' obligations and rights when the contract ends by premature termination or by natural expiration. Provisions may do any or all of the following.

1. Identify the events that trigger premature termination of the entire contract or only certain obligations under the contract.
2. Identify the events that trigger automatic termination or the right to terminate.

---

10. Although the mediator will have the benefit of familiarity with the dispute, permitting the mediator to serve as an arbitral judge may adversely affect the mediation process. For example, parties may be reluctant to divulge information during mediation if the mediator may later serve as the arbitral judge.

11. Typically, both parties will have a right to select one neutral arbitral judge; then the two chosen judges will select the third neutral arbitral judge.

12. *See, e.g., supra* n. 8.

3. State whether the party causing the triggering event has the right to remedy the problem within a stated period of time.
4. Identify the effect of termination or expiration of the contract, such as the award of monetary damages to the nonbreaching party, the payment of outstanding debt to the nonbreaching party, the disposition of inventory, or the discontinuance of the right to use intellectual property.

4. Miscellaneous provisions

Miscellaneous provisions are placed at the end of the contract, after the core and exit provisions. These provisions cover matters not addressed elsewhere in the contract, including but not limited to, administration, enforcement, interpretation, and execution of the contract. Because these provisions appear in most contracts, it may be tempting to take a provision found in one contract and insert it into another contract without considering the wording of the provision and how it might affect other provisions in the immediate contract or a party's interest. Miscellaneous provisions are just as important as the core and exit provisions in the contract. Therefore, cautiously use miscellaneous provisions and give adequate attention to the language contained in these provisions.

The following are short explanations of miscellaneous provisions commonly found in contracts. Some should be of particular concern to international parties. A detailed discussion of miscellaneous provisions, including special drafting problems and ways to remedy these problems, is beyond the scope of this book. Interested readers should refer to *Negotiating and Drafting Contract Boilerplate*.[13]

a. Notice

Provisions in the contract may require that parties give each other notice in designated circumstances. The notice provision addresses this requirement by providing delivery information for each party, including to whom and where to send the notice. It also states the method of delivery, which may include postal mail, overnight courier, fax, e-mail, or any combination of these methods.

b. Force majeure

Sometimes a party's performance under a contract may be disrupted or prevented by situations beyond that party's control. The purpose of a force majeure clause is to permit suspension of a party's performance without incurring a penalty. This period usually lasts for the duration of the interrupting event. Events triggering excused performance may include natural disasters, fires, war, labor disputes, embargoes, or changes in government policies or laws. There are many variations of force majeure clauses. Include a clause that does not conflict with the parties' intentions or other

---

13. *Negotiating and Drafting Contract Boilerplate* (Tina L. Stark, ed., ALM Publishing 2003).

provisions in the contract. For example, if the parties intend to excuse only those instances that are not foreseeable, then the clause should be restricted to reflect this intent. Also, carefully word the force majeure clause so that it does not conflict with any contract provisions that provide for damages in the event of a party's nonperformance under the contract.

c. Choice of law

Ideally, the parties attempt to address every conceivable event that may arise from a contract relationship. Realistically, however, it may not be possible to foresee every possibility. Therefore, a contract should include a provision that designates what law (e.g., treaties, federal or state laws or regulations, local ordinances, or rules[14]) will govern when the provisions are unclear. The designated governing law will fill any gaps left in the contract provisions, and in certain instances, the designated governing law may even override agreed terms in the contract. Therefore, the parties should carefully consider how the laws or rules might affect their interests before agreeing on the law that will govern the contract. If a party is unfamiliar with the law proposed to govern the contract, the party should consult with experts on the law. In any event, laws can change from the time of contracting to the time a dispute arises. For this reason, the parties should consider including a clause restricting the governing law to the law in effect at the time the contract is executed.

If the parties elect to use law in the United States as the governing law, then the parties should be aware that private contract relationships are generally governed by state law, and, depending on the subject matter of the contract, some terms may even be governed by federal law. For purposes of designating a state law, the choice of law provision should expressly reference a particular state's law as the governing law for the contract and generally reference federal law, as applicable.

If a treaty affects the contract, additional concerns may need to be addressed. For instance, in an agreement for the sale of goods between merchants from different countries, the United Nations Convention on Contracts for the International Sale of Goods (commonly referred to as the CISG) may be applicable. The CISG automatically becomes a part of the national law of a country when that country ratifies the CISG. Generally, the CISG applies to a contract for the sale of goods between merchants residing in different countries that have ratified the CISG, unless the parties fully or partially exclude the application of the CISG from the contract.[15] Therefore, when the CISG applies to a contract, the parties must consider whether it would be preferable to fully or partially opt out of the CISG and, if it is preferable, include a provision in the contract stating this. If the parties opt out of the CISG, they must consider what law would serve as the governing law for the contract in place of the CISG and explicitly designate this law in the choice of law provision.

---

14. For example, the parties could agree that the UNIDROIT Principles will govern the contract.

15. *United Nations Convention on Contracts for the International Sale of Goods*, arts. 1(1)(a), 6 (Apr. 11, 1980), http://www.uncitral.org/uncitral/en/uncitral_texts/sale_goods/1980CISG.html.

d. Choice of forum

A choice of forum clause designates where the parties will litigate or arbitrate in the event of a dispute. Logically, the forum clause may designate the country of one of the parties as the appropriate forum. If the United States is chosen as the forum, then a particular state must be designated. It is common for the parties to settle on a forum that bears no connection to either party to ensure the forum court's objectivity.

e. Controlling language

When the contracting parties speak different languages, a problem of understanding contract terms and translation arises. The following, for example, are selected differences in legal expression between English and French.

English	French
compromise	transaction
agreement to arbitrate	compromise
execution	signature
performance	execution[16]

To assist in the interpretation of a contract, include a provision that designates the language that will be used to interpret the provisions.

As part of the negotiating and drafting process, the respective parties may want the contract terms translated into their native languages. To avoid misunderstandings, it is better to agree on a language for negotiation and drafting purposes at the beginning of any discussions. The party whose language is not used should hire a lawyer to represent it in the deal. If a translation of the contract is made, the "controlling language" provision in the contract should acknowledge that, although there may be translations of the contract, only one designated language will control the interpretation of the parties' agreement.

f. Severability

A severability clause merely states that in the event any part of the contract is determined invalid, the remaining provisions will continue in effect. This provision should be drafted with extreme caution. The parties should consider including a right to terminate the contract if the invalid provision destroys the core of the contract relationship. For instance, if sunglasses imported under the example distribution agreement are later legally prohibited for import in the United States, then the parties should be able to terminate the contract.

---

16. William F. Fox, Jr., *International Commercial Agreements* 129 (2d ed., Kluwer 1992) (quoting Georges R. Delaume, *Transnational Contracts* vol. 5, 28 (1983)).

g. Assignment and delegation

The parties may agree to permit or restrict assignment of their respective rights under the contract. The parties also may agree to permit or restrict delegating their respective performance obligations under the contract. Identify the party or parties subject to the provision, and if an assignment or delegation is permitted, any condition for permitting the action. A condition for permitting an assignment or delegation might be requiring the prior written consent of the other parties. The provision should also state that any impermissible attempt to assign a right or delegate a performance obligation is void.

h. Integration or merger

This provision states that the contract reflects the entire agreement between the parties and supersedes all previous negotiations and agreements made by the parties on the subject matter. Parties who want the written contract to serve as the sole testament to the parties' agreement should include this provision in the contract. Under U.S. law, this provision in the contract evidences that the parties intended the contract to be a full and complete expression of their agreement for purposes of invoking the parol evidence rule, generally summarized in section A of this chapter.

The parties also may consider adding a clause stating that the parties did not rely on any representations made prior to the execution of the contract. Reliance is an element of fraudulent misrepresentation, and fraud is an exception to the parol evidence rule. In order to avoid the possibility that a party may file a fraud action and use parol evidence to support its claim, a no-reliance clause should be included in the contract.[17]

i. Waiver or amendments

A waiver occurs when a party fails to enforce or agrees not to enforce a right given to it under the contract. An amendment occurs when the parties modify, add, or delete an agreed term after the contract has been executed. The parties may agree that any provisions in the contract cannot be waived or amended by the parties unless made in writing and signed by both parties. Although this type of restriction is often included in a contract, a U.S. court nevertheless may determine a waiver or amendment valid even if it is not in writing. Knowledge of the law governing the contract is important to determine the effectiveness of this provision.

j. Counterparts

A counterparts provision allows for the contract to be signed by the parties using separate original copies of the contract. This is particularly convenient when the parties

---

17. *See, e.g.,* Vigortone AG Prods. v. PM AG Prods., Inc., 316 F.3d 641, 644-645 (7th Cir. 2002): A no-reliance clause may be effective to preclude a fraud suit, "at least when the contract is between sophisticated commercial enterprises. . . ."

are located great distances from each other. The separately signed pages may be gathered together and attached to a copy of the contract to form a completely signed document. When contracts are signed in counterpart, a blank date line is included next to the signature line for each party so that the party can insert the date that he or she signed the contract. The date in the introductory statement should reflect an "as of" date because the parties will likely be signing the contract on different dates.

 ## I. *Concluding Statement*

The concluding statement formally ends the substantive provisions of the contract and transitions to the signature lines. The following is an example of an archaic form of a concluding statement found in U.S. contracts.

> IN WITNESS WHEREOF the parties have caused these presents to be signed by their duly authorized officers on the date and year first hereinabove written.

This concluding statement, filled with legalese,[18] should be replaced with a simple statement.

> The parties are signing this Agreement as of the date stated in the introductory statement.

If the parties are signing at different times, the concluding statement may merely state: Agreed.

 ## J. *Signatures*

1. *Signature lines*

The format of the signature line varies according to whether the signatory is an individual or a business entity. For an individual, the name of the person (the same name used in the introductory statement) appears under the signature line.

> _____
> Robert R. Jones

---

18. Avoiding the use of legalese in a contract is discussed in Chapter 19.

For signatories that are U.S. corporations or limited liability entities, the entity's full name (the same name used in the introductory statement) is inserted as a heading above the signature line. The signature line is prefaced by the word "By:" to signify that the individual signing on behalf of the entity is acting in an official capacity as an agent for the entity. If the name and title of the individual is known, then this information should be typed underneath the signature line; otherwise, leave this information blank so it can be filled in at the time of signing.

◆ *Example of a corporation*

> Ecklander Corporation
>
> By: _____
>   Name:
>   Title:

A general partner always signs on behalf of a U.S. partnership.

◆ *Example of a general partnership*

> Ecklander, a general partnership
>
> By: _____
>   Name:
>   General Partner

For signatories that are U.S. limited partnerships, a slightly different format is used when the general partner is a corporation.

◆ *Example of a limited partnership*

> Ecklander, a limited partnership
>
> By: Ecklander, Incorporated,
>   General Partner
>
> By: _____
>   Name:
>   Title:

2. *Electronic signatures*

In certain instances, electronic signatures and contracts are enforceable in the United States.[19] As of the date of this writing, the United States has not ratified the United Nations Convention on the Use of Electronic Communications in International Contracts.[20] States, however, have adopted the Uniform Computer Information Transactions Act[21] or the Uniform Electronic Transactions Act (UETA).[22] Federal statutory law, codified as the Electronic Signatures in Global and National Commerce Act, applies in states that have not yet adopted UETA.[23] This relatively recent development in U.S. law simplifies the signing of contracts between distantly located parties.

 ## K. *Seals*

In the United States, the requirement of a seal (melted wax dripped onto the document and impressed with a symbol) has been widely abolished and, where still in effect, is often limited to specific transactions.[24] The parties should check the law of the governing state to determine whether a seal is needed and, if so, what type of seal will satisfy the requirement.

 ## L. *Attachments*

All schedules and exhibits referenced in the contract provisions must be attached at the end of the contract. Schedules contain information that is considered part of the agreed terms of the contract. Information placed in schedules may include (1) information subject to frequent changes, such as price lists; (2) lengthy, technical

---

19. A discussion of laws governing electronic signatures is outside the scope of this book. For a general discussion, see John M. Norwood, *A Summary of Statutory and Case Law Associated with Contracting in the Electronic Universe,* 4 DePaul Bus. & Com. L.J. 415 (2006).

20. U.N. Commn. on Intl. Trade L., *Status 2005 United Nations Convention on the Use of Electronic Communications in International Contracts,* http://www.uncitral.org/uncitral/en/uncitral_texts/electronic_commerce/2005Convention_status.html (accessed Dec. 9, 2007).

21. Unif. Computer Info. Transactions Act §§ 101-905 (2002). As of 2006, only Maryland and Virginia had adopted this act. Norwood, *supra* n. 20, at 416.

22. Unif. Elec. Transactions Act §§ 1-21 (1999) (UETA). As of 2006, UETA had been adopted in 46 states, except Georgia, Illinois, New York, and Washington, the District of Columbia, and the U.S. Virgin Islands. National Conference of State Legislatures, *Uniform Electronic Transactions Act,* http://www.ncsl.org/programs/lis/CIP/ueta-statutes.htm (accessed Dec. 9, 2007).

23. 15 U.S.C.A. §§ 7001-7903 (West 2005).

24. *See generally* Eric Mills Holmes, *Stature and Status of a Promise under Seal as a Legal Formality,* 29 Williamette L. Rev. 617 (1993).

information, such as a long list of product models and stock numbers; or (3) if there are exceptions to a party's representation, a disclosure statement of any exceptions.[25]

Exhibits contain information that is not part of the agreed terms but nevertheless is relevant to the contract. Other contracts, forms, illustrations, and maps are examples of information that may be attached as an exhibit to a contract.

Schedules should be identified separately from exhibits. For example, if there are two schedules attached to a contract and three exhibits, the contract provisions will reference the schedules as "Schedule 1" and "Schedule 2" in the contract provisions, and the provisions will reference the exhibits as "Exhibit 1," "Exhibit 2," and "Exhibit 3." The schedules and exhibits must be labeled identically to the reference used in the contract provisions. References to schedules and exhibits in the contract provisions may be underlined to facilitate locating where they are mentioned in the contract.

> Distributor shall notify Manufacturer of orders of the Product by completing a written purchase order in the form attached as <u>Exhibit 3</u>. The current prices and minimum order quantities for each model of the Product is shown in the attached <u>Schedule 5</u>.

 ## M. *Using Contract Forms*

A transactional lawyer sometimes refers to contract forms when beginning a draft, especially when the lawyer has not had previous experience drafting a contract for the type of business deal contemplated by the parties. Contract forms covering a wide range of transactions are available on the Internet as well as in books. It is not plagiarism to use portions of these forms or the entire form when they are intended for the practitioner's use. Other helpful resources for beginning a draft are contracts created by members of the lawyer's own law firm for similar transactions involving other clients.

Using forms or model contracts as rough guides for drafting the contract in the current deal can save the lawyer time that she would otherwise spend creating a completely new contract. These resources can also help spot possible issues or important points or provisions that the parties might want to address in their ongoing negotiations. A lawyer may also use these resources to identify provisions that are customary to use in certain types of transactions. This quick start to the drafting process may save the client money.

But, at the same time, a lawyer should recognize that forms and model contracts are often quite limited in their usefulness. These resources never cover all the agreed

---

25. For more discussion on disclosure statements, see Kenneth A. Adams, *A Manual of Style for Contract Drafting* 69-70 (ABA 2004).

terms between parties to a business deal. And even when the documents include provisions comparable to the agreed terms in the present deal, a lawyer would be wise to use these sample provisions with great caution. Many of these sample provisions may not be drafted as favorably for the client as they could be if the lawyer carefully considered the provision's effect and revised accordingly. For this reason, a lawyer may need to make extensive revisions involving deletions, additions, and rewording to adequately address the unique aspects of the present business deal and to maximize the protection of the client's interest. Equally troubling, form contracts (and sometimes previous contracts) can be poorly written and may not reflect current law applicable to the present business deal.

Ideally, the lawyer should create a contract for the present business deal that she can use as a resource in future deals. The author of a draft is intimately familiar with the provisions because she will have created the contract's organization, weighed all aspects of the provisions, conscientiously chosen the words, carefully structured the sentences, and considered the interaction between the provisions. Using a familiar contract will hasten the drafting process in future projects because the lawyer is knowledgeable about the provisions in the template, which ones were particularly negotiated by the parties in the previous deal and perhaps why other provisions were omitted that may be desirous to include in the present business deal. By applying the skills discussed in the following chapters, a lawyer can draft a contract that is far more clear and precise, and protect the client's interests better than any published form or other model contract.

CHAPTER
18

An Overview of Basic Contract Provisions

HIGHLIGHTS

- The first step in creating a contract is to determine the type of contract provision that will clearly and precisely communicate the parties' intent.
- Parties can use contract provisions to allocate risk, such as in the case of representations, disclaimers, or indemnifications.
- Definitions assign special meaning to words or phrases used in the contract.
- Action statements convey a party's performance that takes place contemporaneously with the parties' signing of the contract.
- Covenants impose an obligation on a party to perform, or to refrain from performing, an action.
- Discretionary powers give a party the option to act or refrain from acting.
- Conditions are possible future occurrences that, if they occur, will either
  - create an obligation, a discretionary power, or a situation; or
  - terminate an obligation, a discretionary power, or an existing situation.
- Representations are statements made by a party regarding present or past facts, or both, to induce another party to enter into a contract.
- Disclaimers repudiate warranties implied by the law governing the contract.
- Exceptions limit a party's obligations or rights created in the contract.
- Procedural statements provide rules or policies governing the contract relationship.

A. The Importance of Choosing the Right Contract Provision

Provisions that commonly appear in U.S. contracts include action statements, covenants, discretionary powers, conditions, exceptions, representations, disclaimers, and procedural statements. Determining which contract provision best expresses the parties' intent is a primary concern that begins in negotiations and continues through the drafting process.

1. Promoting clarity and precision

The parties' intent can be expressed in a variety of ways. For example, let's say that the manufacturer of a product wants the distributor of that product to provide it with a report of the distributor's monthly sales of the product. It is possible to express this point either (1) as a covenant creating an obligation imposed on the *distributor* or (2) as a stated right of the *manufacturer*:

Example of the point stated as covenant:	Example of the point stated as a right:
On or before the 15th day of each calendar month, Distributor shall provide Manufacturer with a complete and accurate report of Distributor's sales of the Product during the preceding calendar month.	Manufacturer is entitled to receive from Distributor, on or before the 15th day of each calendar month, a complete and accurate report of the Distributor's sales of the Product during the preceding calendar month.

Clarity and precision influence the choice of whether this point should be expressed as a covenant or as a stated right in the contract. The statement imposing an obligation on the distributor by way of a covenant (discussed more fully later in this chapter) infers that the manufacturer receives a right that the distributor will provide a sales report. Similarly, the statement of the manufacturer's right infers that the distributor is obligated to provide a sales report. Either way, it accomplishes the same result. But, because the primary purpose of a contract is to create obligations and because stating the point as a right may lead to unnecessary wordiness, it is more clear and precise to express the point as a covenant.

2. Imposing legal remedies

Another consideration in determining the appropriate provision to use in a contract is whether and when a party will be entitled to a legal remedy if the provision is not satisfied. For instance, if a party makes a false representation of fact in the contract, the other party who relied on that representation may be entitled to damages. Similarly, a party's failure to perform a covenant may make that party liable for damages to the party receiving the right. A contract provision often will specify the damages available to the wronged party, such as monetary damages or specific performance. If damages are not specifically made available in the contract, then the law governing the contract may permit a wronged party to recover certain kinds of damages.

Conversely, other provisions do not provide for any right to recover damages. For example, if the agreed point is expressed as a discretionary power, giving the empowered party the choice to act or to not act, the empowered party is not liable for damages for simply making its choice.

3. Determining risk allocation

The parties' desire to allocate risk also influences the types of provisions that will be included in a contract. In addition to covenants, one of the primary methods for allocating risk is through a party's representation of past or present fact. A party may make representations to induce another party to enter into the contract.[1] Other contract provisions that allocate risk between the parties include disclaimers of implied warranties, indemnifications, and exceptions. The choice of words or phrases used in a provision also can serve to allocate risk, as discussed in Chapter 19.

No matter how the parties choose to allocate risk, however, they should be mindful of the law governing the contract. Governing law may limit the extent to which, or the manner in which, risks are allocated.

B. A Note about Definitions

The need for brevity, clarity, and precision in a contract may require that certain words or phrases be defined within the document. Consider providing a defined term for words or lengthy phrases that are used repeatedly in the contract or that are assigned a special meaning in the contract. Providing a defined term ensures consistency in interpretation. And, in the case where a defined term is taking the place of a lengthy phrase, it can also shorten the length of the contract.

---

1. Representations are more fully discussed later in this chapter.

Two common methods for presenting definitions in a contract are (1) creating a separate section for definitions or (2) embedding a definition in the text of a contract provision. If the contract includes numerous definitions, consider presenting the definitions in a separate section of the contract. Here, the term and its accompanying definition are presented in sentence format. Each definitional sentence is listed alphabetically according to the defined term in the definitions section. Within each definitional sentence, the defined term is the subject of the sentence, followed by the verb *means*, and then the definition or explanation of the term is provided.

> "Product" means Rio sunglasses.
> "Territory" means Canada and the United States of America.

Be careful to limit the provision to the definition of the term. Never include a point of substantive agreement between the parties in a definition provision. Consider the following sentence.

> "Territory" means Canada and the United States of America, *and Distributor shall promote, advertise, and distribute the Product in this area*?

The italicized passage is a substantive point of agreement and should be placed in a separate provision in the contract.

Alternatively, the defined term can be embedded within the text of a contract provision *the first time the word or phrase is used in the contract*. Here, the definition or explanation is followed by the term being defined.

> Distributor shall promote, advertise, and distribute Rio sunglasses (the "Product") within Canada and the United States of America (the "Territory").

To ensure that the defined term will be consistently construed, make certain that the defined term is used properly throughout the contract. Thus, in the distribution contract example, always refer to Rio sunglasses as the "Product." To further ensure consistency in interpretation, capitalize the defined term throughout the contract. Word processing programs typically include a Find or Search function, which can be used to locate the term wherever it appears in the document to ensure it is properly capitalized.

C. Action Statements

Action statements document a party's performance that takes place contemporaneously with the signing of the contract. Action statements are drafted using active voice,[2] and the verb is drafted in the present tense. Thus, in the case of the distribution agreement for sunglasses, the action statement documents the manufacturer's granting to the distributor the right to sell the sunglasses.

> Manufacturer hereby grants to Distributor for the period of this Agreement and subject to the provisions of this Agreement the exclusive right to sell and distribute the Product in the Territory.

The adverb *hereby* is used to convey the immediacy of the action, that the act is being accomplished by the execution of the contract.

 ## D. Covenants

The primary role of a contract is to create obligations by the parties to perform or to refrain from performing certain actions. These obligations are expressed through covenants. To create a covenant, U.S. lawyers commonly use the verb *shall* followed by the base form of the verb describing the action. Although in British English, *shall* is usually reserved for use when framing the sentence in the first person, U.S. English uses *shall* in first, second, and third person sentences. Drafting third person sentences is common in U.S. contract drafting. When used in the context of third person sentences, the definition of *shall* states an obligation or a necessity.

> Manufacturer shall assist Distributor in the sale of the Product by providing advertising material.

Some drafters prefer to use the term *must* instead of *shall* to create an obligation, but according to one authority, "*[m]ust* does not create a duty; it only asserts that a duty exists. By contrast, using *shall* in a contract provision conveys that the duty derives from that provision."[3] Another authority argues that using the word *must* to create a duty "disqualifies the word . . . from being used to create conditions, thus forcing drafters to

---

2. A sentence is written in active voice when (1) the subject of the sentence refers to the one performing the action of the verb and (2) the verb of the sentence refers to the action taken by the actor. (For a discussion of active voice versus passive voice, as well as examples, see Chapter 20.)

3. Kenneth A. Adams, *A Manual of Style for Contract Drafting* 24 (ABA 2004).

find yet another word or phrase to accomplish that legal consequence."[4] (See Section F in this chapter for a further discussion of conditions.) Therefore, consistently using *shall* as the operative word to create a duty promotes clarity in the contract.

Will also could be used to create a duty, but it also can express an action in the future and not a present obligation. To avoid confusion, it is better to use the term *shall* whenever creating an obligation.

A covenant should be drafted in active voice so that the subject of the sentence is the person or entity that has undertaken the obligation created by the covenant. Using passive voice[5] makes the identity of the obligor unclear and creates a longer, more complex sentence. This might result in greater difficulties when interpreting the covenant. A well-drafted covenant also identifies who has the obligation, what the obligation is, how the obligation will be carried out, and when the obligation will be carried out.

Covenants can be used to create a duty to act, sometimes referred to as an affirmative covenant, or they can be used to prohibit or restrict performance of an action, sometimes referred to as a restrictive or negative covenant. The following provision creates an affirmative obligation in the distributor and is stated in active voice.

> Distributor shall promote and advertise the Product in the Territory.

The following example of a restrictive covenant, taken from another section of the same distribution agreement, imposes a prohibition on the party from performing an action.

> During the term of this Agreement, Distributor shall not design, manufacture, or market, or act as a distributor for, any goods that compete with the Product in the Territory.

Sometimes covenants apply to more than one party or even to all the parties to a contract.

> Manufacturer and Distributor shall contribute to a cooperative advertising fund, which will be used for advertising and promoting the Product in the Territory.

---

4. Thomas R. Haggard, *Legal Drafting* 402 (West 2003).

5. In passive voice, the subject of the sentence is not the one performing the action of the verb, and the verb is a form of "to be." The verb shows the subject as acted upon rather than as acting. One way to identify passive voice is to look for *by* in the sentence, which is often, though not always, used to introduce the actor, for example: "The Product shall be promoted and advertised by Distributor." (For further discussion of active voice versus passive voice, as well as examples, see Chapter 20.)

To further promote clarity, use *shall* only when creating an obligation in those persons or entities who (1) are parties to the contract and (2) are capable of acting. So, for example, do not use *shall* in the following contexts.

Example 1

"The retailers of the Product shall provide good customer service."

Explanation: The distribution agreement is between the manufacturer of the sunglasses and the distributor of the sunglasses. Because the retailers of the sunglasses are not a party to this contract, the contract cannot impose a binding obligation on the retailers. Therefore, do not use *shall* when referring to any person or entity that is not a party to the contract.

Example 2

"New York law and federal law, as applicable, shall govern the terms of this Agreement."

Explanation: "New York law and federal law" are not capable of acting or forbearing from acting, which is required when creating an obligation. Instead of using *shall*, draft the provision as a procedural statement: "This Agreement is governed by the New York law and federal law, as applicable." (See Section J of this chapter.)

A final important note: A covenant creates a corresponding right in the party benefiting from the covenant. Therefore, the party receiving this right will want to ensure that the contract contains appropriate provisions that protect its right or provide it with a remedy in the event the obligor fails to perform the duty imposed by the covenant. Using the distribution agreement as an example, the manufacturer will want to include provisions in the contract that will provide it with a remedy in the event the distributor violates its covenant by selling the sunglasses outside the Territory. In order to protect its right, a party may consider including remedial provisions that will allow for it to terminate the contract and receive monetary damages or to ask for injunctive relief forcing the obligor to comply with the covenant (commonly known as "specific performance") if the obligor breaches its duty imposed by the covenant.

 ## E. Discretionary Powers

Contracts often include provisions that give one or both of the contracting parties the option to act or to not act. Discretionary powers are expressed in active voice and use the verb *may* followed by the base form of the verb describing the action.

Manufacturer may inspect Distributor's place of business and inventory the Product stock to determine whether Distributor is complying the terms of this Agreement.

 F. Conditions

A condition is a possible future occurrence that, if it occurs, will result in a consequence that either

(1) *creates* an obligation, a discretionary power, or a situation (sometimes referred to as a condition precedent); or

(2) *terminates* an obligation, a discretionary power, or an existing situation (sometimes referred to as a condition subsequent).

If the condition is stated within a single sentence, the condition is stated in a dependent clause[6] appearing at the beginning or at the end of a sentence. Placement of the dependent clause in the sentence depends on the length of the clause. Longer clauses should be placed at the end of a sentence to promote readability. A condition is written in the present tense. Never use *shall* in the dependent clause. This clause is stating the condition, not an obligation that may arise from that condition. The consequence caused by the occurrence of the condition is found in the main clause[7] of the sentence. Use *shall* in the main clause when the condition creates or terminates an obligation, and use *may* in the main clause when the condition creates or terminates a discretionary power. If the condition creates a situation or terminates an existing situation, state this consequence in the active voice and use a present tense verb that expresses the intent of the main clause.

Example of a condition creating an obligation

If Distributor rejects any of the Product because it is defective, then Manufacturer shall repair or replace the rejected Product.

Example of a condition creating a discretionary power

If Distributor rejects any of the Product because it is defective, then Manufacturer may repair or replace the rejected Product.

---

6. A dependent clause is not a complete sentence; it relies on an independent clause in the sentence to complete the thought.

7. The main clause can grammatically stand alone as a complete sentence, though as a consequence of a condition this main clause necessarily is connected with the condition clause.

Example of a condition terminating an existing situation

> If[8] Distributor is judged by a court to be bankrupt, then this Agreement terminates.

If the creation of a party's right is conditioned on that party's performance of an obligation, then state the condition in the main clause. The right is stated in a subordinate clause. Use the word *must* instead of *shall* in the main clause, because the party's nonperformance of the obligation should only result in a failure to create that party's right.

> To reject any Product that is defective, Distributor must notify Manufacturer in writing of its rejection of the Product and the reason for its rejection no later than 10 days after receiving the Product.

G. Representations

Representations[9] are statements made by a party regarding present or past facts, or both. A party makes representations to induce another party to enter into a contract.

Statements regarding future situations should not be framed as representations. A statement regarding a future situation where the representing party does not have control over it should be expressed as a condition.[10] A statement regarding a future situation over which the representing party has control is best framed as a covenant.[11]

Generally, there are three types of representation statements that either party can make: (1) representations relating to the contract, (2) representations relating to "the subject matter of the contract," and (3) representations relating to the party that is making the statement.[12] Representations relating to the contract focus on the legal capacity of the parties to enter into the contract. Using the distribution agreement as an example, if an officer of the distributor is signing on behalf of the distributor, there

---

8. A condition that is uncertain to occur begins with *if*, but a condition that probably will occur may begin with the adverbs *when* or *after*.

9. U.S. contracts often refer to representations, as the term is used in this section, in the form of the couplet "representations and warranties." According to one authority, "[f]or clearer, more concise, and more disciplined drafting, you should, except when waiving implied warranties, [avoid using the word] warranty and its verb equivalent and instead refer to assertions of fact as representations and have the parties represent." Kenneth A. Adams, *A Lesson in Drafting Contracts: What's Up with "Representations and Warranties"?* 15 Bus. L. Today 32, 32 (Nov./Dec. 2005).

10. Adams, *supra* n. 3, at 47.

11. *Id.* at 47-48.

12. Charles M. Fox, *Working with Contracts: What Law School Doesn't Teach You* 11-12 (P.L.I. 2002).

may be a representation that the officer has the authority to sign the contract on behalf of the distributor. The distributor's representation relating to the subject matter of the agreement may state that it has the equipment, facilities, and personnel to market the sunglasses as provided under the contract. Lastly, a distributor's representation regarding its own status may state that it is a corporation in good standing in all states within the sales territory.

In a representation, the subject of the sentence is the party making the representation and the present tense of the verb *represent* is used, followed by the fact or series of facts being represented as true. The present tense of the verb is used because the party is stating the truth of the statement at the time of the signing of the contract.

> Distributor represents that it is fully licensed in all states where it will sell and distribute the Product.

For a long series of representation statements, consider enumerating and tabulating the sentence. (See Chapter 20 for enumerating and tabulating contract provisions.)

> Distributor represents that:
>
> (1) . . . ;
> (2) . . . ; and
> (3) . . .

There is some disagreement as to whether, depending on the laws in various states, a statement that merely "represents," as opposed to a statement that "represents and warrants" allows for the party receiving the representation to recover damages in the event the fact is untrue. Deciding which clause to use depends on the laws of the state governing the contract. If there is any uncertainty in the governing law, consider using the statement "represents and warrants." "Warranting" may imply an "indemnification obligation if that fact is false," which may not be construed as existing in a situation where a party merely "represents."[13] Drafting the representation statement so that a party "represents and warrants" as to the truth of a fact arguably removes any uncertainty that the party receiving the representation may recover damages in the event the fact was untrue at the time the representation was made.[14] Nevertheless, as noted by one authority, "[i]n a contract containing specific remedies for false representation and warranties (as is the norm), [the distinction between representations and warranties] is not meaningful."[15] Whether using "represents" or "represents and warrants" to express statements of fact, the party receiving the statements should always

---

13. *Id.* at 9 n. 1.
14. Tina L. Stark, *Nonbinding Opinion*, 15 Bus. L. Today 8 (Jan./Feb. 2006).
15. Fox, *supra* n. 12, at 9 n. 1. *See also* Adams, *supra* n. 3, at 32.

ensure that the contract provides for a specific remedy, such as monetary damages, in the event any or all of the statements are untrue.

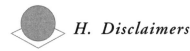 ## H. Disclaimers

A contract may also include a disclaimer that repudiates a warranty, such as a warranty of merchantability or a warranty of fitness, implied by the law governing the contract. Typically, the verb *disclaims* is used in the disclaimer statement. Laws, regulations, and treaties governing the contract, however, may require particular wording in the disclaimer statement and may even require that the disclaimer statement appear in a specific format or be placed in a conspicuous location in the contract.

Using the distribution agreement for the promotion and sale of sunglasses as an example, let's say that the parties opted out of the United Nations Convention on Contracts for the International Sale of Goods[16] as governing law for the contract, instead agreeing that Illinois commercial state laws will govern the contract. Illinois has a version of the Uniform Commercial Code (UCC) in its statutory code.[17] The UCC fills in gaps intentionally or unintentionally left in contract provisions for the sale of goods. Under Illinois' version of the UCC, a U.S. court will interpret a contract for the sale of goods to include a warranty of merchantability regarding the goods, even if this warranty was not expressly stated in the contract. This "implied warranty of merchantability" means that the merchant promises the goods are fit for the ordinary purpose for which they were intended, unless their fitness is expressly disclaimed or modified in the contract.[18]

In the distribution agreement, let's also say that the parties agree to exclude or modify the application of the implied warranty of merchantability (though realistically it is rare to get such a disclaimer because a purchaser would always want this warranty). According to Illinois statutory law, the contract must expressly mention the exclusion or modification, and the provision must include the word *merchantability*.[19] Also, the excluding or modifying provision must be conspicuously placed in the contract.[20]

---

16. *United Nations Convention on Contracts for the International Sale of Goods* (Apr. 11, 1980), http://www.uncitral.org/uncitral/en/uncitral_texts/sale_goods/1980CISG.html. The United Nations Convention on Contracts for the International Sale of Goods is commonly referred to as the CISG. The CISG automatically governs a contract for the sale of goods between parties residing in countries that have adopted the Convention, unless the parties have expressly contracted out of all or part of the CISG. *See* CISG arts. 1(1)(a), 6.

17. In the United States, the sale of goods between parties is governed by the common law, as well as a particular state's adopted version of the UCC. The UCC has been enacted in some form in every state in the United States except Louisiana.

18. 810 Ill. Comp. Stat. § 5/2-314(1) (2001).

19. *Id.*

20. *Id.* at § 5/1-201(10). A term or clause is *conspicuous* when it is written so that a reasonable person against whom it is to operate ought to have noticed it. A printed heading in all capital letters is conspicuous. Language in the body of a form is conspicuous if it is in larger or other contrasting type or color. Whether a term or clause is conspicuous is the court's decision.

Further, Illinois courts interpreting the state's version of the UCC have found a disclaimer of warranty conspicuous when it was written in larger type and capitalized or when it appeared in boldface type.[21] Therefore, the drafter of the agreement would want to ensure that the disclaimer appeared in a similar fashion in the agreement and included the word *merchantability*.

 ## I. Exceptions

Contract provisions, such as those creating an obligation, right, discretionary power, condition, or disclaimer, may be limited by one or more exceptions. A simple exception is often expressed in an independent clause, either at the beginning or end of the sentence. If the exception is lengthy, place it after the basic statement of the provision, or if there are a series of exceptions, state the exception in a separate sentence following the provision that is being limited. Placing a lengthy exception or a series of exceptions at the end of the sentence or in a separate sentence promotes readability and understanding. Begin simple exception clauses with the word *except*. Avoid archaic expressions such as "provided, however, ..." A typical exception removes something from the basic provision. The following example begins with the creation of an obligation within a territory and ends with those areas excepted from the territory.

> Distributor shall promote and advertise the Product within the United States of America, except in the States of Alaska and Hawaii.

 ## J. Procedural Statements

Procedural statements provide rules or policies governing the contract relationship. Ideally, write procedural statements using the active voice, choosing a verb that expresses the intent of the sentence.

> The initial term of the contract ends on the first anniversary date of this Agreement.

---

21. *Bowers Mfg. Co. v. Chicago Mach. Tool Co.*, 117 Ill. App. 3d 226, 234 (1983).

When stating a procedural statement in the passive voice, use the auxiliary verb *is* or *is not* together with the main verb. The doer of the action follows the main verb in a "by the . . ." phrase.

> This Agreement is governed by the laws of the State of New York and federal law, as applicable.[22]

● Exercise 18-A

Appendix M is a memo from the chief legal counsel of In-Play Sports, Inc., to you, as associate legal counsel, listing points for a licensing agreement between the corporation and Paulo Pessoa. For each of the points listed (and there are sometimes more than one agreed term listed in each numbered item), identify a contract provision discussed in this chapter that would best reflect the intent of the parties and protect your corporate client's interests. Briefly state the reason(s) for your choice.

● Exercise 18-B

Appendix N is a memo from the senior partner at Bolton & Associates to you, an associate attorney, listing points for an employment agreement between CID Software, Inc., and John E. Young. For each of the points listed (and there are sometimes more than one agreed term listed in each numbered item), identify a contract provision discussed in this chapter that would best reflect the intent of the parties and protect your corporate client's interests. Briefly state the reason(s) for your choice.

---

22. The example merely shows the appropriate sentence structure for a choice of law statement. Important substantive considerations regarding choice of law, as well as choice of forum, are addressed in Chapter 17.

CHAPTER

19

Word Choice

HIGHLIGHTS

- To promote clarity and precision in a contract, choose simple words and phrases to express the parties' intent.
- Avoid using words or phrases capable of two or more conflicting meanings.
- Carefully chosen words or phrases can qualify contract provisions and allocate risk between the parties.
- Vague words that allocate risk between the parties may be used when it is impossible or impractical to express the parties' intent in detail.

 ## A. Choosing Simple and Concise Words

To promote clarity and precision in a contract written in English, use simple words and phrases that are in common English usage to express the parties' intent. Pretentious or meaningless legal language (*legalese*), needless repetition (*redundancy*), and unnecessarily complicated phrases (*verbosity*) have no place in a contract. Legalese, redundancy, and verbosity can hinder the reader's understanding of the parties' intent. Even worse, it may result in an ambiguity that can lead to misunderstanding and expensive litigation.

Three types of ambiguities can occur in a contract. A *semantic* ambiguity arises when a word or phrase is capable of two or more conflicting meanings. (Examples of semantic ambiguities are discussed in this chapter.) A *syntactic* ambiguity arises when conflicting meanings occur from punctuation or from the order of, or relationship between, words and phrases within a sentence. (Examples of syntactic ambiguities are discussed in Chapter 20.) A *contextual* ambiguity arises from conflicting contract provisions. (Contextual ambiguities are discussed generally in Chapter 17.)

An ambiguity, whether semantic, syntactic, or contextual, is a serious drafting fault. A contract drafter should strive to eliminate all ambiguities because the objective of a contract is to clearly and precisely communicate the parties' intent.

The following discussion focuses on common contract drafting problems that interfere with clear and precise communication of the parties' intent: *legalese, coupled synonyms, coupled words and numerals*, and *nominalizations*. A drafter must be meticulous in eliminating all redundancies and wordiness from a contract.

1. Legalese

The following list provides some examples of legalese. These words are sometimes found in contracts, perhaps because the drafters mistakenly thought these words evoked a sense of professionalism or a lawyerlike tone. In truth, these dull words obscure understanding and readability. A good drafter eliminates legalese from a contract.

above-mentioned
aforementioned
aforesaid
before-mentioned
foregoing
henceforth
hereby (Unless *hereby* is used to convey the immediacy of an action in an action
     statement (*see* section C in Chapter 18), it should be avoided.)
herein
hereinabove
hereinafter
hereinbefore
hereto
heretofore
hereunder
hereupon
herewith
said (When used to indicate something or someone already mentioned; e.g.,
     "said party"; "said agreement.")
same (When used in replacement of a pronoun; i.e., "Distributor shall prepare
     the report and deliver same to Manufacturer.")
such (When used to indicate something or someone already mentioned; e.g.,
     "such party"; "such agreement.")
thereby
therefrom

therein
thereof
thereon
thereto
thereunder
therewith
whatsoever
whensoever
whereas
whereby
wherein
wheresoever
whereupon
whosoever
witnesseth

2. Coupled synonyms[1]

In contracts written in English, the use of *coupled synonyms* dates back over 500 years when both English and French were commonly spoken in England. At various periods in England's history, these languages were used alternatively as the principal language of the law.[2] In those days, coupled synonyms — usually a mix of Latin, French, and English words — clarified meaning to a multilingual society.[3] When English became the primary language in England, contract drafters continued to use coupled synonyms as an ornamental literary style.[4] In today's world, English language contracts may still include coupled synonyms. Coupled synonyms like those found in the following list are relics and have long since lost their initial function. Because coupled synonyms are mere redundancies, choose one of the words in the coupled synonym and omit the others.

any and all	final and conclusive
covenant and agree	free and clear
due and owing	full force and effect
due and payable	furnish and supply
fair and reasonable	just and reasonable
faith and credit	made and entered into

1. *See* David Mellinkoff, *Mellinkoff's Dictionary of American Legal Usage* 129 (West 1992).
2. David Mellinkoff, *The Language of the Law* 120-121 (Little, Brown & Co. 1983).
3. John Gibbons, *Forensic Linguistics: An Introduction to Language in the Justice System* 43 (Blackwell Publg. Co. 2003).
4. Mellinkoff, *supra* n. 2, at 121.

null and void	rest, residue, and remainder
over, above, and in addition to	stipulate and agree
pay, satisfy, and discharge	true and correct
release and discharge	unless and until
represents, warrants, and covenants	void and of no effect

3. Coupled words and numerals

Drafters sometimes present numbers in a coupled word and numeral format. Examples of this usage include the following examples.

on the fifteenth (15th) day of the month

three (3) copies of the report
one-half (1/2) of the original sales price
fifteen percent (15%) of the royalties

The reason for expressing numbers in this coupled format is that, in the event the numeral is incorrect because of a typographical error, the reader may rely on the word to interpret the parties' intent. The logical remedy is to ensure that the numbers are typed correctly, which is one of the drafter's primary responsibilities. Therefore, to avoid redundancy, choose either to express numbers in words (Contract A below) or in numerals (Contract B below) and use the chosen form consistently throughout the contract. The one exception to the consistency rule is that a number should always appear as a written word if it begins a sentence, even when numerals are otherwise used throughout the contract.

If the number appears in the middle or at the end of a sentence:

Contract A	Contract B
. . . on the fifteenth day of the month.	. . . on the 15th day of the month.
. . . three copies of the report.	. . . 3 copies of the report.
. . . one-half of the original sales price.	. . . ½ of the original sales price.
. . . fifteen percent of the royalties.	. . . 15 percent of the royalties.

If the number appears at the beginning of a sentence:

Contract A	Contract B
Three copies of the report . . .	Three copies of the report . . .
One-half of the original sales price . . .	One-half of the original sales price . . .
Fifteen percent of the royalties . . .	Fifteen percent of the royalties . . .

Despite avoiding coupled words and numerals when expressing numbers in a contract, some drafters insist on retaining the coupled word and numeral format when presenting a monetary amount. The reason for this exception springs from the fear of accidentally omitting or misplacing a numeral, comma, or decimal point.

Five Thousand One Hundred Fifty-Seven Dollars and Twenty-Five Cents ($5,157.25)

Five Thousand One Hundred Fifty-Seven and 25/100 Dollars ($5,157.25)

Misplacing or omitting a word that expresses the number, however, is just as easy to do. Attention to detail is critical in any case. To avoid redundancy, use only numerals, which are easier to read than words when expressing monetary amounts. Whether choosing the coupled word and number format or merely numerals, be consistent in presenting monetary amounts.

4. Nominalizations

Nominalizations are prevalent in English language contracts. A nominalization is a verb that has been converted into a noun by adding suffixes such as *-ure, -ment, -ence, -al, -ance, -ity, -tion, -sion*. Using nominalizations unnecessarily complicates ideas, contributes to wordiness, and hinders the reader's understanding. To fix the problem, simply replace the nominalization with the base form of the verb. The following lists some examples of nominalizations and their base verbs.

Nominalization	replace with →	Verb
enter into agreement		agree
enter into arbitration		arbitrate
make a distribution		distribute
make an amendment		amend
make revisions to		revise
make payment		pay

 ## B. Avoiding Ambiguities Arising from Single Words or Phrases

As previously noted, a semantic ambiguity arises when a word or phrase is capable of two or more conflicting meanings. Legalese, redundancies, and verbosity can result in ambiguities, but these are not the only instances where a word or phrase can create an ambiguity. The following subsections address a few of the more common semantic ambiguities that occur in English language contracts.[5]

1. Homophones

Homophones are words that are pronounced the same but have different spellings or meanings. To ensure that the parties' intent is precisely conveyed, take special care not to confuse homophones. The following lists examples of homophones that are usually found in contracts, along with their common definitions.

Homophone	Definition
accept	a verb meaning "to agree"
except	a preposition meaning "other than"
	★★★★★★★★★★★★★
breach	a transitive verb meaning "to break"
breech	a noun meaning the "lower part of the back" or the "rear part of a gun or rifle"
	★★★★★★★★★★★★★
capital	a noun meaning "money or property used for investment," "net worth," or "the center of government," an adjective meaning of "primary importance" or relating to the "financial wealth of a business"
capitol	a noun meaning a "building where a law-making body conducts its business"
	★★★★★★★★★★★★★
currant	a noun meaning a "berry"
current	an adjective indicating "existing at the present time" *Note: "Current" also can be ambiguous within the context of the contract.*
	★★★★★★★★★★★★★
fair	an adjective meaning "reasonable or unprejudiced," an adjective meaning "adequate"
fare	a noun meaning "cost for a person to travel" or "food"
	★★★★★★★★★★★★★

---

5. For detailed discussions and examples of ambiguities, see generally Kenneth A. Adams, *A Manual of Style for Contract Drafting* (ABA 2004); Thomas R. Haggard, *Legal Drafting* (West 2003).

its	an adjective indicating possession by something or a relation to something
it's	a contraction of "it is"

****

guarantee	in law, usually used as a verb meaning "to assure the quality of goods or services," "to promise something," or "to accept responsibility for another's obligations"
guaranty	in law, usually used as a noun meaning either "something used as security for an obligation," or "a pledge of something as security for an obligation"

****

lessen	a transitive verb meaning "to reduce"
lesson	a noun meaning a "learning experience"

****

meat	a noun meaning "the edible soft parts of an animal"
meet	a verb meaning "to come together"
mete	a noun meaning a "boundary"

****

passed	the past tense of the verb *pass*
past	a preposition meaning "to move beyond"
	an adjective meaning "something that took place previous to the present"
	a noun meaning a "time or occurrence that took place before the present"

****

precedence	a noun meaning a "priority" or a "preceding occurrence that is a priority"
precedents	the plural form of the noun "precedent," meaning "prior case decisions that a court is required to follow when adjudicating a current case that involves similar legal issues and facts"

****

presence	a noun meaning "appearance or feeling of the physical existence of somebody or something"
presents	an archaic noun referring to the current legal document

****

principal	an adjective meaning "most significant" or "most important"
	a noun meaning "the most significant individual, party, or group," or "the initial monetary amount invested"
principle	a noun meaning "a basic law or belief" or "a standard of conduct"

****

| some | an adjective meaning "an unspecified number" |
| sum | a noun meaning "total," "aggregate total," or "a definite or indefinite amount of money" |

****

there	an adverb indicating a particular place or a pronoun used to begin a sentence
their	an adjective indicating possession by more than one person or a relation to more than one person
they're	a contraction of "they are"

****

to	a preposition indicating direction or position
too	an adverb meaning "also"
two	a noun meaning the number 2

****

| vary | a verb meaning "to differ" |
| very | an adverb meaning "exceedingly" |

****

| waive | a transitive verb meaning "to give up a claim or a right" |
| wave | a verb meaning "to move back and forth" |

****

weather	a noun meaning "the condition of the atmosphere, including temperature, precipitation, cloud conditions, and wind velocity"
	a verb meaning "to endure an event"
whether	a conjunction that indicates alternatives

****

| you're | a contraction of "you are" |
| your | an adjective indicating possession by "you" or related to "you" |

2. Homographs

Homographs are words that are spelled the same but have different meanings. The meaning of a homograph often can be determined from the word's context. In some instances, however, the intended meaning of the word may not be readily evident from the word's context. For example, in the international distribution agreement, a provision might read as follows.

> **Distributor shall comply with all applicable laws, regulations, and ordinances in the states.**

The word *states* has several different meanings in English. Within the context of this example, *states* could mean either (1) more than one country or nation, or (2) more than one area forming a part of a country or nation. To clarify the parties' intent, replace the homograph with more specific words.

> **Distributor shall comply with all applicable laws, regulations, and ordinances in the United States, Canada, and Solandia.**

If the contract has repeated collective references to the United States, Canada, and Solandia, consider defining *states* the first time it is mentioned. Thereafter, whenever the word is used to reference the United States, Canada, and Solandia, *States* will be capitalized to signify the special meaning assigned to the word in the contract. (See also the discussion under definitions in Chapter 17.)

Domicile and *residence* also are homographs that commonly appear in contract provisions.

Domicile can mean

(1) an individual's dwelling or home;
(2) a place where a corporation is incorporated; or
(3) a place of residence that establishes an individual's or a corporation's legal status.

Residence[6] can mean

(1) an individual's dwelling or home; or
(2) a place where a corporation's offices are located.

---

6. "Despite rigorous efforts to keep domicile separate from residence (one may have many residences at the same time but only one domicile), domicile and residence are frequently equated. Legal residence and permanent residence are synonyms of domicile." Mellinkoff, *supra* n. 1, at 180.

When using a homograph, ensure that the meaning of the word is evident by its context. If the precise meaning is not readily obvious, then either (1) replace the word with a more specific word or (2) specifically define the word the first time it is introduced in the contract and consistently use the defined term throughout the contract.

3. Words and phrases conveying time standards and duration

This discussion is based on the assumption that expressions of days, months, and years in the contract are based on the Gregorian calendar, which is used throughout most of the world. Even so, it should be noted that Muslim countries, with the exception of Turkey, use the Islamic (or Hijri) calendar.

a. Time standards

Ambiguities can arise when referencing the time of day in a contract. The United States and Great Britain commonly use the 12-hour time system to express hours in the day. (See Figure 19-1.) In the 12-hour time system, the first 12 hours after midnight (12:00[7] A.M.) are written with an A.M.[8] suffix, and the 12 hours following noon (12:00 P.M.) are written with a P.M.[9] suffix. It can be confusing, though, because 1:00 A.M. follows 12:00 A.M. and 1:00 P.M. follows 12:00 P.M. Therefore, when using the 12-hour time system, it is clearer to refer to 12:00 P.M. as noon. Referring to 12:00 A.M. as midnight, however, can prove confusing because a day can have two midnights: one that starts the day and one that ends the day.

12-Hour and 24-Hour Time Systems

	A.M.	P.M.
12-hour Clock	1 2 3 4 5 6 7 8 9 10 11 12	1 2 3 4 5 6 7 8 9 10 11 12
24-hour Clock	1 2 3 4 5 6 7 8 9 10 11 12	13 14 15 16 17 18 19 20 21 22 23 24

Figure 19-1

All things considered, it is more precise to use the 24-hour time system when specifying the hour of a day in a contract. (See Figure 19-1.) Using the 24-hour time

---

7. The colon is the U.S. format. The British replace the colon with a period when using the 12-hour time system.

8. The suffix A.M. is the abbreviation for the Latin term *ante meridiem*, which means "before midday."

9. The suffix P.M. is the abbreviation for the Latin term *post meridiem*, which means "after midday."

system also eliminates the need for the suffixes A.M. and P.M. Time zones can be added at the end, though in instances where a time will occur on a distant date, it might be clearer to state the time with reference to a city. This may be especially useful to avoid confusion in those countries that observe daylight savings time during part of the year. Thus, "13:00 CET"[10] could be written as "13:00 Paris time."

There also are different formats for expressing months, days, and years. For example, the 15th day of October 2010 could be expressed in a typical U.S. contract as October 15, 2010. A non-U.S. contract might express the date as 15 October 2010. Which format is used will depend on the drafter's preference. Because the primary focus here is on U.S. contracts, examples of dates will be presented in the format typically used in U.S. contracts.

If time is being expressed in days, the question arises whether *days* means (1) calendar days, which includes all seven days of the week and holidays; or (2) business days, which are only the days the parties are open for business. Unless *days* is specifically defined in the contract, U.S. courts usually interpret the term to mean calendar days.

When a time period is measured by weeks, the question becomes when the week begins and ends. Does *week* mean a seven-day calendar period, beginning in the Gregorian calendar with Sunday and ending on Saturday? Or does it mean a business week, which in the United States typically begins Monday and runs through, and includes, Friday? Or, does it begin on another date relevant to an important starting point in the contract? These ambiguities can be easily resolved by specifically defining *week* in the contract, unless it is otherwise made explicit by the context.

The term *month* also creates ambiguity in a contract. A month usually means a calendar month. According to the Gregorian calendar, some months have 30 days and others have 31 days, and the month of February may have 28 or 29, depending on whether it is a leap year. But when is the month time period to begin in a contract? Does it start on the first day of the calendar month, or does it start on another day relevant to the contract, such as the 15th day in a calendar month? Because of these ambiguities, specifically define *month*, unless the context makes the meaning evident.

Time periods measured by years can also present problems. When does the year begin and end? Does it begin on January 1, using the Gregorian calendar? Or does it begin at another time relevant to an important starting point in the contract? Perhaps the parties intend for the year to mean a "fiscal year." A fiscal year is a 12-month period used for reporting a business's financial condition, which may begin at any point in the calendar year. For example, a fiscal year of a business may begin on July 1 and end on June 30 of the following year. As is the case with other time measurements, define the meaning of *year* as used in the contract, unless evident from the context.

Finally, take into consideration whether a time period begins, ends, or is otherwise affected by any holy day or legal holiday that shifts from year to year according to the Gregorian calendar. For example, Ramadan is observed during the ninth month of the Muslim calendar, which is a lunar-based calendar. Observance of the Christian holy

---

10. *CET* is the abbreviation for the Central European Time zone.

day of Easter depends on a calculation that takes into consideration the date of the first full moon after the vernal equinox. Rosh Hashanah is observed on the first and second day of the seventh month in the Jewish (Tishri) calendar. The Moon Festival (also known as the Mid-Autumn Festival) falls on the 15th day of the eighth lunar month and is a legal holiday in several Asian countries. If at all possible, state precisely the specific year, month, and day when expressing a date in the contract.

b. Miscellaneous expressions of duration

Words and phrases that express time periods also can be ambiguous. Interpretation problems can arise even when specific dates are used, such as in the following examples.

---

from . . . to . . .

Ambiguous:	Manufacturer shall ship the Product *from* January 20, 2012, *to* June 20, 2012.
Problem:	Some U.S. courts may find that *from* does not include January 20, 2009, and *to* does not include June 20, 2009. If the parties' intent is to include these dates, the provisions could be stated more clearly.
Better:	Manufacturer shall ship the Product during the time period beginning on January 20, 2012, and ending on June 20, 2012.

---

through . . . until . . .

Ambiguous:	Manufacturer shall ship the Product *through* June 20, 2012.
	Manufacturer shall ship the Product *until* June 20, 2012.
Problem in both examples:	Whether June 20, 2012, is included in either of these statements is unclear. The beginning date also is not evident. Assuming that the beginning date was specified by a previous provision, the ambiguity of *through* or *until* can be resolved by adding the phrase *and including*.
Better:	Manufacturer shall ship the Product through and including June 20, 2012.
	Manufacturer shall ship the Product until and including June 20, 2012.

by . . .

Ambiguous:	Manufacturer shall ship the Product *by* January 20, 2012, *to* June 20, 2012.
Problem:	The term *by* has the same problem as *through*: It is unclear whether the parties intended the time period to include June 20, 2012. This ambiguity could be eliminated by inserting "on . . . or before . . ."
Better:	Manufacturer shall ship the Product *on* January 20, 2012, *or* before June 20, 2012.

within . . .

Ambiguous:	Manufacturer shall ship the Product *within* 21 days.
Problem:	One problem with this statement is that the starting or ending date of this time period has not been identified. And, even if the starting or ending date were identified, it is unclear whether the 21-day period would include that beginning or ending day. For these reasons, *within* should not be used when specifying a time period.
Better:	Manufacturer shall ship the Product before the 21st day after the day on which the Manufacturer receives Distributor's written request for shipment.

between . . . and . . .

Ambiguous:	Manufacturer shall ship the Product *between* January 20, 2012, *and* June 20, 2012.
Problem:	Most U.S. courts would probably interpret this statement to mean that the dates were not included in the time period. To eliminate doubt, the provision could be rewritten using "beginning on" and "ending on."
Better:	Manufacturer shall ship the Product *beginning on* January 20, 2012, *and ending on* June 20, 2012.

Also, note that the following words are consistently interpreted, at least by U.S. courts, to *not include* the referenced date.

> Manufacturer shall ship the Product 21 days *following* receipt of Distributor's request.
>
> Manufacturer shall ship the Product *after* January 20, 2012.
>
> Manufacturer shall ship the Product *before* June 20, 2012.
>
> Manufacturer shall ship the Product *prior to* June 20, 2012.

4. And/or[11]

The term *and/or* in a contract provision is usually intended as a shortened method of expressing "A or B, or both." Even so, its use can make a contract provision unclear.

> Manufacturer may inspect Distributor's sales records and/or its place of business.

Does the manufacturer have the power to inspect either the distributor's records *or* its places of business? If the intent was also to give the manufacturer the option to do both, then it would be clearer to state the following.

> Manufacturer may inspect Distributor's sales records or its place of business, or both.

5. *"Provided that" and "provided, however, that" clauses*

The phrases *provided that* or *provided, however, that* signal the beginning of a proviso. A proviso is an imprecise clause used in contract drafting to create an exception, a condition, or a limitation that overrides a preceding clause in the sentence. It also can be used to add a substantive provision. The words *provided that* or *provided, however, that*, are sometimes underlined for emphasis. These words create ambiguity because they do not signal precisely to the reader whether the proviso clause is an exception, a condition, a limitation, or a substantive provision. The reader must determine the meaning of the proviso from its context, which can prove a challenge

---

11. This subsection contemplates the use of the term *and/or* in a sentence. But merely using *and* in a sentence or merely using *or* in a sentence can lead to ambiguities, too. See generally Adams, *supra* n. 5, at 8.11-8.52, 8.62-8.67; and Haggard, *supra* n. 5, at 251-257, for detailed discussions and examples.

because the proviso often occurs in long, convoluted sentences. Even worse, more than one proviso may be tacked on to the sentence, thus creating even greater ambiguity. For these reasons, avoid using provisos. The following examples illustrate how provisos can be revised to more clearly express the parties' intent.

An "Exception" Provision

Ambiguous:	Manufacturer may change prices for the Product; *provided, however,* that no price change shall affect purchase orders submitted by Distributor and accepted by Manufacturer prior to a price change.
Better:	Manufacturer may change prices for the Product, except that no price change shall affect purchase orders submitted by Distributor and accepted by Manufacturer prior to a price change.

A "Condition" Provision

Ambiguous:	Distributor may reject any Product that fails to meet acceptance specifications, *provided* that the rejected Product is returned freight prepaid before the 10th day after the day on which Manufacturer receives Distributor's written notice of rejection.
Better:	Distributor may reject any Product that fails to meet acceptance specifications on the condition that the rejected Product is returned freight prepaid before the 10th day after the day on which Manufacturer receives Distributor's written notice of rejection.

A "Limitation" Provision with an Added Substantive Provision

Ambiguous:	Manufacturer may repair or replace the rejected Product promptly after receiving it, *provided, however, that* Manufacturer elect to do so no later than 30 days after receiving the rejected Product; and *provided* further that Manufacturer will pay all transportation costs to deliver the repaired or replaced Product to Distributor.
Better:	Manufacturer may repair or replace the rejected Product as promptly as possible but in no event later than 30 days after receiving the rejected Product. Manufacturer will pay all transportation costs to deliver the repaired or replaced Product to Distributor.

6. *"Notwithstanding" clauses*

Similar to provisos, a clause that begins with *notwithstanding* is intended to override other parts of the contract. The use of these clauses, however, can lead to ambiguities in the contract.

a. *Using a "notwithstanding" clause to override specific parts of a contract*

Sometimes a *notwithstanding* clause expressly identifies the parts of the contract that are intended to be overridden by the provision following that clause.

> 9. Distributor may remedy a breach of this Agreement no later than 20 days after receiving written notice of the breach.
>
> 10. Notwithstanding Section 9, Manufacturer may terminate this Agreement upon written notice to Distributor and without an opportunity for Distributor to remedy a breach of this Agreement upon the occurrence of any of the following events. . . .

In this instance, it would be clearer to reference the exception in Section 9, where the provision overridden by Section 10 is stated, rather than mentioning the exception elsewhere.

> 9. Except as provided in Section 10, Distributor may remedy a breach of this Agreement no later than 20 days after receiving written notice of the breach.
>
> 10. Manufacturer may terminate this Agreement upon written notice to Distributor and without an opportunity for Distributor to remedy a breach of this Agreement upon the occurrence of any of the following defaulting events. . . .

b. *Using a "notwithstanding anything to the contrary" clause*

A drafter may use a *notwithstanding anything to the contrary* clause to override all other provisions in the contract that may conflict with the provision following that clause. In the following example, the manufacturer is not liable for the damages specified, even if other provisions in the contract could be interpreted to impose liability.

> Notwithstanding anything to the contrary, Manufacturer shall not be liable for special, incidental, or consequential damages.

The problem with a *notwithstanding anything to the contrary* clause is that it does not specify the possible conflicting provisions in the contract. Presumably, it applies to *any* possible conflicting provisions. In the above example, the distributor will need to carefully review all the contract provisions prior to signing the contract. The distributor will want to ensure that this *notwithstanding anything to the contrary* clause does not shield the manufacturer from liability in instances where the parties agreed that it would be imposed. Better yet, the distributor should ask that the contract be revised to replace the *notwithstanding anything to the contrary* clause with a specific reference to the overridden provisions.

c. Using a "notwithstanding the foregoing" clause

A *notwithstanding the foregoing* clause is inherently ambiguous because the reader does not know whether the exception applies to the previous sentence, paragraph, contract provision, or all parts of the contract that precede the clause. Never use this type of clause.

 ## C. Choosing Words that Allocate Risk and the Issue of Vagueness

1. Allocating risk

During negotiations, parties identify foreseeable risks that may arise from the contract relationship and discuss who will assume those risks. Each party's goal is to ensure that the scope of the other party's burden is expressed as broadly as possible and to ensure that the scope of its own burden is as narrow as possible. Even so, the law governing the contract sometimes may limit the extent to which risks are allocated or the manner in which risks are allocated.

Who bears the burden of risk and the degree of that risk can be expressed in the contract through the use of carefully worded representations, covenants, and conditions. One of the most hotly negotiated and perhaps dangerous phrases that can shift the risk between parties is "best knowledge" as used in a party's representation.

> Distributor represents that to the best of its knowledge there are no legal actions that could jeopardize its licenses or permits to distribute the Product in the Territory.

In the example, the "best knowledge" standard effectively shifts the risk from the distributor to the manufacturer. If it is later discovered that legal actions existed, the *manufacturer must show* that the distributor knew about this litigation at the time it made the representation in order to recover damages. For this reason, the manufacturer will resist including the "best knowledge" qualification in the distributor's representation. Conversely, the distributor, who does not want to bear risk for something it does not know, will advocate for including this qualification in its representation. Therefore, the "knowledge" standard in representations can be a point of intense negotiations.

A qualifying word or phrase can specify the degree of risk assumed by a party. Consider the following representation that uses the qualifying word *material*.

> Distributor represents that it is under no contractual obligations or other legal obligation that could have a material adverse effect on its prompt and complete performance of its obligations under this Agreement.

The inclusion of the word *material* results in the distributor's bearing less risk than in a case where the word *material* is excluded from the representation. The distributor will breach the representation only if a legal obligation has a *material* adverse effect on its performance.

In addition to representations, a drafter can use covenants or conditions to allocate risk. Here, the focus is on a party's standard of performance, although a standard of performance based on "good faith and fair dealing" is implied in all contracts. The following covenant does nothing more than remind the parties of this unspoken standard.

> Distributor shall make a good faith effort to market the Product in the Territory.

This next example, however, allocates more risk to the distributor by using the term *best efforts*.

> Distributor shall use its best efforts to sell the Product.

The following are other examples of words and phrases frequently used to qualify standards of performance.

adequate	reasonable
convenient	reasonable care
due care	reasonable efforts
due diligence	satisfactory
immediate	substantial
material	sufficient
ordinary course of business	temporary
practicable	to the extent permitted by law
prompt	undue

2. Vagueness

Unfortunately, words or phrases that allocate risk can create vagueness in a contract. But vagueness is not considered a serious drafting flaw, as is the case with ambiguity. Unlike ambiguous words or phrases that give rise to various, often conflicting, meanings, vague words or phrases create only a limited measure of uncertainty.

For instance, what constitutes "best efforts" in the above covenant example? Or what constitutes a "material adverse effect" in the above representation example? The answers to these questions may be easy if the phrases are expressly defined in the contract. Oftentimes, though, these standards are not defined in the contract. If the law governing the contract provides a definition — another important reason for the parties to understand the governing law — then this definition will be applied. But if the governing law does not provide a definition, the answers become more difficult. The parties may have conflicting opinions as to what constitutes "best efforts" or "material adverse effect." What may be the manufacturer's opinion of "best efforts" in promoting and advertising the sunglasses or what constitutes a legal obligation that has a "material adverse effect" on the distributor's performance may be different from the distributor's opinion.[12]

Ideally, precisely state a party's standard of performance. Sometimes, though, it is not possible to do so, either because the standard is impossible to predict at the time of contracting or because it would be impractical to express every detail of the performance. Aside from impossibility or impracticality, there are other reasons why a drafter may elect to keep the standard of performance vague. For instance, parties who have spent many hours negotiating their agreement on larger issues may be content to leave some details out of the contract. In these instances, the parties may settle for performance based on "good faith and fair dealing," a standard of performance implied in all contracts.

Although U.S. lawyers realize that vague words and phrases appear in contracts due to necessity or the parties' preferences, they strive to limit their use of vague words and phrases wherever possible. From the U.S. lawyer's perspective, this is merely good legal drafting practice.

---

12. *See generally* Rob Park, Note, *Putting the "Best" in Best Efforts*, 73 U. Chi. L. Rev. 705 (2005).

CHAPTER

20

Sentence Structure

HIGHLIGHTS

- Short sentences are easier to understand and should be used, whenever possible, in a contract.
- Keeping the subject, verb, and object of a sentence close together will increase readability.
- Sentences using the active voice are clearer and more concise.
- Complex sentences that include an extended list or series of lengthy clauses can be expressed in a more organized and readable format by enumerating the clauses.
- To enhance visual clarity, the drafter can tabulate the enumerated items.

 A. Simple and Concise Sentences

Choosing words that clearly and precisely express the parties' intent is an important component in contract drafting, but the meaning of a well-chosen word can still be obscured in a complicated sentence. Because short sentences are easier for the reader to understand, use short sentences in contract provisions whenever possible. One authority recommends "striv[ing] for an average sentence length of 20 words — and in any event, ensur[ing] that you are below 30 words."[1] While this is a sound

---

1. Bryan A. Garner, *A Dictionary of Modern Legal Usage* 663 (2d ed., Oxford U. Press 1995).

guideline, a drafter should not feel compelled to force every provision into a simple sentence structure. On the contrary, a well-written long sentence may be necessary to adequately express the parties' intent. Also, some variety in sentence length helps maintain the reader's interest. The point is to avoid needlessly complex sentences.

1. Subject, verb, and object placement

The subject, verb, and direct object of a sentence should be placed in close proximity to each other. A dependent clause inserted between the subject and verb or inserted between the verb and object can disrupt a sentence's logical sequence. Fortunately, this problem can be easily remedied by (1) shifting the dependent clause to the beginning or end of the sentence (see Figures 20-1 and 20-2), or (2) removing the dependent clause and conveying the information of that clause in a separate sentence (see Figure 20-3).

Shifting the Dependent Clause to the Beginning of the Sentence

> *Original draft:*
> Distributor shall deliver to Manufacturer, *no later than the 15th day of each calendar month*, a complete and accurate financial statement showing Distributor's sales of the Product during the preceding month.
>
> *Revised:*
> *No later than the 15th day of each calendar month*, Distributor shall deliver to Manufacturer a complete and accurate financial statement showing Distributor's sales of the Product during the preceding month.

Figure 20-1

Shifting the Dependent Clause to the End of the Sentence

> *Original draft:*
> Manufacturer, *on written notice to Distributor*, may change prices of the Product.
>
> *Revised:*
> Manufacturer may change prices of the Product *on written notice to Distributor*.

Figure 20-2

Removing the Dependent Clause and Conveying the Information in a Separate Sentence

Original draft:

Manufacturer, upon receipt of a Purchase Order from Distributor, shall, unless otherwise instructed in writing by Distributor, ship, by marine freight, the Product.

Revised:

Upon receipt of a Purchase Order from Distributor, Manufacturer shall ship the Product. Manufacturer shall ship the Product by marine freight, unless otherwise instructed in writing by Distributor.

Figure 20-3

2. *Active voice*

Sentences written in active voice are usually clearer and more concise than those written in passive voice. The subject of the sentence in relation to the verb determines voice. In active voice, the one performing the action of the verb is the grammatical subject of the sentence. In passive voice, the recipient of the action is the grammatical subject of the sentence.

Passive Voice	Active Voice
The Product shall be promoted and advertised by Distributor.	Distributor shall promote and advertise the Product.

While active voice is preferred in contract drafting, the following situations call for the use of passive voice.

- When the action is more important than the doer of the action.

> All disputes arising out of or relating to this Agreement are to be settled by binding arbitration under the Rules of Conciliation and Arbitration of the International Chamber of Commerce.

Note that the doer of the action is expressed in a phrase beginning with *by*.

- When the doer of the action is obvious, unimportant, or unknown.

> Notices required under this Agreement must be in writing and mailed by registered or certified mail, postage prepaid, to the last known address of the other party.

B. Enumerating and Tabulating Complex Sentences

1. Enumeration and tabulation

Complex sentences that include an extended list or series of lengthy clauses can be expressed in a more organized and readable format by using enumeration. Enumeration, as used in this discussion, refers to organizing a list or series of items so that each item is prefaced by a number in parentheses and the items are presented in sequence, such as (1) ... , (2) ... , (3) .... [2] Figure 20-4 shows a provision without enumeration and the same provision with enumeration.

Passage With and Without Enumeration

Without enumeration:
Distributor shall make a minimum purchase of the Product of $275,000 before the first anniversary date of this Agreement, $300,000 before the second anniversary date of this Agreement, $325,000 before the third anniversary date of this Agreement, and $350,000 before the fourth anniversary date of this Agreement.

With enumeration:
Distributor shall make a minimum purchase of the Product as follows: (1) $275,000 before the first anniversary date of this Agreement, (2) $300,000 before the second anniversary date of this Agreement, (3) $325,000 before the third anniversary date of this Agreement, and (4) $350,000 before the fourth anniversary date of this Agreement.

Figure 20-4

In addition to organizing a list or series of items, enumeration can also be used to remedy ambiguities. In Figure 20-5, it is unclear in the first provision whether the word *polarized* applies only to sunglasses or to both sunglasses and goggles. The following enumerated examples clarify both alternatives.

---

2. Sometimes small letters in parentheses are used instead of numbers, but arguably, it is clearer to use numbers rather than letters when the parties' native languages are different. Also, items should always be enumerated, as opposed to using bullet points, for easier referencing.

Enumeration that Eliminates Ambiguity

Without enumeration:
Distributor shall market and distribute polarized sunglasses and goggles in the Territory.

With enumeration:
Example of provision if "polarized" applies only to "sunglasses":
Distributor shall market and distribute (1) polarized sunglasses and (2) goggles in the Territory.

Example of provision if "polarized" applies to all items:
Distributor shall market and distribute polarized (1) sunglasses and (2) goggles in the Territory.

Figure 20-5

To further enhance visual clarity, the drafter can tabulate the enumerated items. Tabulation, as the term is used in this discussion, is a formatting technique that sets off each enumerated item from the surrounding text by placing it in a separate, indented block. Figure 20-6 shows an enumerated tabulation applied to the provision from Figure 20-4.

Enumerated Tabulation

Distributor shall make a minimum purchase of the Product as follows:

(1) $275,000 before the first anniversary date of this Agreement,
(2) $300,000 before the second anniversary date of this Agreement,
(3) $325,000 before the third anniversary date of this Agreement, and
(4) $350,000 before the fourth anniversary date of this Agreement.

Figure 20-6

Items may be tabulated in a sentence format or a list format. Determining which format to use depends on the drafter's preference and whether one format is more conducive to clearly expressing the intent of the provision.

2. Tabulated sentences

In the tabulated sentence format, the clause that introduces the series (the introductory clause) and the enumerated items in the series are parts of the same sentence. The introductory clause begins the sentence. The punctuation in a tabulated sentence format will be the same as if the sentence had not been tabulated.

Because the series of enumerated items is part of the same sentence as the introductory clause, the first letter of the first word of each item begins with a lowercase letter. The next to the last item in the series ends with a connector, *and* or *or*, to indicate whether the list is cumulative or alternative. All items use the same grammatical structure and are worded so that each item, when connected directly with the introductory clause, constitutes a complete sentence. See Figure 20-7 for an example of a tabulated sentence format.

Tabulated Sentence

Without enumeration and tabulation:

Distributor represents to Manufacturer that it is a corporation organized and existing under the laws of the State of Delaware. Distributor also represents to Manufacturer that it is fully licensed in all States where it will sell and distribute the Product.

Enumerated and tabulated:

Distributor represents to Manufacturer that Distributor

    (1) is a corporation organized and existing under the laws of the State of Delaware, and

    (2) is fully licensed in all States where it will sell and distribute the Product.

Figure 20-7

Tabulation also can clear up ambiguities created by a modifier that appears after the series and thus raises the question whether it modifies one or all items in a series. For example, in the unedited provision in Figure 20-8, it is ambiguous whether the phrase "covering the calendar year immediately succeeding its submission" applies only to "method of distribution" or to all of the items in the series. This is clarified in the enumerated and tabulated version of the provision that follows. By tabulating the items and bringing the end phrase "covering the calendar year immediately succeeding its submission" back to the original left margin, it becomes clear that the end phrase modifies all the enumerated and tabulated items.

Tabulation that Eliminates Ambiguity

Without enumeration and tabulation:

Before December 31 of each year this Agreement remains in effect, Distributor shall provide Manufacturer with a written marketing plan for the sale of the Product that includes a marketing timetable, sales projections, and methods of distribution covering the calendar year immediately succeeding its submission.

Enumerated and tabulated:

Before December 31 of each year this Agreement remains in effect, Distributor shall provide Manufacturer with a written marketing plan for the sale of the Product that includes

(1) a marketing timetable,
(2) sales projections, and
(3) methods of distribution

covering the calendar year immediately succeeding its submission.

Figure 20-8

3. Tabulated lists

In a tabulated list format, the introductory clause carries the burden of signaling by the drafter's choice of words (1) whether the provision is a covenant (*shall*), a discretionary power (*may*), a representation (*represents*), etc.; and (2) whether the list that follows is cumulative, alternative, or open choice, typically by using *all*, *one*, or *one or more* to modify the noun *following*. The introductory clause forms a complete sentence that ends with a colon or a period. Consider the examples in Figure 20-9, showing introductory clauses that may preface a list.

Introductory Clauses

Introductory clause indicating a covenant and a cumulative list:
Manufacturer shall provide to Distributor all of the following:

Introductory clause indicating a discretionary power and an alternative list:
Manufacturer may provide to Distributor one of the following:

Introductory clause indicating a discretionary power and an open choice list:
Manufacturer may provide to Distributor one or more of the following:

Figure 20-9

In tabulated list format, the first letter of the first word in each item on the list is capitalized, and each item ends with a period. The same grammatical structure is used for each item. Because the introductory clause specifies whether the list is cumulative, single alternative, or open choice, the connector *and* or *or* is omitted from the list. Figure 20-10 provides an example of a list format.

Tabulated Lists

Unedited:

To assist Distributor in marketing the Product in the Territory, Manufacturer may provide Distributor with samples of the Product, promotional literature, and price lists; make available to Distributor special purchase offers and quantity discounts of the Product; and make available to Distributor consultation services with Manufacturer's marketing representatives.

Enumerated and tabulated list format:

To assist Distributor in marketing the Product in the Territory, Manufacturer may provide to Distributor one or more of the following:

1. Samples of the Product, promotional literature, and price lists.
2. Special purchase offers and quantity discounts of the Product.
3. Consultation services with Manufacturer's marketing representatives.

Figure 20-10

4. Using tabulation

The following occasions may warrant the use of tabulation:

- When there is a long list of items.
  See Figure 20-6, which shows a sample provision in a tabulated sentence format. The drafter also may express the provision in a tabulated list format.

- When the items are stated in lengthy phrases or clauses.
  See Figure 20-10, which shows a sample provision in a tabulated list format. The drafter also may express the provision in a tabulated sentence format.

- When two or more sentences are closely related.
  See Figure 20-7, which shows a sample provision in a tabulated sentence format. The drafter also may express the provision in a tabulated list format.

- When it is unclear whether a modifier applies to one or all of the items and the items are lengthy phrases or clauses.
  See Figure 20-8, which shows a sample provision in a tabulated sentence format. When the modifier applies to all the listed items, the drafter may express the provision in a tabulated list format if the modifier can be logically inserted in the introductory clause.

5. Avoid overusing enumeration and tabulation

Enumeration and tabulation are helpful organizational tools, but they should not be overused in a document. Excessive use of enumeration and tabulation, especially if they are used more than once in the same section or subsection, can hinder clarity and readability.

● Exercise 20-A

Reread the memo from the chief legal counsel of In-Play Sports, Inc., to you, an associate legal counsel, which appears in Appendix M. Identify agreed terms that might be expressed more clearly in the contract by using enumeration and tabulation. Draft one provision using a tabulated sentence format and another provision using a tabulated list format. When you are drafting these provisions, also apply the other concepts discussed in this chapter and in Chapter 19 (e.g., use active voice, avoid legalese, etc.).

● Exercise 20-B

Reread the memo from the senior partner at Bolton & Associates to you, an associate attorney, which appears in Appendix N. Identify agreed terms that might be expressed more clearly in the contract by using enumeration and tabulation. Draft one provision using a tabulated sentence format and another provision using a tabulated list format. When you are drafting these provisions, also apply the other concepts discussed in this chapter and in Chapter 19 (e.g., use active voice, avoid legalese, etc.).

CHAPTER

21

Checklists and Organizational Format

HIGHLIGHTS

- Making a checklist of agreed terms and other points relating to the deal helps the drafter to develop an outline, create a design layout for a contract, and begin the drafting process.
- Numbering pages; using enumerated paragraphs, headings, and subheadings; and, in lengthier contracts, including a table of contents promotes readability and quick navigation through the contract.

 ## A. Making Checklists

One of the most common problems with drafting a contract is getting started. A good way to begin is to write down a list of all points upon which the parties have agreed. Be sure that relevant *who*, *what*, *where*, *when*, and *how* questions are answered as to each point. For example, in the case of a covenant requiring a party to perform an action, answer the following questions to help ensure all important information is included in the contract.

- Who bears the burden of performing the obligation?
- Who will benefit from the performance of the obligation?
- What is the obligation?
- How will it be performed?
- Where will the obligation be performed?
- When will it be performed?

• What will be the remedy if the party responsible for performing the obligation fails to perform?

These preliminary notes become the drafter's checklist and are the start of a rough outline of the contract provisions. Using this checklist, the drafter can determine whether related terms and points on the list should be grouped together under a general heading that will form a section or subsection in the contract. Eventually, an outline will take shape. The outline can be rearranged and modified, as necessary, during the drafting process. Consider the following list that might serve as a rough outline for the distribution agreement used as the basis for the examples in the previous chapters.

Title
Introductory Statement
Recitals
Transitional Clause
1. Definitions
2. Exclusive Distributorship
    2.1   Grant of Exclusive Distributorship
    2.2   Term
    2.3   Territory
    2.4   Duration
    2.5   Distributor's Representations
    2.6   Independent Contractor
3. Product Promotion
    3.1   Sales Quotas
    3.2   Sales Conduct
    3.3   Manufacturer's Assistance
    3.4   Books and Records
    3.5   Manufacturer's Inspection
    3.6   Sales Forecasts
4. Product Purchase
    4.1   Purchase Orders
    4.2   Amending Orders
    4.3   Manufacturer's Acceptance
    4.4   Prices
    4.5   Price Changes
5. Shipment
    5.1   Method of Shipment
    5.2   Delays in Shipment
    5.3   Insurance
6. Acceptance
    6.1   Product Quality
    6.2   Inspection

As perhaps evident from this outline, contracts drafted by U.S. drafters follow a structural format that may look similar in some respects to contracts drafted by non-U.S. drafters. Note that if this is a lengthy agreement, consider using a cover page stating the title of the contract, followed by a table of contents and a definitions section before the introductory statement, as discussed in Chapter 17.

In more complicated transactions, such as mergers and acquisitions, secondary documents in addition to the main agreement may be needed. In this instance, a lawyer should consider making a master checklist of (1) the information that will be needed to draft the various documents; (2) the documents that will be needed prior to the closing, at closing, and post-closing; and (3) any post-closing actions that will need to be performed. Creating a timeline for when to complete these tasks is also helpful.

Form books and various organizations, such as the American Bar Association, publish sample checklists for different types of contracts and transactions. These checklists can be helpful for beginning your own checklist. But because each business deal is different, a lawyer should revise these checklists by adding, modifying, or deleting items on the lists to meet the special needs of the current deal. (See also section M in Chapter 17 for additional considerations when using form or model contracts.)

 ## B. Organizational Format

Presenting contract provisions in an organized manner aids readability and helps the reader to easily locate specific provisions in the document. Ways to organize contract provisions include numbering pages; using enumerated paragraphs, sections, and subsections; and, for lengthier contracts, including a table of contents. These techniques not only provide organization to the contract but also allow for quick navigation through the contract.

1. Numbered pages

Whether the document is short or long, number each page of the contract to aid in locating particular paragraphs, sections, or subsections appearing in the document. In a U.S. contract, the page number typically appears at the bottom center of the page.

2. Enumerated paragraphs, headings, and subheadings

Enumerated paragraphs, headings, and subheadings are helpful tools for quickly locating information in a contract and for use in a contract provision that references another provision in the contract (commonly referred to as cross-referencing). Enumerated paragraphs, headings, and subheadings also ease the task of amending or revising a contract because the affected provisions can be more precisely identified. Whether to merely use numbered paragraphs or to add headings and subheadings depends on the length and complexity of the contract.

If a document is two pages or less in length, simply organize the contract by consecutively numbering each paragraph. Headings in this instance are unnecessary, though it is more helpful for quick reference to include a plain heading, as shown in the following example. Longer sentences within the paragraphs may be tabulated, as discussed in Chapter 20.

> 3. PURCHASE ORDERS. Distributor shall notify Manufacturer of orders of the Product by completing a written purchase order in the form attached as <u>Exhibit 3</u> ("Purchase Order"). Distributor shall complete the Purchase Order, specifying
>
> (1) the frame colors,
> (2) the type of lenses,
> (3) the quantities, and
> (4) the delivery dates
>
> for each model of the Product. Distributor shall deliver the Purchase Order to the Manufacturer.
>
>   4. ACCEPTANCE. Manufacturer shall not be bound by any Purchase Order received from Distributor unless Manufacturer delivers a written acceptance of the Purchase Order to the Distributor. Manufacturer may accept or reject any order from the Distributor.
>
>   5. PRICES. The current prices and minimum order quantities for each model of the Product is shown in the attached <u>Schedule 5</u>. Manufacturer may change the prices at any time, except that no price change shall affect a Purchase Order submitted by Distributor and accepted by Manufacturer prior to a price change.

For documents three or more pages in length, consider organizing according to enumerated headings and subheadings. Some U.S. lawyers use formats that include a combination of Roman numerals, upper- and lowercase letters in the English alphabet, and numbers. For ease of referencing, especially in contracts between international parties, the simplest format to use is numbers combined with topic headings.

To further assist in readability and referencing, each paragraph should be numbered, and the content should focus on the topic identified in the paragraph heading. In turn, all major headings should reflect the subject matter contained in the sections.

The headings and subheadings should be stated as concisely as possible. Sometimes headings and subheadings appear in a font different from the font used for textual passages, though the decision to do this is based on purely aesthetic, rather than practical, reasons. A more common way to emphasize headings and subheadings is to use a larger font size, all capital letters, bold typeface, underlining, or any combination of these formats. It is imperative that the enumerated system and the headings and subheadings, including formatting, be consistent throughout the contract. Consider the following format.

ARTICLE 4
PURCHASE OF PRODUCTS

4.1. <u>Purchase Orders</u>. Distributor shall notify Manufacturer of orders of the Product by completing a written purchase order in the form attached as <u>Exhibit 4.1</u> ("Purchase Order"). Distributor shall complete the Purchase Order, specifying

(1) the frame colors,
(2) the type of lenses,
(3) the quantities, and
(4) the delivery dates

for each model of the Product. Distributor shall deliver the Purchase Order to the Manufacturer.

4.2. <u>Acceptance</u>. Manufacturer shall not be bound by any Purchase Order placed by Distributor unless Manufacturer delivers written acceptance of the Purchase Order to the Distributor. Manufacturer may accept or reject any order from the Distributor.

4.3. <u>Prices</u>. The current prices and minimum order quantities for each model of the Product is shown in the attached <u>Schedule 5</u>. Manufacturer may change the prices at any time, except that no price change shall affect a Purchase Order submitted by Distributor and accepted by Manufacturer prior to a price change.

Or, a format with a simpler major heading might appear as follows.

4. PURCHASE OF PRODUCTS.

4.1. <u>Purchase Orders</u>. Distributor shall notify Manufacturer of orders of the Product by completing a written purchase order in the form attached as <u>Exhibit 4.1</u> ("Purchase Order"). Distributor shall complete the Purchase Order, specifying

(a) the frame colors,
(b) the type of lenses,
(c) the quantities, and
(d) the delivery dates

for each model of the Product. Distributor shall deliver the Purchase Order to the Manufacturer.

4.2. <u>Acceptance</u>. Manufacturer shall not be bound by any Purchase Order placed by Distributor unless Manufacturer delivers written acceptance of the Purchase Order to the Distributor. Manufacturer may accept or reject any order from the Distributor.

4.3. <u>Prices</u>. The current prices and minimum order quantities for each model of the Product is shown in the attached <u>Schedule 5</u>. Manufacturer may change the prices at any time, except that no price change shall affect a Purchase Order submitted by Distributor and accepted by Manufacturer prior to a price change.

3. Table of contents

As explained in section B2 of Chapter 17, extremely long documents should include a table of contents to help the reader quickly locate specific sections and subsections in the contract. A table of contents lists the enumerated headings and subheadings along with references to the page numbers on which these headings and subheadings appear in the contract. Attachments to the contract also are listed in the table of contents. The table of contents should precede the introductory statement.

● Exercise 21-A

Reread the memo from the chief legal counsel of In-Play Sports, Inc., to you, an associate legal counsel, that appears in Appendix M. Then, do the following.

1. Determine the overall structure of the contract.
2. Decide the design layout you will use for creating the contract. Note that, in addition to numbering the pages and paragraphs, you will need to decide whether you will use headings and subheadings.
3. Using the concepts learned in Chapters 17-21, draft the licensing agreement.

● Exercise 21-B

Reread the memo from the senior partner at Bolton & Associates to you, an associate attorney, that appears in Appendix N. Then, do the following.

1. Determine the overall structure of the contract.
2. Decide the design layout you will use for creating the contract. Note that, in addition to numbering the pages and paragraphs, you will need to decide whether you will use headings and subheadings.
3. Using the concepts learned in Chapters 17-21, draft the employment agreement.

PART SIX

Law School Examinations

CHAPTER

22

Exam-Taking Techniques

HIGHLIGHTS

- The guidelines for essays and multiple-choice questions in this chapter are general ones only; always abide by your professor's guidelines if they differ from these.
- Time management is essential to a successful exam.
- Preparation is also essential: practice, practice, practice.
- Take careful notes to better ensure a complete and organized answer.
- Consider following TRAC when analyzing each legal issue in an essay question.
- Strive to identify the correct answers in multiple choice questions through a process of elimination.

 ## A. Introduction

This chapter gives general guidelines for (1) preparing for an examination, (2) writing answers to essay questions, and (3) writing answers to multiple-choice questions. Of course, if your professor has his or her own guidelines or preferences, you should follow those.[1]

---

1. While it is important to follow the instructions given by your law professor when taking an examination, not all professors provide detailed guidelines. This chapter is designed to fill in those gaps in information.

1. Preparing for an examination

As law students, you are encouraged to combine in one study guide your notes from your reading assignments, classes, and other resources used during the semester, as a way to prepare for an examination. Some call these study guides "outlines," but that does not mean that a formal outline is required. The goal is to organize your materials. Find a system that works for you. What follows are some general suggestions that may help in moving from semester-long notes and materials to an organized, synthesized study guide.

a. Outline in stages

Large blocks of time are not required to make progress on an outline. If you feel obligated, for example, to devote an entire day working on a single outline for one class, you may not start simply because you don't have the time to devote to that one project. Instead, consider setting aside approximately two to four hours periodically to work on an outline for each subject. If you do this throughout the semester — particularly during the second half of the semester when you know what to outline — you will be much better prepared to study for your final examinations.

b. Outline segments of the law at a time

Consider waiting until you have completed a segment of the law before outlining. You may have the urge to outline immediately following each class. This may help you to outline in a timely manner, but you will likely find that you will need to go back and revise your outline as you learn more about the subject matter. For that reason, it is usually better to wait until you have finished the entire discussion of a section of the law before outlining.

For example, let's say that you are studying contracts, and the first section of your contracts course focuses on making a valid offer. You may study many cases to help you understand about the different types of offers and at what point they might be valid. Your time will be spent more efficiently if you wait until you complete your study of the offer concept in its entirety before outlining. At that point, you will likely never focus on valid offers again during the semester, so you will not need to go back later and revise.

c. Organize the outline

Before planning, gather your notes, briefs, casebook, outlines, and hornbooks. The idea is to create a concise study guide from all the resources available to you. Briefly review the area that you are about to outline. Attempt to identify major headings and subheadings. Many times the table of contents of your casebook will be an excellent place to start the outlining process. This can be used as a basic framework to which you attach the substance.

Once you have identified the major headings and the subheadings, you are ready to draft your outline. Try to incorporate the legal concepts discussed in the casebook with the notes that you took in class. Many law professors develop examination questions from their lectures, so you should rely heavily on your notes. Stay focused on what matters.[2]

Many international students in U.S. law schools are uncertain about the proper focus when studying for a final examination. As discussed in Chapter 4, while the study of cases in a law school casebook is a necessary step in a common law system, the cases may not be the focus of examination questions.[3] Rather, exam questions often focus on the *significance* of the legal principles and policies introduced and explained through the study of case law. Consider, therefore, using the legal principles and policies to create the structure of your outline and note the cases as a reminder of how the courts have interpreted and applied these policies and principles. For example, let's say that as you studied contracts you read Cases A, B, C, and D relating to whether a valid offer existed between two parties; Cases E, F, and G focused on the revocation of an offer; and Cases H and I discussed whether there was a valid acceptance. Rather than organizing your outline around the nine cases, focus on the legal topics: offer, revocation of an offer, and acceptance. Your basic outline might look like the following.[4]

A. Offer
  1. Defined; other important policies and principles important to understanding what constitutes a valid offer
  2. Notes on Cases A, B, C, & D
B. Revocation of an Offer
  1. Defined; other important policies and principles important to understanding what constitutes a revocation of an offer
  2. Notes on Cases E, F, & G
C. Acceptance
  1. Defined; other important policies and principles important to understanding what constitutes a valid acceptance
  2. Notes on Cases H & I

If you are uncertain about a concept, refer to one of the resources available to you, such as a hornbook or other guide that focuses on the doctrinal area you are studying. Resist the temptation to merely copy verbatim your class notes or language from other sources. The outlining process should be more than a mere writing function; use the outlining process as an opportunity to better understand the material. Some students

---

2. What doesn't matter are those points discussed in a commercial outline, treatise, or hornbook that were not addressed in class.

3. Many professors do not expect students to discuss in detail cases they have studied in the course; however, other professors may want students to include references to specific cases when answering questions. Always check with each professor to determine what is expected on the exam.

4. Of course, an actual outline would reflect much more detail than what is provided here.

prefer handwriting their outlines, at least initially, because handwriting helps promote thinking.

d. Use your outline for study

Periodically review your outline to refresh your memory about the legal principles covered earlier in the semester. As it gets closer to the end of the semester, try to reduce your outline each time you review it. When you review the reduced outline later, your goal will be to remember the important information from the longer outline just by reviewing the shorter version. A sample partial outline is found at the end of this chapter.

e. Practice writing about the law

Take every opportunity before the exam to practice writing about the law. This is especially helpful when you speak English as a second language. You do not need to find multiple hours to practice; instead, if you have an extra five to ten minutes before or after class or sometime during your day, consider asking yourself a question about the law and then trying to write the answer to the question. For example, if you are waiting for contracts class to begin and the topic for that day is the revocation of a valid offer, try to write what you know about revocation of valid offers without referring to the text or your notes. You can later check your writing for accuracy; if you find mistakes, you can make a note and write about the topic again later.

Another way to practice writing before the exam is to open your book and find a hypothetical question in the notes between the cases in your book. Try to write the answer to a question, and check and review your answer later.

Finally, check to see whether any of your professors have placed exams on reserve in the library or online. These are excellent tools to use for practice since they reveal the types of questions your professor is likely to ask. Oftentimes a professor will include either outlines or sample answers to the questions. Try to answer the questions before referring to the model answers or outline. These questions also will usually provide the time allotted to the question, so you can test yourself to see whether you can adequately prepare to write the answer and write the answer within the allotted time.

There are also multiple Web sites available where sample questions and answers are posted.[5] Going through the exam exercises enables you to determine how much you really know about each area of the law. It also allows you to feel more comfortable about writing about the law in a more formal way. This confidence through practice should carry over to the actual exam.

---

5. A good example is Washburn Law School's site, through which you can access multiple sites. The site is at http://www.washlaw.edu/study/index.html. You may also access an educational site, Computer-Assisted Legal Instruction (CALI), found at http://www2.cali.org.

f. Consider working with others

Consider reviewing your outline with others preparing for the same exam. You will know you have a solid grasp on the subject when you are able to explain a concept to a confused colleague. Many students form study groups, which are small groups of students who meet regularly during the academic year to discuss the substance of one or more classes. If you form a study group, take whatever steps are necessary to make sure that the time you spend together is useful. One way to do this is to find exam questions that address the material you are studying, distribute them to each group member in advance, and then answer the questions individually before meeting to discuss the question as a group. You will then have a better sense of what you covered accurately and what you would have missed when answering the questions on an actual exam.

2. Taking the exam

At the outset of each examination, you will learn how much time you'll have to write your answers. What you may not know, however, is how many sections or questions there are in the examination and how much weight is given to each of the sections or questions. Examinations may be divided by sections when the questions vary in content. For example, your examination may include long essay questions, short essay questions, multiple-choice questions, true/false questions, or any combination of these types of questions.

Take a few moments to set a schedule for your exam so you can properly manage your time. The questions may indicate how many points are allotted to each, or they may include what percentage of the overall exam each question is worth. Based on the points or percentage allocated for each question or section, make a note of how much time you have for each and create an internal clock for moving from question to question, or section to section.

For example, let's say you are taking a three-hour exam, and there are three sections in the exam. Section 1 is worth 50 percent of the total exam, Section 2 is worth 30 percent of the total exam, and Section 3 is worth 20 percent of the total exam. If you begin your exam at 1:10 P.M., you can note that you should be finishing Section 1 around 2:40 P.M. (90 minutes, or 50 percent of the allocated time); Section 2 around 3:34 P.M. (54 minutes, or 30 percent of the allocated time); and Section 3 around 4:10 P.M. (36 minutes, or 20 percent of the allocated time). Some sections may be further divided, which would require you to further subdivide your time. If Section 2 has three short essay questions of equal weight, for example, you could further divide your time for each question, allocating 18 minutes per question.

a. Closed-book examinations

If an exam is closed, you may not bring any materials to the exam. If taking a closed exam, you may want to take a few moments before beginning the exam to write down any notes you believe will help you as you respond to the exam questions. Your notes may include a list of the issues that may be included in the question, definitions you have difficulty remembering, or a short outline of legal points you may need to cover.

You may also want to note any acronyms you created as a way to remember information. Acronyms are created by taking the first letter of many words and combining the single letters into a new word. For example, if you are taking a torts examination in the United States that covers intentional torts, you may remember the different intentional torts using the acronym BATTIFF:

> **B**attery,
> **A**ssault,
> **T**respass to land,
> **T**respass to chattels (including conversion),
> **I**ntentional infliction of emotional distress,
> **F**alse imprisonment, and
> **F**raud

If taking a property exam that includes a question on the concept of adverse possession,[6] you may use OCEAN to help you remember the elements to prove adverse possession. The possession must be

> **O**pen,
> **C**ontinuous,
> **E**xclusive,
> **A**ctual, and
> **N**otorious

The elements of a gift may be remembered through DAD:

> **D**onative intent,
> **A**cceptance, and
> **D**elivery

Of course, the acronyms will make sense only if you understand what the individual terms mean.

b. Open-book examinations

If the exam is open, you are usually allowed to bring your book and notes to the examination. Be careful, however, about relying too extensively on any outside materials. Law school examinations are usually difficult to complete within the time allowed. Insufficient time exists to refer extensively to your text; similarly, there may be little time to browse through your notes, especially if your notes are lengthy or disorganized. If you are allowed to take materials into the exam, consider creating a short outline with a checklist of the issues that may be covered. As an alternative, you

---

6. Adverse possession occurs when one possesses and uses land he does not own in a manner that eventually results in his becoming the rightful owner of the property. The specific rules vary from state to state.

may number the pages of your notes and create a table of contents so you can quickly access information in your notes.[7]

 ## B. Essay Examinations

1. Exam goals

When answering essay questions, you want to identify all the issues that are fairly presented by the facts and applicable law; to present arguments on behalf of both sides, where support for both sides exists; and to express yourself in clear, short, grammatical sentences.

No essay question is exactly like a case in the book. Sometimes, however, you may find a question that is similar to a hypothetical question found in the notes between the cases or one that was discussed in class. Reviewing hypothetical problems is an excellent way to test your knowledge of the law when preparing for an exam.

As you study for your exams, be prepared to analyze a fact pattern that creates a gap in the existing rules. For example, the basic law regarding the right to privacy is always changing as new technology is developed. An exam question might ask about the right to privacy regarding technology that is so new that no statutes or cases have addressed the specific technology before. This type of question would require you to look at the policy reasons for the laws addressing technology already in place and to argue why the new technology should or should not be treated in the same way under the law. These types of questions force you to argue how the rules can be applied to support each position, discussing the relevant policy for a rule's existence.

Strive also to anticipate questions that suggest ambiguities or uncertainties in the application of the rules. Again, when the rules can be interpreted in more than one way, you can create arguments on behalf of both parties, analyzing how the rule would apply to the facts of the exam question under different interpretations. This approach also allows you to emphasize relevant policies for a rule's existence.

In many areas of law, there are conflicts in the rules. For example, there may be a majority rule and a minority rule applied by different jurisdictions; in that case, you would want to discuss the application of both the majority rule and the minority rule to the facts of the essay question. There might also be an older rule that is still recognized in some jurisdictions, such as an English common law rule, and a newer U.S. rule that is likely followed in more jurisdictions. Again, when differing rules such as an English rule and a U.S. rule exist, plan to address both in answering the essay question.

---

7. Not discussed here are take-home examinations, the most open form of an examination. When completing a take-home examination, the examiner usually expects a more finished, professional answer, which is always typed.

2. Strategies for taking the exam

a. Analyze and organize before writing

Use at least one-quarter to one-third of your time analyzing and organizing your exam answer before writing or typing the answer. Sometimes nerves get in the way and you begin writing before you are ready. This urge to begin often occurs when other students around you begin to write in their exam books or type on their computers. Ignore those around you, and stay with the plan you made before you walked into the exam room. As discussed above, the best way to feel comfortable about how you spend your time during the exam is to practice taking timed exam questions. Practicing will allow you to experiment to see how much time you can spend planning and still complete writing your answer.

b. Read the question

Many authorities suggest that you read the examination question completely from start to finish before taking notes while preparing to write your answer. The only problem with this approach is that as you read the question you may begin to think about every possible legal issue raised by the facts. You might reach the end of the essay, however, only to find that the question is not open-ended but one that is more limited. You will then need to refocus your attention on the facts in light of the limited question. Instead, consider reading the first few sentences to get an idea of the story and then skip to the bottom of the essay to read the question. Once you know the specific question, return to the beginning of the essay and read it in its entirety. When reading the question, pay attention to every word and phrase; professors usually take special care in writing essay questions, so you want to take special care in reading the question.

c. Take notes

Use a separate exam booklet or sheet of paper to write your notes and outline prior to writing your exam answer. If writing your exam answer by hand, for example, and you use the same exam booklet for both tasks, you will end up flipping the pages back and forth between the notes and your actual writing. This is not an ideal use of your time.

If you run out of time, some professors will allow you to insert your exam notes that address the points you did not get to in your answer booklet or to clarify what you did write. By keeping separate notes you will be able to more easily insert the relevant notes where appropriate.

More and more students use computers to write examinations. If you are typing your answer, learn in advance about the exam software system used by your law school.[8] If you are using your own laptop, you will likely be required to install the

---

8. Examples of software programs used for examinations are Securexam (http://www.softwaresecure. com), Exam4 (http://64.84.16.214/extegrity/MainFrame.asp), and Examsoft (http://www.examsoft.com).

exam software program prior to the examination. If you are using a computer in one of the school's computer labs, the software program will already be installed on the computers. Since the guidelines for typing and printing an exam vary from one law school to the next, check with your individual school early to ensure you are ready to type your exam.

While reading the essay, note possible legal issues raised by the story; if the legal issues include tests that must be followed to analyze the issue, consider breaking up your notes by the parts of the test. For example, as soon as you realize that the legal issue requires that specific elements be satisfied, divide your preliminary notes element by element. You may find that a single essay question raises multiple legal issues, each with its own test. If so, create outlines of each legal issue. This may take some time, but once your notes are completed, you will be more ready to write and are more likely to stay focused on just answering the question asked and not getting off point. Further, you will write more concisely, which is always appreciated by your professor.

Try to limit your notations to a single word or phrase only, just enough to remind you of the information you need to include when writing or typing your answer. You may prefer to also make notes in the margins of your essay, by drawing an arrow from a specific fact to the margin and noting that fact's potential relevance. This technique can be helpful, but you will usually need to take one more step and create some type of organizational scheme in your notes before you begin writing.

Once you have completed your notes, take a moment to be sure you have identified all the relevant legal issues and used every fact possible in the analysis. One way to check your use of the facts is to underline or draw a box around a fact on the essay exam each time you note its use in the answer. Using this technique allows you to quickly check any facts not marked and to consider whether you missed a way to use that fact in your answer. Be careful, however, not to assume that a single fact can be used only once in an exam answer. You may find you can use a single fact in more than one place.

As a last step before writing, ask yourself whether you have considered all the issues, addressed all the legally significant facts, considered all ways to support each side when the question raises a disputable issue, and considered the importance of policy in answering the question. Ask yourself:

- Is this answer complete in fact, law, and policy?
- Is this answer accurate in fact, law, and policy?

● Exercise 22-A

Consider the following facts in an essay question:

David was walking down the sidewalk one evening when he thought he saw an acquaintance of his, Quinn, fighting with Pete. Both Quinn and Pete were shouting, and David thought he saw Pete rushing at Quinn with a knife. (In fact, Pete held only a rolled-up newspaper.) David, concerned for Quinn's life, picked up a board, ran up to Pete, and shouted, "Stop!" When Quinn saw David holding the board, he ran away. Pete dropped his newspaper and started to say something to David when David swung the board at him, narrowly missing his head. Peter then put his fists up and yelled,

"What are you doing?" David, fearful that Pete would strike him, again swung the board and hit Pete, causing Pete to suffer a head injury. When Pete fell to the ground, he broke two of the fingers on his right hand.

David then began kicking Pete, who was lying defenseless on the ground, and screamed at him, "I should kill you! Your kind is ruining the city! If I ever see you again I'm going to kill you!" David then walked off. Fortunately, Quinn came back, found Pete, and called an ambulance.

Two months after these events, Pete comes into your law office and tells you he wants to sue David for his injuries. Pete's physical injuries have now healed (although he still has medical bills to pay), but he remains fearful that David may harm him if he encounters him again.

Consider for purposes of this exercise only that you have the following relevant legal principles to help you write the exam answer. This is a closed exercise, so other principles and policies may also be relevant in answering this exam question.

1. Assault occurs when one actor intentionally places the victim in reasonable apprehension of imminent harmful or offensive contact.
2. Intent requires that the actor has a purpose or knows to a substantial certainty that a result will occur.
3. The apprehension of harmful or offensive contact must be reasonable. Apprehension is not the same as fear or intimidation.
4. Some overt or open act is necessary to find assault. Words alone do not make an actor liable for assault unless together with other acts they put the victim in reasonable apprehension of imminent harmful or offensive contact.
5. Battery requires (1) an act by the defendant that brings about harmful or offensive contact to the plaintiff's person; (2) intent on the part of the defendant to bring about harmful or offensive contact to the plaintiff's person; and (3) causation.
6. Self-defense is a valid affirmative defense to assault and battery claims. In an affirmative defense the defendant claims that, even though he committed the tort, because of the defense he is not legally liable. When a person has reasonable grounds to believe he is being or is about to be attacked, he may use such force as is reasonably necessary for protection against potential injury. Reasonable grounds to use force may be based on a reasonable mistake regarding the threat of injury.
7. Defense of the third person is when one goes to the aid of another person and uses only as much force as the other person could have used to protect himself.
8. In defending oneself or another, the force used in self-defense must be roughly equivalent to the force of danger being used. If a person escalates the violence beyond the initial scope, that person may lose the affirmative defense.

Instructions.

1. Identify the legal issues raised in this essay question (all causes of action and any affirmative defenses arising from the case).
2. Note the facts that would be relevant in analyzing each legal issue raised in this question.

3. Structuring your exam answer

a. Large-scale structure

If the analysis of the legal issue is based on a legal test, such as a series of requirements or elements that must be met to answer the question, that test creates the basic structure for your answer of that legal issue. You may choose to address those requirements that are not in dispute and then those that are in dispute, or you may move through your answer element by element, in the order provided in the test. For example, let's say that an exam question requires you to determine whether an enforceable contract exists, requiring a valid offer, a valid acceptance, and consideration.[9] You may have concluded that the consideration requirement is easily met and is therefore not in dispute. You may either address consideration at the beginning of the analysis, indicating why it exists, and then discuss the disputable offer and acceptance requirements, or you may analyze (1) offer, (2) acceptance, and (3) consideration, since that is the order of the requirements set out in the main rule.

If the answer requires you to address multiple legal issues, analyze completely one legal issue before moving to the next legal issue. For example, Exercise 22-A requires you to analyze multiple causes of actions involving different intentional torts. You should have organized your outline so each intentional tort is discussed fully before moving on to the next intentional tort.

Consider possible patterns of organizing your answer and select the most appropriate pattern. You may choose to analyze each person's rights and liabilities in order, for example, or the legal significance of each event, one cause of action at a time.

You may also help your exam reader move through your answer by providing headings when you move from one topic to another. These headings may be a word or phrase that simply highlights the new topic. For example, in Exercise 22-A, you may have included headings such as "Assault," "Battery," or "Self-Defense."

● Exercise 22-B

Refer back to the question in Exercise 22-A. Outline the essay question as you would an essay question on an exam.

b. Small-scale structure

The overriding theme regarding structure, whether it's in an objective analysis, a letter, or an answer on an exam question, is to bring in information when it becomes most relevant to your reader. The basic structure introduced in Chapter 7 of this book is the structural checklist of TRAC, which is a good guideline for essay questions. TRAC in an examination context would look like the following.

---

9. Consideration in contract law focuses on the value exchanged by the parties.

Topic/Thesis:

Tell your reader what legal issue you are addressing (you can do this in a sentence or with a heading).

Rule:

Explain the relevant rule and any definitions that are applicable to the legal issue. Some exam questions will include relevant rules, such as a statute to be used in analyzing the exam question. When this occurs, *do not* rewrite the entire statute in the exam answer. Instead, simply refer to the statute generally and then provide the explicit words and phrases from the statute where relevant in the analysis.[10]

Analyze/apply the law to the facts in the hypothetical case:

Apply the relevant rules to the facts in the question and support both sides' position, where possible. Include also any relevant policy considerations or arguments that help explain the law or support each side's position.

Conclude:

You may end with your conclusion on the legal issue. Some professors, however, will instruct you to not include a conclusion since you should have answered the question by this point in your answer, thus making a formal conclusion redundant (and there's no time for redundancy on an examination).

4. Writing the answer

If you have prepared to write your answer by using the above techniques, you can focus solely on writing a clear answer that is easy to read. Strive to make clear the connections between your ideas; don't force the exam reader to piece together your answer. Instead, be explicit and obvious. Regardless of whether English is your first or second language, the best way to be clear is to write simple sentences in simple subject, verb, and object order. The answer to an essay question is really a first draft. There is usually no time to revise your answer; it must make sense after drafting the answer once.

a. Clearly answer the question asked

Make sure you answer the specific question asked. Do not try to impress your exam reader by including information that is not relevant to the question.

---

10. Some professors may instruct you to not provide a separate section that sets out the relevant rules. If so, make sure in the analysis that the rules and their definitions are obvious in your answer.

For example, if a question directs you to analyze the likely damages Party B may recover, do not include information about whether an enforceable contract exists. Adding information beyond what the question asks will not add points but will likely take up precious time better spent on issues that are relevant to the question.

b. Write to the unfamiliar reader

Do not assume that the examiner knows the facts set out in the essay question or the law relevant to analyzing the essay when answering the question. Your examiner will likely not fill in the gaps for you. Instead, you will receive no points for missing information and may lose additional points due to a lack of coherence. Where appropriate, explain the law in your answer; when analyzing the application of the law to the facts of the essay, provide the specific facts from the essay that support your answer. For example, in Exercise 22-A, when addressing whether Pete committed an assault, the facts state that Pete put up his fists and yelled at David, "What are you doing?" If in your exam answer you refer only to Pete's yelling at David, you have omitted Pete's use of his fists (an overt act) and his exact words ("What are you doing," which is not threatening language). All these specific facts are key to the analysis.

Finally, if time permits, review your answer and correct any grammatical or stylistic errors.

c. When in doubt about whether to include a legal issue, include and discuss briefly

There are times when you might read an essay and decide the facts suggest that a specific legal issue may be relevant. Upon further thought, however, you might decide that one of the requirements to establish the test is missing. Instead of omitting any discussion of that legal issue, consider addressing the point quickly, explaining why the test is not met.

For example, if taking a torts examination, you may read an essay where the facts involve a dispute between two friends, Jim and Ken. Jim goes to Ken's house and bangs on the door, screaming threats to harm Ken. This raises a question about whether Jim has assaulted Ken. Assault requires that the actor intentionally place the victim in fear or apprehension of physical harm. As you are reading the essay, however, you read that, unknown to Jim, Ken has left out of the back door of his home to go for a run. This fact eliminates the possibility of assault, since Ken could not be placed in apprehension of physical harm when he was not there to hear Jim's threats. In this example, you would want to at least indicate that Jim's actions support his intent to commit an assault, but there could be no actual apprehension, and therefore no assault, since Ken left and didn't hear what Jim said.

d. Omit an isolated statement of facts and thesis paragraph

Omit rewriting in your exam answer an isolated statement of the facts introduced in the essay question. You simply do not have time to restate the story by itself. While you won't lose points by rewriting the facts, you won't receive any points for an isolated statement of facts. Again, what you will lose is precious time better spent on writing substance that is important to the exam answer. Also, students who rewrite the facts at the beginning of the exam answer tend to then refer only generally to the facts in the analysis. Instead, bring in the specific facts when they are relevant to a point you are making in the analysis.

Also omit a detailed thesis paragraph, where you provide your conclusions on the legal issues at the beginning of your exam answer. Again, while you may write thesis paragraphs in other legal documents, they do not belong in an exam answer. As with isolated statements of facts, you won't lose points for thesis paragraphs, but you will likely receive no points for these statements, so the time is better spent on writing something that will count. If you want to provide an introductory paragraph, consider telling the examiner how you will proceed through the answer (for example, the overall structure followed in the exam answer).

e. Omit references to specific citations

Professors may or may not prefer that you refer to specific statutes and cases; the best approach is to always check with your professors about what they want you to include in your essay exam answers. You may be told that while references to specific cases are not wrong, they are not necessary unless the case is a landmark case and pivotal to answering the question. These landmark cases are cases where the court establishes specific legal principles, such as *Palsgraf v. Long Island R.R. Co.*[11] in the area of torts. Your professor will likely be more interested in the principles and policies that originate from the case rather than the case itself. If you want to refer to a case but can't remember its name, simply describe the case. For example, you may describe *Palsgraf* as the case where a mother sued a railroad for negligence when one of its employees dropped a box of fireworks, causing a series of events that ultimately ended with the plantiff mother's injury. Of course, some professors may instruct you specifically to discuss the cases studied in the course. Again, always follow your professor's instructions. Even when a professor wants you to include case references, however, you will likely not be required to provide official citations.

5. Summarizing the steps

As the above discussion reveals, to answer an essay question, you need to (1) identify the relevant issue(s); (2) remember the applicable law and the requisite rules, whether they be composed of elements, factors, etc., that must be applied in analyzing the legal issue(s); (3) determine which facts in the question are relevant to the legal issue(s) and where they can best be used in supporting each side's position;

---

11. *Palsgraf v. Long Island R.R. Co.*, 162 N.E. 99 (N.Y. 1928). This case is the landmark case in the United States that established using foreseeability as the guide for determining proximate cause.

(4) organize your answer; and (5) write your answer in simple, clear sentences. Preparing to write your answer involves steps (1) through (3); outlining the answer prior to writing your answer occurs in step (4); and actually writing the exam answer is covered only in the last step.

6. Last suggestions

Don't provide a conclusion to a question without thoroughly explaining how you reached that conclusion. Omission of the analysis will always result in a point reduction. Remember that if you don't write it down on the paper, you can't get credit for it. You likely went through a series of logical steps as you analyzed each question. Be sure to write those logical steps in your exam answer.

Strive to include all the legal issues raised by the essay question. You may find that you know more about one legal issue than you know about the others. You may be inclined to write as much as you can about the most familiar issue, allowing little or no time to address the other legal issues raised in the question. You will likely receive no additional points, however, for writing a great answer on one legal issue when you have omitted or not adequately addressed the other legal issues pertinent to the question. If your professor has allocated a certain number of points for each legal issue, you may get all those points for the issue you spent the most time on, but you will lose all the points for those issues you do not address. Statistically, making the decision to focus only on one issue is not a good idea.

Follow a logical structure when answering each question. You are likely to lose points if your answer lacks structure. You do not want to make your examiner work at finding the information because it is not located in the most logical place possible in your answer. If the legal principle you are addressing has a specific test to use in its analysis, allow that test to create the basic structure of your answer.

Answer the question asked. If you are not sure of the answer, do the best job you can. Discussing a different legal point will not enhance your points and, again, may result in a point reduction.

Finally, when asked a question that requires you to apply the law to the specific facts of the essay, integrate references to both the law and the specific facts in your answer. A common problem in exam answers occurs when the student either discusses the law only, without any reference to the specific facts, or discusses the facts only, without any reference to the law.

For example, consider the following sample answers, analyzing whether Pete committed an assault when he put up his fists and yelled at David, "What are you doing?"

Example of an answer comprising all facts:

Pete committed an assault. David thought he saw Pete fighting with his friend, Quinn, and tried to come to his rescue. After he swung a board at Pete (but did not hit him), Pete put his fists up and yelled, "What are you doing?" David thought Pete was going to hit him.

Example of an answer comprising all law:

Pete committed an assault against David. Assault occurs when one actor intentionally places the victim in reasonable apprehension of imminent harmful or offensive contact, which would be a battery if completed. The apprehension of harmful or offensive contact must be reasonable, and some overt act is necessary to find assault. Words alone do not make an actor liable for assault unless together with other acts they put the victim in reasonable apprehension of imminent harmful or offensive contact with his person. Pete intentionally put David in apprehension of imminent contact through both his words and his actions. Pete had to know he was scaring David.

Example of an answer interweaving law and facts:

Pete likely committed an assault against David. Assault occurs when one actor intentionally (with substantial certainty) places the victim in reasonable apprehension of imminent harmful or offensive contact. The apprehension of harmful or offensive contact must be reasonable, and some overt act is necessary to find assault. Words alone do not make an actor liable for assault, unless together with other acts the words put the victim in reasonable apprehension of imminent harmful or offensive contact with his person. Pete's actions included his overt act of raising his fists to David, and Pete should have known with substantial certainty that he would place David in apprehension of imminent contact, especially since they were arguing face to face.

Pete may argue, however, that his words did not support an assault, since he merely asked, "What are you doing," which doesn't support a threat of anything, certainly not of imminent contact.

The outcome may depend on the tone when Pete was yelling at David; however, the volatile nature of the events taking place supports assault.

● Exercise 22-C

Refer to the question provided in Exercise 22-A. Write an answer to the essay question using the relevant legal principles provided. Address all the potential causes of action as well as any affirmative defenses that may arise from this case, based on the relevant law provided above.

● Exercise 22-D[12]

Read and answer the following essay question.

---

12. Students were given 60 minutes to complete this exam question, which was written by James P. Nehf, Professor of Law and Cleon H. Foust Fellow, Indiana University School of Law-Indianapolis.

Benny Cardozo is an elderly gentleman who lived alone in a little house outside a small town in a rural part of the state. Benny worked his entire life at the steel mill in the nearest city (some 20 miles from his home) and after retiring was now living on his pension and modest social security benefits. In December of this year, a bitter cold wave hit Benny's part of the world and, as luck would have it, Benny's old furnace broke down on the coldest day of the year. The temperature in the old frame house quickly fell, and Benny tried to keep warm by keeping a fire going in his fireplace. He also tried in vain to get a furnace repair person to take a look at the furnace. There were only two businesses that offered furnace repair services in the entire tri-county area, and they were unavailable due to the large number of service calls resulting from the bad weather. Benny, who had always been something of a loner and who had no family or true friends in the area, became desperate as he saw his wood supply getting smaller and the temperatures dropping even further.

On the day following the furnace breakdown, Benny finally persuaded one of the local furnace dealers, Cheathem Heating and Air Conditioning, to take a look at his furnace. The business was run by Harry Cheathem, who was new to the area, having just moved from Las Vegas. Harry inspected the furnace and informed Benny that it could not be repaired. Benny asked how much a replacement would cost and when it could be installed. Harry, looking out the window at the blowing snow and the few logs remaining in the wood rack on Benny's porch, responded that the price would be $3,500 and it could be installed later that day. Moreover, the furnace came with a ten-year warranty, meaning that Harry would fix the furnace for no charge if it broke down within ten years after installation. Benny said, "Well, it looks like I really don't have a choice, do I? I either freeze or buy the furnace. Go ahead and install it, but I don't have $3,500. Will you take $1,800 now and the rest in monthly installments?" Harry said, "Sure. It's almost Christmas, and I'm in the holiday spirit. It's a deal." After Benny signed the contract, Harry shook Benny's frigid hand and smiled warmly.

Harry installed the furnace that afternoon and evening, working until 11:00 P.M. Benny withdrew the last $1,800 from his savings account, gave Harry the money, and signed a promissory note for the remaining $1,700, plus interest. The furnace worked well, but only for a week; it then started blowing cold air. Benny tried to reach Harry, but Harry did not return his phone calls. After two days trying to reach Harry, Benny gave up and moved out of his freezing house and into an apartment in the nearest city. Although Benny did not know it at the time, the malfunction in his original furnace was actually rather minor, and it could have been repaired by any qualified person for $50.

The weather became even colder the day after Benny moved out. Due to the lack of heat in Benny's house, some water pipes froze and burst in the basement, resulting in $800 in water damage to Benny's carpet and furniture. Moreover, some of the water leaked into the fuse box and caused a small fire, which destroyed Benny's stamp collection, worth about $2,000.

Benny then discovered that the furnace he purchased had a suggested retail price (installed) of only $1,800. Benny immediately stopped paying installments on the $1,700 he owed Harry. Harry sued Benny for the money. Benny countersued, seeking the following: (1) return of the $1,800 he paid Harry on the day of installation; (2) an injunction forcing Harry to repair the furnace pursuant to the warranty; (3)

reimbursement for the cost of his apartment lease for the period in which he could not live in the house; (4) $800 for the water damage; and (5) $2,000 for the stamp collection.

Who should win the lawsuit and why? What should be the remedies?

Consider for purposes of this exercise only that you have the following relevant legal principles to help you write the exam answer. Again, this is a closed exercise, so other principles and policies may also be relevant in answering this exam question.

1. To avoid a contract provision on grounds of unconscionability, two elements must be proved: (1) a meaningful choice is absent, and (2) the provision is substantially unfair to one party.

2. Economic duress may void a contract. Under one approach, a court will not enforce a contract if the party was constrained to do what he otherwise would not have done. Some courts using this approach require that the "evil" party somehow contribute to the predicament. Under a second approach, courts don't look at the "voluntariness" but at whether the "evil" party's conduct is a type that society should discourage.

3. The remedy for unconscionability and duress is usually to void the contract, with no affirmative damages recovered. Damages will be recovered if a party successfully proves a breach of warranty.

4. **Remedies:**
   a. <u>Restitution</u>: the defendant must return any benefit received under the contract.
   b. <u>Injunctive relief</u>: the court may order specific performance of the contract, usually *not* awarded if damages would adequately compensate the injured party or if supervision of the performance would be difficult.
   c. <u>Consequential damages</u>: damages that are reasonably within the contemplation of the parties when the contract was made. Note, however, that parties cannot recover for damages that could have been prevented by reasonable action (mitigation of damages).

C. Multiple-Choice Questions[13]

Some students prefer essay questions; others declare that they always do better on multiple-choice questions. Students usually don't know why they prefer one type of question over the other. The difference between the types of questions actually reflects an important difference in function. Multiple-choice questions are designed differently to test different aspects of your legal abilities. Cognition is certainly one of those

---

13. Thanks to Lawrence P. Wilkins, William R. Neale Professor of Law, Indiana University School of Law-Indianapolis, who wrote much of the commentary on multiple-choice questions as part of a class handout on taking examinations.

abilities. For example, many multiple-choice questions are created with the assumption that you know the basic material and that you will be able to detect fine distinctions in alternative statements of elements, rules, principles, concepts, policies, and arguments. If the question looks like that type of question, consider the responses carefully, looking for differences while thinking about the significance in those differences.

Some questions may simply test your memory of rules or legal principles. More often, however, multiple-choice questions test your ability to take your knowledge about an area of law and apply that knowledge in determining which choice of answers is correct. Multiple-choice questions may also provide more than one correct answer, requiring you to determine which answer is most correct. Frequently this type of question asks something like, "Choose the most accurate and complete statement of the choices below." Although more than one answer may be correct, one answer is most correct.[14]

This type of multiple-choice question is similar to most U.S. state bar examinations, required in almost every state in order to become licensed to practice in that state. The 100 questions on the multi-state exam usually contain more than one correct answer, which is one of the reasons why the examination is so challenging. Many professors include these types of questions on their exams. They are more difficult to answer than those questions that just ask you to remember information or those questions that have only one correct answer; therefore, they require special care in reading and analysis.

One approach to answering multiple-choice questions is to read the question carefully without reading the choice of answers. Try to answer the question on your own, without looking at the choices. This enables you to think about the question without getting confused by the choices. Once you think through the question, read the choices carefully, looking for what you believe to be the correct answer. If you are not sure which answer is correct, you should be able to at least eliminate one or two answers that are obviously incorrect or weaker than the others in some aspect. Once you have narrowed your choices, make sure each answer remaining is technically a correct answer (even if you don't know yet whether it's the right answer to the question). In other words, ask yourself whether the answer accurately reflects the legal principles and policies you know to be true. This step sometimes eliminates additional choices. If more than one choice remains, consider which choice answers the question more specifically. If one provides a general answer and another provides an answer that more specifically relates to the question asked, the second, more specific answer is likely to be correct.

Be careful, however. In some instances what you concluded is the correct answer before looking at the actual choices is not one of your choices. When none of the responses offered by the question match your preconceived answer, you may become

---

14. In some instances, there may be no correct answers to the multiple-choice question, requiring you to choose which of the bad answers is not as bad as the others. You must be mindful of the distinctions between the proposed responses and evaluate each carefully.

frustrated, and other factors may begin to affect your choice. You don't want to give up on the question and select a response according to some arbitrary criterion (such as "none of the responses I've selected so far have been (c); the law of averages favors (c); so this must be (c)," or some other similarly illogical method). The best protection against this kind of frustration is to keep an open mind.

● Exercise 22-E

Answer the following multiple-choice questions:

1. When David swung the board and hit Pete, he committed a battery. However, David claims an affirmative defense. Which of the following answers is most accurate?

   a. David has a valid affirmative defense, because he can claim that he defended a third person, Pete, who had been fighting with his friend, Quinn.
   b. David has a valid affirmative defense, because his actions in hitting Pete were roughly equivalent to Pete's making a fist and yelling at him.
   c. David does not have a valid affirmative defense because Quinn ran away and wasn't there when David hit Pete with the board.
   d. David would have a valid affirmative defense under the circumstances even if Pete had only yelled at David.

2. If Benny is successful in suing Harry, who replaced the furnace, he is likely to recover:

   a. nothing, since a new furnace would cost $1,800, and Benny paid $1,800 to Harry.
   b. $800 for the water damage to the carpet and furniture, and $2,000 for the stamp collection.
   c. $1,750, the difference between what Benny paid for the new furnace ($1,800) and what it would have cost to repair his old furnace ($50).
   d. $800 for water damage to the carpet and furniture only, because the damage to his stamp collection was unforeseeable.

D. *The Final Suggestion*

Law school examinations often test not only your analytical skills but also your endurance. If you are taking a four-hour exam, for example, strive to get plenty of sleep the night before the exam. Staying up all night to prepare for an exam is rarely productive. You may end up being overly tired and cannot therefore think as clearly as needed. Your analytical processes simply do not work as well as they should. Schedule your time wisely.

Sample Outline of Battery[15]

Intentional torts:

Battery:

1. Contact (with the person of another) which is
2. Harmful or offensive
3. With intent (applies to all intentional torts)

Harmful or offensive:

1. The purpose of battery is to protect physical or personal integrity.
2. Contact does not require actual physical contact, so long as there is contact with clothing or an object closely identified with the body.
3. Tort law provides compensation for the victim; however, if a defendant's actions were willful, wanton, or malicious, the victim may also recover punitive damages, for punishment and to deter the behavior in the future.

Fisher v. Carrousel Motor Hotel, Inc. (defendant snatched a plate from plaintiff, an African American participant at a luncheon and yelled offensive remarks to plaintiff, sufficient to support battery and actual and punitive damages).

Intent:

1. **Test:** Plaintiff can prove intent by showing either a (1) purpose to cause contact, or (2) knowing with substantial certainty that an action will cause a contact. *Garrett v. Dailey* (boy pulled out woman's chair while she was trying to sit down).
2. **Mental impairment or age** does not automatically protect an actor from liability. But mental impairment or youthfulness might make it more difficult for a plaintiff to prove the actor knew with substantial certainty that an action would cause a contact. When mental impairment is involved, the result may be a strong negligence case based on reckless behavior.
3. **Intent focuses on the mental state of the defendant.** Also, intent need not be directed toward causing harm but only the interference (or invasion) at issue in the case. Note, however, that the idea that there is no need to prove "intent to harm" is not agreed upon by everyone.

---

15. This sample is shorter than what is contained in a complete outline but should provide a workable structure for outlining.

Competing policy for battery actions:

1. **To provide compensation to the innocent victim.** If intent to harm is not required, more victims will recover.
2. **To deter risky behavior in the future.** If intent to harm is required, fewer victims will be compensated.

If the second policy had been applied to *Garrett*, the court may have found the defendant child's behavior in pulling out the chair from the plaintiff woman arguably not "risky," so there would be nothing to deter.

APPENDIX

A

Shrader v. Equitable Life Assurance Society

Supreme Court of Ohio.
Shrader, Appellee,
v.
Equitable Life Assurance Society
of the United States;
Wolford et al., Trustees, Appellants.
No. 85-184.

485 N.E.2d 1031
Nov. 27, 1985

[Jean M. Shrader was strangled to death in a parking garage in downtown Columbus, Ohio. No criminal charges were filed. Jean's husband, John J. Shrader, and Dale Wolford, Jean's father, both claimed a right to the decedent's life insurance proceeds. Equitable Insurance deposited the proceeds with the court to pay out once the rightful owner was determined. Shrader filed a Motion to Dismiss, asserting that he could not be denied the insurance money unless he had pled guilty to or been convicted of aggravated murder, murder, or voluntary manslaughter. Shrader's motion to dismiss was denied.

The only disputed factual issue appeared to be whether Shrader intentionally and feloniously killed his wife. * * * "The common pleas court rendered judgment against Shrader on his claim and ordered that the money Equitable had deposited with the court be paid to the Jean W. Wolford Charitable Trust," as directed by Dale Wolford.

A sharply divided panel of the court of appeals reversed. The majority recognized the well-settled rule in Ohio that the beneficiary of a life insurance policy cannot recover when the death of the insured is caused by the intentional and felonious act of the beneficiary. The court also held, however, that a civil case cannot be used to determine whether the beneficiary actually killed the insured. The majority concluded that "[p]ublic policy supports the determination that the identity of the killer be established in a criminal proceeding, if available, rather than in a civil proceeding."]

* * *

Douglas, Judge.

I

The first issue in this case is whether Ohio Revised Code 2105.19, dealing with persons prohibited from benefiting from the death of another, is applicable in this case. That provision states: "(A) No person who is *convicted* of or *pleads guilty* to a violation of or complicity in the violation of section 2903.01 [aggravated murder], 2903.02 [murder], or 2903.03 [voluntary manslaughter] of the Revised Code * * * shall in any way benefit by the death. All property of the decedent, and all money, insurance proceeds, or other property or benefits payable or distributable in respect of the decedent's death, shall pass or be paid or distributed as if *the guilty person* had predeceased the decedent * * *." (Emphasis added.)

It is undisputed that John Shrader has never been convicted of, or pled guilty to, any of the homicides enumerated in the above provision. Indeed, he has never been charged with any criminal homicide offense. Since Shrader is presumed innocent of any criminal violation until his guilt is established by proof beyond any reasonable doubt, *see Taylor v. Kentucky*, 436 U.S. 478, 483 (1978), he cannot be said to be a "guilty person." Since R.C. 2105.19 only operates to prevent certain *criminals* from reaping the fruits of their crimes, and since John Shrader does not fall into that category of persons, the statute is not applicable in this case.

Shrader argues that section 2105.19 provides the exclusive method for disqualifying a beneficiary from receiving life insurance proceeds. A familiar principle of statutory construction, however, is that a statute should not be construed to impair pre-existing law in the absence of an explicit legislative statement to the contrary. *Isbrandtsen Co. v. Johnson*, 343 U.S. 779, 783 (1952); *Frantz v. Maher*, 155 N.E.2d 471 (Ohio App. 1957). All that section 2105.19(A) does is eliminate the necessity to prove that the beneficiary of a policy of life insurance committed such an act, when the beneficiary has been convicted of or has pled guilty to one of the specifically enumerated homicide offenses. There is no indication that the General Assembly or any case law intended or requires that the statute be construed to be the *exclusive* method to determine whether a person should be barred from recovering as a beneficiary under a policy of insurance on the life of a decedent alleged to have been killed by the beneficiary. Thus we find Shrader's argument regarding the statute unpersuasive.

II

The second issue in this case is whether the common law will bar a beneficiary of a life insurance policy from receiving the proceeds of that policy when the beneficiary intentionally and feloniously caused the death of the insured.

The well-established policy of the common law is that no one should be allowed to profit from his own wrongful conduct. The court in *Schmidt v. Northern Life Assn.*, 112 Iowa 41, 44 (1900), said that "[i]t would be a reproach to our system of jurisprudence if one could recover insurance money payable on the death of the insured, whose life he had feloniously taken.

* * *

Ten years after the Iowa Supreme Court decided *Schmidt*, this court announced its decision in *Filmore v. Metropolitan Life Ins. Co.*, 82 Ohio St. 208 (1910), holding that a beneficiary of a life insurance policy cannot recover thereon where the death of the insured is caused by the intentional and felonious act of the beneficiary.

III

The third issue in this case is whether the identity of one who intentionally and feloniously causes the death of another can be established in a civil proceeding, thereby preventing the wrongdoer from receiving the proceeds of the deceased's life insurance policy.

In *Huff v. Union Fidelity Life Ins. Co.*, 470 N.E.2d 236 (Ohio App. 1984), the litigants were decedent's widow and decedent's son (who was not the son of the widow). The widow alleged that the son was barred from recovering his father's life insurance benefits because he intentionally and feloniously caused his father's death. The son was never convicted of a homicide, nor did he plead guilty to any homicide offense. In a deposition in the *civil suit*, the son admitted he stabbed his father and thereby caused his

civil
criminal degree of proof ≠ → beyond a reasonable doubt.

1033

death. However, the court described his conduct as that which could be justifiable. Even though the identity of the wrongdoer was known, the appellate court nevertheless found in essence that the identity of the father's killer could be established in a civil suit, and held that the question of whether the killing was intentional and felonious was one for the civil trier of fact. *Id.* at 238.

It is possible that the defendant on a murder charge may be found not guilty and acquitted, *but if the same person claims as an heir or devisee of the decedent, he may be found in the probate court to have feloniously and intentionally killed the decedent and thus be barred under this section from sharing in the estate.* An analogy exists in the tax field, where a taxpayer may be acquitted of tax fraud in a criminal prosecution but found to have committed the fraud in a civil proceeding.

The concept that no one should be allowed to profit from his own wrongful conduct is a *civil* concept. Civil courts are, therefore, a proper forum to determine the identity of one who has been alleged to have caused, intentionally and feloniously, the death of another, and if that person is the beneficiary of the proceeds of insurance held on the life of a decedent, then to deprive such person of the proceeds and thereby prevent gain through the person's bad acts.

IV

The appellate court in this case took the position that:

"Public policy supports the proposition that the identity of a murderer be proved beyond a reasonable doubt in available criminal proceedings rather than by a lesser degree of proof in a civil proceeding. John J. Shrader should be charged with murder in a criminal court if there is sufficient evidence to civilly prove that he committed murder, at least if his alleged guilt is to disqualify him from recovering the insurance proceeds to

which he was otherwise entitled as the primary beneficiary."

It is respectfully submitted that the problem with the appellate court's decision is that it fails to recognize that the instant case is *not* a murder trial, and that John Shrader faces absolutely no loss of his life or liberty as a result of this lawsuit. This is a civil case where the issue has been raised whether John Shrader is *liable* (not whether he is *guilty*, but whether he is _civilly liable_) for the intentional and felonious killing (not murder) of his wife. Shrader brought this action to recover the proceeds of insurance on the life of his wife, and a counterclaim was filed. Upon the evidence before the court, the trier of fact determined that John Shrader failed to defend against the counterclaim of appellants which alleged that Shrader "intentionally and feloniously" caused the death of his wife. This case then is like any other civil case. The trial court applied the law to the facts, granted judgment for the Wolfords, on their counterclaim, and determined that Shrader was not entitled to the insurance proceeds both because he had failed to prove his claim and because he had _unlawfully terminated_ the life of his wife. While Jean Shrader is not a party to this lawsuit, her specific fundamental interests and those of the public in general are involved. It would be manifestly against those interests to allow one who has intentionally and feloniously killed Jean Shrader, or anyone else, to profit thereby.

For all of the foregoing reasons, we therefore hold that the identity of a person who intentionally and feloniously caused the death of another can be established in a civil proceeding in order to prevent the wrongdoer from receiving the proceeds of the deceased's life insurance policy. To hold otherwise would be to deprive aggrieved parties of a remedy, and the law will always give a remedy.

The judgment of the court of appeals is hereby reversed and the final judgment of the court of common pleas is hereby reinstated. *Judgment reversed.*

APPENDIX

B

Brief of Shrader v. Equitable Life Assurance Society

Shrader v. Equitable Life Assurance Society, 485 N.E.2d 1031 (Ohio 1985).

F: Wife was strangled to death in a parking garage, and husband was the suspect. No criminal charges were filed. The husband and his wife's father both claimed a right to the wife's life insurance proceeds. The husband argued that he couldn't be precluded from taking the insurance proceeds because he had not been charged with or convicted of a crime.

PH: Court of common pleas: Husband is precluded from taking.

   Ct. App.: Rev'd. Civil case cannot be used to determine whether husband killed wife.

SI: (1) Does the statute that determines whether someone will be prohibited from benefiting from the death of another, based on that person's being convicted or pleading guilty to a crime, apply to this case?

   (2) If not applied, will the common law bar a beneficiary of a life insurance policy from receiving the proceeds when the potential beneficiary intentionally and feloniously caused the death of the insured?

   (3) Can the identity of one who intentionally and feloniously caused the death of another be established in a civil proceeding?

PI: (1) Did the court of appeals properly determine that a civil court cannot determine whether one intentionally and feloniously caused the death of another?

H:

   SI: (1) No.
       (2) Yes.
       (3) Yes.

   PI: (1) No.

J: Rev'd.

Relevant Rules:

SI (1):

1. R.C. 2105.19: "No person who is *convicted* of or *pleads guilty* to a violation of or complicity in the violation of section 2903.01 [aggravated murder], 2903.02 [murder], or 2903.03 [voluntary manslaughter] of the Revised Code * * * shall in any way benefit by the death. All property of the decedent, and all money, insurance proceeds, or other property or benefits payable or distributable in respect of the decedent's death, shall pass or be paid or distributed as if *the guilty person* had predeceased the decedent * * * *." (Emphasis added.)

2. A statute should not be construed to impair preexisting law in the absence of an explicit legislative statement to the contrary (citations omitted).

SI (2):

1. No one should be allowed to profit from his own wrongful conduct.

2. It would be a reproach to our system of jurisprudence if a beneficiary could recover insurance money payable on the death of the insured, whose life the beneficiary had feloniously taken.

3. A beneficiary of a life insurance policy cannot recover thereon where the death of the insured is caused by the intentional and felonious act of the beneficiary.

SI (3):

1. *Lex simper dabit* remedium — the law will always give a remedy.

Court's Reasoning:

SI (1): The statute covers those who have been found "guilty" and prevents certain criminals from benefiting from their crimes. The statute provides only one way to preclude a killer from taking by relying on a criminal conviction. However, nothing in the legislative history supports the conclusion that this is the exclusive method for precluding a killer from taking. The husband has not been tried or found guilty; therefore, the statute does not apply. However, the statute is not the exclusive method for determining whether one who intentionally and feloniously caused the death of another can benefit from that act.

SI (2): The common law supports the conclusion that a potential beneficiary of a life insurance policy cannot recover where that potential beneficiary intentionally and feloniously caused the death of the insured. *Filmore.*

SI (3): The idea that no one can benefit by his or her wrong is a civil concept (*see Filmore*) and therefore civil courts can determine whether one intentionally and feloniously killed another. The court cites *Huff v. Union Fidelity Life Ins.*, 470 N.E.2d 236 (Ohio App. 1984), where a civil court determined whether a son had killed his father, which would bar the son from recovering his father's life insurance proceeds. The son admitted killing his father, but the court stated that the trier of fact had a right to determine whether the son's action was justified as self-defense. The court also found that a lower burden of proof in a civil case (preponderance of the evidence rather than beyond a reasonable doubt, which is the burden of proof in a criminal case) is not a violation of public policy since the accused does not risk losing his life or liberty.

APPENDIX
C

Everett v. Rogers

*1030

Everett v. Rogers[1]
836 F. Supp. 1030
(S.D.E.C. 1995)

Plaintiff Steven Everett seeks recovery of the title to and possession of "Winter," an eighteenth-century masterpiece painted by Corrado Giaquinto (the "Painting"), currently possessed by defendant, John Rogers.

Findings of Fact

On July 24, 1960, the Painting was stolen from the home of John Rogers in Washington, D.C. Rogers was a foreign service officer with the State Department until 1963, having spent twenty-five years with that agency. He is neither an art collector nor a participant in ***1031** the fine arts community. He does not subscribe to or read periodicals on the fine arts.

On July 25, 1960, Rogers reported the theft of the Painting to the Metropolitan Police Department (the "Police Department") and provided them with a photo of the Painting. The Federal Bureau of Investigation ("F.B.I.") was also informed of the theft on the same day and started an investigation. The F.B.I. maintained frequent

---

1. This edited case is based on *Eristoty v. Rizik*, 1995 WL 91406 (E.D. Pa. Feb. 23, 1995).

contact with the Police Department through October 1960. The F.B.I. also advised Interpol, a European investigative agency, of the theft. Local law enforcement authorities discouraged Rogers from hiring a private investigator, assuring him that the Police Department, F.B.I., and Interpol were doing everything and more than a private investigator could do.

At various times in 1961, 1966, 1972, 1974, and 1979, Rogers contacted the F.B.I., or the F.B.I. contacted Rogers regarding the status of the investigation or possible leads to discovering the Painting. But, from July 9, 1979, through August 2, 1993 (when the F.B.I. informed Rogers that the Painting had been located), there had been no further contact between the F.B.I. and Rogers.

In 1972, Rogers notified the Art Dealers Association of America ("ADAA") about the Painting. But until September 1992, Rogers never published any announcements or notices of the theft of the Paintings in any newspapers, magazines, art journals, or other periodicals. From 1961 through 1991 Rogers periodically visited museums to look for the Painting. He never provided museums, auction houses, art galleries, scholars, or experts on Giaquinto with photographs of the Painting or information identifying the Painting.

In March 1988, a woman who owned a home in East Carolina City removed furniture and objects from her home and hired a cleaning company to remove all other furnishings. While removing the furniture, one of the owners of the cleaning company, Mr. Kern, discovered the Painting, torn in five pieces, in a plastic trash bag behind a dresser.

Kern showed the Painting to an antiques dealer, who contacted the East Carolina Museum of Art ("ECMA") to identify the Painting's history and value. The ECMA examined the Painting. Although art experts were called in, no one was able to give information about the history of the Painting.

In March 1989, Kern turned over the Painting to an East Carolina City auction house to be sold. The plaintiff, Steven Everett, a professional conservator of paintings, purchased the Painting for $60,000 at an auction on April 16, 1989. Everett never contacted the International Foundation for Art Research ("IFAR"), the ADAA, or any law enforcement agency to determine whether the Painting had been missing or stolen. He was not required by law to do so. He later spent substantial time and money restoring the Painting.

In 1992, Rogers learned from a friend about IFAR, a nonprofit organization dedicated to preventing the circulation of stolen, forged, and misattributed works of art. Since IFAR's establishment in 1976, owners of stolen art have been able to register their losses with IFAR. IFAR publishes a magazine, *IFAR Reports*, that reports on stolen or lost art. The magazine circulates to art dealers, law enforcement officials, insurance agencies, museums (including the ECMA), and private collectors throughout the world.

Rogers filed a report with IFAR about the theft of the stolen Painting. The September 1992 issue of *IFAR Reports* included an announcement about the theft of the Painting and a photograph of the Painting. A conservator from the ECMA identified the Painting. He advised the proper law enforcement authorities, who tracked down the Painting. The F.B.I. retrieved the Painting from Everett's home and returned it to Rogers.

On September 20, 1993, Everett's attorney sent a letter to Rogers demanding the return of the Painting. Rogers' attorney

*1032

refused the demand. The Painting remains in the possession of Rogers.

Discussion

Everett contends that Rogers has no right to the Painting because the statute of limitations, which states how long a claim can be brought in court, had ended. Two potential issues relating to the statute of limitations are present in this case: First, what is the applicable statute, and, second, when did it begin to run?

To put the matter in context, the applicable statute of limitations is the replevin statute, which governs the time within which an original owner can sue for recovery of a stolen item. Given the instant factual setting, the statute would permit Rogers three years following Everett's acquisition of the painting in April 1989 to bring an action for recovery of the painting. E.C. Code § 4-201.[1] Since Rogers did not act within the period, he will be prevented from recovering the Painting "unless equitable principles justify tolling the statute of limitations." *Schuler v. Baldwin*, 594 F.2d 1285, 1287 (13th Cir. 1987).

Courts favor statutes of limitations because they "stimulate [claimants] to activity and punish negligence" and "promote peace by giving security [against stale claims] and stability to human affairs." *O'Keeffe v. Snyder*, 416 A.2d 862, 868 (N.J. 1980) (quoting

---

1. E.C. Code § 4-201 (2007) provides: "An action for taking, detaining, or injuring personal property, including actions for specific recovery thereof, must be commenced within three years after the cause of action has accrued." In the case where the owner is proceeding against a good faith purchaser of the property, the cause of action does not accrue until the time when the good faith purchaser acquired the property. *Schuler v. Baldwin*, 594 F.2d at 1287.

Wood v. Carpenter, 101 U.S. 135, 139 (1879)). "A statute of limitations achieves those purposes by barring a cause of action after the statutory period." *Id.* at 868.

The statute of limitations will not begin to run if strict enforcement would work an injustice, such as where an original owner is unable to locate stolen artwork for many years despite reasonable search efforts. Under the discovery rule, an original owner's cause of action does not accrue "until the injured party discovers, or by exercise of reasonable diligence and intelligence should have discovered, facts which form the basis of a cause of action." *Id.* (quoting *O'Keeffe*, 416 A.2d at 869). In the stolen art context, such facts include "the identity of the possessor of the paintings." *Id.* at 870. In *O'Keeffe*, the Supreme Court of New Jersey described the focus of the discovery rule as follows: "The discovery rule shifts the emphasis from the conduct of the possessor to the conduct of the owner. The focus of the inquiry will [be] whether the owner has acted with due diligence in pursuing his or her property." *Id.* at 872. In stolen art cases, where a court finds that an owner has diligently searched for a painting "but cannot find it or discover the identity of the possessor, the statute of limitations will not begin to run." *Id.* The discovery rule fulfills "the purposes of a statute of limitations and accord[s] greater protection to the innocent owner of personal property whose goods are lost or stolen." *Id.* at 875.

In the present instance, the Painting could probably not have been discovered for nearly 30 years after its theft. The Painting may well have remained all the while in a trash bag — torn in five pieces — in the house in East Carolina, from 1960 until 1988. Usually an artwork has been resting comfortably with a new owner for many years before the original owner arrives on the scene; in this case the Painting was with Everett for a relatively brief four years before the whereabouts of the Painting became known.

The burden of proving due diligence under the discovery rule logically rests with the original owner as the party "seeking the benefit of the rule to establish facts that would justify deferring the beginning of the period of limitations." *Id.*, at 873.

*1033

Rogers relies on the discovery rule as grounds for preserving his claim to title to the Painting beyond the normal three-year statutory period. As such, the burden of proof as to this issue properly rests with Rogers.

Two precedents provide a helpful basis for applying the discovery rule to the present facts. The *O'Keeffe* court recognized that "[t]he meaning of due diligence will vary with the facts of each case, including the nature and value of the personal property." 416 A.2d at 873. Thus, the court explained, "with respect to jewelry of moderate value, it may be sufficient if the owner reports the theft to the police. With respect to artwork of greater value, it may be reasonable to expect an owner to do more." *Id.* In *Autocephalous Greek-Orthodox Church v. Goldberg & Feldman Fine Arts, Inc.*, 917 F.2d 278 (7th Cir. 1990), the Seventh Circuit followed *O'Keeffe* and adopted the discovery rule. In that case, the court emphasized that an original owner's obligation to search for missing property is a continuing one: "[W]e note that any 'laziness' this rule might seem to invite by the plaintiffs is heavily tempered by the requirement that, all the while, the plaintiff must exercise due diligence to investigate the theft and recover the works." *Id.* at 289.

After careful consideration of the law and the facts of this case, the court finds that Rogers' search efforts were reasonably diligent for discovery rule purposes. Several factors contribute to this conclusion. First, the evidence demonstrates that Rogers did make an affirmative, sustained effort to locate the Painting.

Foremost in this effort was Rogers' reporting of the theft to the F.B.I. and continued contact with the F.B.I. through the late 1970s. Rogers was reasonable to conclude on the advice of the police that the F.B.I.'s and Interpol's involvement constituted the best investigative channels available for locating his missing artwork. Indeed, in light of

Rogers' status as a government official and the highly responsive service he received from the F.B.I., culminating in its personal delivery of the Painting in 1993, Rogers' reliance on that agency was all the more reasonable.

Nor was Rogers' apparent lack of contact with the F.B.I. after 1979 necessarily unreasonable. The evidence indicates that Rogers and the F.B.I. communicated with each other from time to time over a 19-year period, usually occurring when either came into possession of potentially relevant information. Presumably no leads arose from 1979 until after the IFAR report was published in 1992. That assumption aside, it is quite understandable that one's efforts to search for a lost item would lessen somewhat as the years passed. Indeed, it would be unusual for theft victims such as Rogers to keep in frequent contact with law enforcement officials 20 to 30 years after the fact. Rather, it seems the more plausible approach for victims in Rogers' position is to keep their eyes and ears open and to expect that the police or F.B.I. would be in touch should any leads arise.

Furthermore, that Rogers did not discover IFAR sooner should not be fatal to his claim. Rogers is not a serious art collector; he is merely a man in search of lost artwork that decorated the walls of his home. This court focuses on Rogers' exercise of diligence after discovering the IFAR registry — namely, Rogers' registering the Painting in 1992 — rather than his arguable lack of diligence in discovering IFAR's existence.

Additionally, the balance of equities weighs in Rogers' favor. Everett purchased the Painting without inquiring as to the painting's prior ownership or the identity of the consignor, without making any inquiry of art or law enforcement agencies, and with the knowledge that the Painting was in five pieces — suspicious circumstances to say the least. Everett took the risk that an original owner could appear at any time. In short, Everett took a gamble — he used his savings to purchase what he felt was a masterpiece — hoping to gain tremendous benefits by selling the restored Painting for a substantial profit.

*1034

Rogers, on the other hand, suffered an intrusive crime, subsequently contacted the F.B.I. and remained in contact with that agency for many years, and, finally, set in motion the process of recovering the Painting through his diligence in contacting IFAR when he became aware of its existence. The fact that the Painting was located within a few years of purchase, yet many years after being stolen, was due specifically to the revived efforts of Rogers in 1992; this constitutes a continuing effort rather than a weak effort that lapsed in 1979.

The discovery rule is fact sensitive so as to adjust the level of scrutiny as is appropriate in light of the identity of the parties; what efforts are reasonable for an individual who is relatively unfamiliar with the art world, for example, may not be reasonable for a savvy collector, a gallery, or a museum. While Rogers could certainly have been more aggressive in his search — for example, making inquiries at galleries and museums rather than merely visiting them — Rogers' occasional visits to galleries and museums, his follow-up on tips, and his reliance on the services of the F.B.I. (and, through it, Interpol) constitute a a reasonable search effort under the discovery rule.

Notably, the standard is not whether Rogers did everything that might have been done with the benefit of hindsight, but whether his efforts were reasonable given the facts of the case.

In light of all the above factors, this Court finds that Rogers exercised reasonable due diligence in searching for the Painting and has satisfied the demands of the discovery rule. Accordingly, the statute of limitations did not begin to run until 1993 when Rogers discovered the whereabouts of the Painting and the identity of the possessor. Rogers' claim to the Painting is thus timely and will be honored by this Court.

APPENDIX
D

Mats Transport v. ABC Corporation

**Mats Transport, Plaintiff, v.
ABC Corporation, Defendant.**

sold (purchase agreement)
CNC

*824 S.E.2d 1467
(E.C. App. 1992)[1]*

Miller, Chief Justice.

The plaintiff, Mats Transport, sued the defendant, ABC Corporation, alleging the defendant violated a covenant not to compete which was part of a purchase agreement it had signed when the defendant sold a part of its business to the plaintiff. Defendant moved for summary judgment, claiming that the covenant not to compete is unreasonable because it is broader than necessary for the protection of the plaintiff's business and therefore is unenforceable. Following a hearing, the trial court granted the defendant's motion. We affirm.

Both plaintiff and defendant are trucking firms. On May 1, 1989, plaintiff and the defendant entered into a purchase agreement which provided that the defendant would sell to the plaintiff all goodwill associated with or related to its business, its trade name, its customer list, and its operating permits. The purchase agreement included a covenant not to compete with the plaintiff under the terms of which the defendant agreed that for a period of five years it would not compete directly or indirectly with the plaintiff's trucking business in the United States.

In consideration for the defendant's sale of its business and the covenant not to compete, the plaintiff paid $50,000 to the defendant.

Shortly after the Agreement went into effect, the defendant leased seven trucks to Todd Stern ("Stern"), who had been a truck driver for the defendant. Stern began operating his own trucking firm. Plaintiff argues that Stern's operations compete with it, and that the defendant's leasing of trucks to Stern violated the covenant and has substantially diluted and impaired the value of the goodwill purchased by the plaintiff and resulted in lost revenues and lost profits for the plaintiff.

Under Rule 56(c) of the East Carolina Rules of Civil Procedure, summary judgment is proper "if the pleadings, depositions, answers to interrogatories, and admissions on file, together with the affidavits, if any, show that there is no genuine issue as to any material fact and that the moving party is entitled to a judgment as a matter of law." E.C. R. Civ. Proc. 56(c). In passing on a motion for summary judgment, the judge's role is not to evaluate the weight of the evidence or determine the truth of the matter, but it is instead to decide whether there is a genuine issue for trial. Summary judgment is especially appropriate where the issues in dispute are purely legal. In these circumstances, the need for trial is avoided because there are no genuine issues of material fact that must be resolved. The defendant argues that summary judgment should be entered in its favor because the CNC is unreasonable as a matter of law.

This court begins its analysis by noting that covenants not to compete are not favored by the law. The reason for this is not difficult to fathom; they impede trade and distort the market mechanism which allows our

---

1. Created from *Ridgefield Park Transp. v. Uhl,* 803 F. Supp. 1467 (S.D. Ind. 1992).

economy to function. Covenants not to compete consequently are strictly construed against the party seeking to enforce them. They are not per se unlawful, however, and will be enforced if they are reasonable, which is a determination made by the court.

Courts in this state apply a three-pronged test to determine whether a covenant not to compete ancillary to the sale of a business is unreasonable: (1) the covenant must not be broader than necessary for the protection of the covenantee's[2] legitimate business interest; (2) the covenant cannot have an adverse effect on the covenantor;[3] and (3) the covenant cannot adversely affect the public interest. *Hanson v. Albright*, 539 S.E.2d 500, 501 (E.C. App. 1989). If the covenant not to compete fails any prong of this test, then it is unreasonable as a matter of law.

This court finds that the covenant not to compete contained in the purchase agreement signed by the defendant fails the first prong of the test because it is broader than necessary to protect the plaintiff's interest. Whether a covenant is overly broad depends, in part, on the extent of the territory restricted. *See id.*

> When a party sells a business to another, the seller often will agree not to compete with the buyer for a certain period of time within a certain area. This covenant not to compete protects value of the business's goodwill, which represents the value of the customers' relationship with the business at the time of the sale.

---

2. The party for whose benefit the covenant not to compete is made.

3. The party who agrees not to compete.

Matthews v. Acme Tax Consultants, 470 S.E.2d 756, 763 (E.C. App. 1984).

While the trucking operation which the plaintiff purchased had permits to operate in 48 states, the record indicates that the defendant was primarily a regional shipper that operated out of a terminal in the southern part of East Carolina. Although the defendant at times hauled freight across the United States, this activity was sporadic; its business consisted primarily of serving a handful of major clients over established routes in East Carolina and the states on its border.

All parties were aware at the time of sale that the defendant was not a national concern and that it did not preside over an elaborate shipping network. This was implicit in the fact that the defendant had only one truck terminal and a small number of trucks. The covenant not to compete, however, constrains the defendant in a way that contemplates a far different organization — one that has its own developed markets coast to coast and a shipping infrastructure to support them. Nothing in the record supports such a finding.

The covenant not to compete signed by the defendant prevents the defendant from competing, directly or indirectly, anywhere in the United States. The activity that it seeks to prohibit is far more encompassing than is necessary to protect the plaintiff's interests, because it amounts to a total prohibition on the defendant's entry into any trucking market in the United States.

Because the covenant not to compete fails the first prong of the *Hanson* test, this court need not examine the other two prongs. We uphold the trial court's finding that the covenant was unreasonable as a matter of law and affirm the trial court's summary judgment.

APPENDIX

E

Checklist for an Objective Discussion of a Fact-Based Issue: One Issue and One Case

NOTE: The purpose of this checklist is to help you think critically about the structure and content of your paper. The checklist is not an exhaustive list of everything that must be included in your paper.

Framework Paragraph

____ Have you told your reader the issue you are addressing in your discussion?

____ Have you provided *only* those facts necessary to set up the legal issue and saved the other detailed facts for the analysis?

____ If this is the first time you have mentioned the parties involved in your client's case, have you introduced the parties by their full names?

____ Have you not only provided the substantive issue but also placed that substantive issue in the proper procedural context?

____ Have you included any rules that will be needed to answer the question or that are helpful as general information? And have you quoted the key language of those rules and provided citations to the authorities where you found those rules?

____ (Optional) Have you told your reader your outcome in this case (turning this first paragraph into a thesis paragraph)?

Organization

A. Read the first sentence of each paragraph to check your structure.

____ Did you make the structure of your discussion obvious through clear topic or thesis sentences?

B. Check your placement of your rule explanation.

____ Have you provided the rule explanation after setting out the main rule and *before* applying the case facts to the facts of your client's case?

Rule(s)

____ Did you bring up a rule as it became relevant in your discussion?

____ Did you quote the rule(s) or, if you paraphrased the rule(s), were you careful not to change the meaning of the rule(s)?

____ Did you cite to the authority where you found the rule(s)?

Rule Explanation

____ Does the rule explanation contain the following information?

    ____ The parties in the case, identified by generic names that reflect the relationship of the parties in the legal dispute (e.g., seller/buyer, slayer/deceased, husband/wife).

    ____ The facts of the case relevant to the issue being analyzed.

    ____ The court's holding on the issue being analyzed.

    ____ The court's reasoning for the holding on the issue being analyzed.

____ Did you *complete* the rule explanation before mentioning the facts of your client's case and how the facts of your client's case are similar to or different from the facts in the rule explanation?

Analysis

____ Were your references to your client's facts as explicit and specific as possible? Remember, you are writing to an unfamiliar reader. Don't rely on the reader's knowledge of the facts.

____ When you stated similarities or differences between the facts of the case law and the facts of your client's case, were you explicit about the facts you were comparing?

NOTE: It is not acceptable to make a reference too general, such as, "Similar to *Mats Transport*, Ana . . ." You must state the *specific facts* of the case law and the *specific facts* of your client's case.

Draw an arrow connecting the facts of the case law and the facts of your client's case. The facts should be connected within the same sentence or in adjacent sentences.

____ When you bring up facts from case law in your analysis, did you review the preceding rule explanation to make sure you first mentioned those facts in that rule explanation?

____ Did you mention any additional facts present in your client's case (which may not be directly comparable to or distinguishable from the facts present in the case law) that could logically support the position in your analysis?

____ Did you draw reasonable inferences from your client's facts and the similarities/differences between your client's case and the case law to support your analysis? Use facts and similarities/distinctions to draw reasonable inferences that support your analysis. Do not simply indicate the important facts and similarities/distinctions and then conclude. Make a clear connection between the facts and the law.

_____ Did you avoid comparing the holding of a court in the case law to what the holding may be in your client's case?

NOTE: It is not an analysis to compare a case holding to the anticipated holding in your client's case, such as, "Similar to *Mats Transport,* where the court found the CNC unreasonable, the CNC that Ana has been ordered by the court to sign is unreasonable." Rather, you must compare the similarities or differences of the facts of the case law to the facts of your client's case.

_____ Have you avoided creating new facts or speculating about events not present in your client's case?

_____ Did you avoid stating a conclusion at the end of the stronger position analysis before beginning the weaker position analysis? (Stating a conclusion at the end of the stronger position analysis can be confusing to the reader because the reader will think you have completed your discussion of the issue.)

Conclusion

_____ Have you provided a quick overall conclusion that answers the main question posed by the supervising attorney, indicating the main reasons supporting your conclusion?

_____ Have you *not* included new law and analysis in the conclusion? (If important, this information belongs in the discussion.)

_____ Have you omitted references to authority?

_____ Have you omitted statements such as "I believe," "I feel," and "It is my opinion that"?

Citation
Note: See Chapter 15 for the basic citation rules.

_____ Did you give a full cite to a case the first time you mentioned it?
Did you either
_____ provide the complete cite at the end of the sentence?
_____ provide the full name of the case in the sentence and wait until the end of the sentence to give the citation?

_____ Did you give a pinpoint cite to a case each time you quoted from the case?

_____ Did you give a pinpoint cite to a case each time you told the reader what the court did in that case (held, stated, reasoned, found, etc.)?

_____ Did you give a pinpoint cite to a case each time you paraphrased a rule or an idea from the case?

_____ If you took something from a case where the court quoted from authority, did you use the proper citation format showing this to the reader?

_____ If you use the "*id.*" short citation format, did the last cite refer to the same authority that you are referring to now?

Format and Style

1. **Check your quoted text.**

   ____ Have you quoted key language
      ____ from the rule?
      ____ from the court's reasoning?
   ____ Do the quoted passages embedded in your sentences make sense within the context of your sentence. (Did you change the tense of verbs, change words, add words, or omit words, if necessary, so that the quoted passages read logically within the context of your paper?)
   ____ If the quoted text comprises 50 words or more, have you placed the quote in block form (indented, single-spaced, with no quotation marks)?
   ____ If the quoted text is 49 words or less, have you placed quotation marks around the quoted text?
   ____ Have you provided ellipses where you have excluded language from the middle or end of a quoted text?
   ____ Have you provided brackets around letters or words that you added to or changed from the original text?

2. **Check grammar, style, punctuation, and typographical errors.**

   ____ Did you avoid using first person, unless you are referring to "our client"?
   ____ Did you avoid using word contractions such as *wouldn't, didn't, can't*?
   ____ Did you underline or italicize all case names?
   ____ Did you use past tense for verbs when referring to information from the case, describing what a court did in a case (e.g., *held, reasoned, stated*), or stating the facts of your client's case?
   ____ Did you use objective-type verbs when describing a court's action (e.g., *reasoned, held, found, stated*)?
   ____ Did you use the pronoun *it* when referring to a company, court, or organization?
   ____ Did you avoid using the adverbs *clearly* or *obviously* in your analysis? If a statement truly reflects something that is clear or obvious, you don't need the adverb.
   ____ Did you avoid posing rhetorical questions in your paper? Rhetorical questions do not add to the reader's knowledge of the subject matter. At best, they are unnecessary space fillers; at worst, they may lead the reader to a different answer than the one you are supporting with your analysis.
   ____ For a party's name in your client's case, did you give the full name of the party the first time you mention the party (e.g., *Ana Hart*), but thereafter use a short name to refer to the party (e.g., *Ana, Hart,* or *Ms. Hart*)? Were you consistent in using the same short name when referring to this party throughout the paper?
   ____ Were all periods or commas correctly placed inside quotation marks?

APPENDIX
F

Loch v. Blue Sail Cayman, Ltd.

234

Loch v. Blue Sail Cayman, Ltd.

105 F. Supp. 2d 234 (S.D.E.C. 2000)[1]

The plaintiff, Linda Loch, filed this diversity action on behalf of her minor son, Robert Dean Loch, against Blue Sail Cayman Ltd., a corporation organized under the laws of the Cayman Islands ("Blue Sail Cayman"). The plaintiff claims that Blue Sail Cayman is liable for negligence, strict products liability, and breach of warranty, pursuant to the East Carolina Product Liability Act, E.C. Code §§ 82-572 to -585, arising from a jet ski accident while vacationing in the Cayman Islands. The plaintiff seeks compensatory and punitive damages, as well as costs and attorneys' fees. Blue Sail Cayman moved to dismiss for lack of personal jurisdiction. For the reasons set forth below, Blue Sail Cayman's motion to dismiss is denied.

According to the plaintiff's complaint, on September 7, 1998, plaintiff Linda Loch, her husband Robert Loch, and their son, Robert Dean Loch, all residents of East Carolina, were registered guests at the Paradise Grand Resort & Villa. At noon that day, they arrived at Rum Point, a beach area close to the resort. Robert Dean Loch and his father waded into the ocean near several jet skis and other vessels

and recreational equipment owned or operated by Blue Sail Cayman, which were available for rent. Robert Loch placed his son on one of the jet skis, which then propelled forward unexpectedly and struck a breakwater. Robert Dean Loch was propelled over the handlebars of the jet ski and struck the breakwater. As a result of the accident, he suffered permanent disabling injuries.

The parties in this case have completed discovery on issues relating to personal jurisdiction, and the defendant has challenged the sufficiency of evidence underlying the plaintiff's allegations of jurisdiction. "On a motion to dismiss for lack of personal jurisdiction, it is the plaintiff who bears the burden of showing that the court has jurisdiction over the defendant."

Hall v. Gates, 21 F. Supp. 2d 349, 351 (S.D.E.C. 1998); *see also Metro. Life Ins. Co. v. Robertson-Ceco Corp.*, 84 F.3d 560, 566-567 (2d Cir. 1996). "To survive the motion, the plaintiff must make a prima facie showing through affidavits and other evidence that the defendant's conduct was sufficient for the court to exercise personal jurisdiction. After discovery, a plaintiff must submit an averment of facts that, if credited by the trier, would suffice to establish jurisdiction over the defendant." *Hall*, 21 F. Supp. 2d at 342. "Regardless of the controverting

---

1. Created from *Szollosy v. Hyatt Corp.*, 2000 WL 1576395 (D. Conn. Sept. 14, 2000).

evidence put forth by the defendant, the court must resolve all doubts in the plaintiff's favor." *Am. Med. Corp. v. Altamont Med. Tech., Inc.*, 26 F. Supp. 2d 50, 54 (S.D.E.C. 1998).

> [I]n resolving questions of personal jurisdiction in a diversity action, district court must conduct a two-part inquiry. First, it must determine whether the plaintiff has shown that the defendant is amenable to service of process under the forum state's laws; and second it must assess whether the court's assertion of jurisdiction under these laws comports with the [federal constitutional] requirements of due process.

Metro. Life Ins. Co., 84 F.3d at 567.

In ruling on the motion to dismiss, the Court must consider the application of E.C. Code § 33-939(f)(2) as to Blue Sail Cayman.

1. East Carolina's Long-Arm Statute

East Carolina's long-arm statute provides, in relevant part, that

> [e]very foreign corporation shall be subject to suit in [East Carolina], by a resident of this state or by a person having a usual place of business in this state, whether or not such foreign corporation is transacting or has transacted business in this state and whether or not it is engaged exclusively in interstate or foreign commerce, *on any cause of action arising* as follows:
> ... (2) *out of any business solicited in this state by mail or otherwise if the corporation has repeatedly so solicited business, whether the orders or offers relating thereto were accepted within or without the state.* ...

E.C. Code § 33-939(f) (emphasis added).

The plaintiff's claims in this case arise out of Blue Sail Cayman's allegedly extensive advertising and marketing in East Carolina. The plaintiff argues that Blue Sail Cayman solicited business in East Carolina, which renders it subject to personal jurisdiction in East Carolina pursuant to E.C. Code § 33-939(f)(2).

In opposing jurisdiction, Blue Sail Cayman denies that it repeatedly solicited business in East Carolina. The parties agree that Blue Sail Cayman is a Cayman Islands corporation. Blue Sail Cayman offers an affidavit in support of its contention that it is not licensed to conduct business in East Carolina; does not maintain an office or employees or an agent in East Carolina; and does not own real estate in East Carolina. In addition, Blue Sail Cayman alleges that the plaintiff and her family did not travel to the Cayman Islands for any reason having to do with Blue Sail Cayman, and that the plaintiff had not heard of Blue Sail Cayman prior to the jet ski accident.

The plaintiff argues that Blue Sail Cayman "engaged in a major advertising campaign in East Carolina in order to induce East Carolina residents . . . to visit its facilities in the Cayman Islands." Pl.'s Mem. at 16. The plaintiff offers affidavits and other evidence in support of her contention, such as advertising and promotional materials, which indicate that Blue Sail Cayman "advertised through a variety of print media, such as magazines, pamphlets, and brochures — all of which are distributed to East Carolina residents on a daily basis through travel agencies, bookstores, and dive shops." *Id.* at 17. The plaintiff also presents evidence that Blue Sail Cayman mails promotional materials throughout the United States, including to East Carolina travel agencies, and that it maintains customer lists for advertising purposes, which lists include East Carolina residents. *See id.* at 7-9, 18. Blue Sail Cayman also allegedly solicited East Carolina residents through the Internet, by creating, purchasing, and maintaining an "interactive" Web site that allow consumers in East Carolina to purchase services from their homes. *See id.* at 16-17.

The plaintiff also presents evidence that Blue Sail Cayman maintains an "interactive"

236

Web site. The Web site offers a toll-free telephone number and an e-mail address, through which East Carolina residents are able to obtain more information and make reservations for Blue Sail Cayman's services. *See id.* at 6.

The plaintiff contends that Blue Sail Cayman encourages East Carolina residents to visit Blue Sail Cayman's facilities and use its services. *See id.* at 7. Blue Sail Cayman concedes that Blue Sail Cayman sends postcards and promotional materials to East Carolina customers, travel agents, tourist boards, dive shops, and other travel-related individuals and businesses on behalf of Blue Sail Cayman. Prior to the incident giving rise to this case, Blue Sail Cayman sent advertising material to Robert Loch. *See id.* at 18. Blue Sail Cayman also sends bulk e-mail messages and circulates newsletters throughout the United States. Blue Sail Cayman advertises in national publications such as *Skin Diver* magazine, which are available in East Carolina. In addition, there is no dispute that Blue Sail Cayman maintains mailing lists and client lists for solicitation purposes, which include East Carolina residents. Finally, the plaintiff presents evidence that Blue Sail Cayman has received e-mail inquiries from East Carolina residents through its Web site. *See generally id.* at 7-9, 17-18.

Blue Sail Cayman argues that its Web site is "passive" and cannot be used directly to purchase Blue Sail Cayman's services. Blue Sail Cayman also argues that the fact East Carolina travel agents, dive shops, and other similar businesses distributed Blue Sail Cayman brochures and information to East Carolina residents is not, without more, determinative of personal jurisdiction over Blue Sail Cayman; national advertising alone is not sufficient to establish a basis for personal jurisdiction. *See* Reply Br. Def. Blue Sail Cayman, Ltd.

The Court concludes, however, that Blue Sail Cayman solicited business sufficiently in East Carolina to bring it within East Carolina's jurisdictional statute. Blue Sail Cayman has engaged in a national marketing and advertising campaign involving in-state travel agency promotions and brochure circulation that is likely to prompt a significant number of East Carolina residents to utilize its services and visit its facilities. *See Polo v. Club Med, Inc.*, 19 F. Supp. 2d 912, 916 (S.D.E.C. 1998); *Delong v. Holiday Inn, Inc.*, 815 F. Supp. 68, 75 (S.D.E.C. 1993). Blue Sail Cayman also hosts an interactive Web site, the Court concludes, through which East Carolina customers can obtain information and make reservations for Blue Sail Cayman's services. *Cf. Mink v. AAAA Dev. LLC*, 190 F.3d 333, 336 (5th Cir. 1999) (looking to the nature and quality of the commercial activity conducted over the Internet). Also, as indicated, the plaintiff presents evidence that Blue Sail Cayman receives and responds to e-mail inquiries from East Carolina residents, and maintains client lists and mailing lists that include East Carolina residents. The plaintiff presents evidence that Robert Loch received at least one promotional letter from Blue Sail Cayman prior to his family's trip to the Cayman Islands. Although a single promotional letter might not be sufficient to subject a defendant to personal jurisdiction under E.C. Code § 33-939(f)(2), the Court considers the letter in this case as one factor among many in concluding that Blue Sail Cayman is subject to personal jurisdiction in East Carolina. Moreover this evidence is relevant to the issue of solicitation. Accordingly, based on the totality of evidence presented by the plaintiff, the Court concludes Blue Sail Cayman is subject to jurisdiction in East Carolina under E.C. Code § 33-939(f)(2).

2. Due Process

The court must next determine whether the statutory reach of the long-arm statute violates constitutional due process. Under the due process standard, a nonresident must have "minimum contacts" with the forum state. To have these minimum contacts, "a defendant must purposefully avail himself of the privileges and benefits of the forum state. . . . [T]he defendant's conduct and connection with the forum state should be such that he should reasonably anticipate being haled into court there." *Am. Med. Corp.*, 26 F. Supp. at 54-55. Due process requires that the defendant be given "fair warning" that its activities in a state may subject it to suit there. *See Metro. Life Ins. Co.*, 84 F.3d at 567. The minimum contacts inquiry rests upon the totality of the circumstances.

Based on the evidence presented in this case concerning Blue Sail Cayman's active solicitation of business in East Carolina, the Court concludes that the plaintiff has made a prima facie showing that the exercise of jurisdiction in this case is consistent with due process. The acts of Blue Sail Cayman set forth in the preceding section of this ruling represent sufficient minimum contacts with East Carolina such that it could be said to have purposefully availed itself of the privileges of conducting activities in the forum state. Based on the totality of Blue Sail Cayman's conduct in connection with this case, including patterns of advertising, sales promotion, and Internet communication directed at East Carolina, Blue Sail Cayman could reasonably have anticipated a viable and growing sales market in East Carolina, thus supporting the Court's conclusion that Blue Sail Cayman knew its goods or services would enter East Carolina.

Having concluded that the necessary minimum contacts exist between Blue Sail Cayman and East Carolina, the court proceeds to the second part of the jurisdictional analysis: "whether the assertion of personal jurisdiction would comport with 'traditional notions of fair play and substantial justice.'" *Rodriguez Paint Co. v. Found. Express, Inc.*, 818 F. Supp. 1028, 1033 (S.D.E.C. 1993). As part of its

"reasonableness" analysis, the Court must consider:

(1) the burden that the exercise of jurisdiction will impose on the defendant; (2) the interests of justice of the forum state in adjudicating the case; (3) the plaintiff's interest in obtaining convenient and effective relief; (4) the interstate judicial system's interest in obtaining the most efficient resolution of the controversy; and (5) the shared interest of the states in furthering substantive social policies. . . . While the exercise of jurisdiction is favored where the plaintiff has made a threshold showing of minimum contacts at the first stage of the inquiry, it may be defeated where the defendant presents "a compelling case that the presence of some other considerations would render jurisdiction unreasonable."

Metro. Life Ins. Co., 84 F.3d at 568 (quoting *Burger King Corp. v. Rudzewicz*, 471 U.S. 462, 477, 105 S. Ct. 2174, 2185 (1985)).

The import of the "reasonableness" inquiry varies inversely with the strength of the "minimum contacts" showing. Therefore, a strong showing by the plaintiff on the "minimum contacts" reduces the weight given to "reasonableness"; on the other hand, a weak showing by the plaintiff on the "minimum contacts" increases the weight given to "reasonableness." *See id.* at 568-569. Here, the plaintiff made a strong showing that Blue Sail Cayman had sufficient minimum contacts with East Carolina.

a. Burden on the Defendant

In this case, Blue Sail Cayman contends that it will be burdensome and offensive to traditional notions of fair play and substantial justice for it to defend this case in East Carolina because it has no property, office space, or employees or agents in East Carolina. Nor are many of the potential witnesses found in East Carolina; they are in the Cayman

Islands, which will result in great expense to Blue Sail Cayman. Also, the jet ski involved in the accident is in the Cayman Islands. The cost of bringing the jet ski to East Carolina also would be unduly burdensome. Certainly, there are many difficulties associated with requiring Blue Sail Cayman to defend this suit in East Carolina. This factor cuts in favor of Blue Sail Cayman.

b. Interests of Forum State

The forum state (in this case, East Carolina) has a "manifest interest in providing effective means of redress for its residents." *Hallwood Realty Partners, L.P. v. Gotham Partners, L.P.*, 104 F. Supp. 2d 279, 283 (S.D.N.Y. 2000). This factor, therefore, weighs strongly in the plaintiff's favor.

c. Interests of Plaintiff in Obtaining Convenient and Effective Relief

Litigating in East Carolina would be more convenient for the plaintiff. "The plaintiff's choice of forum is the best indicator of his own convenience." *Scott v. Jones*, 984 F. Supp. 37, 46 (D. Me. 1997). Furthermore, the plaintiff maintains that hearing the case in the Cayman Islands would create a significant financial burden of traveling to the Cayman Islands, and of retaining counsel and producing American witnesses there. This factor, as well, supports the plaintiff.

d. Efficient Administration of Justice

"In evaluating this factor, courts generally consider where witnesses and evidence are likely to be located." *Metro. Life Ins. Co.*, 84 F.3d at 575. In this case, the principal witnesses, Robert Dean Loch and his father, are located in East Carolina, as are several of the physicians who have treated plaintiff Robert Dean Loch since the accident. Robert Dean Loch's medical records are also located in East Carolina. Further, it is far more efficient to proceed in East Carolina than in the Cayman Islands, given its relatively remote and inaccessible location in the "middle of

the Caribbean Sea." On the other hand, the jet ski involved in the accident is in the Cayman Islands. And, viewing the scene of the accident would be impossible if the case were tried in East Carolina. Because more witnesses are likely to come from East Carolina, this factor weighs slightly in favor of the plaintiff.

e. Policy Arguments

"This factor requires [this Court] to consider the common interests of the several states in promoting substantive social policies." *Kernan v. Kurz-Hastings, Inc.*, 175 F.3d 236, 245 (2d Cir. 1999). Blue Sail Cayman contends that the Cayman Islands has a significant interest in hearing this case because of its strong interest in tourism. East Carolina, however, has a stronger interest addressing injuries to its citizens caused by Blue Sail Cayman who has purposefully conducted or solicited business in East Carolina. This factor weighs in favor of the plaintiff.

Our consideration of the reasonableness factors shows that they weigh more in favor of asserting jurisdiction over Blue Sail Cayman. While the first factor (the burden on the defendant) cuts in favor of Blue Sail Cayman, this court recognizes that, taken alone, it falls short of overcoming the plaintiff's strong threshold showing of minimum contacts. The fact that Blue Sail Cayman maintained no physical presence in East Carolina does not mean that it did not purposefully avail itself of the jurisdiction or that this Court's exercise of jurisdiction of Blue Sail Cayman would be unjust, unfair, or unreasonable. The defendant has failed to make a "compelling" case that this Court's exercise of jurisdiction over it would be unreasonable under the circumstances. Consequently, the constitutional principles of due process are not offended by asserting jurisdiction over Blue Sail Cayman.

For the reasons set forth above, Blue Sail Cayman's motion to dismiss is denied.

APPENDIX
G

Langford v. Emerald Beach Resort and Marina

Langford v. Emerald Beach Resort and Marina

24 F. Supp. 2d 85[1]
(S.D.E.C. 1998)

The plaintiff, Merle Langford, commenced this action against the defendant, Emerald Beach Resort and Marina, to recover damages for personal injuries he allegedly sustained while he was vacationing at the defendant's resort in St. Thomas, U.S. Virgin Islands. The one count complaint alleges that while the plaintiff was a guest at the defendant's hotel from February 25, 1997, to March 5, 1997, he became ill and suffered injuries after eating dinner at the Sea Grape Restaurant, which is owned and operated by the defendant. The plaintiff claims that his injuries were caused by the defendant's negligent food preparation and inspection. The plaintiff also alleges that the defendant is subject to suit in East Carolina under General Statutes § 33-939(f), the foreign corporation long-arm statute. The defendant now moves to dismiss this action on the grounds that this court lacks personal jurisdiction.

In support of its motion to dismiss, the defendant filed a memorandum of law and the affidavit of Nouvella Barbier, the

defendant's director of marketing. The affidavit attests that in 1997, 728 East Carolina residents stayed at Emerald Beach; that Emerald Beach has placed a total of three advertisements in the Arcady Courant, one on September 20, 1996, another on February 7, 1997, and one on September 11, 1997; that Emerald Beach has received bookings from a total of sixty-six East Carolina travel agents in the past two years; and that Emerald Beach has no officers, agents, representatives or conducts any business of any kind in East Carolina.

In opposition to this motion, the plaintiff submitted a memorandum of law. The plaintiff did not submit any counter-affidavits and did not request the evidentiary hearing that is required when issues of fact are necessary to the determination of a court's jurisdiction. Instead, the plaintiff argues in his memorandum that the facts contained in the defendant's affidavit support his contention that this court has personal jurisdiction over the defendant. Since the plaintiff relies on the defendant's affidavit and has not submitted any further evidence to assist the court in determining this jurisdictional question, the court concludes that there are no issues of fact and, thus, due process does not mandate an evidentiary hearing. The sole question before the court, therefore, is whether the facts

---

1. Created from *DeLuca v. Holiday Inns, Inc.,* 1993 WL 512432 (Conn. Super. Dec. 3, 1993).

attested to in the defendant's affidavit are sufficient to support a determination that this court has personal jurisdiction over the defendant.

To survive a Rule 12(b)(2) motion to dismiss for lack of personal jurisdiction, the plaintiff is required to make only a prima facie showing that each defendant is amenable to personal jurisdiction in East Carolina. *S.M. Trade Fin., Inc. v. Piva Bank*, 990 F.2d 86, 89 (2d Cir. 1993). "Prior to discovery, a plaintiff challenged by a jurisdiction testing motion may defeat the motion by pleading in good faith . . . legally sufficient allegations of jurisdiction." *Ball v. Metallurgie Hoboken-Overpelt, S.A.*, 902 F.2d 194, 197 (2d Cir.), *cert. denied*, 498 U.S. 854, 111 S. Ct. 150, 112 L.Ed.2d 116 (1990). As in a motion to dismiss for failure to state a claim, the court must construe all allegations in the light most favorable to the plaintiff and doubts must be resolved in his favor, "notwithstanding a controverting presentation by the defendants." *S.M. Trade Fin., Inc.*, 990 F.2d at 89-90; *Tenmilo Ltd. v. MAS Group PLC*, 931 F. Supp. 46, 50 (D.E.C. 1996).

Personal jurisdiction in this diversity case is governed by East Carolina law. *Inter'l Computers, Inc. v. Sahar, Inc.*, 127 F.3d 375, 380 (2d Cir. 1997). Analysis of a procedural challenge to personal jurisdiction over a foreign corporation is a two-step process. *Little v. Brown*, 303 S.E.2d 805, 807 (E.C. 1986). The court must first inquire whether, under the facts of the case, the state's long-arm statute may be asserted as a basis for jurisdiction over the defendant. *Id.* Once jurisdiction has attached under the long-arm statute, the court must then determine whether the exercise of jurisdiction satisfies the federal constitutional requirements of due process. *Id.*

Under subsection 33-939(f)(2) of the East Carolina General Statutes, a suit may be brought against a foreign corporation:

> whether or not such foreign corporation is transacting business in this state . . . on any cause of action arising . . . out of any business solicited in this state by mail or otherwise if the corporation has repeatedly so solicited business, whether the orders or offers relating thereto were accepted within or without the state. . . .

This subsection confers jurisdiction over designated causes of action without regard to whether a foreign corporation transacts business in East Carolina and without regard to a causal connection between the plaintiff's cause of action and the defendant's presence in this state. The language of subsection 33-939(f)(2) requires inquiry not only into the various elements of the plaintiff's cause of action but also into the totality of contacts which the defendant may have with the forum. *Edwards Bros., Inc. v. El-Tek, Inc.*, 461 S.E.2d 490, 496 (E.C. 1992).

The statute does not permit the exercise of jurisdiction over this defendant. The court is not convinced that the defendant "repeatedly so solicited business" in this state. The plaintiff relies on *McGinley v. Executive Int'l, Inc.*, 355 F. Supp. 1177 (D.E.C. 1973), but in that case the defendant placed six advertisements over a six-month period in newspapers with East Carolina circulations. Here, the undisputed facts as set forth in the defendant's affidavit, do not satisfy the statutory requirement that the cause of action "arise[s] . . . out of . . . business solicited in this state. . . ." The only evidence of business solicited in this state is that the defendant placed a total of three advertisements in the Arcady Courant, a newspaper of general distribution in the town of Arcady, from September 1996 to September 1997. Neither party submitted the contents of these advertisements, although they presumably sought East Carolina residents to stay at the defendant's resort. In *Stoll v. Circle Bank*, 662 S.E.2d 535, 545 (E.C. 1995), the East Carolina Supreme Court based its determination that the trustee bank "repeatedly so solicited business" in this state on the defendant's numerous advertisements in newspapers and magazines;

87

its substantial number of mortgage transactions in East Carolina; and its large credit card business in East Carolina. Additionally, the court concluded that the defendant's activities could be characterized as an "organizational network that is likely to prompt a significant number of East Carolina" residents to place business with the bank. *Id.*

In the present case, the plaintiff presented no evidence of such an "organizational network." The plaintiff claims in his memorandum of law that the defendant established such an organizational network by supplying travel agencies with brochures. The court is not convinced that bookings from sixty-six East Carolina travel agents in the past two years demonstrates an "organizational network" or even repeated business solicitation in this state.

There simply is no evidence for the court to conclude under what circumstances these bookings were made and therefore whether they constitute repeated business solicitation under subsection 33-939(f)(2). Viewing the totality of the defendant's contacts and connections with this state, this court is not convinced that the defendant reasonably could anticipate being haled into court here.

Because the requirements of East Carolina's long-arm statute have not been satisfied, this court does not need to discuss the second prong of the jurisdictional analysis, whether the exercise of jurisdiction over defendant would violate the due process clause.

For these reasons, the defendant's motion to dismiss is granted.

APPENDIX
H

Hanson v. Albright

Hanson v. Albright   **500**

539 S.E.2d 500 (E.C. App. 1989)[1]

Plaintiffs-appellants-sellers John and Karen Hanson (the Hansons) appeal the trial court's grant of a permanent injunction in favor of defendants-appellees-buyers Asad A. Albright, Employee Benefit Consultants of America, Incorporated (EBC), enforcing a covenant not to compete in connection with the sale of a business.

Hanson and Associates (H&A) was a pension consulting firm owned and operated by John and Karen Hanson. John held 80% of its stock. Albright wanted to take his 118 clients from a pension consulting firm he owned, buy H&A, and merge the two. Albright, after meeting John and Karen, began negotiations to purchase H&A. At that time, H&A had approximately 600 clients.

During these negotiations, Albright agreed to pay the Hansons a total of $1,000,000: $850,000 for John's stock and $150,000 for the covenant not to compete set forth below. Albright also agreed that John and Karen would become employees of EBC, Albright's new pension consulting firm. The CNC covered twelve states and lasted for three years, which coincided with the duration of Karen's employment contract (John's ran for fifteen months).

The covenant not to compete read:

(a) For a period of three years from the date of closing, neither Sellers Karen Hanson nor John Hanson shall, directly or indirectly, engage in any activities within the States of East Carolina, Michigan, Ohio, Illinois, Kentucky, Missouri, Louisiana, Oklahoma, Wisconsin, Tennessee, Pennsylvania, or West Virginia, either as an owner, shareholder, director, officer, employee, or in any other capacity, on behalf of himself or herself or any third party, which are competitive with the services provided by the Seller prior to closing.

Approximately one year later Karen was terminated for insubordination, and John resigned. They formed another pension consulting business, naming it Actuaries and Benefit Consultants, Inc. (ABC). The Hansons began competing with Albright by contacting their former clients.

The Hansons filed a complaint, alleging that Albright materially breached the Stock Purchase and Pledge Agreements by firing Karen. Albright answered and filed a counterclaim for injunctive relief, requesting the court to enforce the CNC. After a trial on the merits, the trial court granted a permanent injunction against the Hansons, finding that the covenant not to compete was reasonable. The Hansons appeal. The only issue

---

1. Created from *Fogle v. Shah*, 539 N.E.2d 500 (Ind. App. 1989).

SI

before this court is whether the covenant not to compete is reasonable.

Covenants not to compete created in connection with the sale of a business reflect the value of the customers' affiliation with the particular business, which is part of the bargain sought by the buyer. This "goodwill" is the protectable interest upon which the covenant not to compete focuses. The goodwill of a business is an intangible asset which may be transferred from seller to purchaser, and it becomes the buyer's right to expect that the firm's established customers will continue to do business with the newly purchased company. The seller reentering the market and competing with the buyer for customers prevents the buyer from receiving all that has been sold to him. Agreements in partial restraint of trade in connection with the sale of a business appear to be sanctioned because of the value of the goodwill purchased.

R

In East Carolina, the first step in analyzing a covenant not to compete in connection with the sale of a business is determining whether a protectable interest has been purchased. The parties here agree Albright has a protectable interest in the goodwill of H&A.

A three-pronged test is then applied in determining whether a covenant not to compete in connection with the sale of a business is reasonable. The factors of the test are:

(a) whether the covenant is broader than necessary for the protection of the covenantee (here, Albright) in some legitimate interest,

(b) the effect of the covenant upon the covenantor (the Hansons), and

(c) the effect of the covenant upon the public interest.

The Hansons present one issue for our review, that is, whether the three-year, twelve-state geographical restriction contained in paragraph 19(a) of the stock purchase agreement is broader than necessary to protect the goodwill purchased from the Hansons and the territories they serviced as employees of EBC.

H&A is a business that provides services. A covenant not to compete connected with the sale of a service-oriented business normally will be localized because services generally are performed within a small geographic area. However, there will be cases such as this case where the territory covered reasonably may extend over several states because of the nature of the business.

The undisputed evidence establishes that the pension consulting business depends on the employees' familiarity with clients. Customers have many consulting needs that occur time and again. Prompt service, integrity, and loyalty are of great importance to customers. Customers tend to rely on key personnel who have demonstrated these qualities in the past. The record here establishes that John and Karen had a successful relationship with their clients. Their clients kept returning and referred their friends to John and Karen. As a result, H&A grew as a business. If the Hansons were allowed to solicit their former pension consulting customers, the goodwill Albright purchased would be destroyed.

Albright notes that he paid valuable consideration, approximately $150,000, for the covenant and $850,000 for the goodwill and business, which included the Hansons' good working relationships with their former clients. Albright gave the price the Hansons wanted and sought to protect his purchase by having the Hansons' good name and expertise associated with his business. He did not want the Hansons competing for the clients he had purchased, those new clients he could attract, or those who did business with EBC. Clearly, a broad spatial restraint is justified here.

The Hansons contend it was unreasonable to preclude them from competition in twelve states in their geographic entirety. In states one through nine, H&A had a maximum of four clients; in states ten and eleven, H&A had approximately 583 clients; and in the twelfth state H&A had no clients. The Hansons argue that territorial restraint

502

is greater than necessary to protect the goodwill of H&A. We disagree.

The person who purchases a business with the purpose of extending its scope is entitled to bargain with the seller against competition within the territory into which he plans to extend his business. This type of contract does not violate public policy where the area it covers is not greater than that which the parties may fairly anticipate the extended business will cover.

It is readily evident the parties thought EBC would geographically expand throughout the whole of the twelve states listed in the covenant. That Albright was attempting to expand EBC's client base is shown by negotiations with a major client in the twelfth state. John Hanson knew this fact and agreed to include that state in the purchase agreement. These facts establish that EBC was a growing business with plans to extend throughout the entire territory covered in the covenant. Further, by the plain words of their contract, the parties contemplated expansion into these areas.

Finally, Albright argues that with respect to the extent of the purchaser's original business, EBC's 128 clients in eleven states further support the argument that this covenant is territorially reasonable. John and Karen were employed by EBC immediately after H&A was sold to Albright. The record establishes that they would have contact with many of EBC's clients. Albright had a protectable interest in those clients, in addition to the goodwill purchased from H&A.

The second prong of the test to determine reasonableness addresses the effect of the promise upon the covenator (the Hansons). While the influence of this factor on the enforceability of employer-employee restraints is great, its importance in the sale or transfer of property is rather negligible.

The seller of a business, in determining the sale price, definitely puts a separate value on the goodwill of the business. Once specifically paid for his promise not to compete, the seller, whose bargaining power is usually similar to the purchaser's, has little appeal to the courts in a claim that the covenant is unduly harsh and covers too much territory. Courts are reluctant to help a "person who has voluntarily entered into an agreement not to compete, accepted the (frequently very considerable) consideration for his promise, and afterward wants to be absolved of his part of the bargain." Annotation, 46 A.L.R.2d 114, 261 (1951). Thus, policy supports every individual's right to work; however, policy also supports allowing any individual the option to sell anything he wants, including that right to work.

We find the covenant is reasonable as to the Hansons.

The third factor, considering the reasonableness of the CNC as to the general public, is also met in this case because any restraint on trade will be minimal at best. Albright testified pension consulting firms are everywhere and noted that there are twelve such firms in Flora, East Carolina, alone. Thus, the general public will not be harmed here by a restraint of trade. We find no error here.

Affirmed.

APPENDIX

I

Schuler v. Baldwin

This appeal concerns a dispute over ownership of a painting by Claude Monet that disappeared from Germany at the end of World War II and has been in the possession of a good-faith purchaser for the last thirty years. The issue on appeal is whether the plaintiff-appellee exercised reasonable diligence in trying to locate the painting in order to postpone the running of the statute of limitations in a suit against a good-faith purchaser, the defendant-appellant. The issue arises on an appeal from a judgment of the District Court for the Southern District of East Carolina, awarding recovery of the painting to plaintiff-appellee Katherine Schuler, a citizen of West Germany who owned the Monet from 1922 until 1943, from defendant-appellant Martha Baldwin, an American citizen who purchased the painting in East Carolina in 1957 and who has possessed it ever since. We conclude that the undisputed facts show that Schuler failed to exercise reasonable diligence in locating the painting after its disappearance,

---

1. This heavily edited text is based on *DeWeerth v. Baldinger*, 836 F.2d 103 (2d Cir. 1987).

and that her action for recovery is untimely. We therefore reverse the judgment of the district court.

Background

The oil painting is an impressionistic landscape painted by Monet. The painting's estimated worth is in excess of $500,000.

Plaintiff Katherine Schuler is a citizen of West Germany. Schuler kept the painting in her home from 1922 until 1943.

In August 1943, Schuler sent the Monet and other valuables to the home of her sister for safekeeping during World War II. Schuler's sister lived in a castle in southern Germany. Her sister hung the painting in the castle. In 1945, at the end of the war, American soldiers were stationed in the castle. Following the soldiers' departure, Schuler's sister noticed that the Monet was missing. She informed Schuler of the painting's disappearance in the fall of 1945.

Schuler contacted several authorities concerning the lost Monet. In 1946, she filed a report with the military government administering the Bonn-Cologne area after the war. The report no longer exists, but Schuler testified that it was a standard government form in which she briefly described items she had lost during the war. In 1948, in a letter to her lawyer regarding insurance claims on property she had lost, Schuler expressed regret about the missing Monet and inquired whether it was "possible to do anything about it." Her lawyer wrote back that the Monet would not be covered by insurance; he did not begin an investigation. In 1955, Schuler sent the 1943 photograph of the Monet to an art expert and asked him to investigate the painting's whereabouts. The art expert responded that the photo was insufficient evidence with which to begin a search, and Schuler did not pursue the matter with him further. Finally, in 1957 Schuler sent a list of art works she had lost during the war to the West German federal bureau of investigation. None of Schuler's efforts during the period 1945-1957 helped her to locate the Monet. Schuler made no further attempts to recover the painting after 1957.

In the meantime, the Monet had reappeared in the international art market by 1956. In December of that year, Galwyler & Co., Inc., an art gallery in Carolina City, acquired the Monet on consignment from an art dealer in Geneva, Switzerland. From December 1956 until June 1957, the painting was in the possession of the Galwyler art gallery in East Carolina, where it was shown to several prospective buyers. Defendant Martha Baldwin eventually purchased the painting in June 1957 for $30,900. The parties agree that Baldwin purchased the painting for value, in good faith, and without knowledge of any adverse claim.

Since 1957, Baldwin has kept the Monet in her Carolina City apartment, except for two occasions when it was displayed at public exhibitions. From October 29 to November 1, 1957, it was shown at a benefit at a local hotel, and in 1970 it was loaned back to the Galwyler art gallery for a one-month exhibition.

Schuler learned of Baldwin's possession of the Monet through the efforts of her nephew, Max Kern. In 1981, Kern was told by a cousin that Schuler had owned a Monet that had disappeared during the war. Shortly thereafter, Kern identified the painting in a published

book of Monet's works. The book indicated that the painting had been sold by the Galwyler art gallery in 1957 and that the gallery had exhibited it in 1970. In 1982, Schuler retained counsel in East Carolina and requested that the Galwyler art gallery identify the current owner. By letter dated December 27, 1982, Schuler demanded the return of the Monet from Baldwin. By letter dated February 1, 1983, Baldwin rejected the demand.

Schuler filed the present action to recover the Monet on February 16, 1983. At the conclusion of discovery, the parties submitted the case to the district court judge for decision on the record. The district court adjudged Schuler the owner of the painting and ordered Baldwin to return it. The judge found that Schuler had superior title and that the action was timely as she had exercised reasonable diligence in finding the painting.

Discussion

In this diversity action, we must apply the substantive law of East Carolina. *Klaxon Co. v. Stentor Elec. Mfg. Co.*, 313 U.S. 487, 61 S. Ct. 1020, 85 L. Ed. 1477 (1941). The East Carolina statute of limitations governing actions for recovery of stolen property requires that suit be brought within three years of the time the action accrued. E.C. Code § 4-201. Where the owner proceeds against one who innocently purchases the property in good faith, the statute of limitations period begins to run when the good faith purchaser acquired the property. Because Schuler did not bring an action within the three-year time period, her action will be barred unless equity justifies tolling the statute of limitations.

In order to avoid unjust results that might be caused by a strict application of the statute, we hold that under East Carolina law an original owner's "cause of action will not accrue until the injured party discovers, or by exercise of reasonable diligence and intelligence should have discovered, facts which form the basis of a cause of action." *O'Keeffe v. Snyder*, 416 A.2d 862, 869 (N.J. 1980).

Rule Explain

1287

The question of what constitutes due diligence that tolls the statute of limitations depends upon the circumstances of the case. When the action is for the return of stolen property, one of the key circumstances is the nature and value of the property at issue. *See id.* at 873. It has been recognized that when the property is valuable art, the search efforts that may reasonably be expected of an owner may be more exacting than where the property is of a different kind or of a lesser value. *Id.*

Reasons Schuler's investigation was minimal. The "reports" filed with the military government and West German federal bureau of investigation amounted to no more than a standard form listing personal items lost during the war and a one-sentence letter submitting a list of works that read only, "I lost during and after the war." Neither of these reports gave any details as to how, where, or when the Monet had disappeared, nor any other information that would be essential to a credible search. Schuler's contacts with her lawyer and the art expert were no more meaningful. She wrote to her lawyer regarding her insurance coverage. She mentioned that the Monet was among the art she had lost and inquired generally, "Is it possible to do anything about it?" It is not clear whether this was a request to find the painting or simply a question about insurance coverage. In any event, when her lawyer wrote back that the Monet would not be covered by insurance, Schuler let the matter drop. Schuler did ask the art expert to find the Monet. But, as with her lawyer, the investigation never was started; the art expert replied that he had insufficient information on which to proceed, and Schuler then abandoned the effort.

More revealing than the steps Schuler took to find the Monet are those she failed to take. Conspicuously absent from her attempts to locate the painting is any effort to take advantage of several mechanisms specifically set up to locate art lost during World War II. One such mechanism was a program initiated by the allied forces in Europe to handle works of art looted during the war. Under this program, Central Collecting Points (CCPs) were established throughout Germany where works of art turned in to the occupying forces were catalogued and stored until claimed by

their rightful owners. In 1949, administration of the program was transferred to the German government, and the paintings then located in the CCPs were given to a Trust Administration of the Federal Republic of Germany. Another program was run by the United States Department of State, which engaged in its own independent effort to locate stolen art. Schuler informed none of these agencies about the Monet, although she was aware of the CCPs; her family had attempted to recover other art from them. Nor did Schuler publicize her loss of the Monet in any one of several available listings designed to keep museums, galleries, and collectors vigilant for stolen art.

Most indicative of Schuler's lack of diligence is her failure to conduct any search for 24 years, from 1957 until 1981. Significantly, if Schuler had undertaken even the most minimal investigation during this period, she would very likely have discovered the Monet, since there were several published references to it in the art world. First, the Monet was pictured in the catalogues of two public exhibitions at which the painting was shown. Finally, the Monet is included in a published book that led to the painting's discovery by Kern. Consultation of any of these publications would likely have led Schuler to the Monet, as each one is connected to the Galwyler art gallery, which sold the painting to Baldwin.

X search. < investigation 24y.

The district court excused Schuler's failure to search for the Monet after 1957 on the grounds that she was elderly and that published references to the Monet were not generally circulated. But in 1957, when Schuler made her last attempt to locate the painting, she was only 63 years old. Moreover, though the published references may not have been generally circulated, they were accessible to anyone looking for them. Finally, although an individual, Schuler appears to be a wealthy and sophisticated art collector; even if she could not have mounted a more extensive investigation herself, she could have retained someone to do it for her.

→ PH.

→ Reason

The judgment of the district court, therefore, is reversed. *J*

APPENDIX

J

Objective Analysis Checklist of a Fact-Based Issue: Multiple Issues and Multiple Cases

NOTE: The purpose of this checklist is to help you think critically about the structure and content of your paper. This checklist is not an exhaustive list of everything that must be included in your paper.

I.   Framework/Introductory Section:

_____ Have you told your reader the issue you are addressing in your memorandum, and have you provided enough factual context when introducing that issue so your reader understands *why* you are addressing the issue, without reading anything else? You should be able to set this up in one sentence, two at the most.

_____ Have you included any main rule that would be helpful as general information, and have you cited to the source of that rule?

_____ Have you told your reader what will follow? That is, have you set out the legal issues in the introductory section so your reader knows what you will be focusing on?

_____ (Optional) Have you told your reader your conclusion in this case (turning this first paragraph into a thesis paragraph)?

_____ Have you provided an initial framework/introductory section at the beginning of the discussion but have also provided introductory paragraphs at the beginning of your discussion of any legal requirement that involves an analysis of more than one legal point?

_____ Have you left until later in your discussion any information that is more helpful and relevant to your reader when providing TRAC for one of the specific legal questions you are addressing, rather than including it in this introduction? For example, have you waited to explain each factor or requirement and those cases relevant to the factor or requirement until you are ready to provide the complete TRAC of the factor or requirement?

II. Large-Scale Structure:

A. *Read the first sentence of each paragraph to check your structure:*

____ Do you make the structure of your discussion obvious through clear topic, thesis, or transitional sentences? Check each time you move from one legal point to the next or from your stronger position to your weaker position within the analysis of a disputable issue. Is the transition logical and clear to your reader?

____ If you begin a paragraph explaining a case name, have you first stated *why* you are explaining the case? For example, if you are explaining a case because you have introduced a new legal point, introduce that new legal point first in a topic sentence and *then* explain the case. In other words, lead with the law.

____ Have you avoided a case-by-case analysis? If you find that while addressing the same legal requirement you are explaining one case, then applying it to your client's facts, then explaining a second case, then applying it to your client's facts, you have probably created a case-by-case analysis. Instead, explain the cases together and then apply to your client's case.

B. *Check your placement of the explanation of the cases (rule explanation):*

____ Have you provided the explanations where they are most relevant and helpful in your analysis and for your reader?

____ Have you provided each rule explanation *before* applying the facts of that case to the facts of your client's case?

C. *Check your discussion of any legal point in dispute:*

____ When you provide a TRAC with an analysis of both a stronger and a weaker position, do not conclude until you finish analyzing the weaker position. Then provide the conclusion for your entire TRAC of the legal point. If you conclude after analyzing your stronger position and then continue with an analysis of the weaker position on the same point, your reader will likely be confused (thinking that the TRAC ended after analyzing the stronger position and concluding).

> **For example, don't do this:**
> A court is likely to find that Party A made a valid offer.
>
> [analysis/support for valid offer]
>
> Therefore, Party A's offer was valid.
> [new paragraph] However, Party A may not have made a valid offer.
> [You have now provided two sentences back to back, a conclusion and a transition, which contradict each other substantively. Omit the conclusion of the stronger position, and carefully word your transition to the weaker position.]

D. *Check your transitions from one legal point to the next legal point.*

____ Check each time you move from one legal point to the next. Is the transition logical and clear to your reader? For example, if you concluded that Party A did not make a valid offer, you must provide a logical transition to the discussion of the next legal point, e.g., "However, should a court find the offer valid . . . ," and then move on to the next requirement, such as the acceptance requirement.

III. Discussion/Analysis:

A. *Check any legal point that is not in dispute:*
____ Have you provided only as much of a TRAC as is necessary?

    ____ a topic or thesis sentence telling the reader what legal point you are addressing?

    ____ any helpful definitions or explanations of the legal point, if necessary?

    ____ any explanation of a relevant case, if required?

    ____ the specific relevant facts from your case that support what is the obvious outcome regarding this legal point?

B. *Check any legal issue that is in dispute:*
____ Support both positions. However, do not make up facts or speculate about events not provided in the assignment. Use only what's provided to you in the cases and in your client's facts. If a legal point is in dispute, use more than one case. Additional cases may be explained in full or cited with a parenthetical that provides the factual holding of the relevant issue.

    1. Check the placement of the rules or definitions of the rules

    ____ The rules or definitions of the rules should be placed after the topic or thesis sentence and before you explain the relevant case(s). Provide the key language word for word and in quotes.

    2. Read the first time you mention a *cited case* that you will use in your analysis:

    ____ Have you provided a complete explanation of the case, including

        ____ **key facts** regarding the legal point you are addressing, including any quoted testimony or other relevant language that is vital to the legal analysis. Include also enough facts to give your reader a quick visual picture of what happened relevant to the legal point you are addressing.

        ____ **the court's holding** regarding the specific legal point you are addressing.

        ____ **the court's overall reasoning** (why it held as it did).

        ____ **the overall holding** in the case.

    ____ Have you used neutral names or generic references to the parties in the cited cases (e.g., buyer/seller, parent/child, etc.)?

_____ Have you provided the specific facts here in the rule explanation and again in the analysis, where you are comparing or contrasting those case facts to the facts in your client's case? This is the one situation where repetition is needed.

3. **Read the first time you discuss *your client's facts* in your analysis:**

_____ Make sure your references to your client's facts are as explicit and specific as necessary. Remember, you are writing to an unfamiliar reader. Don't rely on the reader's knowledge of the facts.

_____ You should be referring to the client's facts only (1) in any introductory paragraph, to provide some factual context for the legal issue you are addressing; or (2) after providing the explanation of a legal point along with the relevant case(s), so the law can be applied to the client's facts.

_____ Have you provided direct quotes when a party's statement is essential to the analysis?

_____ Have you used personal names when referring to the parties in your client's case?

4. **Check your use of the facts and your case analogies and distinctions:**

_____ **Check your case analogies and distinctions:** When comparing and contrasting facts from your case to the facts in the cited cases, provide the explicit, key facts from both cases. Be sure to make a clear connection between the facts of your case and the facts of the cited case(s). For example, you do *not* want to say, "Similar to *Case B*, Party A . . ." You must state the *specific* facts you are comparing. Draw an arrow connecting the cited case facts and your case facts with a pen. The facts should be connected within the same sentence or in adjacent sentences.

For example:
"Similar to the condition in *Case B*, where the buyer said he would purchase the goods, but only if they arrived on a certain date, here Simpson agreed to buy the towels as long as they reached the company's warehouse by November 12."

_____ **Have you indicated the *significance* of those facts and case analogies and distinctions?**
Use the facts from your case (that cannot be compared or contrasted to the facts in cited cases) and the case analogies/distinctions to draw *reasonable inferences* that support the legal point you are making. Do not simply state the important facts, and

case analogies and distinctions, and then conclude. Make a clear connection between the facts and the law.

5. **Check your placement and use of public policy:**
   ____ Have you provided relevant policy only if necessary and only where it is most relevant to your analysis and therefore to your reader?

6. **Check for completeness and accuracy:**
   ____ Have you provided all rules, definitions, and other general explanations to help explain the legal point you are analyzing?
   ____ Have you considered all possible ways to use the facts, law, and policy to support each side?
   ____ Have you accurately stated the facts, law, and policy throughout your document?

IV.   Conclusion(s):

____ Does the conclusion summarize the key points in your analysis, providing reference to the key law, facts, and policy necessary to support your conclusion (if you have the space)?

____ Have you written this conclusion so it will make sense if read first?

____ Have you answered the question asked by the supervising attorney?

____ Have you *not* included new law and analysis in this conclusion? (If important, that law or analysis belongs in the discussion section.)

____ Have you omitted references to authority, unless pivotal to an understanding of the summary?

____ Have you omitted statements such as "I believe," "I feel," "It is my opinion that" (here and throughout your paper)?

V.   Format, Style, and Citation:

A.   Check your quoted text:
____ Have you quoted key language
   ____ from any statutes, rules, or definitions, where necessary?
   ____ from the court's reasoning?
   ____ from public policy, if relevant?
   ____ from witness testimony or other language from the cited cases that is essential to the analysis of a legal point?

____ Have you properly integrated any quotes within the larger sentence? When integrating quotes into a sentence, make sure the overall sentence is grammatically correct if read without quotation marks.

Use of brackets: Quoted language — "Every good boy does fine."

Example of the quote integrated into the sentence: I remember my mother teaching me the notes on the white spaces of a musical scale by telling me to remember the phrase that says that "[e]very good boy does fine."

Or

I remember my mother teaching me the notes on the white spaces of a musical scale by telling me to remember the phrase, "**E**very **g**ood **b**oy **d**oes fine."

____ **Have you used ellipses (three spaced periods) properly to show where original quoted language has been deleted?**

When introducing a quote that starts in the middle of the quoted sentence, you do not need to provide ellipses at the beginning of the quote. Your reader will know this language was not at the beginning of the sentence simply because the first quoted word is in a lowercase rather than a capital letter.

When providing a quote where additional language was found at the end of the quoted sentence, provide the three ellipses and add a fourth period to show the end of the sentence.

____ Quotation marks always go

____ outside commas and periods.

____ inside colons and semicolons.

____ inside or outside question marks and exclamation points, depending on whether the question mark is part of the quote.

B. Check for Grammar, Style, Punctuation, and Typographical Errors:

Suggestion: Read your paper out loud, sentence by sentence backwards, and check a grammar book where necessary. You may also want to check your past papers for comments to be sure you have corrected in this paper any problems noted in those past papers. Here are some additional guidelines.

____ Do not include rhetorical questions.

____ Do not use contractions.

____ Write out numbers to ninety-nine.

____ Refer to the court as an *it*, not a *they*.

____ Prefer nouns over pronouns, unless doing so makes your sentence awkward.

____ Check the clauses around your commas. If you find an independent clause (subject and verb) on either side of a comma, with no conjunction separating the two, you have written a run-on sentence. To fix this, you need to either (1) change the single sentence into two sentences; (2) change the comma to a semicolon; or (3) if appropriate, add a conjunction (such as *and* or *but*) after the comma and before the second independent clause.

For example:

The railroad station is nearby, it is always crowded.

To correct, we can write either

(1) The railroad station is nearby. The station is always crowded.

(2) The railroad station is nearby; it is always crowded.

(3) The railroad station is nearby, and it is always crowded.

APPENDIX
K

Small v. United States

Small v. United States
544 U.S. *385 (2005)

. . .

*386 Justice Breyer delivered the opinion of the Court. [Justices Stevens, O'Connor, Souter, and Ginsburg joined.]

*387 The United States Criminal Code makes it "unlawful for any person . . . who has been *convicted in any court*, of a crime punishable by imprisonment for a term exceeding one year . . . to . . . possess . . . any firearm." 18 U.S.C. § 922(g)(1) (emphasis added).

The question before us focuses upon the words "convicted in any court." Does this phrase apply only to convictions entered in any *domestic* court or to *foreign* convictions as well? We hold that the phrase encompasses only domestic, not foreign, convictions.

I

In 1994 petitioner, Gary Small, was convicted in a Japanese court of having tried to smuggle several pistols, a rifle, and ammunition into Japan. Small was sentenced to five years' imprisonment. *United States v. Small*, 183 F. Supp. 2d 755, 757, n. 3 (W.D. Pa. 2002). After his release, Small returned to the United States, where he bought a gun from a Pennsylvania gun dealer. Federal authorities subsequently charged Small under the "unlawful gun possession" statute here at issue. *United States v. Small*, 333 F.3d 425, 426 (3d Cir. 2003). Small pleaded guilty while reserving the right to challenge his conviction on the ground that his earlier conviction, being a foreign conviction, fell outside the scope of the illegal gun possession statute. The Federal District Court rejected Small's argument, as did the Court of Appeals for the Third Circuit. 183 F. Supp. 2d at 759; 333 F.3d at 427, n. 2. Because the Circuits disagree about the matter, we granted certiorari. *Compare United States v. Atkins*, 872 F.2d 94, 96 (4th Cir. 1989) ("convicted in any court" includes foreign convictions); *United States v. Winson*, 793 F.2d 754, 757-759 (6th Cir. 1986) (same), *with United States v. Gayle*, 342 F.3d 89, 95 (2d Cir. 2003) ("convicted in any court" does not include foreign convictions); *United States v. Concha*, 233 F.3d 1249, 1256 (10th Cir. 2000) (same).

*388 II

A

The question before us is whether the statutory reference "convicted in *any* court" includes a conviction entered in a *foreign* court. The word "any" considered alone cannot answer this question. In ordinary life, a speaker who says, "I'll see any film," may or may not mean to include films shown in another city. In law, a legislature that uses the statutory phrase "any person" may or may not mean to include "persons" outside "the jurisdiction of the state." *See, e.g., United States v. Palmer*, 3 Wheat. 610, 631 (1818) (Marshall, C.J.). . . .

In determining the scope of the statutory phrase we find help in the "commonsense notion that Congress generally legislates with domestic concerns in mind." *Smith v. United States*, 507 U.S. 197, 204 (1993). This notion has led the Court to adopt the legal presumption that Congress ordinarily intends its statutes to have domestic, not extraterritorial, ***389** application. . . . That presumption would apply, for example, were we to consider whether this statute prohibits unlawful gun possession abroad as well as domestically. And, although the presumption against extraterritorial application does not apply directly to this case, we believe a similar assumption is appropriate when we consider the scope of the phrase "convicted in any court" here.

For one thing, the phrase describes one necessary portion of the "gun possession" activity that is prohibited as a matter of domestic law. For another, considered as a group, foreign convictions differ from domestic convictions in important ways. Past foreign convictions for crimes punishable by more than one year's imprisonment may include a conviction for conduct that domestic laws would permit, for example, for engaging in economic conduct that our society might encourage. *See, e.g.,* Art. 153 of the Criminal Code of the Russian Soviet Federated Socialist Republic, in Soviet Criminal Law and Procedure 171 (H. Berman & J. Spindler transls. 2d ed. 1972) (criminalizing "Private Entrepreneurial Activity"); Art. 153, *id.*, at 172 (criminalizing "Speculation," which is defined as "the buying up and reselling of goods or any other articles for the purpose of making a profit"); *cf., e.g.,* Gaceta Oficial de la Republica de Cuba, ch. II, Art. 103, p. 68 (Dec. 30, 1987) (forbidding propaganda that incites against the social order, international solidarity, or the Communist

State). They would include a conviction from a legal system that is inconsistent with an American understanding of fairness. *See, e.g.,* U.S. Dept. of State, Country Reports on Human Rights Practices for 2003, Submitted to the House Committee on International Relations and the Senate Committee on Foreign Relations, 108th Cong., 2d Sess., 702-705, ***390** 1853, 2023 (Joint Comm. Print 2004) (describing failures of "due process" and citing examples in which "the testimony of one man equals that of two women"). And they would include a conviction for conduct that domestic law punishes far less severely. *See, e.g.,* Singapore Vandalism Act, ch. 108, §§ 2, 3, III Statutes of Republic of Singapore p. 258 (imprisonment for up to three years for an act of vandalism). Thus, the key statutory phrase "convicted in any court of, a crime punishable by imprisonment for a term exceeding one year" somewhat less reliably identifies dangerous individuals for the purposes of U.S. law where foreign convictions, rather than domestic convictions, are at issue.

In addition, it is difficult to read the statute as asking judges or prosecutors to refine its definitional distinctions where foreign convictions are at issue. To somehow weed out inappropriate foreign convictions that meet the statutory definition is not consistent with the statute's language; it is not easy for those not versed in foreign laws to accomplish; and it would leave those previously convicted in a foreign court (say of economic crimes) uncertain about their legal obligations. . . .

These considerations, suggesting significant differences between foreign and domestic convictions, do not dictate our ultimate conclusion. . . . They simply convince us that we should apply an ordinary assumption about the reach of domestically oriented statutes here — an assumption that helps us determine Congress' intent where Congress likely did not consider the matter and where other indicia of intent are in approximate balance. We consequently assume a congressional intent that the phrase *391 "convicted in any court" applies domestically, not extraterritorially. But, at the same time, we stand ready to revise this assumption should statutory language, context, history, or purpose show the contrary.

B

We have found no convincing indication to the contrary here. The statute's language does not suggest any intent to reach beyond domestic convictions. Neither does it mention foreign convictions nor is its subject matter special, say, immigration or terrorism, where one could argue that foreign convictions would seem especially relevant. To the contrary, if read to include foreign convictions, the statute's language creates anomalies. . . .

For example, the statute specifies that predicate crimes include "a misdemeanor crime of domestic violence." 18 U.S.C. § 922(g)(9). [T]he language specifies that these predicate crimes include only crimes that are "misdemeanor[s] under Federal or State law." 18 U.S.C. § 921(a)(33)(A). If "convicted in any court" refers only to domestic convictions, this language creates no problem. If the phrase also refers to *392 foreign convictions, the language creates an apparently senseless distinction between (covered) domestic relations misdemeanors committed within the United States and (uncovered) domestic relations misdemeanors committed abroad. . . .

*393 The statute's lengthy legislative history confirms the fact that Congress did not consider whether foreign convictions should or should not serve as a predicate to liability under the provision here at issue. Congress did consider a Senate bill containing language that would have restricted predicate offenses to domestic offenses. *See* S. Rep. No. 1501, 90th Cong., 2d Sess., p. 31 (1968) (defining predicate crimes in terms of "Federal" crimes "punishable by a term of imprisonment exceeding one year" and crimes "determined

by the laws of the State to be a felony"). And the Conference Committee ultimately rejected this version in favor of language that speaks of those "convicted in any court, of a crime punishable by a term of imprisonment exceeding one year." H.R. Conf. Rep. No. 1956, 90th Cong., 2d Sess., pp. 28-29 (1968), U.S. Code Cong. & Admin. News 1968, 4426, 4428. But the history does not suggest that this language change reflected a congressional view on the matter before us. Rather, the enacted version is simpler and it avoids potential difficulties arising out of the fact that States may define the term "felony" differently. And as far as the legislative history is concerned, these latter virtues of the new language fully explain the change. Thus, those who use legislative history to help discern congressional intent will see the history here as silent, hence a neutral factor, that simply confirms the obvious, namely, that Congress did not consider the issue. . . .

The statute's purpose *does* offer some support for a reading of the phrase that includes foreign convictions. As the Government points out, Congress sought to "'keep guns out of the hands of those who have demonstrated that they may not be trusted to possess a firearm without becoming a threat to society.'" Brief for United States 16 (quoting *Dickerson v. New Banner Institute, Inc.*, 460 U.S. 103, 112 (1983)). . . . *394 And, as the dissent properly notes, one convicted of a serious crime abroad may well be as dangerous as one convicted of a similar crime in the United States.

The force of this argument is weakened significantly, however, by the empirical fact that, according to the Government, since 1968, there have probably been no more than "10 to a dozen" instances in which such a foreign conviction has served as a predicate for a felon-in-possession prosecution. [Citation omitted.] This empirical fact reinforces the likelihood that Congress, at best, paid no attention to the matter.

C

In sum, we have no reason to believe that Congress considered the added enforcement advantages flowing from inclusion of foreign crimes, weighing them against, say, the potential unfairness of preventing those with inapt foreign convictions from possessing guns. The statute itself and its history offer only congressional silence. Given the reasons for disfavoring an inference of extraterritorial coverage from a statute's total silence and our initial assumption against such coverage, we conclude that the phrase "convicted in any court" refers only to domestic courts, not to foreign courts. Congress, of course, remains free to change this conclusion through statutory amendment.

For these reasons, the judgment of the Third Circuit is reversed, and the case is remanded for further proceedings consistent with this opinion.

It is so ordered.

The Chief Justice took no part in the decision of this case.[1]

Justice Thomas, with whom Justice Scalia and Justice Kennedy join, dissenting. ***395** . . .

[T]he Court distorts the plain meaning of the statute and departs from established principles of statutory construction. I respectfully dissent. ***396** . . .

II

The plain terms of § 922(g)(1) prohibit Small — a person "convicted in any court of, a crime punishable by imprisonment for a term exceeding one year" — from possessing a firearm in the United States. "Read naturally, the word 'any' has an expansive meaning, that is, 'one or some indiscriminately of whatever kind.'" *United States v. Gonzales*, 520 U.S. 1, 5 (1997) (quoting *Webster's Third New International Dictionary* 97 (1976)). . . . ***397** The broad phrase "any court" unambiguously includes all judicial bodies . . . with jurisdic-

tion to impose the requisite conviction — a conviction for a crime punishable by imprisonment for a term of more than a year. Indisputably, Small was convicted in a Japanese court of crimes punishable by a prison term exceeding one year.

The clear terms of the statute prohibit him from possessing a gun in the United States.

Of course, the phrase "any court," like all other statutory language, must be read in context. *E.g., Deal v. United States*, 508 U.S. 129, 132 (1993). The context of § 922(g)(1), however, suggests that there is no geographic limit on the scope of "any court." [Footnote omitted.] By contrast to other parts of the firearms-control law that expressly mention only state or federal law, "any court" is not qualified by jurisdiction. . . . ***398** Congress' explicit use of "Federal" and "State" in other provisions shows that it specifies such restrictions when it wants to do so. . . .

III

Faced with the inescapably broad text, the Court narrows the statute by assuming that the text applies only to domestic convictions, criticizing the accuracy of foreign convictions as a proxy for dangerousness, finding that the broad, natural reading of the statute "creates anomalies," and suggesting that Congress did not consider whether foreign convictions counted. None of these arguments is persuasive.

*399 A

The Court first invents a canon of statutory interpretation — what it terms "an ordinary assumption about the reach of domestically oriented statutes," to cabin the statute's reach. . . . The extraterritoriality cases cited by the Court do not support its new assumption. [The cited cases] restrict federal statutes from applying outside the territorial jurisdiction of the United States. . . . ***400** These straightforward applications of the extraterritoriality canon, restricting federal statutes from reaching conduct *beyond U.S. borders*, lend no support to

---

1. Chief Justice Rehnquist was ill and unable to participate.

the Court's unprecedented rule restricting a federal statute from reaching conduct *within U.S. borders.* . . . Aside from the extraterritoriality canon, which the Court properly concedes does not apply, I know of no principle of statutory construction justifying the result the Court reaches. Its concession that the canon is inapposite should therefore end this case. . . . *401*

B

In support of its narrow reading of the statute, the majority opines that the natural reading has inappropriate results. It points to differences between foreign and domestic convictions, primarily attacking the reliability of foreign convictions as a proxy for identifying dangerous individuals. . . . *402* Surely a "reasonable human being" drafting this language would have considered whether foreign convictions are, on average and as a whole, accurate at gauging dangerousness and culpability. *403* . . .

C

The majority worries that reading § 922(g)(1) to include foreign convictions "creates anomalies" under other firearms control provisions. It is true, as the majority notes, that the natural reading of § 922(g)(1) affords domestic offenders more lenient treatment than foreign ones in some respects. *404* . . .

These outcomes cause the Court undue concern. They certainly present no occasion to employ, nor does the Court invoke, the canon against absurdities. We should employ that canon only "where the result of applying the plain language would be, in a genuine sense, absurd, *i.e.*, where it is quite impossible that Congress could have intended the result . . . and where the alleged absurdity is so clear as to be obvious to most anyone." *Public Citizen v. Department of Justice*, 491 U.S. 440, 470-471 (1989) (Kennedy, J., concurring in judgment). . . .

[T]he majority abandons the statute's plain meaning based on results that are at most incongruous and certainly not absurd. As with the extraterritoriality canon, the Court applies a mutant version of a recognized canon when the recognized canon is itself inapposite. *405* Whatever the utility of canons as guides to congressional intent, they are useless when modified in ways that Congress could never have imagined in enacting § 922(g)(1). . . .

D

The Court hypothesizes "that Congress did not consider whether the generic phrase 'convicted in any court' applies to domestic as well as foreign convictions," and takes that as license to restrict the clear breadth of the text. Whether the Court's empirical assumption is correct is anyone's guess. Regardless, we have properly rejected this method of guesswork-as-interpretation. . . . *406* Here, . . . "our task is not the hopeless one of ascertaining what the legislators who passed the law would have decided had they reconvened to consider [this] particular cas[e]," [*Beecham v. United States*, 511 U.S. 368, 374 (1994)], but the eminently more manageable one of following the ordinary meaning of the text they enacted. That meaning includes foreign convictions. . . .

I do not even agree, moreover, that the legislative history is silent. As the Court describes, the Senate bill that formed the basis for this legislation was amended in Conference, to change the predicate offenses from " 'Federal' crimes" punishable by more than one year's imprisonment and "crimes 'determined by the laws of a State to be a felony' " to conviction " 'in any court, of a crime punishable by a term of imprisonment exceeding one year.' " The Court seeks to explain this change by saying that "the enacted version is simpler and . . . avoids potential difficulties arising out of the fact that States may define the term 'felony' differently." But that does not explain why all limiting reference to "Federal" and "State" was eliminated. The revised provision would have been just as simple, and would just as well have avoided the potential difficulties, if it read "convicted in any Federal or State court of a crime punishable by a term of imprisonment exceeding one year." Surely that would have been the natural change if *407 expansion beyond federal and state convictions were not intended. The elimination of the limiting references suggests that not *only* federal and state convictions were meant to be covered.

IV

The Court never convincingly explains its departure from the natural meaning of § 922(g)(1). Instead, it institutes the troubling rule that "any" does not really mean "any," but may mean "some subset of 'any,'" even if nothing in the context so indicates; it distorts the established canons against extraterritoriality and absurdity; it faults without reason Congress' use of foreign convictions to gauge dangerousness and culpability; and it employs discredited methods of determining congressional intent. I respectfully dissent.

APPENDIX
L

Citation Chart

The following chart provides a quick reference to basic citation forms using the *ALWD Citation Manual*. Note: The bullet points are used for examples of short citation forms. This chart does not include how to refer to a source in a textual sentence. Even though this text focuses on citation to sources included in office memoranda and court documents (when the citation is part of the regular text), each source in the following chart includes an example of how that same source would be properly cited in other documents where footnotes or endnotes are used.[1] Always check your citation manual for specific rules when citing.

(1) Constitutional provisions:

Text and footnote form:

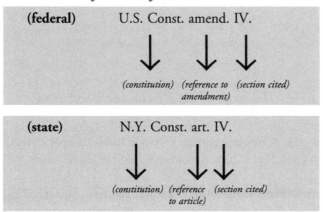

---

1. Always cite to the official source, where possible. The citation manuals provide the various resources in which a source is located; the citation manuals also state to which resource to cite first, second, third, and so on.

- If referring to a specific section of a constitutional amendment or article, add a section symbol and the appropriate section number.

For example:

U.S. Const. amend. IV, § **2.**

- If the reference is also to a clause within a section, indicate by adding "cl. x" after the reference to the section.

For example:

U.S. Const. amend. IV, § 2, **cl. 3.**

(2) Statutory provisions:

Text and footnote form:

(federal)   23 U.S.C. § 1331 (2005).

(title) (code)   (section #) (year of publication)

(state)   810 Ill. Comp. Stat. § 5/2-14(1) (2001).

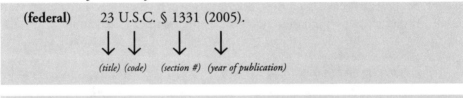

(title)   (code)   (section #)   (year of publication)

Computer Assisted Legal Research (CALR) (in both text and footnote form):

(federal)   23 U.S.C. § 1331 (Westlaw current through 2005 1st Spec. Sess.).
                23 U.S.C. § 1331 (Lexis current through 2005 1st Spec. Sess.).

(state)   810 Ill. Comp. Stat. § 5/2-314(1)(Westlaw current through 2001 Reg. Sess.).

Short-form citations to statutes:

Once you have provided the complete citation to a statutory provision, you may thereafter use one of the short citation forms, depending on where the subsequent citation is located.

"*Id.*" indicates that the citation is to the same source as the immediately preceding citation.

Text form and footnote form:[2]

(federal)   If the next citation to the same statute immediately follows the full citation:

• *Id.* at § 1331(a).

If other citations are provided between the first full citation to the statute and the next citation to the same statute:

• 23 U.S.C. § 1331(a).

(state)   If the next citation to the same statute immediately follows the full citation:

• *Id.* at § 5/2-314(1)(a).

If other citations are provided between the first full citation to the statute and the next citation to the same statute:

• 810 Ill. Comp. Stat. § 5/2-314(1)(a).

(3) Case law:

Text and footnote form:[3]

(federal)

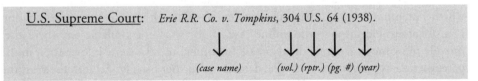

U.S. Supreme Court: *Erie R.R. Co. v. Tompkins*, 304 U.S. 64 (1938).

↓   ↓ ↓ ↓   ↓

(case name)   *(vol.) (rptr.) (pg. #) (year)*

Federal Circuit Court:

Lopez v. Immig. & Nat. Serv., 775 F.2d 1015 (9th Cir. 1985).

↓   ↓ ↓ ↓   ↓

(case name)   *(vol.) (rptr.) (pg. #) (circuit & year)*

---

2. The *ALWD Citation Manual* provides extensive rules on citing case names. Check *ALWD Citation Manual* Rule 12.2 and Appendix 3.

3. The *ALWD Citation Manual* allows you to use either italics or underlining when writing the case name.

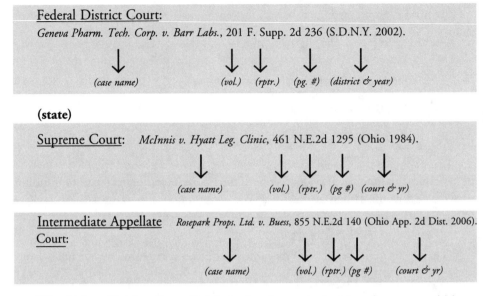

Federal District Court:

Geneva Pharm. Tech. Corp. v. Barr Labs., 201 F. Supp. 2d 236 (S.D.N.Y. 2002).

↓ (case name)   ↓ (vol.) ↓ (rptr.)   ↓ (pg. #)   ↓ (district & year)

(state)

<u>Supreme Court</u>:   *McInnis v. Hyatt Leg. Clinic*, 461 N.E.2d 1295 (Ohio 1984).

↓ (case name)   ↓ (vol.) ↓ (rptr.) ↓ (pg #) ↓ (court & yr)

<u>Intermediate Appellate</u>   *Rosepark Props. Ltd. v. Buess*, 855 N.E.2d 140 (Ohio App. 2d Dist. 2006).
<u>Court</u>:

↓ (case name)   ↓ (vol.) ↓ (rptr.) ↓ (pg #)   ↓ (court & yr)

If both the official and unofficial citation is required, this reference would be:

Rosepark Prop., Ltd. v. Buess, 167 Ohio App. 3d 366, 855 N.E.2d 140 (2d Dist. 2006).

Note: In the above example, the court designation is no longer included with the parenthetical information because it is obvious in the official citation.

CALR (for both text and footnote form):

You need to cite to an online case only when the case is not available in a printed source. This usually occurs when a case is published online but is not an officially reported case. If you plan to use an unreported court opinion to support a legal point you are analyzing, always check the court rules in that jurisdiction to determine whether an unreported case has any precedential value. Otherwise, the proper citation is easily accessible through the online case. If a case is not available anywhere else, provide the same case name, the database identifier, and the same information in the parenthetical as provided above. The database identifier usually includes the year, the name of the database, and the document number. Check the *ALWD Citation Manual*, Rule 12.12.

For example:

McIntyre v. McIntyre, 2005 WL 3536419 (Ohio App. Dec. 23, 2005).

↓ (case name)   ↓ (year) ↓ (Westlaw identifier)   ↓ (court)   ↓ (date decided)

Pinpoint pages:

When referring to a specific reference in a case, provide the page on which the referenced information is located. For example, in the following text form the pinpoint citation is page 68:

> *Erie R.R. Co. v. Tompkins*, 304 U.S. 64, **68** (1938).

If you acquire your case from an online source, you will need to follow carefully the system for pinpoint references, known as star pagination. All citations to the same case will be located at the top of the case, in the heading. For example:

> ***304 U.S. 64, **58 S.Ct. 817, ***82 L.Ed. 1188**
>
> Supreme Court of the United States.
>
> ERIE R. CO.
>
> v.
>
> TOMPKINS.
>
> No. 367.
>
> Argued Jan. 31, 1938.
>
> Decided April 25, 1938.

The official reporter citation, the United States Reports (U.S.), is preceded by a single asterisk (*); the Supreme Court Reporter citation (S. Ct.) is preceded by two asterisks (**); and the United States Supreme Court Reports, Lawyer's Edition citation (L. Ed.) is preceded by three asterisks (***). You need cite only to the United States Reports in your document; however, the online version of the case will track all three reporters. You must be especially careful, therefore, that you follow the correct star pagination throughout the case and note the correct pinpoint page. When you see a new page number, this indicates that the official page has just changed and all the text that follows can be found on that page in the official reporter, until yet another page number is set down in star pagination form.

◆ *For example:*

> ***69** Mr. Justice BRANDEIS delivered the opinion of the Court.
>
> The question for decision is whether the oft-challenged doctrine of Swift v. Tyson[1] shall now be disapproved.
>
> Tompkins, a citizen of Pennsylvania, was injured on a dark night by a passing freight train of the Erie Railroad Company while walking along its right of way at Hughestown in that state. He claimed that the accident occurred through negligence in the operation, or maintenance, of the train; that he was rightfully on the premises as licensee because on a commonly used beaten footpath which ran

for a short distance alongside the tracks; and that he was struck by something which looked like a door projecting from one of the moving cars. To enforce that claim he brought an action in the federal court for Southern New York, which had jurisdiction because the company is a corporation of that state. It denied liability; and the case was tried by a jury.

*70 The Erie insisted that its duty to Tompkins was no greater than that owed to a trespasser. It contended, among other things, that its duty to Tompkins, and hence its liability, should be determined in accordance with the Pennsylvania law; that under the law of Pennsylvania, as declared by its highest court, persons who use pathways along the railroad right of way — that is, a longitudinal pathway as distinguished from a crossing — are to be deemed trespassers; and that the railroad is not liable for injuries to undiscovered trespassers resulting from its negligence, unless it be wanton or willful. Tompkins denied that any such rule had been established by the decisions of the Pennsylvania courts; and contended that, since there was no statute of the state on the subject, the railroad's duty and liability is to be determined in federal courts as a matter of general law.

The trial judge refused to rule that the applicable law precluded recovery. The jury brought in a verdict of $30,000; and the judgment entered thereon was affirmed by the Circuit Court of Appeals, which held (2d Cir., 90 F.2d 603, 604), that it was unnecessary to consider whether the law of Pennsylvania was as contended, because the question was one not of local, but of general, law, and that 'upon questions of general law the federal courts are free, in absence of a local statute, to exercise their independent judgment as to what the law is; and it is well settled that the question of the responsibility of a railroad for injuries caused by its servants is one of general law. . . . Where the public has made open and notorious use of a railroad right of way for a long period of time and without objection, the company owes to persons on such permissive pathway a duty of care in the operation of its trains. . . . It is likewise generally recognized law that a jury may find that negligence exists toward a pedestrian using a permissive path on the railroad right of way if he is hit by some object projecting from the side of the train.'

*71 The Erie had contended that application of the Pennsylvania rule was required, among other things, by section 34 of the Federal Judiciary Act of September 24, 1789, c. 20, 28 U.S.C. § 725, **819 28 U.S.C.A. § 725, which provides: 'The laws of the several States, except where the Constitution, treaties, or statutes of the United States otherwise require or provide, shall be regarded as rules of decision in trials at common law, in the courts of the United States, in cases where they apply.'

In the above example, pages 69, 70, and 71 of the United States Reports are shown using a single asterisk. Page 819 of the Supreme Court Reporter is shown with a double asterisk. When the only citation is to an online database, pinpoint references are made to the appropriate page reference online rather than the actual page of a reported case. To provide a pinpoint page, add an "at" after the database identifier, and then provide the pinpoint page(s).

For example:

McIntyre v. McIntyre, 2005 WL 3536419 **at *3** (Ohio App. Dec. 23, 2005).

Short-form citations to cases:

Once you have provided a full citation to a case, you may thereafter use one of the short citation forms, depending on where the subsequent citations are located.

(1) *Use of Id.*
A citation to "*Id.*" indicates that the citation is to the same source as the immediately preceding citation.

(a) *Id.* is used alone if the information in the second reference is found on the same page as the information provided in the immediately preceding citation.

(b) "*Id.* at xxx" is used if the information in the second reference is located in the same case as the immediately preceding reference but is found on a different page. In place of "xxx" provide the actual page number where the information is located.

For example:

- *Id.* at 70.

This would be the proper citation to information found on page 70 of *Erie Railroad Co. v. Tompkins*, where the immediately preceding citation was also to *Erie*, but the second reference is on a different page than the first reference.

(2) *Use of the short citation form:*
Short citation forms are used when you have already provided the full case name and citation to a source, and you want to cite to that case again. The subsequent citation, however, does not immediately follow a citation to the same case, so the use of "*Id.*" is inappropriate.

You may shorten the case name once provided in full. Thus, "*Erie R.R. Co. v. Tompkins*" could become "*Erie.*" The shortened name is followed by the volume and name of the reporter where the case is found, along with "at xxx." The "xxx" is replaced with the pinpoint page to where the information you are citing is located.

For example:

- *Erie*, 304 U.S. at 70.

<u>Note:</u> The above two examples are the only times "at" is used when citing. You will *never* provide a citation that looks like one of the following:

Wrong: *Erie* at 70.
Wrong: *Erie R.R. v. Tompkins*, 304 U.S. 64 at 70 (1938).
Wrong: *Erie*, 304 U.S. 64 at 70.

(4) Law review articles:

Text and footnote form:

Caleb Nelson, *What Is Textualism?* 91 Va. L. Rev. 347 (2005).

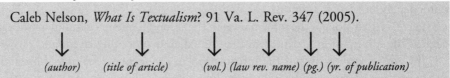

CALR:

If an article is provided on the Internet, provide the same information as with a footnote: the author, *the title of the article* (in italics), the volume number, the abbreviation for the periodical, any necessary article number, and the date (in parentheses). In addition, at the end provide the URL. See Rule 23.1(i) of the *ALWD Citation Manual.*

For example:

Caleb Nelson, *What Is Textualism?* 91 Va. L. Rev. 347 (2005), http://www.virginialawreview.org/content/pdfs/91/347.pdf.

Short-form citation to law review articles:

Text form:

When the citation follows immediately after a citation to the same source:

• *Id.* at 348.

When the citation does not immediately follow a citation to the same source:

• Nelson, 91 Va. L. Rev. at 348.

Footnote form:

When the citation follows immediately after a citation to the same source:

• *Id.* at 348.

When the citation does not immediately follow a citation to the same source:

- Nelson, *supra*[4] n. 5, at 348.
  (The notation "n. 5" refers to the previous footnote where this book is cited.)

(5) Restatements of law:

Text and footnote form:

Restatement (Second) of Torts § 402A (1995).

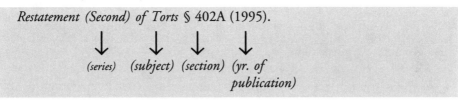

(series) (subject) (section) (yr. of publication)

Short-form citation to Restatements:

When the citation follows immediately after a citation to the same source:

Text and footnote form:

- *Id.*

When other citations are provided between the last cite to the same Restatement:

- Restatement (Second) of Torts § 402(A).

(6) Books:

Text and footnote form:

William N. Eskridge Jr., *Dynamic Statutory Interpretation* (Harv. U. Press 1994).

(author) (title of book) (publisher) (yr. of publication)

---

4. The term *supra* means literally "above" and is used to refer to material found earlier in the document. The term *infra* means literally "below" and is used to refer to material found later in the document. *See* Rule 10.0 of the *ALWD Citation Manual*.

If citing to a particular page in the book, for example, page 45 of the Eskridge book, above (using textual form):

William N. Eskridge Jr., *Dynamic Statutory Interpretation* **45** (Harv. U. Press 1994).

Short-form citations to books:

Text form:

When the citation follows immediately after a citation to the same source:

- *Id.* at 45.

When the citation does not immediately follow a citation to the same source:

- Eskridge, *Dynamic Statutory Interpretation* at 45.

Footnote form:

When the citation follows immediately after a citation to the same source:

- *Id.* at 45.

When the citation does not immediately follow a citation to the same source:

- Eskridge, *supra* n. 14, at 45.

(7) Other World Wide Web sites:

Any citation to a World Wide Web site contains the following: (1) name of the author; (2) title (in italics); (3) pinpoint reference (if available); (4) URL; (5) access or update information; and (6) exact date. See Rule 40.0 of the *ALWD Citation Manual*.

For example:

Legal Writing Institute, *Plagiarism Exercise*, www.lwionline.org/publications/plagiarism/exercise.asp (accessed March 19, 2008).

APPENDIX

M

Memorandum to Prepare a Licensing Agreement

In-Play Sports, Inc.
One Athletic Forum Drive
Boulder, Colorado

TO: Associate Legal Counsel
FROM: Chief Legal Counsel, In-Play Sports, Inc.
RE: Licensing Agreement with Paulo Pessoa

I have been meeting with the attorney for Paulo Pessoa, the Brazilian international soccer superstar, about giving In-Play Sports, Inc. an exclusive license to use his name, likeness, or both, on soccer cleat shoes and soccer balls, as well as for advertising and promoting this merchandise in the United States and Canada. Please draft the licensing agreement between Paulo and the corporation. The parties agreed to include the following terms in the contract.[1] The terms are not presented in any particular order.

---

1. Licensing agreements range from simple memoranda of understanding to complex, formal agreements. Particularly, terms for payment of royalties in international agreements can become complicated where, for example, some countries become involved in negotiations and sometimes require certain royalty rates, payment of withholding tax, approval of the agreement, or filing with a government agency. In addition, other terms (including, but not limited to, provisions relating to intellectual property) may become problematic depending on the laws and regulations of the countries affected by the licensing agreement, especially when manufacturing or distribution, or both, is to take place in a market other than in your country. Before drafting the agreement, become familiar with the laws and regulations of any country impacted by the agreement, as well as any international trade agreements that may affect the licensing relationship. Hiring local counsel familiar with a country's laws to review the agreement can prove invaluable in ensuring your client's interests are protected.

The goal of this exercise is to introduce you to contract drafting skills as commonly practiced in the United States, as opposed to studying various countries' laws. Therefore, the terms of this agreement have been created to emphasize drafting techniques taught in the chapters, including writing, tabulating, and organizing. The listed terms for the agreement in this assignment do not necessarily comply with current law, an international trade agreement, or a treaty that may govern a licensing agreement between a Brazilian citizen and a U.S. corporation.

You must determine how to group these terms into provisions and in what order the provisions will appear in the contract. Ensure that you draft the provisions so that they accurately and concisely state the agreed terms. Consider providing definitions for some terms and tabulating some provisions if this will make the agreed terms clearer. The language of the agreement will be English.

1. In-Play Sports, Inc., is a Delaware corporation. Its principal office is One Athletic Forum Drive, Boulder, Colorado 98743, U.S.A. In-Play Sports is in the business of developing, producing, packaging, and marketing sports equipment and apparel. Robert C. Weiss, President, will sign the agreement on behalf of the corporation.

2. Paulo Pessoa is a resident of Rio de Janeiro, Brazil. He was a member of the Brazilian national soccer team when it won its most recent World Cup. He wants all notices or statements under the agreement to be mailed to his attorney, Andre Silva, Avenida Rio Branco 23, Rio de Janeiro, Brazil 20090-003.

3. In-Play Sports has the exclusive right to use Paulo's name and likeness in connection with the development, production, marketing, and distribution of soccer cleat shoes and soccer balls.

4. The territory covered by the agreement is the United States of America and Canada.

5. The period of the license: The first day of next month, ending in five years. In-Play Sports wants to retain the right to renew the agreement for one successive five-year renewal period. The corporation's election to extend the license must be given in writing to Paulo 30 days prior to the expiration of the agreement's initial term.

6. In-Play Sports agrees to comply with all recording requirements and any other provisions of the intellectual property laws of the countries covered by this agreement.

7. Breach will occur if In-Play Sports violates any of the terms and provisions of the agreement. Paulo will notify In-Play Sports in writing of his intention to terminate if there is a breach. If Paulo gives notice, In-Play Sports has 30 days to remedy its breach. If In-Play Sports fails to remedy the same, the agreement and the license will cease and terminate. Notwithstanding termination, Paulo's rights arising out of the agreement or in connection therewith shall nevertheless continue in full force and effect, including his rights to receive earned but unpaid royalties.

8. If In-Play Sports becomes insolvent or if a petition for bankruptcy or for reorganization is filed by or against it, or if it discontinues it business, the license granted automatically terminates without any notice required by Paulo. If this occurs, In-Play Sports, its receivers, representatives, trustees, agents, administrators, successors, or assigns, have no right to sell the merchandise unless Paulo provides his written consent.

9. Upon expiration of the license or termination of the agreement, all rights granted to In-Play Sports will revert to Paulo, who then can license his name and

likeness to others. In-Play Sports will have the right to dispose of all inventory upon expiration of the agreement for a period of 120 days thereafter, but only if royalties are paid and statements provided to Paulo under the terms of this agreement.

10. All notices and any statements to be provided under the agreement must be in writing and sent by overnight courier to parties' addresses, unless a party notifies the other of a change in writing at the addresses noted in paragraphs 1 and 2. Notice is deemed given as of the date of mailing by overnight courier.

11. In-Play Sports agrees to pay a royalty of 10 percent on all net sales by In-Play Sports to its customers and distributors of the licensed merchandise. Payments are to be made in U.S. currency.

12. Royalty computations are to be made on the basis of the net sales price of the merchandise. The net sales price is the invoiced billing price for the merchandise, less any returns for damaged goods.

13. All royalties for an accounting period computed in other currencies must be converted into U.S. dollars at the selling rate for bank transfers from such currency to U.S. dollars as quoted in New York City at the close of business on the last day of each calendar quarter (or the next business day if such last day is not a business day) during the term of the agreement.

14. Royalties are to accrue when the merchandise is sold by In-Play Sports. This occurs on the date when the merchandise is billed, invoiced, shipped, or paid for, whichever occurs first.

15. Royalties for any calendar quarter will be paid within 30 days following the end of the calendar quarter. All royalty amounts are to be stated, and all payments are to be made in U.S. currency.

16. At the same time as payment of royalties, In-Play Sports promises to provide a statement, certified to be accurate by an authorized officer of the corporation. The statement must show the number of each type of merchandise sold during the quarter and the net sales price for each merchandise sold.

17. When the agreement is executed, Paulo will receive a nonrefundable advance royalty of U.S. $100,000. This will be set off as a credit against the percentage royalties.

18. No later than 60 days after the execution of the agreement but before each one-year anniversary of the agreement a written marketing plan regarding the merchandise will be provided by In-Play Sports to Paulo. The marketing plan is to include for each type of merchandise sales projections, methods of distribution, the expenditures for advertising, and any other information that Paulo may reasonably ask In-Play Sports to include. Each market plan must include specific information for the following one-year period and include general estimates and projections for subsequent periods during which the agreement remains in effect.

19. Accurate books of accounts and records showing all transactions related to the merchandise will be kept by In-Play Sports. Paulo, or his authorized representative, can examine these books at any time at the offices of In-Play Sports.

20. In-Play Sports will agree not to produce any products using the name or likeness of any professional soccer player for distribution in the United States and Canada during the term of the agreement or for two years thereafter.

21. The agreement does not prevent Paulo from granting other licenses for the use of his name and likeness, except Paulo cannot give a license for the use of his name and likeness in connection with soccer cleat shoes and soccer balls in the territory covered by this agreement while this agreement is in effect.

22. In-Play Sports agrees to manufacture the merchandise at its own expense in sufficient quantities to meet reasonably anticipated demand. The merchandise must be of good quality, consistent with the reputation and accomplishments of Paulo. In-Play Sports agrees to exercise reasonable efforts to advertise and promote the merchandise at its own expense and to use its best efforts to sell the merchandise in the United States and Canada.

23. Paulo is concerned about the quality of the merchandise. To ensure that the merchandise is of high quality In-Play Sports agrees to provide to Paulo, free of cost, for his written approval, a sample of each piece of merchandise, including any packaging or wrapping material. Paulo agrees not to unreasonably withhold his approval. If he doesn't give notice of his approval within 30 days of the date of submission, his approval is assumed to have been given. In-Play Sports will not change approved merchandise without Paulo's prior written consent. If he rejects any merchandise, In-Play Sports can elect to redesign and resubmit said merchandise for his approval in accordance with the foregoing.

24. Paulo will state that he owns the rights to his name and likeness, that he has the right to grant the license to In-Play under the terms of this agreement, and that there are no other agreements with third parties that will conflict with the grant that he is making to In-Play Sports.

25. The agreement shall bind and inure to the benefit of Paulo's successors and assigns.

26. New York law will govern the agreement. Disputes will be resolved in the applicable state or federal court in New York.

27. In-Play Sports will agree to indemnify Paulo, defend him against, and hold him harmless against any claims, suits, losses, costs, and expenses (including reasonably attorneys' fees and costs) arising out of violations of the agreement by In-Play Sports or defects in the merchandise.

28. Paulo agrees to indemnify In-Play Sports, defend it against, and hold In-Play Sports, its officers, directors, employees, and agents, harmless against any claims, suits,

losses, costs and expenses (including reasonable attorneys' fees and costs) arising from a breach by Paulo of any representations he made in this agreement.

29. In-Play promises to obtain and maintain during this agreement, at its own expense, product liability insurance providing protection at a minimum in the amount of U.S. $4 million for each single occurrence for any claims, suits, losses, costs, or expenses arising out of any violations or alleged violations of the agreement by In-Play Sports or defects or alleged defects in the merchandise.

Within 30 days after execution of the agreement, In-Play Sports agrees to submit to Paulo a fully paid certificate of insurance naming Paulo as an insured party, confirming the policy has been issued and is in full force and effect, providing coverage of Paulo as required by the agreement. The certificate will provide that before any cancellation, modification, or reduction in coverage of the policy, the insurance company will give Paulo 30 days' prior written notice of the proposed cancellation, modification, or reduction.

30. In-Play Sports cannot directly or indirectly assign, transfer, sublicense, or encumber any of its rights or obligations under the agreement.

31. The agreement can be signed in two counterparts. Each one shall be considered an original, but the counterparts will together constitute one and the same agreement.

32. Consider other provisions that might be necessary for this contract. Discuss these additional provisions with me.

APPENDIX
N

Memorandum to Prepare an Employment Agreement

Bolton & Associates
Attorneys at Law
One Bank Tower, Suite 3401
Seattle, Washington 98188

TO: Associate Attorney
FROM: Senior Partner
RE: CID Software, Inc. — Employment of John E. Young

We have been asked by Jane Crossland, Senior Vice President of Executive Recruiting for CID Software, Inc., to draft an employment agreement for a new sales executive, John E. Young. Ms. Crossland provided me with the agreed terms for the proposed contract.

Please use the following agreed terms to draft the provisions for the agreement.[1] You should consider how you will format the agreement (i.e., headings, sections, and/or articles). The terms are not presented in any particular order. You must determine how to group these terms into provisions and in what order the provisions will appear in the contract. Ensure that you draft the provisions so that they accurately and concisely state the agreed terms. Consider providing definitions for some terms and tabulating some provisions if it will make the agreed terms clearer.

1. New employee: John E. Young. He lives in Seattle, Washington.
2. Employer: CID Software, Inc. This entity is incorporated under the laws of the State of Delaware and licensed to do business in every state. It has offices in Colombia (Bogotá), European Union (all major cities), Nigeria (Abuja),

---

1. The information is not presented in clear and concise language. You will need to redraft this information in light of the drafting concepts covered in this book.

Egypt (Cairo), Russia (Moscow), Bahrain, China (Beijing), Shanghai, Guangzhou), Singapore, Thailand (Bangkok), Japan (Tokyo), South Korea (Seoul), Australia (Perth and Sydney), Malaysia, Indonesia, and the Philippines.

3. CID Software, Inc., is a wholesale distributor of computer Software.

4. Young's position with the corporation will be Vice President, Sales and Senior Account Executive. His sales territory will be Singapore, Thailand, Philippines, Indonesia, and Australia. He's expected to work out of the Southeast Asian home office in Singapore.

5. The agreement can be terminated for cause. For cause situations include when there is a disclosure of confidential information or other violations of the agreement, dishonesty, inability to perform job duties, neglect of duties, illegal conduct, including a violation of the policies of the corporation, international law, or the laws of any country where Young is living, visiting, or doing business.

6. Young gets an exclusive right to sell software in his territory during the first year of employment. He is to keep this right for a second year, but only if he has sales in the first year amounting to more than U.S. $1 million. If his sales in the second year are over U.S. $1.5 million, Young gets to keep this exclusive right through the third year.

7. He is to receive a base salary of U.S. $50,000 annually. The salary is to be paid on the first business day of every month.

8. He is to receive a commission of 10 percent of collected gross revenues for sales of computer software attributed to him.

9. Commission payments are to be paid on the first business day of every month, based on an accounting computed on the first business day of the previous month that reflects the collected revenues for the calendar month preceding the accounting.

10. Payments of salary and/or commission are to be paid in U.S. currency.

11. For purposes of calculating commission payments, revenues will be based on the current and fair rate of exchange for currency of the countries where the revenues were generated.

12. There is to be a review of Young's commission payment percentage in 6 months. The regional manager for Southeast Asia and Australia gives all reviews. Reviews are to be made every 6 months until the agreement is terminated.

13. Young is to promote to the distributors the sale of software. Sales are to take place in his territory. As an account executive, Young's duties are to be those that are usual and customary for account executives in the same industry.

14. Young reports to the regional manager for Southeast Asia and Australia.

15. Contract term: 3 years, May 1, 20XX–April 30, 20XX. There is to be a provision for early termination. We'll address this in the endgame provisions of the contract.

16. Young wants 160 vacation hours annually plus Singapore national holidays and Christmas and New Year. CID is agreeable to this. Young has to request the specific time of his vacation. The vacation that he requests is to be allowed unless he is needed by the company.

17. Housing is to be paid by the company, but only up to U.S. $1,500 montly. Young pays for furnishing his residence, as well as for the utilities in his residence and the taxes for his residence.

18. Young can participate in the following employee benefits. His participation will be in accordance with the plan documents set by the company and in effect from time to time: medical and dental plans, disability benefit insurance plans, a 401(k) savings and investment plan, an employee stock purchase plan, term life insurance, whole life insurance, long-term care insurance, accidental death and dismemberment insurance, and any other plan offered by the company so long as Young is qualified to be a participant in the plan.

19. The company agrees to pay for necessary travel expenses. This includes costs for baggage, passport photos, passports, visas, hotel accommodations, ground transportation, or housing, meals, gratuities, airplane tickets, and baggage transfers.

20. All applicable U.S. taxes are to be paid by Young, but any taxes in the countries where Young will be residing and/or doing business on behalf of the company are to be paid by the company.

21. Before departure from the United States, Young must submit to a physical examination and (at his own risk) vaccinations as may be required by the company. He must furnish a report from the examining physicians regarding his physical examination and vaccinations. The examining physicians are to be designated by the company.

22. The company is concerned about hiring people who do not have the proper qualifications. The company wants Young to state that he received his Masters in Business Administration (M.B.A.) from Indiana University in 20XX. The company also realizes that Young is employed by its main competitor, Simple Software, Inc. The company wants Young to assure it that he is not prevented by his employment agreement with Simple Software, Inc., from working at the company and is not under any restriction of a non-competition clause in the agreement with Simple Software, Inc. or any other employment agreement, from marketing software for the company in the proposed sales territory.

23. Jane Crossland, Senior Vice President of Executive Recruiting for CID Software, Inc., will be signing on behalf of the company.

24. Governing law for the agreement will be the State of Washington. Disputes will be resolved in the applicable state or federal court in Washington.

25. The agreement can terminate prior to the expiration of the term, upon the occurrence of death, incapacity, or disability of Young.

26. The agreement also can terminate without cause at the company's election upon at least 30 days prior written notice delivered to Young.

27. The agreement can terminate for cause at the election of the company by providing Young with written notice that states the reason for the company's action, provided Young does not correct the problem within a reasonable time after notification. "Cause" is any act of dishonesty to the company, violation of the established policies of the company, conviction of a crime

(other than for traffic violations), or a material breach of any obligation under the agreement by Young.

28. The agreement can terminate for cause at the election of Young by providing written notice to the company stating the reason for Young's action, provided the company does not correct the problem within a reasonable time after notification. "Cause" is the failure of the company to pay when due any amounts owing to Young under the agreement or a material breach of any obligation under the agreement by the company.

29. If Young breaches the contract, the company does not have to pay any travel expenses or other expenses incurred by Young after the date of termination. Any of Young's salary that is due and owing at the time of his termination of employment must be paid by the company.

30. The company will be required to pay Young's return transportation to the United States if the agreement expires or if it is terminated without cause by the company. The company also pays any reasonable relocation expenses incurred (e.g., moving furnishings to the United States).

31. Include a provision that Young cannot compete with the company for three years after termination of employment with the company; he cannot compete (directly or indirectly) in geographic areas where he has been doing business for the company.

32. Any notices to the company required under the agreement are to be sent by overnight carrier to the attention of the regional manager at the Singapore offices, Millennium Tower, Level 9, 34 Temasek Avenue. Any notices to Young required under the agreement are to be sent by overnight carrier to Young to the attention of his attorney, William Dailey, 450 Union Street, Suite 223, Seattle, WA 98188. Notice in either instance will be effective only upon receipt.

33. Any amendments or modifications are to be made in writing and signed by the parties; otherwise, they are not effective.

34. To the extent any provision of the agreement is considered illegal or unenforceable, the parties will consider the provision deleted under the agreement and the remainder of it will be considered by the parties to be unaffected and will continue in full force and effect.

35. If Young's employment is terminated, Young is required to deliver to the company copies and originals of all documents, data, materials, and property, including hard copy and electronic form, that are considered property of the company or relate to the business of the company.

36. The company can assign its rights and delegate its performance. Young cannot assign his rights or delegate his performance.

37. The entire agreement between the parties is contained in the agreement. It will supersede all prior agreements and understandings.

38. Consider other provisions that should be included in this contract. Discuss these additional provisions with me before drafting them in the contract.

Glossary

ADR: An abbreviation for alternative dispute resolution. *See* "alternative dispute resolution."

Absurd result: A ridiculous or illogical outcome.

Acronym: A word created by taking the first letter of each word in a phrase and combining those single letters into a new word.

Action statement: In the context of a contract, a clause documenting a party's performance that goes into effect contemporaneously with the signing of a contract.

Active voice: In grammar, the subject of a sentence is the person or entity performing the action of the verb and the verb describes the action taken.

Adjudication: A judicial decision-making process; the act of entering a judgment or a decree in a lawsuit.

Administrative agency: A department or commission in state or federal government that regulates and monitors a particular industry or public interest (e.g., the Federal Communications Commission) as provided under the law.

Admissible evidence: Evidence permitted by the court to be introduced at trial and considered by the trier of fact when making its decision.

Adversary: An opponent.

Adversary legal system: Adversary legal systems involve parties who oppose each other and state their views and arguments regarding how their dispute should be decided before an independent decision maker, usually a court. The lawyers representing the parties provide evidence, witness testimony, etc., before the court in order to prove their case. The lawyer for the opposing party may ask questions to challenge the strength of the other side's case.

Adverse possession: A system where landowners lose their legal rights to real property by allowing another to use the property in a way and for a period of time that the other acquired title to the property.

Affiliation: To be associated with; for example, to be a member or part of an organization or group.

Affirm: To uphold the decision of a lower court.

Affirmative covenant: A contractual obligation that creates a duty to act.

Affirmative defense: A defense raised by a party in a lawsuit; the party admits that the cause of action is established, but because of the defense, the party cannot be held legally liable. Examples of affirmative defenses include self-defense in a criminal case or necessity in a trespass to property case.

Aggravated: To make worse, as in "aggravated assault" in criminal law.

Aggrieved: One who is injured or has sustained a loss.

Allegation: A claim stated in a pleading that the party making the claim intends to prove at trial.

Alternative dispute resolution: An alternative method for settling disagreements without requiring the parties to engage in formal litigation. Examples of alternative dispute resolution methods include mediation and arbitration. *See* "ADR."

Ambiguity: Lacking clarity; a term or provision is capable of two or more mutually conflicting meanings.

Analogy: A comparison that states similarities between two or more things.

Answer: A pleading that is a defendant's written response to a plaintiff's complaint; it specifically responds to each allegation raised in the complaint by either admitting, denying, or pleading that the defendant lacks sufficient knowledge to respond to the truth of the allegation.

Appeal: A legal process by which a party in a lawsuit requests a higher court to review the final judgment of a lower court within that higher court's jurisdiction.

Appearance: In a legal context, an act of coming into court or filing documents with a court by which a party to a lawsuit, in person or through its attorney, indicates an intent to participate in the lawsuit.

Appellant: The party who initiates an appeal.

Appellate court: A court in the state or federal court system that has the power to review the decisions of lower courts in its jurisdiction and decide whether these lower court decisions should be upheld, modified, or reversed.

Appellate review: The process by which an appellate court reviews a decision made by a lower court in its jurisdiction.

Appellee: The party who opposes an appeal.

Arbitration: An alternative to a court adjudication of a dispute. The opposing parties agree on a neutral person or group of persons to hear the parties' arguments and settle the dispute by issuing an award.

Arbitrator: A person or one of a group of persons chosen by opposing parties in a dispute to hear the parties' arguments and settle the dispute by issuing an award.

Assault: When one person intentionally puts another person in fear or apprehension of imminent contact.

Attribution: The process of giving credit for a thought, idea, or statement to the creator of that thought, idea, or statement. Proper attribution requires that 1) the writer must accurately report the borrowed words or ideas in the writer's paper; 2) the writer must notify the reader about any quoted words, phrases, or passages by either placing quotation marks around the quoted text, or, if the quotation is fifty or more words, by placing the quoted text in block format; and

3) the writer must accurately cite to the original source at all necessary points in the writer's paper where the writer has borrowed text or ideas.

Background: In the context of a contract, a series of fact statements that set up the circumstances for the agreement, e.g., the parties' backgrounds, their relationship to each other, or their motives for entering into the contract.

Balancing of equities: The process by which a fact-finder in a dispute considers notions of fairness as they relate to the particular circumstances of the parties in the dispute.

Battery: Intentional and harmful or offensive touching of another.

Bench trial: A trial in which there is no jury and the judge decides issues of fact and makes rulings of law.

Beneficiary: A person who receives a benefit from someone or something, such as a person who receives property under the terms of a Last Will and Testament.

Bilateral: Two-sided, as in bilateral offers.

Bill: When the term is used in connection with legislation, it means a writing that is introduced to a legislative body as a proposed law; the legislative body considers whether it should be enacted into law.

Bill of Rights: The first ten amendments to the United States Constitution, mandating fundamental rights and protections for the people.

Binding: In the law the term "binding" is often used when discussing statutes and cases that must be reconciled in reaching a decision in a present case, e.g., binding authority.

Block format: A form for presenting a quotation of fifty or more words; the right and left margins are indented, and the quoted text is single-spaced.

Bona Fide Purchaser (BFP):   One who purchases goods with a good-faith belief that the seller has a legal right to sell the goods to the purchaser.

Brief: In a legal context, a summary of a case that states the relevant facts of the dispute, the procedural history, the procedural and substantive issues raised in the case, the court's holdings on the procedural and substantive issues, the rules favorably applied by the court, and the court's reasoning.

Burden of proof: The responsibility of one party to prove a legal assertion in court.

Canons of construction: Persuasive rules or principles used by courts to help give meaning to ambiguous statutory language.

Case of first impression: A legal issue raised where there is no controlling law in the jurisdiction.

Cause of action: A claim or claims of wrongdoing (e.g., breach of contract, negligence, or fraud) that entitle the victim to a remedy as provided under the law.

Chattels: Personal property; things.

Choice of forum provision: In a contract, a provision that designates where the parties will resolve their issues in the event of a dispute.

Choice of law provision: In a contract, a provision that designates what law will govern in a dispute between the parties.

Chronological: In order, starting from the oldest date to the most recent date. For example, the steps in a lawsuit, in chronological order, begin with filing a complaint with a court through the trial and appellate process.

Circuit court of appeals: An appeals court in the federal court system.

Claimant: A person who makes a claim, e.g., a plaintiff in a lawsuit.

Closing: In connection with a sale, the action(s) that conclude a transaction. Actions may include, but are not limited to, any or all of the following: the delivery of personal property or real estate, the payment of a purchase price, or the signing of a contract.

Closing argument: An attorney's final presentation to the court that summarizes the evidence presented at trial that is favorable to the attorney's client and that attempts to persuade the fact-finder to decide in favor of the attorney's client.

Collection agency: A business hired to collect debts owed by one party to another.

Commercial outlines: Commercial publications of outlines and other materials designed to help law students understand legal doctrine and study for examinations.

Common knowledge: Information that that the average educated person should know or be able to locate.

Common law: A body of rules and principles created by the judiciary to respond to legal issues not addressed by statute.

Complaint: In the context of a legal action, a pleading filed in a court by a plaintiff that begins the formal litigation process. The complaint establishes the jurisdiction of the court, outlines the plaintiff's claims, names the defendants, and designates the remedy sought by the plaintiff.

Computer Assisted Legal Research (CALR): Computer programs used to research the law online.

Concurrence: In reviewing lower court decisions, when one or more judges agree with the outcome by the majority of the judges but do not agree with how the court reasoned to the decision. The concurring judge(s) may or may not write a concurring opinion.

Condition: In the context of a contract, it is a possible future occurrence that, if it occurs, will result in a consequence that either 1) gives rise to an obligation, a discretionary power, or a situation, or 2) terminates an obligation, a discretionary power, or an existing situation.

Condition precedent: In the context of a contract, a condition that gives rise to an obligation, a discretionary power, or a situation.

Condition subsequent: In the context of a contract, a condition that terminates an obligation, a discretionary power, or an existing situation.

Conditional gift: A gift made on condition that something will happen as a result of the gift. For example, in the United States engagement rings are often given by a man to a woman, with the condition that the couple gets married.

Confidentiality covenant: In the context of a contract, it provides that a party obtaining private information about the other party by means of the contract relationship may not disclose the information, unless specific exceptions are stated. *See* "covenant."

Congressional hearings: Proceedings held by various committees of the United States Congress to collect evidence in order to evaluate proposed legislation or other governmental action.

Consequential damages: Monetary damages awarded if reasonably within the contemplation of the parties when the contract was made, less any monies that could have been prevented through the plaintiff's mitigation.

Conservator: An individual who guards or preserves, such as one who preserves art.

Consideration: An agreement to exchange performances or promises between two or more parties that requires the parties to act, forbear from acting, or give up a present or future right.

Constituent: One component of a larger whole, as in constituent requirements.

Constituents: The population that a legislative representative is charged to represent. For example, a U.S. senator from New York represents the interests of New York citizens (constituents) in the U.S. Congress.

Constitutional provision: A clause in a state or federal constitution. For example, the First Amendment to the United States Constitution includes a clause providing for the separation of church and state.

Contextual ambiguity: In the context of a contract, an ambiguity arising from conflicting contract provisions.

Counterclaim: A claim made by a defendant against a plaintiff in a lawsuit that may or may not relate to the subject matter raised in the plaintiff's complaint.

Counterpart provision: In the context of a contract, a clause allowing the contract to be signed by the parties using separate original copies of the contract.

Countervailing: Opposite, as in arguments that are in opposition to others presented.

Coupled synonyms: Words that have the same meaning and are paired together in a sentence or clause, creating a redundancy.

Court of last resort: The highest court of appeals within a state court system or a federal court system.

Covenant: In a contract, an obligation to perform or to refrain from performing certain actions; a promise.

Covenant not to compete: An obligation by which the obligor promises not to engage in specific conduct that competes with the interests of the obligee for a specified period of time and within a specified geographic area.

Covenantee: The party for whose benefit the covenant is made; the party receiving the covenant or promise.

Covenantor: The party making the covenant.

Credibility: The degree to which one is believed; reliability; truthfulness.

Cross-claim: A claim made by a party against any co-party arising out of the subject matter of the lawsuit.

Cross-examination: At trial, the process by which the attorney for the opposing party questions a witness called by the other party to testify. This questioning takes place after the direct examination of the witness by the attorney for the party who called the witness to testify. The cross-examination can address only matters raised during the direct examination.

Decedent/deceased: A person who has died. The term is often used when discussing the Last Will and Testament of a party who has died.

Declarant: A party making a statement.

Declaratory judgment: A decision made by the court during the course of a trial that can be appealed immediately.

Deductions: Conclusions that must flow from a set of circumstances.

Default judgment: A judgment entered in favor of the prevailing party when the opposing party fails to respond to the claims made by the prevailing party.

Dependent clause: In grammar, a statement that does not form a complete sentence and thus is incapable of standing alone; to be grammatically correct, it must be accompanied by an independent clause.

Deposition: A means of acquiring information during the litigation process during which a party or witness is questioned either orally or in writing about matters related to the controversy; and responds orally.

Descent and distribution: The process of passing property after a party dies without a Last Will and Testament.

Dicta: Statements by a court in its opinion that are not part of the direct holding of the case.

Direct examination: The process at trial by which the attorney for the party who called the witness to testify questions that witness.

Direct object: In writing, a noun or pronoun that receives the action of the verb in a sentence and answers the question *what*? or *who*? (e.g., Jack threw a knife; knife is the direct object).

Directed verdict: *See* judgment as a matter of law (JMOL).

Disclaimer: In the context of a contract, a clause that denies a warranty.

Discovery: The evidence gathering stage of formal litigation during which each party investigates and collects information related to any claims or defenses raised in the pleadings.

Discretionary: Optional, not required.

Discretionary powers provision: In the context of a contract, a clause giving one or both contracting parties the option to act or not to act.

Dissent: To disagree with, as a judge who disagrees with, or dissents to, the majority opinion in a case.

District court: A trial court in the federal court system.

Docket: The official record of a court; records all of the cases, the filings of documents by parties in the cases, and the actions taken by the court in the cases.

Drafter: The party who writes a document, e.g., a contract.

Due diligence: The degree of care a party must exercise to meet a legal requirement or obligation.

Duty of care: A level of care and caution that is owed by one party to another in certain situations. If the party fails to provide this standard of care, then the other party may be liable for the resulting harm.

Dynamic statutory interpretation: A theory of statutory interpretation that promotes the use of traditional tools of statutory construction but permits considering what the statute ought to mean if the original legislative outlook does not reflect current political, legal, or societal customs.

East Carolina: A fictitious state in the United States created for the purpose of the exercises in this book.

East Carolinians: Citizens of the fictitious state of East Carolina.

Economic duress: Pressure to take certain actions because of financial needs (for example, signing a contract).

Ejusdem generis: A canon of construction used when interpreting a statute, providing that general words following specifically listed words apply only to those items "similar in nature" to the listed words.

Elements: In the law, requirements, usually part of a test that must be met in order to establish liability in a cause of action.

Ellipsis: A set of three periods used within a quotation to indicate the omission of quoted material.

Enact: To pass into law, as in a statute or amendment.

Enumeration: In a contract, organizing information in a series, such as (1) . . . , (2) . . . , and (3) . . . .

Equity: An ideal of justice relating to the fair treatment of individuals.

Estate: The quality and quantity of a person's ownership interest in personal property or real estate; the property owned by a decedent upon his death as well as the property acquired or received by the estate from the time of the decedent's death until the final distribution of the property to the beneficiaries.

Exceptions: In the context of a contract, provisions limiting the scope or effect of an obligation, right, discretionary power, condition, or disclaimer.

Execute: To perform; to sign.

Executive branch: One of the three branches of state government or federal government; its primary role is to enforce the statutes created by the legislative branch.

Exhibits: Documents attached to a contract that contain information not part of the agreed terms but are nevertheless relevant to the contract (e.g., other contracts, illustrations, maps, or forms).

Exit provisions: Clauses in a contract stating the parties' respective obligations, discretionary powers, and rights when the contract ends, either by premature termination or by natural expiration of the contract.

Expression unius est exclusio alterius: A canon of statutory construction providing that mentioning one or more items of a class implies the exclusion of other items that are not mentioned.

Extrinsic source canons: A canon of construction used when interpreting a statute by looking to agency interpretations of a statute, legislative history, or common law rules of other courts that have interpreted the same (or similar) statute.

Fact-based issue analysis: A discussion to determine whether the facts of a case satisfy an applicable statute, rule, or principle.

Fact-finder: In the U.S. judicial system, the party deciding the facts in a case presented to the court. The fact-finder may be a jury or, if no jury, a judge serving as the fact-finder.

Fact sensitive: Influenced by the facts.

Factors: Considerations; in a legal test, factors are multiple items that are not required but are considered and weighed in determining whether a legal test has been met.

Fair market value: The price at which a seller is willing to sell an item and a buyer is willing to buy the item.

False imprisonment: A tort that occurs when one party intentionally confines another party to a bounded area, with the party's knowledge and without the other party's consent.

Felony: A crime that can result in punishment for more than one year.

Final judgment: A judgment by a court that settles a disputed issue and may be appealed.

Floor debate: A debate between legislators that takes place in the hall of the legislative body, when the legislators argue in favor of or against proposed legislation, or other governmental action.

Force majeure provision: In the context of a contract, a clause that provides for the suspension of certain obligations under a contract without incurring a penalty upon the occurrence of an event outside the control of the contracting parties, e.g., natural disasters, fire, war, or embargoes.

Foreign courts: Courts outside the jurisdiction of the court presiding over a dispute.

Forum: The court or jurisdiction where the legal dispute will be litigated.

Fraud: Intentional misrepresentation.

Free market system: A system in which the prices for goods and services are set by the buyer and seller (e.g., supply and demand), instead of by law or by the government.

Fully integrated contract: A contract that is intended by the parties to be, and in fact is, a final and complete expression of their agreement.

Fundamental right: A right expressed in the provisions of the United States Constitution.

Future earning capacity: A person's ability to make money in the future.

General jurisdiction court: A court that can hear cases raising many different types of disputes.

Generic names: In the context of an explanation of a case, the names identifying the relationship of the parties to the dispute at issue, e.g., "buyer" and "seller" in the case of a dispute involving a sale.

Goodwill: An intangible asset of a business arising from the approval or patronage of customers because of the business's good business practice.

Gross negligence: When an actor either does something in a conscious, voluntary manner, or omits to do something in reckless disregard of a legal duty and the consequences to another party.

Hearsay: A statement made by someone other than the person testifying at trial.

Heir: A person who stands to inherit property from an estate.

Hierarchy: A classification system that ranks people or objects based on their characteristics or powers.

Holding: The answer to the issues raised in a case, based on the legal principle drawn from the opinion. *See ratio decedendi.*

Homicide: The killing of a person by another.

Homographs: Words that are spelled in the same way but have different meanings.

Homophone(s): One or more words that are pronounced in the same way, but have different spellings and meanings.

Hypothetical: In law, a fictitious story created to explore the law's policies and principles; theoretical.

In pari materia: A canon of construction used when interpreting statutes, providing that statutes relating to the same subject matter should be interpreted similarly to avoid inconsistencies.

Indemnification: An agreement providing that a party who breaches a contract provision agrees to compensate the nonbreaching party for any loss or damages arising out of the breach.

Independent clause: In grammar, a clause that includes both a subject and a verb and can, therefore, stand on its own.

Inference: A conclusion of fact reasonably deduced from facts already shown to be true.

Inheritance: In the context of an estate, the personal property, real estate, or money one receives upon the death of the owner.

Injunction: A court order requiring a party to a dispute to take a specific action or to refrain from a specific action.

Instructions of law: Instructions given by the judge to the jury advising the jury about the law relevant to the case.

Intangible: Something that is not physical, that cannot be touched (e.g., intellectual property).

Integration clause: In the context of a contract, a provision stating that the written contract reflects the entire agreement between the parties and supersedes all previous negotiations and agreements made by the parties on the subject matter.

Intentionalism: A theory of statutory interpretation that focuses on determining a legislature's intent. The intentionalist looks at the words of a statute as an expression of the legislature's meaning that can be clarified through the use of outside sources.

Interrogatories: A method of acquiring information in the litigation process through a series of written questions relating to the dispute submitted to the opposing party, who must respond in writing.

Intestacy: A situation in which a person has died without a valid Last Will and Testament.

Introductory statement: In the context of a contract, the first textual paragraph in a contract that formally introduces the name of the contract, indicates the date of the contract, and identifies the parties to the contract.

Involuntary manslaughter: When one kills another without intending to do so; the death is a result of criminal negligence or occurs while another unlawful act is taking place. Deaths occuring as a result of an automobile accident are oftentimes ruled as involuntary manslaughter.

Issue of fact: A question regarding the truth of an item, occurrence, or situation claimed by a party in its pleading and disputed by another party in its response pleading.

Issue of first impression: A question of law that has never been decided in a jurisdiction. *See* Case of first impression.

Issue of law: A question regarding what law should be used to resolve a legal dispute or how a law should be interpreted to resolve a legal dispute.

JMOL: Judgment as a matter of law ("JMOL"). *See* "motion for a judgment as a matter of law."

Judgment: The final decision of a court regarding a legal dispute.

Judgment as a matter of law (JMOL):   *See* "motion for a judgment as a matter of law."

Judgment notwithstanding the verdict (JNOV):   Outdated terminology for "judgment as a matter of law."

Judicial branch: One of the three branches of state government or federal government; its primary role is to interpret and apply statutes and to create laws in situations not addressed by statutes.

Judicial efficiency: A public policy concern that the judicial system function economically by avoiding duplicative actions and wasting judicial resources.

Judiciously: Using sound judgment or discretion.

Jurisdiction: The power of the court to assert authority over parties in a case (*see* personal jurisdiction) and the authority of the court to hear and decide the issues arising from the pleadings in a case (*see* subject matter jurisdiction); the geographic area in which a court may assert this authority.

Jurisprudence: The study of legal theory.

Jurist: A legal scholar.

Jury trial: A trial where the jury serves as the fact-finder in a case (as opposed to the judge) and decides issues of fact.

Just: In the law, based on notions of justice; lawful; correct; deserved.

Justice: A judge who sits on the United States Supreme Court, or on the court of last resort in the state judicial system; a principle of fairness and equity.

Landmark decision: Major, as in a "landmark case"; a case that establishes a new rule that is then followed and subsequently cited.

Law-based issue analysis: A discussion to determine whether a statute, rule, or principle applies to a dispute or, if competing rules exist that may apply to a dispute, determines which rule should apply.

Law review article: A scholarly paper published in a law school-sponsored periodical, edited by law students at that institution.

Legalese: Pretentious or meaningless legal language.

Legislative act: In the context of legislation, a law enacted by the legislature.

Legislative branch: One of the three branches of state government or federal government; possesses law-making powers and enacts statutes that are subject only to constitutional restraints.

Legislative history: The official records of the legislative process that pertain to a particular piece of legislation.

Legislative intent: The reason legislators enact a bill into law.

Limited jurisdiction court: A court that can hear only disputes raising certain issues (e.g., a small claims court may hear only cases involving claims for small debts).

Living law: The legal principle that the common law is constantly evolving to integrate advances in science and technology, as well as to integrate changes in social customs and economic considerations.

Long-arm statute: A state statute that mandates that a court may exercise personal jurisdiction over a party who is outside the territorial boundaries of the court's jurisdiction, provided the party has certain contacts with the state, as stated in the statute.

Malice aforethought: Planning in advance to do something wrong.

Mandate: When used as a verb, it means to command, dictate, or require.

Mandatory precedent: Prior case decisions that must be followed by a court (e.g., a state trial court is bound by the previous decisions of the higher courts within its jurisdictional borders, as well as federal statutory and constitutional decisions of the United States Supreme Court).

Manslaughter: The killing of another. Voluntary manslaughter is an intentional killing; involuntary manslaughter is an unintentional killing.

Maxims: Rules of law.

Mediation: A non-binding method of alternative dispute resolution where the parties seek to resolve their issues through mutual collaboration and problem-solving with an unbiased third party.

Mediator: An unbiased third party who assists disputing parties in resolving their issues.

Merger clause: In the context of a contract, a provision stating that the contract reflects the entire agreement between the parties and supersedes all previous negotiations and agreements made by the parties on the subject matter.

Merits: A case decided "on the merits" is one that is fully tried at the trial level and is not dismissed on a procedural motion.

Model Rules of Professional Conduct: A set of ethical guidelines for U.S. lawyers published by the American Bar Association. The guidelines include some rules that are mandatory and others that are only advisory. Many states have adopted the Model Rules of Professional Conduct.

Molestation: Illegal physical contact made by one person to another.

Motion: In the context of a legal dispute, an oral or written formal request made by a party to the dispute to the court, to make a ruling or enter a judgment in the dispute.

Motion for a judgment as a matter of law (JMOL):   At the end of an opposing party's presentation of its case at trial, another party may make a motion to the court to enter a verdict in the moving party's favor on the basis that "there is no legally sufficient evidentiary basis for a reasonable jury to find for [the opposing party]." Fed. R. Civ. P. 50(a)(1). If the court grants the motion, then a judgment is entered in favor of the moving party.

Motion for a judgment on the pleadings: A motion by a party made anytime between the close of pleadings and prior to the trial, asking the court to enter judgment in the moving party's favor because, based on the pleadings filed by the parties, the moving party is entitled to judgment as a matter of law.

Motion to dismiss: Responding to a pleading, a party moves the court to dismiss a claim raised in the pleading on the basis that even if the facts alleged in the pleading are true the claim raised by the pleading must be dismissed because there is no legal basis for the claim.

Moving party: A party to a legal dispute who makes a motion to the court.

Named party: A party who is named in a lawsuit, e.g., a defendant or plaintiff.

Neurosurgeon: A medical doctor who performs surgery on a person's nervous system.

No contest plea: A plea entered by a criminal defendant that allows the defendant to accept responsibility for the charge without admitting guilt. Also known as a "nolo contendere plea."

Noscitur a sociis: A canon of construction used for interpreting statutes; the meaning of a word or phrase can be deduced from the words surrounding the word in question.

Nuisance: In a legal context, something that interferes with another's use and enjoyment of his property; an annoyance.

Obiter dicta: That part of a court opinion that is not necessary to the holding in the case.

Objective legal analysis: A type of analysis that requires a writer to consider and present the support that exists for both sides of a disputable issue. The goal of objective legal analysis is to inform the reader of the law on a particular issue and to predict the issue's probable outcome in a client's case.

Opening statement: An attorney's presentation at the beginning of the trial; provides an outline of the case to the fact-finder and states what the attorney intends to prove in the case.

Opposing counsel: The attorney representing the other party in a case. For example, an attorney representing the wife in a divorce proceeding is opposing counsel to the attorney representing the husband in the same divorce proceeding.

Oral argument: An oral presentation by an attorney to the court regarding a disputed issue in an attempt to establish the validity and superiority of her client's position and persuade the court to rule in favor of her client.

Ordinary course of business: Conducting business in a way that is in accordance with the customary way to operate that type of business.

Orthopedic surgeon: A medical doctor who performs surgery on muscles and the skeletal system.

Overrule: To set aside or reject a prior court decision in a different case to reject an objection made by a party during the trial.

Parenthetical: A term used to refer to the factual holding of a case, when it is provided in parentheses after the case citation.

Parol evidence rule: A rule that addresses whether a court will admit evidence intended to interpret disputed terms in an executed, written contract. Parol evidence includes evidence relating to an oral statement or extraneous writing made prior to the execution of a written contract. It also includes evidence relating to oral statements and sometimes extraneous writings made contemporaneous with the execution of a written contract. The parol evidence rule prohibits admission of outside evidence to contradict, supplement, or explain terms in a written contract (1) when the contract is intended by the parties to be and, in fact, is a fully integrated agreement or (2) when the contract is not a fully integrated agreement and the term is determined by the court to be clear and unambiguous. Conversely, if the contract is not a fully integrated agreement and the term at issue is deemed unclear or ambiguous, the court may admit parol evidence to supplement or explain that term to the extent the evidence is consistent with other terms in the contract. The admitted parol evidence is recognized as part of the contract only if the fact-finder decides that the evidence is credible.

Passive voice: In grammar, the subject of the sentence is not the one performing the action of the verb and the verb is a form of "to be."

Pension: An account set up on behalf of a party that becomes available upon retiring from employment.

Personal jurisdiction: The power of the court to assert authority over parties in a case, which is necessary for any judgment rendered by the court to be enforceable over the parties.

Personal representative: One party who acts on behalf of another, oftentimes a party acting on behalf of the estate of one who is deceased.

Persuasive authority: Legal sources that are not binding on courts deciding future cases but which may help persuade the court to reason to a decision in a certain way. Persuasive authority may be primary authority that originates in a nonbinding jurisdiction, or it can be any non-primary source.

Persuasive precedent: Decision-making rules a court may follow from lower courts in its jurisdiction or from courts outside the jurisdiction.

Plagiarism: The intentional or unintentional use of someone else's written or spoken words or ideas without proper attribution to the source.

Plain Error Doctrine: A doctrine providing an exception to the general rule that if a party fails to object, the alleged error is considered waived. If a party can establish the existence of exceptional circumstances that affect substantial rights resulting in a miscarriage of justice, then the alleged error may not be waived.

Plain Meaning Rule: Rule of statutory interpretation that states a court will first look to the language of the statute itself to determine its meaning, and, if the statute is clear in its plain meaning, the court will not look outside the language of the statute to determine the statute's meaning. Under the Plain Meaning Rule a court will consider commonly accepted English principles of grammar, syntax, and punctuation to determine the meaning of a statute's words, as understood by a reasonable person.

Pleading: Documents filed with a court at the beginning of a formal litigation process that establish the claims and defenses of the parties. A pleading includes documents such as a complaint, answer, cross-claim, counterclaim, and any replies to cross-claims or counterclaims.

Precedent: Holdings in prior cases used by a court to reach a decision in a current case.

Predeceased: A person who has died, or is treated as though he or she died, before the decedent.

Preempt: To override; to take the place of.

Preponderance of the evidence: A majority; more than fifty percent. For example, the burden by some plaintiffs to prove their case is by a preponderance, or majority, of the evidence.

Pretext: Pretext occurs when persons say they are doing something for one reason, but they are really doing it for a different reason that they are unwilling to admit. For example, in an employment situation an employer may claim to have fired an employee because the employee did not arrive to the office on time, when the firing really occurred because the employee reported to the government that the employer was doing something illegal.

Pretrial conference: A conference between the attorneys involved in a case and the judge that is held before the trial of the case to assist in the management and speediness of the trial.

Primary authority: The main source of the law: constitutions, statutes, case law, and administrative regulations based on statutes.

Private investigator: A detective that is not acting on behalf of a government agency but is hired by a private party to obtain information for that private party.

Procedural law: Laws governing the process for determining the parties' rights and obligations in a legal dispute.

Procedural posture: The identification of the motion that is the basis for the appeal for review of a case. For example, if a case was fully tried at the trial level, the appeal will be based on the final outcome in the case (also known as a "decision on the merits"). If the case was dismissed based on one of the procedural motions available to a party, such as a summary judgment motion (*see also* motion for judgment as a matter of law; motion for judgment notwithstanding the verdict), the procedural posture on appeal will be whether the summary judgment motion was properly granted.

Procedural statements: In the context of a contract, a clause that provides rules or policies governing the contract relationship.

Proceeds: In the law, usually refers to money or assets.

Promulgate: To proclaim, announce, or make public.

Prong: One part of something larger, as in one requirement of a three-pronged (requirement) test.

Property settlement: In a dissolution of marriage proceeding, an agreement that divides the property of the divorcing couple between them.

Prototypes: Original models designed and created prior to the mass production of goods.

Provision: Condition; limitation. A clause found in a contract or statute. *See* "contract provision" and "statutory provision."

Proviso: In the context of a contract, an imprecise clause creating an exception, a condition, or a limitation that overrides a preceding clause in the sentence, or adds a substantive provision.

Proximate cause: One of the requirements to prove negligence, specifically, that an actor's breach of a duty resulted in an injury that was reasonably foreseeable.

Prudential considerations: Factors that seek to ensure accurate, consistent, and efficient judicial decision-making that weigh on a court's interpretation of a statute.

Public policy: Principles that concern the society as a whole; a principle of law that promotes the protection of the public's well-being as opposed to the interests of a private person, entity, or group.

Purposivism: A theory of statutory interpretation that focuses on determining the purpose or goal of a statute. After determining the purpose of the statute, the purposivist interprets the statute consistent with that purpose.

RJMOL: *See* "renewed motion for a judgment as a matter of law."

Ratio decidendi: The court's decision on a contested legal issue in a case. *See* holding.

Rebuttal: Evidence that disproves or contradicts any evidence.

Recitals: In the context of a contract, a series of fact statements that set up the circumstances for the agreement, e.g., the parties' backgrounds, their relationship to each other, or their motives for entering into the contract.

Reconciled: How one thing is consistent with another; for example, showing how the decision in a new case is consistent with the holdings in prior cases binding on the court in the new case.

Remand: In the context of a legal dispute, a decision by a higher court to send the case back to a lower court for the lower court to take additional action in the case.

Remedy: In the context of a legal dispute, a means by which a wrong is made right or compensation is given to the victim of the wrongdoing, e.g., an injunction or payment of money.

Removal: In the context of a legal dispute, the process of having a case that was filed in one court moved to another court. For example, a defendant may request the removal of an action originally filed in a state court moved to federal court if the case involves a question of federal law. Only the defendant can request a removal.

Renewed motion for a judgment as a matter of law ("RJMOL"): A renewed motion made by the losing party after the jury returns its decision; requests that the judge enter a judgment in the moving party's favor, despite the jury's verdict against that party.

Representations: In the context of a contract, statements made by a party regarding present or past facts, or both.

Res judicata: A judicial doctrine that prevents the parties from litigating the same issues again when a final judgment has been issued by a court with appropriate jurisdiction over the parties and over the subject matter of the action. Res judicata is an affirmative defense to any second action on the same issue involving the same parties.

Restatement of Law: A collection of common law rules covering various areas of law, such as contracts and torts, published by the American Law Institute and written by scholars in the field, with commentary.

Restitution: When the party must return any benefit received under the contract.

Restrictive covenant: A contractual obligation that prohibits or restricts performance of an action.

Reverse: In the context of an appeal of a case, to overturn or set aside the ruling of the lower court in that case.

Rule explanation: A concise description of a relevant court decision, used to help the reader better understand the rule by showing how a prior court applied the rule in an issue identical or similar to the issue being analyzed.

Schedules: Documents attached to a contract that contain information considered to be part of the agreed terms of the contract (e.g., price lists, product models, or stock numbers).

Seal: Melted wax dripped onto a document and impressed with a symbol.

Secondary sources: Anything that is not primary authority. The most common legal secondary sources include legal encyclopedias, law review articles, books, and restatements of law.

Semantic ambiguity: A word or phrase having two or more conflicting meanings.

Sentimental value: Non-monetary value given by a person to an object or event because it evokes strong emotional feelings in that person.

Service of process: The formal process where all defendants to an action are served with a copy of the complaint (or some other legal notice), along with a summons to appear in court and respond to the plaintiff's claims.

Severability clause: In the context of a contract, a provision stating that in the event any part of the contract is determined invalid, the remaining provisions will continue in effect.

Signing in counterpart: The signing of a contract by the contracting parties at different times and sometimes on different originals of that contract.

Slayer: Someone who has killed another.

Slayer statute: Statute that prevents a person who kills another to benefit from the victim's death. The specific requirements vary from state to state.

Socratic method: A teaching method through which a professor instructs by asking questions of students, rather than just lecturing.

Sovereign authority: The power of each nation to decide its own course of action and govern its own people and territory.

Specific performance: A remedy in a contract dispute that forces a party to satisfy its contractual obligations under the contract; available only if monetary damages would be an inadequate remedy.

Stare decisis: A legal doctrine that requires a court to reconcile a new decision with that court's prior decisions and higher court decisions in the same jurisdiction involving similar issues and substantially similar facts.

Statute of Frauds: A U.S. statute designed to avoid fraudulent acts by setting out certain requirements that must be met to enforce contracts for the sale of goods over $500.

Statute of limitations: A statutorily-imposed time limit for filing a complaint.

Statutory provision: A clause in a statute.

Statutory scheme: The statutory scheme of a statute may include 1) any statutory definitions of terms used in the statute in question, 2) other statutory provisions related to the statute in question, 3) any codified preamble that pertains to the statute in question, and 4) the title of a legislative act that includes the statute in question.

Stay: In the context of a legal dispute, a court's action to stop or suspend the proceedings.

Strictly construe: To interpret a term or clause narrowly.

String citation: To place one or more cites immediately after a previous cite.

Subject matter jurisdiction: The authority of the court to hear and decide the issues arising from the pleadings in a case.

Substantive law: Law found in statutes, regulations, constitutions, and common law; helps determine the parties' rights and obligations at issue in a legal dispute.

Substantive policy canons: Canons of construction used in interpreting statutes that focus on matters such as constitutional concerns, the common law prior to the statute's enactment, and specific statutory policies; these canons do not focus on the meaning of statutory text or what the legislature intended when it drafted the text.

Summary judgment: A judgment entered by a court, upon a party's summary judgment motion, dismissing a lawsuit because no genuine issue of material fact existed as to any or all claims or defenses, so the moving party is "entitled to judgment as a matter of law." Fed. R. Civ. P. 56(c).

Syntactic ambiguity: Conflicting meanings occurring from punctuation or from the order of, or relationship between, words and phrases within a sentence.

Tabulation: A formatting technique that sets off each enumerated item from the surrounding text by placing it in a separate, indented block. For an example, see Figure 20-6 in Chapter 20.

Target audience: The people or segment of the population that a writer is attempting to reach with her writing.

Textual canons: A canon of construction used in statutory interpretation focusing on the legislature's choice of certain words, the syntax used in the statutory language, or the relationship of the words or phrases in the question to words or phrases found in other provisions of the same statute or similar statutes.

Textualism: A theory of statutory interpretation that focuses on the plain meaning of a statute and textual canons.

Thesis statement: A statement that introduces a legal issue and also provides the conclusion on that legal issue.

Thirteenth Circuit: A fictitious federal circuit that includes the fictitious state of East Carolina; used for purposes of examples and exercises in this book.

Threshold issue: An issue that should be decided by the court first.

Transcript: In the context of a legal dispute, the official record of a proceeding.

Transitional words: Words used to notify the reader that a change in focus (transition) is taking place.

Treatise: Books that contain a thorough scholarly analysis of a specific topic.

Trespass: To invade.

Uniform Resource Locator (URL):   An Internet address; the string of letters, words, and numbers that usually begins with "http."

Unilateral: One-sided; in a contract, unilateral performance means performance by one party to the contract.

Vacuum: In the law, writers may refer to something being considered "in a vacuum." This means that the reference is being considered in isolation of everything else — it will be considered on its own.

Venue: The location of the suit; out of all the courts with personal and subject-matter jurisdiction over the dispute, where the lawsuit may be brought.

Verdict: A jury's decision on issues of fact in a trial.

Voir dire: An examination of potential jurors by the attorneys or the judge to determine whether the potential jurors will be fair and impartial when weighing the evidence in a trial.

Voluntary manslaughter: When one kills another intentionally, but there are reasons to lessen the crime that would otherwise be considered murder. Deaths occurring during a heated fight, for example, may fall within voluntary manslaughter.

Waiver: In the context of a contract, occurs when a party fails to enforce or agrees not to enforce a right given to it under the contract.

Warrant: In the law, a formal document that authorizes someone to take a certain action, such as a warrant for a person's arrest.

Writ of certiorari: An order issued by an appellate court after exercising its discretion to review a lower court's decision in a case. The writ orders the lower court to certify the record of the case's legal proceedings in that lower court and present the certified record to the appellate court.

Index

Contracts